The Letters / *Part Three*

Fifty years of correspondence between a missionary in Africa and her family

By Christine Helen Cheal / Transcribed by Ruth Fiona Cheal

Orange Hat Publishing
www.orangehatpublishing.com - Waukesha, WI

The Letters / Part Three: Fifty years of correspondence
between a missionary in Africa and her family
Part Three of Three

ISBN 978-1-64538-060-3
First Edition

The Letters / Part Three: Fifty years of correspondence
between a missionary in Africa and her family
by Christine Helen Cheal, transcribed by Ruth Fiona Cheal

For information, please contact:

Orange Hat Publishing
www.orangehatpublishing.com
Waukesha, WI

Cover design by Kaeley Dunteman with select photographs by David Cheal

Orange Hat
PUBLISHING

www.orangehatpublishing.com

To Almighty God
Who first called Christine Cheal to a life of serving Him.

Before Her First Journey To Africa

Mr & Mrs Hayward left Nigeria for home leave furlough in 1919 and ill health prevented them returning. Their colleague Miss E. Webster returned instead. Another missionary soon died, and much itineration (visiting the outstations) was done by Evangelists and two English clergy who arrived in 1922. In 1930 Rev CH Wedgewood retired, leaving Miss Webster almost alone. Mr H. Jump and Mr J. Spencer were the first SUM – Sudan United Mission – missionaries to arrive in Panyam to start the first leprosy clinic and work alongside Miss Webster. Miss C.H. Cheal followed at the end of 1930.

Introduction

Christine Helen Cheal [1905-1985] eldest child of Ernest and Annie Cheal of Crawley, Sussex, England, knew without a doubt that God had called her to be a missionary. In 1928 she pencilled a now faded note of promises to God and prayer requests she made while at the Keswick Convention: I have asked of God, and received by faith, that He will preserve me from ever backsliding into a life apart from His choice for me; that He will make me a shining light by life, deed, work and face, wherever I go; that He will make me a prayer warrior; that He will keep me abiding in Christ and filled with the Holy Spirit so that the love of God may be shed abroad in my heart for Himself, for fellow Christians, and for lost sinners. In August that year she returned to Overstrand on the Norfolk coast to help with the CSSM Children's Special Service Mission. There are two letters on crumbling CSSM headed paper, dated 1926 and '27 thanking her for her earlier contributions.

Chris went to North London to study at the Medical School for Missionaries and in a letter home, dated Oct. 3rd 1928, she wrote, 'there is no extra fee for the Dentistry course so the total fee is 14 guineas (£14.14 shillings) to be paid as soon as you like please Father.' Chris and a friend Marie took rooms with a Mrs Arundel who served a solemn 4 course dinner the first evening to all her lodgers, an old lady, a Dutch girl, & two boys also studying medicine. There was also a lady housekeeper-cook and two other maids. After the meal the girls talked and sewed in the drawing-room till bedtime. The next day they went into the City by tube train which 'cost only 4d the whole way.' The remaining students had assembled: 2 Norwegian girls, one Swiss, a missionary from China, another English girl, 'and 11 men – one really quite old and two are not gentlemen.' One of the younger lodgers seemed, 'to be inwardly splitting with laughter most of the time,' and two visitors were also very jolly, Ping Chun and Ping Wun, both studying law at the London University. Some of the first medical lectures were on terminology; anatomy of cranium, chest, abdomen; and the eye.

In April 1929 Chris pencilled in a notebook: 'I have asked the Lord that the power of the Holy Spirit will fill me in greater measure, that the Lord will draw me nearer to Himself, even 'though it be a cross that raiseth me'. Also that He will work in me such selflessness that I shall count not my life dear unto myself. I have confessed and claimed His power against carelessness, laziness in prayer, lack of love, and love for the things of this world.

In September of that year Chris moved on to new lodgings to study at the Bethnal Green Medical Mission. In another letter to May she writes, 'You know the sort of longing after you've had a ripping time anywhere to share it with someone; that's what I feel like now...nearly decided me to come home...writing is much too feeble & slow to tell you all about everything. How can I describe the wonderful, illuminating times at High Leigh; Dr Scroggie's teachings were marvellous eye openers to me, what I've been longing for – that grip of the Bible as a whole. Miss Hooker's & Mrs Burton's talks on practical problems for Christians were again priceless; Dr Deck too, his ripe & mellow wisdom has I'm sure blessed many – I had been rather worried about that besetting sin I spoke to you of, vulnerable points hanging around in my mind.' Other struggles included, ' we had a run of very sick people on the District to nurse these last few weeks & one has died & another is dying or dead. I verily hope no more turn up.' And at the end, 'Thursday is supposed to be our free day – could you make business in London that day & we might have lunch together possibly? Now I should stop, I have to send some notes and must let down my navy dress. Do write soon.'

One letter addressed to 'my darling Mother' contains several gems: 'we went out to see two women, one with an operation wound for cancer to be dressed daily, Mildred has given me this to do on my own. Did I tell you that I have to wear the most annoying headdress, a sort of afternoon tea-cloth which gives the appearance of wings & a flowing thing down my back! Our windows here are just over the road and the traffic noise Mother is truly awful, I've never heard anything like it before, the trams, buses & lorries keep up a constant din except for an hour or two at night.' And this, 'On Tuesday I helped in the Clinic then Dr Balfour kindly asked M & me to go out with him in his car to the country. We went to Epping Forest which is beautiful, then to a tea garden, it was so nice after the heat & squalor of Bethnal Green. I sang a solo & also in a trio at that evening's meeting. At 10.30, ready for bed, we got called out to a woman ill after miscarriage; we had to come back & phone for instructions about medicine & treatment, then go again and do it. It was after 12.0 before we finally got back. The next day's surgery I did alone, it was very interesting; I gave a hypodermic injection, changed dressings & chaperoned patents for the Dr's examinations.' And finally this, 'This afternoon we went to Oxford Street to buy hats! I got a very nice brown felt in the sale at Peter Robinson for £1 it is a really good one.' Mother replied tenderly, including a glimpse of her firmness with Rene, the youngest of the three girls: '(she) wanted to sit down & write to you directly after breakfast, forgetting that there were a few jobs to be done such as beds to be made & dishes to wash and her own clothes to be washed...she gets a good many enjoyments, she ought to be a happy girl. She has a strange mixture in her makeup – many good impulses, but easily turned aside.' And this, 'Father might possibly travel up on Thursday taking your parcel & some apples, if not I will send them either by Carter Patterson or the post.' And on the last page, 'We must pray much for one another, I feel what a responsible place you are in, but that the authorities have not troubled much about arrangements for you. Father & I don't like the idea of your sleeping alone in the place, it does not seem right or suitable…however dearie, this may all just be a taste of the 'fellowship of Christ's sufferings, He was so often alone from human companionship…your way will not be easy, but if all you do is done for love to the Lord Jesus He will reward you in His own most blessed way. Now I commend you to Him, may you be kept, blessed, & find all your need met abundantly in Him.'

Towards the autumn of 1930 when Chris' travel plans must have been nearly ready, many letters of farewell were sent to her; here are some snippets from them:

*So you're going to join the merry throng of missionaries, I'm so glad & wish you every joy in it, you are in for the finest time of your life, the greatest joy of all – work for the One Who gave His all for us. Be sure to write a full journal from the first. Ever your loving Uncle P.

*We the women of Lowfield Heath Sewing Class ask your acceptance of this little gift to remind you of our love & prayerful interest as you leave for the work to which God has called you at Panyam. Isaiah 41:10. (14 signatures including Parsons, Willmott, Willis, Riley & Tullet)

*…assure you of our loving remembrances over all the way the Lord has led you from His first dealings with you – sent forth by the Spirit of God, will He fail you? Never! From your affectionate friend Vivian G Banham.

*Be assured that God will give abundance in grace sufficient for the day of parting. Please buy a travelling rug with the enclosed cheque, or a clock, or anything else you would like to take with you – rat poison perhaps! Yours CHM.

*I shall be thinking of you & your loved ones left behind knowing the Lord will meet every need in His own wonderful way. Much love to yourself, E J Inwood.

*As I can't come up to Liverpool to see you off & say goodbye, I'm sending this wee note & praying that you may have a good & happy journey & especially a very real sense of the Master's Presence with you every day, all the time. A letter cannot tell you all my prayers that you may be kept in peace & safety all the time. Exodus 23:20 & all the love & kisses I can send you, your ever loving Prebity.

*Whether tests in the physical or spiritual realm, prayer is the best defence, often your only resource, but sometimes so difficult in expression that victory lies in simply living in the attitude of prayer, the attitude of believing God & His Word when all around you & all within you seems going the wrong way. Do remember, when the evil one is working most powerfully in our consciousness God is at that very same moment working in our unconscious being. And Hudson Taylor didn't wait till he landed but began his work on board ship. God's richest blessing be with you as you leave home, throughout the journey and all your years of service. Yours sincerely, James Middlemass.

*I shall think of you spending your first Christmas away from home and I am sure that you will be so busy making others happy that you will not be troubled with homesickness (signature illegible)

*There are only 17, no 16, days left. I am sending this letter to greet you when you arrive at Sierra Leone; you will need no assurance of our unceasing thought & prayers for you. We want to know about everything, life on board ship, travelling companions etc. I am so sorry that I have nothing special to give you for your 25th birthday…I wish I could tell you of the joy your coming brought to our home, you came as God's gift and we gave you back to Him before you were 24 hours old; so that we feel about your going to Africa – it is just the fulfilling of His plan for your life, & we wish nothing better His Way is Best. But we shall miss you darling more than I can tell you & we will live 'looking' for the day you return to us, DV. I will close now with all the love I can send my own darling, praying God's rich blessing may be given you in preparation for your new life work. As always your loving Mother.

*It is funny to think that when your eyes rest on this page you will be in Lagos in tropical heat & sunshine I suppose, so unlike Ireland and England! Take all reasonable care to keep yourself well & fit, don't go (as Miss Bennington did) without your sun helmet & so court sunstroke. I will give you a verse that came to me early this morning while thinking of you, Ezekiel 11:16 may you find it to be increasingly true. With all my heart's love Mother.

*What a joy it must be to you dear Annie & your husband to 'let go' such a precious treasure as your eldest daughter to the mission field. L.V. Hamilton

*I think the correct way to address one's sister on the mission field must be: My beloved sister – at any rate it will look well in the book when it comes out (!!)...can't you see the heading of, say, Chapter VII Panyam-First missionary sphere-first impressions-language study-'grace enough for every need' even the rats!-fellow workers, and so on & so forth, it will make a very interesting chapter, please send full particulars at your earliest convenience. It does feel positively weird to think you will actually be in Panyam when you read this...rather awe inspiring. Tuddy dear you are there, in the thick of things, on the King's business – keep looking forward not back; get a hold of the vision of Panyam as a completely Christian place. If the Lord returns before you come back here I wonder whereabouts we shall meet in the air! Yours as ever, May.

*You go to the Field as a Probationer Missionary...a report of your progress will be made to the Executive Committee by the Missionary in charge of the Station and the Field Secretary. This will cover language study, fitness for the work, ability to get on with colleagues and the people. If these reports are favourable the Committee will then accept you as a Missionary...The only rule laid down by our Lord whereby we His people are to be recognised as such, is that we are to love one another. Think of it at all times and may that wonderful love of Christ, fruit of the Holy Spirit's indwelling, fill your heart and manifest itself unconsciously in all you think, say and do...If the sea is kind you will enjoy your trip, study the map as you go; we shall be remembering you. Every good wish, yours very sincerely Gilbert Dawson, Sudan United Mission, Fleet Street, London.

*I trust when you open this you will have found your sea legs and the

fear of fog will be past. I am very glad to be having a niece go to Africa, the land I hoped would be my own field one day, but the way did not open. Over these past weeks you have lived somewhat in the limelight around the British Isles but it will have faded by the time you open this. You may have much joy but I believe for you testing times will come. I can't stop to write more now, read this with a great deal of love & longings for you, from your old Auntie Jo.

*You will be greatly feeling the parting with your dear ones when you read this I do pray that the Lord Himself will be your Comfort. God-speed on the journey, it will be cold on the water for the first few days; I hope you will not be ill. Daisy C-B.

*Beloved child I want to send this with all the love it is possible to put into words. You are so dear to us all & the parting does mean a good deal, but all the same I hope I can make you realise that we feel honoured by God – that He should have chosen you & led you out into this grand work & our daily prayer will be the He will bless you & make you a blessing. While kneeling down to pray for you last night Job's words were with me for you, 'He that is perfect in knowledge is with thee; mighty in strength & wisdom.' Can we want more than that? Everything we need or can ever need is in Christ for us. The joy is in knowing you are not going alone & that He is with you withersoever you go – brings such comfort to us. God bless you my darling & keep you well & strong, guide you, fit and prepare you for everything He is preparing for you – this is the prayer of your loving Mother.

*The weather here has been terribly rough but somehow I haven't been uneasy that you had it unpleasant. How I wish I could take a peep to see if you are alright. Such a lot of tension & strain while staying with the W's – more & more I think our family must be exceptional in our unity & happiness!! I must get some foreign paper so be able to write more next week to you because I can only send 1 ounce for a penny-halfpenny. I asked little Frank where you were & he replied, "Cousin Chrissie gone right away on a big boat." Tons of love from your May.

*Surely it is more than 4 days since you left us. We have had gales ever since with warnings to shipping given out on the wireless so you can imagine how my heart has followed you & how often you have been re-committed into the Father's care & how often I have needed for myself to roll my anxieties about you onto Him, the only One who can help. I do pray you are in calmer waters now. As I write Wilfrid, May & Rene are singing 'Oh for a thousand tongues to sing' and Frank on the piano stool is making a joyful noise unto the Lord…Mrs Morphew has invited us to the babies' dedication service – just a few close friends and of course the servants! Miss L is unable to attend – I was not very sorry to hear that. Poor Nurse Moorhead stepped off a bus at 9.30 the other evening & fell into the ditch in the darkness & cut her head on a stone, Doctor had to stitch it. Rene has been like an angel in the house while May was away& has just called us to supper so I'll say goodnight my own dear love, Mother.

*Father met Dr Richardson on the train the other day & he was very interested to hear about you. I find from his book that he was pioneering out in the Sudan at one time. Oh if there was a chance of establishing a transatlantic telephone or television apparatus out there! I'm longing to hear your voice and how you are getting along & how you like Panyam. Tons more love with very best Christmas wishes & for New Year too, yours as ever May.

*This first Christmas in the place of your life work – may you lose any sense of homesickness, may it be a blest time – the first time Jesus has called you to spend His birthday away from all you know, with Him, & with so many new people, may He have some special birthday token for you as He establishes you there. Mrs Mac.

Preface

Many of the following letters throughout the next forty years, both from family and friends mostly in England, a few from other countries also, and from Chris in Nigeria, had to be shortened, leaving out some lesser daily doings. Where necessary I have added brief explanations in brackets of things possibly unfamiliar to younger generations and Americans. But these wonderful communications remain, to glorify God and to acknowledge the devoted service gladly given to Him by so many mentioned here, mainly of course Christine Cheal.

Her siblings used several nicknames: Chris – Chedlet, Tuddy, Tudhams; her sister Mary – May, Mipsie; their youngest sister Irene – Rene, Prebity; and brother Wilfrid – Bilter. Their mother, Annie Grace, came from Ireland so there are many visits back there and place names and Irish expressions also. May poured out her heart to Chris, and made a few comments, somewhat tongue in cheek, about their memoirs one day becoming published. My father, Wilfrid Cheal, although not a frequent letter writer, wrote many studies with deep Biblical understanding. It is my huge privilege to have had the opportunity to transcribe all these letters, thereby honouring my relatives, the unsung heroes, with this, their magnum opus. 1 Thess. 1:2,3.

SUM Great Portland St, London

Aug 5th '54

Dear Chris, the days are going by rapidly & soon you will be going back to Africa. You will soon be assuming full responsibility for the work at Panyam; I know how you feel about it Chris but the Lord is able to make all grace abound toward you and to make you fruitful in every good work. We have been in contact with 2 students either in their last year at Emmanuel or actually finished; one is Joan Onions, very highly spoken of by the school staff & she is willing to go to Gindiri believing her calling is to Teacher/Evangelistic work, much the same as Pixie Caldwell is doing at Langtang. The other is Joyce McQuone, a fully qualified nurse midwife from Leicester, especially interested in Vom, & you'll be interested to know she received her call through you, which came so clear there has never been any looking back. It would be a great joy to see both these girls going forth & I hope that will be realised. I am enclosing a list of the subjects of further pictures we would love to purchase from you if you possibly could find the time to take them then send them back here. We shall be thinking of, and praying for you, most sincerely W. Richmond.

Kano Airport Hotel

Aug 25th 54

My Darlings all including of course Rene & the Clyro family – the journey was excellent, I caught glimpses of the French Alps from 19000 ft up & the sunset over the Mediterranean was utterly marvellous pink-tipping the clouds below us as a reflected rainbow of all colours swirled about us. We were served afternoon tea at 5pm then dinner at 7.30 in a cunning little hot plate divided into sections for the meat pie vegs and mashed pots. We stopped at Tripoli for less than an hr then on to Kano by 5.45 with the first streaks of light in the eastern sky. You can imagine my disappointment when told there was to be no plane to Jos and I have to wait till tomorrow. I managed to phone through & heard Gordon Muir & Nakam were just ready to leave to collect me so now they will wait till tomorrow. While still at the Airport I was greeted in Sura & found Francis Naule who was our houseboy when I first arrived & now he works at the Eye Hospital here! We intrigued a few Officials with the language we were conversing in! And now darlings thank you all so very much for all your love & kindness yesterday and throughout the whole furlough; I feel so rich in your love & it made yesterday feel all wrapped around in loving kindness – I trust you too all shared in that feeling. I was glad Wilfrid went with you Rene & I just hope you caught your train alright, and not least I thank you NonaJane for the packet – the rubber dollies in bed are sweet & so are the pictures, & I know they will make some children very happy. Rene dear your lovely letter & packet needs an answer all to itself, thank you so very much, now goodbye dears blessings on you, C.

On the sand dunes at Portrush

Aug 29th '54

My Darling it was such a joy to get your letter from Kano Airport direct to us here at the Esplanade Hotel, thank you for such thoughtfulness & I'm so so glad your flight was good even though you had to wait there, that must have been trying. Mother seems very happy here yet in looking back I feel I should not have brought her so immediately after your farewell then the strain for her of the flight; she has been upset internally which I'm sure is reaction but she is more settled today. Our room has glorious views out over the sea & we can rest here quietly when not visiting or being visited by so many welcoming & eager Irish relatives, & Jimmy, Isabel & Bernard who came to stay several days in this same hotel! We have walked up to Ranmore Head & had a gorgeous time out on the rocks with the waves throwing up mountains of spray catching the sunlight. I had an unexpected phone-call asking me to speak; in place of Dr Erskine suddenly taken ill; at dear Susan's memorial on Oct. 10th. I have found this very difficult & asked for a few days to think & pray before consenting. Last night was one of unwelcome wakefulness and yet suddenly in direct answer to my specific prayer for words that would perfectly fit Susan, came into my spirit's ears, "The angel of God Whose I am and Whom I serve;" this came with that clear sense of coming from outside myself, not at all from my own conscious thinking; not only Paul's testimony but Susan's own, summing up the witness of her life with its emphasis on personal surrender followed by willing service. Now goodbye my dear darling & my prayer for you is that you will be specially helped to settle back into all that awaits you, through the first few difficult days of adjustment, & given all the wisdom & grace you need; my heart's love as always is yours, May.

Panyam

Sept 2nd 1954

Darlings Nakam has agreed to post this as soon as she gets to England so I must write hastily. Thanks indeed for the letter from

Moira telling of the hot sunny days in Portrush; I trust your homeward journey today will be good & uneventful. My heart is full for it seems you are yes always close, but so far away, with all the little nooks & crannies of Brookfield & familiar sounds & so on, yet here I am 3500 miles away & feeling just as much at home here in all these familiar sights & sounds. We've just been listening to the records of Billy Graham & G Beverly Shea choir, they are really nice & got here just before I did, all 6 records fine but 10/- duty to pay! And my case from Griffiths McAlisters arrived safely in Lagos and is now on its way up country. Mr Marshall came to take us out for a lovely day, 22 miles along the new road to the Jibam River and back along another bit of road still being built out to Chip – when it is finished we shall be able to get there in one hour's drive instead of a two day trek! At Communion today Nakam spoke again, a very good word, and there were many reports some good & others disappointing as is often, but several new places have been opened up while I've been away & that is really encouraging. I want to go visiting them all as soon as I can get ahead with the office work; which leads me to pray especially for you May as you start work again with so many meetings & responsibilities. Now Father dear Rene's letter yesterday brought me the sad news of further disappointment over the Business, I am so very grieved about this especially when you have not been well, and have not had Mother & May with you, or Wilfrid, this past week. I trust that Mr Compton's contribution as Director will bring some benefit & perhaps new ideas. I shall continue to pray for these needs, remembering Matt 7:25 for both you and those before you who founded the Business so firmly upon the Rock. Just then Mwantet put his head through my window asking me to send his special greetings to you & Mother, & he was quite charmed to see the colour photograph of you both. He wants you to know the little church they've finished building in his village of Milet is already in use & about 100 folk gather there each Sunday with others coming in from Mongu to lead the services. With my dearest love to you Father specially and of course to all the others also as they come home, yours Chris.

Panyam

Sept 13th–16th '54

My Darlings, firstly a wee note to you Mother in hopes you are feeling rested after all that good Irish air & not too weary from the strains of plane travel and partings. I know this will cheer you: Katya, Senlat, Datilik & Bibwahat all came through the other day and we exchanged much joyful greeting. They were deeply touched when I told them how I often found you in the early mornings with your Bible open and their names on your slip of paper for prayer. Major Marshall has been so kind – he gave one of the lorries to take 20 people to the Airport to join the huge crowds gathered to see Nakam off and would take no money for it; he came himself and presented her with a bottle of Eau de Cologne! He helped rearrange some of our loads in the cars for safety and has said I am to contact him with any motoring problems that might arise in future. You know that I felt quite apprehensive about the delicate situation of taking over completely after so many years, specially the car, but everything went off as smoothly as could be, Nakam was most sweet throughout & left in a positive halo of glory & generosity & I am so very grateful to God for this. She gave me so many of her things, like her lovely clock, and fine bed linens & blankets, & stuff she would not need in England, & would not take a penny for them. Our garden has not done well this year & Peter Batchelor (now with a fantastic ginger beard!) has advised on soil conditions, but I do think Old Lot's goats & sheep are more likely the cause of the failure. A most distinguished African is staying in our RestHouse tonight, The Hon. Abubakar Tafawa Balewa Minister for Transport. He's from a Northern village about 100 miles away but lately living in Lagos. Frances & I went to greet him and talk for half an hour; he is very clever, has spent a year at London University & has taught in 3 London

Secondary Modern Schools, and back to England again last year with David for the Conference. He said "you will laugh when you hear what I taught there, Scripture (he is a Moslem) and English!" David is taking him to see our Fish Farm tomorrow then bringing him here for Tea. David got back Kaduna on Saturday having made a broadcast in Hausa about Nakam's life in this country; to be heard in Hausa on Thursday then on Friday translated into English – how I wish you could listen in also! Isabel has been helping the Teachers prepare for the new term and now our schools are underway and going on well, despite poor attendance on the first day due to several uncrossably swollen rivers after a night of downpours, and our boarders have all arrived back safely too, it is nice having them about again. Frances & I went out to take the evening treatments to the Cerebro-spinal meningitis patients, and she was keen to have a go as she is very mechanically minded although has never driven using the steering wheel gears. It was odd for me to be in position of instructor! But after scraping them a bit, just as I used to, she did alright. I have now written to our charming young ADO asking to meet to discuss with him the hope for Agricultural Grants for some of our Std 6 boys who really want to take the agri course for land development; I'm praying our Pankshin Div of Native Admin will provide these grants. May darling thank you for writing so fully & I am thrilled you are taking that solemn & wonderful opportunity on Oct 10th, I shall be with you in prayer as you prepare, believing that promise in 2 Cor. 9:10 that the Lord, having given you that word, will multiply it & increase the fruit of it; & I'm certain you will be given grace to overcome all nervousness of the crowds who will be there. I've just had a marvellous letter from Nakam since she got home, for which I think even Daisy might warm to her now – isn't that lovely; blessings on you all my very dearest dears, yours Chris.

29 Marlborough Pk, Lisburn Rd, Belfast

Oct 14th '54

Dear Miss May Cheal in amongst the crowds you had 18 of our large family out to hear you speak & they said that you were like an angel & you were as good as their Teacher for you know how to drive it home. I can tell you they took in everything & one even got it all down in shorthand. I believe you know they are not often like that. I do hope that you were not too tired after that for I recall Miss Park telling me it takes a lot out of you to speak like that as you did. I feel it was well worth coming over to hear you. Many cried and one lady in the front row was crying all through the whole Service; yours very sincerely ML.

Panyam

Oct 26th '54

Darlings I really am most uncomfortable with such long gaps for you to wait between my letters, I am so sorry, but I do know you understand the situation, especially dear May with your busy days too, but I still wish there was more time to sit & chat like this with you all, to keep up my normal sort of letter-writing. Thank you each so much for your lovely letters, even when you don't hear from me; that is so appreciated. I took Frances P – with whom I have had such dear fellowship during her stay here, for one day's rest while I had meetings in Daffo. Soon after I left here there a woman came to the doorstep and had an unfortunate miscarriage there – it would be F to have to cope with an emergency like that when on holiday! She was such a help to me as we drove many nerve-wracking miles under drenching rain-clouds and necessarily through young rivers flowing fast across much of the road, parts of which were unspeakable. I have heard now that the Native Admin Comm at Pankshin has agreed and will pay £2 per month to every student in the Agricultural Training, we are so very glad about this. A letter came from a young church member at Niyes telling me of a dream he had in which I helped him overcome an evil spirit – how I wish that much more of one's help could be given as easily as that! Thank you so much for sending me the reports of May's talk in Belfast – just what I wanted to know, I am so thankful about it; ever yours C.

Panyam

Nov 5th '54

My Darlings as always your loving greetings rejoice my heart & I do thank you & another lovely letter came this morning too, and as today I start my jubilee year I'm thanking God for all you Mother & Father have been to me these past 49 years. Both books have arrived & already I'm deep into the Arthur Rendle Short one – very well written & the Billy Graham I'm sure will be as good, thank you May for that. Mother your news from the Dr is rather staggering but I believe you must make your own decisions (as I did in 1945) about telling or not telling those around you; I don't suppose at all it was caused by pills and I very much hope nothing more will occur. Now please do not worry about sending gloves, even for weddings they are hardly worn any more anyway, especially in this heat! Please dears forgive me for not writing our Convention news to you as I wanted to, but I had to make Nakam the priority this time, so I have asked her to pass that letter on to you as there is simply no time for me to write it again. She has been so kind & thoughtful, sending advice & suggestions for everything, & much grateful appreciation of everything I can tell her, 'revelling in any news' & continuing to pray faithfully for the work here. I believe she must miss it all dreadfully. I expect it was the weight of the responsibility that made me apprehensive, and I have heard since from several folk to whom the messages were blest.

Later 11th now: must tell you more of Rendle Short: he stayed a night at the Arundels when I was there & spoke at Chomeley Hall & the next day we travelled up to town together, so one rubs shoulders with greatness! I didn't realise he was such a distinguished surgeon & scientist. Mother the gloves have arrived and they are beautiful so I will wear them although it is not usual; and the bride says she will wear gloves also! I have sent you a packet of Christmas cards for folks whose addresses I'm afraid I can't remember but you see them regularly so would you be so kind as to deliver them? The few days in Gindiri went off well, particularly the Open Day with vast crowds of Africans & Europeans – cars buzzed about like Piccadilly! Each Department was open exhibiting their work & most of it was really splendid especially at the Blind School where the children have only been a few months. The remainder of my time was business meetings usually over meals – so many folk I had to see for discussion & decision making, plus some wonderful times of prayer. David has to attend an important business meeting in Jos tomorrow but unfortunately he has let his motor tyres get worn right down, & with no other transport available at all there's nothing for it but to lend him our car. I know Nakam would not approve but it has to be, so I have just taken him out for some gear practice in it. I shall be extremely glad to see him & the car safely back; yours always C.

Panyam

Dec 5th '54

Darlings it has been ages since I had the time to write properly to any of you, I am so sorry & trust you will continue to understand this situation although I'm sure you don't like it any more than I do. Your letters keep coming and bring me such joy, thank you everso much. How good it was to hear Rene's condition seems to be understood at last and treated seriously; and her boys doing well & even asking for prayer for some friends. Father you appear to be improving, and May happy & very busy, & the Clyro family alright as far as I know – we have a lot to be thankful for do we not! And I have truly felt the powerful support of the Lord's hand & your prayers during these last weeks through an almost overwhelming burden of work & responsibility especially when David is away so much. Two specific difficulties have been: in one outstation the 100 or so Christians have turned against their Evangelist Joshua Fwanchin (for whom Wilfrid used to pray) & he came to me as a broken man. At Jibam I had to read the riot act to the Christians there, none of whom bothered to help the builder I'd sent there to finish the new school they have built, so the builder moved on to other jobs in another near Chip. So if Jibam have not completed the work themselves by opening day Jan 10th I will have to remove their 2 Teachers Ishaku Dabiring & Yilhi to other schools. This is a big disappointment & most frustrating after the progress reaped there in previous years & so many Jibam boys now in Gindiri Training. As a little light relief Frances B & I made a wonderful 8lb wedding cake, which then sank right down in the middle so won't so at all for the occasion. About 10 days after I last wrote (yes David & the car both returned in fine shape!) Isabel & I motored off at 7am to make several visits to see some Chiefs & sort out a few palavas in 5 different villages. All accomplished, we returned by mid afternoon, after what would have been at least a 3 day trek before the new roads! Also that week a young ex GLB woman, Hajaratu, died of her TB. David was with her & later spoke of the lovely testimony she gave quoting 2 texts from John's Gospel & praying beautifully; he said he had never before heard such a bright witness from a dying person. Frances & I motored to Jos for another day's meetings, dentist & shopping; on the way back I gave the wheel to F until Mongu where we were stopped by a police patrol checking licences. Frances' was out of date – she'd forgotten to renew it last year, so they took it from her & now she must go to the P Station in Jos next time she's in! Last Sunday we had a shock coming back after church to find our cold bacon for lunch gone and greasy finger marks all over the bars on Frances' window – the thief must have been exceptionally thin to squeeze in there then out again with loot, which included some keys and a little cash. Rather unsettling & more police involvement required. How blessed we are though, to have many encouragements to help offset these unpleasantries. On Friday I joined with the Pankshin Edu Comm to visit Butura to measure out for a new school building there as the old one is falling down, and I had to ask several questions about other necessary repairs – please pray about this with me for I am so ignorant of building requirements. Also I need your prayers for a difficult meeting in a few days just when you should be getting this letter. A man who is so proud & selfish has been creating minor havoc & discontent which if left unchecked will only spread. I must talk to him and I pray for ability to meet him with loving calm rather than dread & dislike & at the same time that I may be given wisdom with firmness. I am so thankful for you all, with dearest love from Chris.

Greenbank, Grange-over-Sands, Lancs

19.xii.54

Very Dear Chris, we follow as well as we can your doings in your African town. Our congratulations are due to you for the fine start you have made as Commanding Officer; and we rejoice with you in that so far the political upsets that are marking all parts of Africa seem in God's mercy to leave you and your flock unhurt. We pray that it may go on like it so far as your work is concerned and that no let or hindrance may be allowed to interfere with the peaceful carrying out of your mission. Not of course, that we don't include others in our prayers, but we know more of your work & of yourself and so are able to pray more definitely. I was intending before you left England to send you £10 to help you along but then it occurred to us that the money might be more useful to you here in England as a reserve fund and I thought to ask you about it but apparently did not. So please now tell me whether an English cheque is negotiable in your part and I will send it with our love. We both, as you know, are more or less under the weather these days although really are keeping wonderfully well. Auntie Edie suffers a lot in the legs & I am troubled among many things with the eyes, the result of which you can see in this letter-writing that is not particularly straight, and difficult to read! We hope the cheque will reach you safely (is there any other way of sending money out?) & prove to be of divine ordering. Auntie joins me in love and prayer for 1944 no 54 no 55 to be your best year yet, your loving Uncle Edward.

SUM Gindiri

Dec 30 '54

My darlings I am eschewing 'indoor games' as being a non-priority activity here this evening in order to write to you 3 at Brookfield with my dear love to Wilfrid & family & Rene & family also. How I have longed for time to be with you on paper at least, but there has been none. Your cards came 2 days before Christmas Mother & were all much appreciated, as is the utterly lovely Beautiful Britain calendar, it will be a perpetual joy, thank you everso much. We did get through the Regional Church Council alright, even with the Fiyam complaints against us which are now to be thrashed out locally with Pastor Damina before we all meet again on Jan 12th. These petty matters have to be given time just as all the other topics, even when they are as untrue as this. The charge is against me & is that when last there I only spoke with the Suras whereas in fact, of the 4 Fiyam homes there are, I went into & spoke with the women present in two of them. Pastor Damina is the one who was with David on the Jos road when they had the head-on collision with a lorry on a corner – we are thankful God spared their lives again – that is the 3rd car David has wrecked from slightly reckless driving, & he's still hopefully awaiting insurance help. I think we all enjoyed having Miss Noakes & Miss Craven to stay over Christmas although they arrived a day earlier than expected! For me it was hardly a holiday but all the special programmes went off alright, including the usual 4.30am carol singing, and particularly the Bible Sunday ones May, how I wished you had been here to participate and to hear the children recite their learned verses. David asked for testimonies of special help received from Scriptures & gave his own as: 'As I was with Moses so shall I be with thee' and 'Lo I am with you always' and how he is always so conscious of being 'in Christ' and with Him & what a blessing that is. Major Marshall came to Christmas Dinner with us for he had given us a wonderful great duck! Miss Noakes told me some of her experiences as a counsellor at Harringay; unwilling, even antagonistic at first but she then sent in her name. While counselling three times a week through the whole Crusade she was able to help so many people & was amazed by the rich blessing she herself received. Then it was soon time to pack up to come here for the OTC but not till I had prepared our house for the Morris family to stay in our absence. Here there are 26 of us, 14 Europeans & 12 Africans: 4 have come from Etinan (Qua Iboe) 3 from Ilorin (2/3 of the way to Lagos) & 2 from Numan (350 miles) Miss Noakes has brought messages from all sorts of high-up GLB folks at home including one from our Royal Patron the Duchess of Gloucester! She said she was delighted to have this direct link to us in Nigeria, and ended with, 'May God's blessing rest upon all your efforts to fulfil the aim of the Girls Life Brigade in Nigeria.' I have never sent such a long telegram before but here's what we sent back: 'GLB Officers African & European, in training at Gindiri, Nigeria, under Miss KE Noakes, received with joy the message from our Royal Patron. They send loyal & affectionate greetings & best New Year wishes.' Now I will go over for the evening's Epilogue so it must be goodbye once again, with dearest love as always from your own Chris.

Panyam

Jan 18th 1955

Darlings All I do so hope my scribbled note arrived in time to greet you Mother on the 11th and with the knowledge of my thoughts & prayers surrounding you on that day specially; and now Father the same coming for you on the 26th. More than anything I would so love to hear of some big & permanent relief of the Business anxieties that I know have been burdening you – may you be filled with God's love & remembrance. Rene told me of Mrs Potten's tragic end; but I am thankful Tim is free to go to Grange to help the two old dears there. I was sorry to read of B's asthma returning & W's fibrositis & the extraordinary tale of Lizzie running off after all the kindnesses you've shown her! How I wish I could come back & take her place with you! And this dreadful weather you are having with snow and flooding; I do pray for May in all her travelling about & that you all will be kept. Last summer together seemed also to be all cold & rain didn't it?! I can answer your 4 questions: the wedding went off really well, even with the hen getting into my room & needing to be chased out, and there being nearly twice as many guests as we prepared for! Yes, Miss Noakes is just the person we needed here & she's been grand in every way & most efficient, wise & authoritative on committees. Although she has got me appointed as GLB Commandant thereby relieved, I hope, of most of the donkey work, I have earnestly requested that the official title of Major will not be used because as a member of the Society of Friends I am quite sure that would not be approved, so do not worry Father! Miss N will also, with Miss Craven as Secy, take over much if not all of the communications between the London HQ and other Battallions, & ourselves; a great relief to me. I have discovered that it is good to shut myself away in our Guest House to get essential office work done, and with fewer interruptions. Now to the thieves and yes we have been 'visited' by them again, the most recent time when I was away in Gindiri. They were found to be a few quite small boys from a school camp nearby & as they all owned up in the end we had to punish them. Each got a flogging in front of the whole school (only six strokes, ten for the ringleader) and three of them have to do work as well. Their fathers insisted they should be dealt this punishment even though they all come from dreadfully poor homes – all in the same Compound where David was born! Goodbye now my dearest dear loves especially Father at this time, yours as ever Chris.

Brookfield

Jan 19th 1955

My beloved Chris thank you so dearly for your letter of birthday greetings; I worry that you are dreadfully overstrained in your work, but it only determines me to be sure we must not fail you in prayer, for you, like each of us need that greatly. Things are rather trying here with Barbara still in bed all the time, May attempting two days' work into each day, and still we have no sign of anyone to replace Lizzie here although we keep asking around. Last week I went to Crawley Hospital to visit poor Aunt Grace as there seemed no-one else to go; as Mr Yetman was also in there of course I went to see him too, he seemed very low & tired from too many visitors I gather! It is so loud & worldly there, I found myself quoting Quaker doctrine to them both, "You will just have to make a little quiet place in your heart to which you can resort when other voices speak too loudly," and then we had a little prayer which I think was received gratefully. And now this afternoon we were at his funeral conducted very nicely by Mr Brignall, using the order of service written out by Mr Y himself over 20yrs ago, with his chosen hymns. We all acknowledged the truth of the words for him, 'I have fought a good fight, I have finished my course, & I have kept the faith.' Remarkable news has come from Braeside that when the ambulance taking dear crippled Auntie Edie from the Nursing Home, it became stuck fast in the snow on the hill up to Rodborough. A minister came out of his gate to offer help but what think ye?! Edie walked with the help of two nurses to Inglewood and said she was not a halfpenny the worse for it, indeed better, after being indoors for so long! Dear Rene came down today to help us here, it is good of Erik to spare her but I am sure it was not altogether agreeable to him but it is a great comfort to us. She has already been twice to Clyro to help them. May has to go by road in these conditions to Woking & Farnham. Father expected to meet a gentleman at Gatwick today, arriving in his own plane (!) but the fog in London has put a stop to it. He is a Christian man, acquainted with Mr Brooks, wanting us to grow here some special plants he needs in his business, so of course we will meet him to consider this. It may be another of God's wonderful ways of helping us just now; with dearest and best love, Mother.

SUM Alohom

Jan 30th '55

My Darlings it is 8.45pm & I wonder if you are sitting round the parlour fire having supper! I was touched to hear of dear old Sam Yetman's happy passing – a faithful soul indeed, I am glad you were able to see him so near the end Mother. I do hope B is now improving and that you & Rene have had a little time to enjoy each others company. I have been much aware of the help wrought by your faithful prayers, thank you so much; no more so than in the office work where I do seem at long last to be getting my head above water a bit with the accounts & book keeping. I'm sitting in one of our funny little outstation churches, a place I'd never seen until yesterday but one I've wanted to visit for a long time. Every time I can do this sort of thing I make up my mind to do it more often as it really is a delight & the dear people seem so appreciative. This place was only opened 2 yrs ago but there were 130 folk crammed in here and standing outside this morning for the service, some used to attend the nearest village before this was up & running. Now there is one baptised fellow here, two in training for it & fourteen in Enquirers Class. We are the first Europeans here so of course have been under great scrutiny; dozens of small boys, women & girls simply stand & stare, and my eating seems to be intriguing, with more heads poking through each window space to gaze at me! The Evangelist here is a nice fellow with a wife & 3 little ones; his brother & their elderly mother live with them. Before coming here David & I attended the monthly Gindiri gathering & the elections for the new Church Council. We felt that prayers were answered because the 2 most difficult Fiyam men did not get enough votes, athough one even voted for himself. 5 other names were then put forward but it turns out 3 of them were coerced into it by the two troublesome ones who really are fishy characters & I don't feel that they can be trusted at all for you never know where you are with them. Please continue to pray with me about this matter. The other two really seem keenly genuine & we are pleased with them. David arrived back from Kaduna last Saturday with a huge Pontiac – a terrific American car, so big & long that he had to knock down a wall of his garage to make room for it! He had a special service of dedication for it on Sunday afternoon in the playground. Many of us wish he had been content with a less expensive car (it cost £1000) but all the ministers seem to go in for this sort now. Ethel came with me to Daffo on Tues & coped very well with the Teachers & their timetables & school fees; and David Daika our new BB man was also really helpful with the book work. Our Panyam Teachers are trying to persuade me to open another school to cope with the ever growing crowd of would-be pupils; several have had to be turned away from our Beginners Class. It is a big problem which I think must wait for discussion of the implications until Mr Bristow gets back. Now I need to get to bed as I hope to leave here by 6am tomorrow to get back for breakfast, to start the difficult 'month-end' process once again. There is a little motor road to this place off the main road near Mongu, and I do have the car here. David will post this in Jos for me tomorrow & if you get it quickly please pray specially for Payday on Wed, Reports etc Thurs & Church Council on Friday so goodbye my darlings with blessings on you each, C.

Panyam

Feb 4th '55

Darlings before I drop right off to sleep I must tell you a note has come through from my London Bank that £10 was paid in by you Father in December. I feel overwhelmed by your generosity when I think of all you have done for me in these past years – thank you a thousand times but I should hate to think of you going short of anything you might need or find a comfort so please don't put anything more in my bank for a very long while! I wrote last from the village of Alohom where I was on a short trek, determined to return here by 7am breakfast & did; knowing one of the problems awaiting me was Katya's school out in Dimwai where only 12 children turned up. The others were there but their fathers would not pay the fees. 15 is the minimum for a Teacher so it was obvious although difficult that we would have to close that school, just leaving Enoch the Evangelist who was very sad about it. But Katya took his new marching orders well & went happily off to Abwor where they have 60 children & Teachers Nathan Benle & Luther Dabiring who were glad of more help. The next big decision was to open another school as a relief for the colossal number of new children in our Stnd1 here. This new one, only for beginners, will be at Kopal, just 3 miles away, as so many of these new children come from there, held in their nice new church building. I'm going to send a boy who has already completed his probationary teaching year, so cannot expect more than a very small salary until he's gained more experience & training. We get no Govt grant for them until the second year of well established running, so our Churches have to bear the financial responsibility for the initial years. On Payday it was nice to see 'my' boys getting their first salaries, well earned & much prayed over, and every one of them gave me back their tenth to go towards their fees for further training at

Gindiri. When Dafwash collected his he said he would give the tenth but first he wanted to take it all home to pray over it with his family, for its wisest use. Wasn't that sweet! But then he did leave me his tenth anyway. Every single one of these transactions, however small, I must carefully note in the correct book beside the correct name. He was asking so warmly after you all & repeated that in a note he wrote me, ending with 'from one of your sons.' And when the Reports were given, 2 were particularly excellent regarding Yilhi & Yadang. There is also good news from Gwoza via Ishaya D who writes that after his third trip up into the hills the Chief there has agreed to build him a house so he can stay – the chief's own suggestion, and that has thrilled our people here who have been specifically praying for this. There is great activity, and growth, in every department, for which we give thanks, particularly the big work in our own Dispensary which has now expanded into 7 smaller clinics in outstation villages, and in 4 of these leprosy clinics are also held, & in addition, Frances Barnden has recently started an Infant Welfare Clinic right here in Panyam to which more & more women are coming, both Christian & non-Christian. Ethel Foreman has been kept tremendously with the growing numbers in schools and Teachers writing to us begging for help from probationary teachers; she is now going around visiting & inspecting and I am so grateful for their help. Several of my old GLB girls are now opening up schools for women & young wives of the Teachers/Evangelists; it is grand to see them taking on work like this & being a blessing to other women & girls. It does rejoice my heart to see Africans now doing what had hitherto been jobs assigned to the European Missionary – one such being the long talked & dreamed of Bible study Courses for men, led by our 3 Pastors in Training, firstly for those already Evangelists, but growing now to include any men who are hungry to learn more of the Way of God & His Word – a priority in this work. Now, lest you should think 'everythin' in the garden's comin' up roses,' let me add I've had a horrid time of it with 2 (Christian, & one a Church member) builders wanting a large contract price for building

Butura School and I will not give in to unpleasant demands like this; and Danko, our old houseboy, has upped and left the work after being a most satisfactory Teacher for years, in order to take a second wife; and our big Convention is at the end of this month; so I know you'll be remembering these, dearest love Chris.

SUM Milet

11 Feb 55

My Dear Mrs Cheal I hope you and family are well as we are all at Milet well. Dafwash is preparing for going back to Gindiri, but he writes this for me. We are very happy for having an Evangelist with us here he is now teaching us very well and more & more people are still coming to know the Lord Jesus as their Saviour, we have over 300 people coming to our church now! Did you know the church we built was broken down? We are now preparing for a new building & I hope it will be finished before rainy season comes. Dafwash and I were very glad to have the Cards you sent to us for the Exmas we hope we may use them in the service of the Lord. How is your family and how are you getting on in life? I hope that the Lord will bless you in all that you do that you may be a help for those living in your place and to us too, may He bless you amen your friend Mwantet.

Panyam

Feb 21st 1955

My Dear Darlings Father, Mother, May, Rene, Erik, Wilfrid, Barbara, Ant & Mouse, and Alison, David, Nona & Jonathan!! I include you each one as it seems quite impossible to make the time I long to do to write individually personal letters, but as dear Uncle Alex said, "The love's just the same," and so it is. I think of you all so very much & have just heard on the 7pm news of more snowy weather you poor dears; and May has to be out driving, and Barbara still so unwell, I long to hear of improvements as I continue to ask God to bless you & keep you safe. Work continues unabated but I must say I believe your prayers do also for I do feel uplifted and enabled to cope with it all. Last weekend I was in Gindiri & after the meetings I planned to write copiously but what actually occurred was that I wrote 2 short business notes and fell deeply asleep – so I am enabled to rest well also, thank you! Back here during one recent sorting out of several palavas at once, one old heathen chief had marched in full of complaints and anger and as I looked at his livid face, something about it reminded me of Uncle Arthur (!!) and in a pause I told him so to his & everyone else's intense amusement. We all than had a good laugh which cleared the air wonderfully & when he went off I said, "Goodbye Father!" – uncle is almost the same as a real father out here. So that was another day at Daffo again without David but with Ethel's stalwart efforts, and Joel & Manasseh too, we got through all that had to be done. And another good Teachers Meeting here where they all come in for cups of tea & we discuss problems & needs in each school & finish up with prayer. The next day Ethel & I left early for a short trek to visit & check on schools in the Chip area but only motored as far as the big river, as yet un-bridged, but when the engineers have finished we shall be able to get to Chip all the way by car. We stopped at Kopal, Abwor, Jing where the evangelists in charge are doing awfully well with growing numbers of pupils, & now asking us for more equipment and more teachers to help! The rest of the way we were driven in style upon Major Marshall's great lumbering tractor, crowds of people along the way coming out to watch our progress. We ate our picnic at Yardang's house & Ethel stayed for a proper school inspection & I took my bike on to Longkat but it was terrifically hot by then, the air as if off a furnace. Showul ran out to meet me, with a few of the babies with him & I met up with Dabohon & Sila the Evangelist who is doing his very best for all his pupils, & took me to see Datep the crippled man. Major M had collected Ethel then drove us both on his lorry to Jibam where we were to spend the night. She & I were so hot but there were no facilities for a bath for us so we went down to a branch of the big river & as there was no-one around we bathed & it was simply wizard! I had nothing but a nylon slip though E had brought her bathing costume. After that & our meal, a few other Christians wandered down so we shared jolly good long crack with them. I chose to sleep on the ground with just a groundsheet & it wasn't too bad! After early morning prayers we left to visit a few more villages & their schools, talk with the head engineer who was inspecting the bridge designs with his wife & 2 sons. We stopped again briefly at Abwor & from the car heard Katya teaching singing to a class of small children – the scale in perfect tune! This was the first time I'd driven down and up the big hill on the new road & it was fine. Goodbye now my own darlings with all my love, Chris.

10 Harewood Rd, South Croydon

Feb 22nd '55

My Dearest Chris, many thanks for your letters & the lists, all most welcome, and I did send on to your Mother just as you asked me to. The news sounds all most encouraging & I have been repeatedly remembering you & will continue especially during the Convention days; I hope that David is with you & all continues to go well, for if he is not I am sure it will be hectic. I think the idea of a quiet room in which to help individuals & to pray is an excellent plan & I love the thought of my old round hut being used for that. A great many heartfelt prayers were offered up from there so perhaps now many will be helped there through to decision & victory. Such is my homesickness still for Panyam that when reading your letter tears rained down for awhile; all very silly I suppose but there it is. It is wonderful the way Abwor has shot forward and that the young wives are getting schools going – that is just what is needed. You simply must have someone to take over supervision of schools or I cannot think what will happen when Ethel's 3mths are up. We are in our 9th day of snow & ice & biting winds, fresh snow every day & night. It really is ghastly & the cold has penetrated all outer defences & got to my very marrow & core; flu is raging around but thank God I am kept well, just so very cold; much love & prayer, Nakam.

As from: Brookfield (but the I. of W. really)

March 13th '55

My dearest darling, please forgive this scrawl but I have such a weather cut on my thumb I can hardly write. I'm still thrilling at your happy descriptions of the Convention & especially using that Quiet Room – just exactly what was needed to bring to birth the vague aspirations stirred in hearts by such terrific messages; and the team sitting around outside it under the trees in deep conversations with the seekers, Bibles open, then one going off into the QR hut & the team member coming back for another. That picture in my mind is as clear as a photograph in my hand. God will surely bring much fruit from this as you do your part in helping to grow His Kingdom. Do you remember I had to be here last year while you were at home? But this yr I'm only staying 4 days but even so there are 10 meetings to attend within that time. At this moment I'm sitting outside & it is so wonderful to feel the warmth of the sun without the dreadfully biting NE wind we've had at home for so long. Last Tues I had 3 meetings in Kingston, Chislehurst & Tonbridge. The roads were bad and it was snowing hard by the time I got to C'hurst so after that one I returned to Redhill and went by train to Tonbridge. There was further heavy snow during the evening & I was thankful for the train & that I only had to drive home from Redhill although it was freezing by then & the journey required great care. The drawing-room meeting (C'hurst) is run by Peggy Watson every month & despite the weather conditions & that her road is not made up, the room was absolutely full with women from several different churches or none. Peggy is doing such a great thing, it was a stimulating & happy time, & there have been several conversions. I met Mrs Warner who used to give the wireless talks on 'Lift up your Hearts' she is so brave with her husband still in hospital she looks after their 4 boys, things are not at all easy for her. So many seem to be in the midst of the stress & strain of very hard times – which brings me to Father; I have given away some of the tenth of Susan's legacy and intend the rest for him. But he would not accept it, even as a loan. Reading through 2 Cor.9 again I felt strongly it would be right so I sent it to him and on that very day a man called to see him about selling off some of our frontage. You probably have not heard this yet but the big petrol people have offered £4000 for the land between the cottages & the mill. How I hate to think of it sometimes but we do recognise with thankfulness that it surely must be the Lord's answer to our prayers; all my love for ever yours May.

Panyam

Mar 19th '55

Thank you, my Darlings, for all of your lovely letters, each one so very dear to me, as you know. I took Ethel to Munpun – 17 miles in the car then walking on rough ground down a beautiful valley for 3 more miles – E is excellent at her job. She knows just what to look for, & tells the Teachers their faults so nicely, & their good points too. There are 3 Teachers there for the 50 pupils, and they have nearly 300 in to Sunday services. Leaving her there I went on 2 further mls up very steep hillside with Ishaku to Asa, another recently opened outstation where I was glad to see they are doing so well with 40 children in school, happily taught by dear Zakariyas. He is the horticulturalist & I noticed he has a row of little Cassia trees growing there. Returning for Ethel we then had the long climb back to the car & were extremely hot & weary by the time we got there! On Friday I went to Gindiri to collect Frances after her short holiday & also Miss Mary Riley who has now been with us a week & we are enjoying her company. Mary is the new Youth Worker from England, keen to see & do everything & happily fell in with the little programme I had in mind. Ethel was going to spend the weekend at Jing – 20 miles along the new road, & walk from there to Katul on Mon, cycle to Jibam on Tues then by lorry to Jibilik on Wed so Mary & I dropped her off, staying about half an hr, then we carried on to Abwor where Katya looked after us very well & we had a lovely time. Mary was impressed by all the wee schoolboys & their admirable behaviour! In the evening we joined the Teachers & their wives & Mary was intrigued to see them finishing their meal outside under the stars. As each family group finished they got up washed their hands & cleaned their teeth then sat down again. Then we had gramophone, some of the old records than some from Harringay – they specially liked 'To God be the Glory'! Two of the Teachers speak good English so Mary was able to chat with them & of course we used Sura too for the others & the wives. Mary had my camp bed & my brainwave worked – to use the seat of the car which came out easily, with the back also & was quite comfy. After breakfast we set off for Gu two miles on, an outstation opened 9 yrs ago & very hard to begin with. Really it is a miracle when I think of the time Nakam & I camped there with a tent, there was not one follower; now there are nine communicants & over 300 in to Sunday services! Mary spent her last Sunday in England with Nakam & brought a message from her for these people, which was much appreciated. On our return to Abwor Mary preached at the afternoon gathering & I interpreted for her. The next morning we set off at 5.30 to walk to Jinkam another newish outstation so I could talk with the Evangelist Eliya Davil who wrote a note to me saying he wanted to leave the work but without any explanation. We also stopped at Lingpang to pray with the few Christians there; & learned that the R.Catholics have opened new stations very close to several of ours & seem to be rather keen to take over, as in other places sadly. Katya & Luther are turning Abwor into a hive of happy activity & learning; they work well together & set such good examples of bright cleanliness & enthusiasm. On Monday they gladly presented a BB Drill for Mary to see, and took her to meet the women running the school for wives. It was truly an impressive visit, hard work but such a delight, and we were overwhelmed with gifts of eggs & chickens as we departed, just in time before a huge thunder & hail storm hit them. Back in Panyam the 2 large cockerels were just enough to feed us plus 2 unexpected visitors & during that meal there was an emergency call out to fetch a seriously ill woman from Baron, so Frances went to her. David has come home from Kaduna & it is good to have him here once more. We've had little time to talk but he told me of a growing sense of opposition to the preaching of the Gospel in Moslem provinces so we set Sunday aside for special intercessions along these lines. It does not affect us here in Plateau Province but it does affect Bornu, Maiduguri & Gwoza, Numan & all our Danish branches. I brought Mary into Jos with me for the Field comm. & our staffing needs are to be discussed; I think we may be given Kay Maxwell when Frances goes on furlough. I know you will enjoy the enclosed letter from Katya I've not corrected his few mistakes, dearest love to all as ever your own Chris. Have realised I never mentioned the offer from Esso which does seem like an answer, although the thought of another big petrol station & garage so close is not appealing, yet I don't think you could refuse such an unexpected thing. It may be a means of blessing to them as well as to us in ways we cannot see at present. Yes, we are to have Kay M who has excellent Hausa, when she gets back here in June (I've written asking her to call in & see you before she leaves to come here) and also Dorothy Somerville for schools at least till December; I am very pleased with both; blessings on you all C.

SUM Abwor

19.3.55

Dear Mrs Cheal, I am very glad to write these few lines to you & hope you are well. Thank you very much for your kindness & the beautiful verses you sent me & cards which you sent to my father and he sent his greetings to you. After I left Gindiri I went to Dimwai village to work but not enough pupils and was transfer to here Abwor village where we have 60 pupils & I work with Luther D and Nathan B. I have 19 boys in my class & enjoyed my teaching very much. This week our Miss Cheal brought us a visitor from England, a newcommer to this land, came to see our Mission Station Schools. Remember will you please the people of Dimwai in your quiet time they seem to be difficult to receive our Lord into their hearts. Give my greetings to your family & other friends in Christ, Nishe & her little boy sent their greetings to you, your loving son in Christ, Katya.

Panyam

Mar 31st '55

Mother darling thanks for your recent letter with the happy news of your London day out with Father; I'm sorry about poor old Percy Tullett, he & I used to be on duty together during the V1 raids, give him my greetings if you should go to visit him. The same post brought me a letter from Auntie Lena with restrained news of the Annetts; and from Rene telling of Erik's plan for a Swiss holiday with Mouse & 2 others –

sounds wizard & I hope will do M a lot of good. Last Thurs night I was awakened by Frances at 1.30am saying our nice BB man David Daika was in a coma following 'a mysterious accident' in which he fell down a steep bank into the river late at night. He had been busily preparing for the BB Camp at Tahas, so surely this was a direct attack by the enemy against this effort. We prayed over him in the Dispensary where he was laid, Pastor David & many others joining us for this. Ernest Killer brought over the Doctor from Mongu LS who decided it was 'only' concussion & he should soon recover, but it was 2 hours before he was fully awake. He was able to walk to his home but has been directing the final preparation from his bed. We may never know the cause of his accident for, as is often the case, he has no memory at all of the evening it happened, but he is at the Camp & I hear it is going well. Despite this & other delays we got through end of month business satisfactorily & this evening 4 new evangelists were officially accepted, 2 as replacements & 2 to open new villages. Now we are getting ready for Ethel's wedding on Saturday; just a simple affair in our sitting room with 12 guests for the reception, a simple meal on small tables. Tomorrow, Friday, I must make a chocolate cake for it, to compliment the wedding cake which arrived yesterday a bit bashed about in transit but still it should taste good! Forgive any more now but I am nearly blotto with sleep, sending my dearest love as ever Chris.

Easter Sunday 1955: Darlings it was a special delight to me to get your letter of the 28th on Good Friday when I had more time than usual to read & re-read it & now I'd give anything to slip in beside you all to share the rest of this lovely Day with you in your family gathering & the wireless tells me you have at last some warm weather to add to the joy. And it is so good to hear of the Billy Graham relay film & the preparations, and Mother, no need to worry, I can't think of anyone more fit than you to be one of the Counsellors! I eagerly await further news of the permit for the Esso people & I'm sure you are being kept from worry & as it so clearly bears the stamp of answered prayer that we may confidently expect to see it working out alright or something better than expected. It's a great pleasure to me that my report of Mary Riley's visit here so cheered & encouraged you to write your thought about May coming out here for a similar sort of visit which fills me with happy visions – that would be perfectly wizard! Of course if you could all come, better still, but seriously it would be reasonable to hope the Bible Soc might cooperate & be willing to send her for 3mths to assess the need & value of womens work in this country, & then a month's holiday with me...kai oh kai how my castles in the air are growing!! Ethel's wedding went off quite happily; David is getting very good in marrying folk in English! The bride & her bridesmaid were dressed very simply in light green, white & grey. The eats were nice and well appreciated & we soon cleared up after the 13 visitors had left & Frances & I have been finishing off cake ever since! We have had a busy time with another Edu Comm & a Field Council mtg also, both helped now by the formation of a new committee to serve with me & promote an Assistant Schools Manager to be understudy to me to learn the ropes, and everyone approved this! And we have been allowed to submit new proposals for simple school building starting with our 3 hoped for new school sites. So things are slowly moving in the right direction. This morning I had the privilege of preaching the glorious Easter message to a packed full church, but now darlings my writing time has truly gone, dearest love as always Chris.

Panyam

April 16th 1955

My Darlings I am in the unusual position of being alone here for the weekend so it feels as if I have a lot of time & space in which to write first to you & then many other overdue letters. I do feel sad thinking about poor Uncle Ed & Aunt Edie being so shut in there & apparently not very happy; & I was surprised to read of Alison having an Xray for her back, I knew of no trouble there & trust it is nothing too serious. One of our boarders has just come to me saying he cannot return to school on Monday because he only has managed to get 16/- of the £1 fee, and has no extra for his food, and almost worse, last night white ants have eaten his one shirt into ribbons & he has no other garment. I went to fetch the one cotton pullover we have left from Christmas but as he is by far the tallest boy in class, it is of no help to him. I shall have to come up with something better for him. Last week Frances and I went off for a day of school inspections and measuring up sites for new schools mainly in Jing, Longkat and Kopal – always a happy task; however, not so this time. At Longkat I left Frances dealing with medical patients & went to find Chief Showul & measure the site. An air of tension gradually developed into a palava which increased into an angry & beligerant shouting match – when Africans get angry over a farm you're for it. I tried to intervene & calm & difuse but to no avail. It turned out the Chief had graciously given me Sila's farm land for the new Mission school & Sila had said nothing until he realised what poor land he was to get in exchange. I felt absolutely awful & quite helpless, and ashamed for there were so many heathen men gathered around to watch this spectacle of Christian men behaving in such a dreadfully un-Christlike manner. Finally an unoccupied farm the other side of the road was agreed upon & I managed to grab hold of Sila & not let go until we got to his house where I ordered him to stay until he had cooled down. Then I gave him a serious talk. Showul was still shaking with fury at Sila but I told him what he himself looked like and had said & that his immediate need was to repent of his fault then forgive Sila, or between them they could wreck the entire work of God in that place. He did slowly quiet down so then he & Katya & I could measure out the new site & then I fetched Frances so that we could sit & eat our meal for I was utterly spent & it was blazing hot by then. Going back to Sila's house I found both men sitting together calmly talking with several others who had witnessed all, as if nothing had happened; they welcomed me and we talked deeply. I have told you all this horrid incident so you can understand how crafty the enemy is to attack like that 'out of the blue' just when things seemed to be growing & prospering at such a fine rate; and how desperately we all need your continuing prayer support & protection, as does this very necessary new school which has not got off to a very good start. Perhaps the devil is afraid of the blessing that surely will come from this place & so is opposing it as hard as he can. There were no other such problems that day except that the promised lorry did not show up so we had to push back up those 4 long miles that felt like 6 to chose & measure the final site of the day. We got safely back here at 5pm & at 5.30 the heavens opened & a real tornado gave us nearly 2ins of rain from very black clouds.

Sunday pm now with apologies for falling asleep & writing no more then! After all the services & SS & Tea I then walked exactly 2 mls up the new road to Niyes to visit a young communicant & church member who went off to join the army 2yrs ago leaving his young wife at home. He returned on leave a few weeks ago & the Niyes Evangelist told me he has heard this chap is planning to leave his lawful wife again to go to the barracks at Kaduna with a different young girl. The wife came to me, very troubled, asking me to speak with her husband so that he would take her with him. We agreed that David should speak to the soldier but if D is not back then I should. I went & found all the men communicants finishing the day's worship with prayer together & specifically remembering this soldier. They too wanted David to see him but one of them recalled hearing the man in question was leaving tomorrow; so we all prayed then I took Ignatious having decided if the man was home I was to speak to him & if not, to leave it to David. We got to his compound & found he had just gone out to Kopal, so my mind was clear & I returned with Ignatious, leaving the job to David as soon as he possibly can. My efforts to help the lad with the ant-eaten shirt produced nothing but dear David had arranged for a parcel of old things – which has just arrived, as has the lad, who has now gone away delighted! He could not face Church today in nothing but rags. Back to yesterday & the Pankshin Local Education Comm which was rather tedious as these meetings so often are. The RC priest was not there so his application didn't even get discussed; and my 3 applications for schools were argued over though I was nicely backed up by a visiting teacher who stated the great need for new schools, but without the LEC approval we cannot proceed. It is an impossible situation really: everyone agrees the country wants & needs education, but the Edu Dept insists on fine buildings & equipment (our grass roofed buildings and dried mud desks are no longer considered suitable we are told) so that it is not possible for local people or us poor Churches & Mission Stations to bear the cost. I think now I shall have to get David to bring this up in the House & tackle the Minister of Education & see if he can't do something! Now I must stop & write to the Plastics Lady – so sorry I can't remember her name, can you please send it quickly & her address on an envelope – for the toys have arrived & very nice they are! About 10 doz little motorcars, & some paint boxes, and two very special television sets though I hardly know how to use them. The mail has just come with your dear letter Mother, so many thanks & so glad you had a happy Easter time and that TV added to your enjoyment! Goodnight my dearest dears with all my love, Chris.

Panyam

May 3rd 1955

Darlings, perhaps you can tell by the too-long gaps between my letters, that this seems to have been another overly-long time of increasing palavers; but I am kept well & strong and for that, and much else besides, full of gratitude. And your dear letters continually bring great cheer & delight. Yes, the soldier from Niyes, Ifraimu Mape, did meet with David for a most serious talk & warning not to abandon his young wife Christiana again, especially as she so recently miscarried their first baby. However on the following Friday he did leave home without his wife, called in at a friend somewhere who had hidden the girl for him, and took her off, leaving his poor wife no option but to return to her father's compound. I went up to talk with her & join in the prayers with the friends surrounding her – a sweet & precious time; so in her sorrow she does at least have the sympathy & help of her Christian friends. Humanly speaking, how can she possibly remain faithful to this man now? I know you will be praying for her also, thank you so much. On a better note, Adamu tells me that all is now quite peaceful between Chief Showul & Sila, since that dreadful time I was involved in with them. Interestingly Sila did not come in for end of month reports but sent Damen in his place. David asked me to go with him to the Pankshin School Advisory Committee which was pretty awful and made us long for the changes we trust will come when the Local Edu Comm is set up. At present it appears that the taxes from our District's people are simply feeding into their school finances enabling them to provide new buildings & fine equipment. What couldn't we do here with that kind of money?! It is very hard. But, David Daika has agreed to take on the Schools Managership, subject to Mr Whale's agreement; this is hopeful & I plan to go to Jos to talk with him about this. I really do try to make the Scripture lessons simple & vivid but I've just had a bleak afternoon examining the GLB girls – only 1 out of 14 passed; dearest love as always from Chris.

Jos

May 17TH '55

My darlings I am here today stocking up foodstuffs and for meetings so will make sure to post this if I can get it written in time during lunch. I am fully recovered from a couple of days in bed with a spot of fever & feeling rather squeamy; and Frances also is fine but was under the weather last week. We all enjoyed Mr Caldwell's 6dy visit and a bit of the Blarney Stone too & he loved going out shooting with David; touring the Fish Farm, and the picnics we all went on while climbing the gorge en route to showing him the nearest outstations. The great New Bridge is nearly completed, at least the enormous concrete pillars are, upon which will rest the Bailey bridge. So we shall soon be able to motor across it & all the way to Chip, so now the plans are to establish a Church down there initially for monthly gatherings and then weekly. At Jing Mr C was tremendously pleased to organise a squad to make a buttress support for their Church wall which had just made an ominously large crack, forcing the new young Teacher to get all the children outside in a hurry. The Christian men went out for supplies & returned remarkably speedily with huge tree trunks to shore up the wall from outside. The work at that school is beyond praise – after only 4mths all the 37 children are reading, writing and doing neat & correct sums! I did have a chance to read your lovely fat mail before starting out this morning but so sorry about the postscript added re Erik – how strange that that sort of operation should cause a set-back; do hope he's better by now & anxieties relieved. And Mother I repent in dust and ashes for my vulgar English, thank you for your check – it is good to have such now & again! News of Dietgard (?) is interesting, I do hope she will soon settle in & be of real help to you; I can't imagine anyone being in our home & not being the better for it! And I should have mentioned long before this the packet of magazines arrived safely – apologies dear May – & particularly enjoyed her article on the Bible in the World. Another confession: I received a letter from the Chief of Katul recently released from prison, full of praising God for His mighty power & thanking us for our prayers – I'm afraid mine were for his poor wife rather than for him. And there is good news of Christiana: one of her friends gave birth to twins and could not manage so gave one infant to be adopted by Christiana who is so wonderfully cheered and her breast milk has fully returned! You will remember we have been in favour of divorce only in special circumstances & in all these past years our Church has only granted it to 5 people whose partners had proved repeatedly unfaithful. All 5 have been re-married to Christians & 3 are now Evangelists. However the Regional Church Council brought this up and we have been put on the carpet (sorry Mother, is this vulgar also?!) & told this is un-Scriptural and, despite both David & I defending it, it cannot be allowed any longer. Remembering & lifting up the wonderful Wembley goings on, & sending dear love, Chris.

Panyam

May 31st '55

My darlings the recent letters from Mother, May & Rene, all eagerly devoured & my heart goes out to you each one in your various trials: R&E in this most anxious time, May's increasing workload, W with that bad extraction & headaches of general Business worries & that Esso hasn't not materialised into anything worth while yet, and on top of all that the rain & cold. But what wonderful news from Wembley & the thousands blessed in the rain, including, we hear from this end, Sir John

& Lady Hunt (of Everest fame) came out in tears & stood in the rain, and that the Queen & the Duke were there on the quiet on the Thursday night! And from here too, I have a holiday booked from Aug 1st-21st in Miango; and this which I know will cheer you: one of our nice new boarders is called Andrew, baptised into that name, already a Church member, told me his story one evening as we sat on the verandah under the stars. Born in Jing of heathen parents who both died years ago, so A went to live with a heathen uncle near Langtang; there the son of the Evangelist told Andrew about the Gospel. He was thrilled & determined to become a Christian but his uncle did all he could to stop this, finally locking him up for 3 days without food. After that he ran away to Kwalla in the very south of our District, to an older brother who had become a Christian. Here he went forward & learned all he could & in 1952, with several other unmarried fellows were the first to be baptised. In 1953 he started at Chip School then passed the Entrance exam to come here & he should progress to Stnd6 by 1957! Both David & Yariyep had to go to Makurdi last week for a very important political meeting. All the small non-Moslem parties have decided to join together to give a united front against what seems to be increasing Moslem pressure. In their absence I had to cope with the usual Saturday business in Gindiri on my own but I think it all went well; I know I was helped. Also, Christopher just took off for the weekend having made no provision for his Sunday classes; we just found him not there so had to take them ourselves. Sadly this is not the first time he has showed this unreliable behaviour. David was most put out about it when he heard, and C was very fed up with me when I ticked him off. Jo Spencer & Joyce Milverton returned with me from Gindiri to have a few days holiday with us; they are both very nice & so good at their respective jobs of training teachers & domestic science. I do hope Barbara is better again by now and that you are all well, and not too much bothered by the wretched strike; as ever yours with dear love Chris.

Panyam

June 8th 1955

My Darlings it is 9am, not my usual time to sit & write, but there has been no time in the evenings, and I am awaiting the arrival of Miss Leonard from Bristol where she is SUM Local Secy, our next English visitor! Coming out for 2 months at her own expense of course to see the work which has so interested her for years, with an itinerary planned for her, starting at Forum, coming here today for 6 days then I'm to take her on to Gindiri. I do not know her, only that she is not young, so I hope I can entertain her satisfactorily. Naturally this sort of thing does take a lot of time, although I do enjoy it, especially as things here are not quite so rushed nowadays, which is a blessing. Your letter took 8 days to get here which I suppose isn't too bad in strike conditions. To quote Florence Allshorn, "I'm tired of things being so hard for everybody." What with Barbara still being so unwell, making life so difficult for her & poor Wilfrid and all of you who see but can actually do so little – even though I know you go round often to do all you possibly can; and how I long to hear of some relief in the Business trouble which does not seem to be lessening at all. At least Erik is out & better & I hope the time at Eastbourne will really set him up again.

June 15th now & I'm determined to add a bit before the last post goes, as there has been absolutely no time to write in the evenings for ages I'm so sorry, yet yours continue faithfully arriving plus the recent inclusion of my photos back again, thanks so very much. One of our guests has needed careful handling & much time ensuring her comfort because she is afraid of much in this country and almost everything here with us; she shows little understanding of what goes on here & little interest in finding out; I am not entirely sure of the purpose of her visit. Dorothy Somerville has arrived & seems very pleased to be here which is so pleasant; and next we expect Anna Esler from Ballymena to be based at Gindiri, & Peter Bradford coming to Kabwir. Last week I saw Mwantet again who told me they do now have enough grass cut to finish the church roof & hope to do it on Saturday; and Dafwash has promised to try to be a more positive influence in his Training class. I told him about you Mother being one of the Counsellors during the Crawley showing of the Billy Graham film – the blessing you have received while taking part, and he was so pleased. He is such a dear fellow; now my dear love to you all Chris.

Panyam

July 10th 1955

My very dear ones, my recent letters to you have been brief, rushed & infrequent, please forgive; I do not like it to be so but here are more brief lines – the best I can do for the moment. I was remembering Jonathan on his birthday last week and Anthony on his Commissioning & picturing how good he must've looked in his uniform. I spent an evening at Mongu Leper Col with the Hamiltons, so enjoying their company & their lovely soft Belfast accents! Dorothy S is settling in well, very busy in the schools, and picking up Sura extremely quickly – such a gift! After a terrible journey over slippery muddy roads & waiting for the delayed lorry at Gindiri I was able to meet Kay Maxwell who'd only left London the previous afternoon. She was really tired but gave me your message right away! The four of us are getting along very happily with much good talk and laughter. A letter came to me & brought much joy for its beautiful English as well as content, from Katya. He says some of his class are troubled for they are not right with

God so he told them to come to him after school & he talked & had prayer with them. He finished with, "I hope our Lord will let them know Him as their Lord." He is busily responsible & doing very well for the whole school at Abwor. Now Mother I know you particularly have been praying for the troublesome marriages I told you of some time ago, well here is a clear answer about one couple that will please you. The Bidol Evangelist's wife came to me asking to be released to go off anywhere she pleased with whoever she wanted. She knew perfectly well I would not but tried for a long while to convince me how impossible it was for her to stay. I knew he was doing her no harm. I told her to look well at my photo of you, handing it to her – you who pray for her. I explained that my parents had occasionally had words, sometimes you get on Father's nerves & sometimes he on yours, but you soon forget about it and the only thing we your children remember is the great love you have for each other & how you are always happy to be together – this is what Christ does for two people who belong to Him, committed to each other & to Him. She began to soften & I then added my thought that she was so silly to want to go to another man when she had such a tall, handsome husband. We then prayed together & finally she agreed to go find her friend – another wife who wanted a new man – and they would each go home. That really was a great wonder, in which you have a considerable share Mother & I thank you. Dorothy brought a fridge with her so for the first time in Panyam we are having the benefit; I got a leg of mutton 2 days ago & put it in the cold & this evening we had it & nothing could have been tenderer or nicer, specially with masses of mint sauce! May dear I have an urgent need of a couple of hairnets, please slip them into your next envelope; and Mother your noble example of preserving has inspired me & I have managed to bottle 3 jars of mangoes using the Porosan tops I got in Crawley last yr; also 9lbs marmalade from our own trees & 9lbs of marrow jam too. On Sunday afternoon man was brought in from Kopal terribly mauled by a leopard, & an older man wounded but not so badly.

Neither Kay nor I would attempt to stitch such deep gashes so we put him in the car straight to Pankshin Hospital. He is young & strong & should recover, but it's a long time since any human casualties from leopard etc. dearest love to each of you as ever from Chris.

SUM HQ Jos

Aug 3rd 1955

Well, here I am Darlings – on holiday! I didn't get away till Tues after all as there was a big Moslem festival & no shops open here; but it was good to have the extra day to finish up all accounts etc & Dorothy got back from her 6 days in Mongu so she will keep an eye on poor Kay who has been unwell since she arrived but says now she is feeling a bit better. Good news before I left was that the two troublesome Bidol wives are back with their lawful husbands & all seems to be well; & Katya with 23 others were all passed & ready now for baptism. The car has had a full overhaul so I'm off to Miango.

Later, the 7th: it is very quiet here so wonderful rest times, until tomorrow when the Missionaries Conf is here for the next 4 days. I've enjoyed playing volleyball and a sort of darts, & the Sunday communion service here was packed full into their new Church & help partly in their vernacular Iregwe & partly in Hausa. Your letters caught up with me here & as always lovely to receive, & thank you for the hairnets…but I've not worn grey ones before! And poor Rene with her trouble, oh she does have a time of it doesn't she.

Now it's the 12th & I'm marvelling at the speed of your latest letter Mother – you posted it Tuesday teatime & it arrived today, Friday at noon! Darlings I have felt specially burdened in prayer for you this week

& now you write of the great Business disappointments with the loss of the Ifield job, and the Esso and the Hyders plans, I am so sorry, for these do feel like crushing blows don't they, yet we know the Lord has heard all our constant united petitions, so we can be confident He will make His own provisions for the need in His own perfect timing. My faith has been tremendously strengthened by the treat we had on Weds evening when some SIM folk brought a cinema projector & 3 very fine films, one being the Moody Faith & Fact, Dust or Destiny featuring a species of fish brought up on the highest yearly tide of the California coast; in a matter of seconds the females burrow into the sand, lay their eggs & then get carried back out on the next huge wave. Then a microscope showed the eggs in salt water growing in a laboratory; it was the miracle of timing that staggered me – if our Almighty Father God can arrange with such precision the moment when fish spawn, surely we must marvel afresh at the Divine forces called into action for every human spiritual rebirth in His name. It encourages me to ask you all to join with me in special prayer for fruitful new birth from our Convention in October. I've just heard from Panyam that Dorothy's amazing fridge has smoked out, filling the dining rm with the smoke, apparently she turned it up too high. But I did like to hear that Barbara is at last well again, & that May's due back from the North, & Anthony should be somewhere between India & Malaya; none of our relations have been that way since Uncle P left Formosa I think. Dearest & best love to you all C.

SUM Jos

Aug 21st 1955

Darlings my Miango holiday was fine – even playing (& losing rather badly) a few games of chess, and those 4 days of special fellowship, and driving through such cloudbursts that several small rivers swelled up & over the new road & had to be driven very slowly through. I met a young SIM girl who is also going through the fires; she was very happily married to a fellow from her own home town & they were working together up near Nguru when he suddenly developed symptoms of mania. He is no longer hospitalised & can go about a bit but is quite irresponsible and does very queer things. Added to this the poor wife heard news that her mother is having an operation for a brain tumour. Much prayer was going up for her, and him, at Miango. But really this letter is to assure you of my warm & loving remembrances for the 26th & most special greetings to you both Mother & Father on another Anniversary in which we all rejoice! Also of course I yearn that there might be some lifting of the heavy load of anxiety & care to mark the Day. You have been so much on my mind in this respect for it is a burden on my heart to think of you being so hard-pressed and brought to the end of all human resource like this. Daily Light of last night, Aug 20th was a challenge & a comfort & I thought of you reading it in bed together & hoped it was being thus to you too. Whatever happens, you have always the great & solid comfort of knowing that our Nursery Business has been carried on upon honest & God-fearing lines and as your hope & trust has ever been in Him, so it is surely His responsibility to bring you to a solution of the present crisis. And whatever happens you know that we shall always stand together in love & mutual aid; but I do wish there was more I could do, & sending very dearest love & constant remembrances, your own Chris.

Brookfield

August 22nd 1955

My beloved Chris just to think we are still 2dys off a year since we left you at Gatwick, it seems so much longer. I feel you are very near to us at this time & your dear letters have been such a comfort. The roses have been especially beautiful this year I wish you could see them. I remember you always with much longing & desire to see you. How lovely that you were able to see those films, and the detail about those fish does indeed bring home in a new way the power & might of our All-wise God. The land previously allotted for Esso, Father has now offered to the Povey Cross garage but Mr L there wants enough acreage for Sam's Cafe also so we await decisions on that. Wilfrid has pocketed his pride and been to see Mr Ledgard who said all his affairs are in the hands of his wife (the one who had been his secretary you remember) but did invite W to return. This he did, even with one of his bad heads, but the answer was still a definite nil. We return to our knees and can only leave it in Higher Hands. Several folk say our work is quite as good if not better than other firms and they do so hope we shall stay in business & continue working. I lost one of my chicks last Saturday, I fear it was sun-stroke for they had no shade but Paice has moved them so so we hope there will be no further casualties. Still waiting for this man in the Office with Father discussing accounts, I do feel rather strung up & tense about it & need patience in the waiting. I do hope Father will realise this and soon tell me. 7.40pm now & the verdict is as poor as suspected, so now we must see what the Bank will say; you may be sure we have explored every avenue, but our expectation is from God and He never faileth, we will praise Him for all that is past and trust Him for all that is to come. Now sending you all the love it is possible to send my darling, your Mother.

Panyam

Aug 25th '55

Just a quick note Darlings to tell you 2 things; David came to tell me of the gruelling time he had in Kaduna for it seems the Moslems in Govt are now trying hard to get rid of him. The 2 wks seemed like 2yrs to him & there was no other Christian to talk with but he proved the Lord's help & presence with him in a new & deeper way; his daily readings were such a help, esp the stories of Asa & Jehosaphat. Finally the Governor, Sir Bryan Sharwood-Smith called him in, with the 2 Christian Chiefs of Kagoro, & they had a very helpful talk. And this evening I went out to the parents – not Christians – of a little girl about 6 who died this morning. They told me she had a pain in her chest during the night & she prayed to God to take her, "But Lord please not till the morning," and to her mother, "But if I go who will help you with the baby, you will have trouble," and to her father, "In the morning take me out & bury me with my brothers," then she sang hymns & prayed until daybreak when she passed on. So sad and yet so wonderful to hear of such staunch faith in one so young; she had been at school & to church but has been ill much of the time so very little chance of learning. Her mother was in my SS class when I first came out, and of course I took that opportunity to talk with her & her husband; ever yours, Chris.

As from: Panyam

Sept 21st '55

Dearest Mummy thank you so much for your dear letter of yesterday & I posted one to May also yesterday in which I referred to Barbara's word to me about the calm faith of Father & Wilfrid which surely must give deep satisfaction to the Lord. As I read your letter I thought that you come not one whit behind them in calm & courageous faith & I'm sure the way that you have all faced up to the difficulties & huge burden of anxiety during these long months will be a witness to many of His power to uphold His own in their dark times. When I got home from Daffo yesterday afternoon I found Kay, so recently back from hospital, looking unmistakably jaundiced about the eyes & skin, feeling rotten again & vomiting. Jaundice is a serious disease & needs careful handling so we decided to get her straight back to hospital. Whether she had this in her when she went in initially or whether it is something new I don't know but it is strange how she has been ill with one thing & another since she came to us. She's not been able to keep down food, however light, so we got her in the car with a pot in case of need. Mercifully the Govt Hospital had a spare bed so took her in and I'm staying at our HQ overnight.

Now it is Thurs morning & I'm thankful for a good refreshing sleep after too many hectic days, more than a month's worth anyway. GLB opens again on Tuesday & the plan was for me to hand it all over to Kay this season but that is not looking likely.

Friday morning & I'm back home having got through everything including dental checkup & seeing Kay & Dr Branch who tells me she has a pukka jaundice and will need to stay in for at least a fortnight, but this is probably not related to her previous fever & symptoms. This will make a lot more work for us but I had another example of the Lord's kindness over the car on the way back, so I can hardly doubt that His grace will be sufficient & He will supply all our need. The handbrake didn't seem quite right & we were heavily loaded with two nice fellows Ishaku & Aristarkus, 7 bags of cement, 8 galls of petrol & 12 of kerosene, so on the way I stopped in at Barakin Ladi at the Motor Workshop only to find the back wheel was very hot. A white mechanic put an African on to it and in 5 minutes he had fixed the rear brake tension & all was well. If I'd gone on driving much longer some serious damage would have ensued. Now goodbye my dears all of you with much love from Chris.

SUM Jos

10.10.55

Dear Chris I've now rec'd both your letters via Pastor David & Chief of Jos. I am very concerned about Kay and have written to Dr in Charge of Plateau Hospital, Dr Branch, asking for an explanation for surely if she is well enough to nurse a mental patient then she is well enough to return to her work with you where she is very much needed. I understand she left Hospital on the Monday & returned there on the Friday. In reply I had a real snorter from him declaring he will now be withholding certain privileges. It is a strange business and gives cause for concern; I am not satisfied with his actions or excuses. I think in any further illnesses we should consult Vom. I am sorry about all this but I do not think Kay will now leave Hospital until the weekend & if this is so I will bring her out with me on Tuesday. I am so sorry that you have been so troubled and overworked by these irresponsible actions. Please greet Dorothy for us; they still only have Dec 20th for her flight. Mollie sends her love & we both send prayerful remembrances, sincerely, Bill.

31 Queens Rd, Immingham

Oct 23rd '55

Darling how especially good of you to write when we know you are so dreadfully busy; I was so pleased to get your letter yesterday – Sat'y, thank you very much for it. So you have had your hair cut off, I'm sure it looks fine! And I'm trying to grow mine. I wonder if you are back yet from your trek or if you are preaching out in any of the villages today. It really is most strange about Kay, I'm sure you must feel rather uneasy about her & the whole business. I do hope & pray that her presence at Panyam is not going to be an added burden as you have so much of everything to see to; I am specially remembering this problem. I did think she seemed unusually nervy when I saw her for a short while at Brookfield just before she went out. Bless you for asking darling but no I'm afraid I've not done anything definite about Cousin Fred's suggestion yet for I do so loathe the thought of any more examinations etc. and while I feel well, as at present, I would rather just carry on. And Dr S does not seem to think anything of the continuing frequency of the other…pause whilst I answer the door…it's Jehovah Witness people again, they are very busy around here selling books & holding public meetings & so on. Erik went to Lincoln to fetch a Swedish steward from the mental hospital where he's been for about a month but the doctors say he is fit now to leave & should go home to Sweden for further treatment on his kidneys, toxins from which affect his brain it is thought. He has nowhere else to go so we housed him here until E can get him onto a boat. It was a strange experience however he was quite alright & very grateful indeed. Yesterday they both left for London to get him on a Swedish Line & E is still there to meet the Lutheran Pastor & talk about a different church or mission. I doubt if the present Mission will stand up to another winter. And poor E had his dentures on

Thurs & is finding it very hard to keep them in; he's to see the London surgeon again Nov 11th so I hope we can spend that weekend at home although May will be away in Ramsgate then. Please greet David & everyone, I think of you all constantly, God bless you always darling, as His love surrounds & unites us all, ever yours Rene.

Brookfield

Oct 28th '55

My beloved Chris I am missing your regular letters but I most certainly understand the reasons for your lack of time to write and I've been remembering you on those two treks, and all the preparation for the Convention, and the new GLB girls, & the rather confusing problem with Kay, on top of all your normal daily doings and businesses. Now this one of mine should reach you for the 4th though it won't go now till tomorrow, so let it bring you my very dear love & many happy returns – you have lived through half a century – just think of that! I do pray the next half will bring more stability & peace in the world with a great movement toward Christ & His way of Life & your own part in that great work opening out step by step before you. So once again I lift my heart to the Lord in thanksgiving & praise for His gift to us of you & His continuing graciousness to us as a family. May has heard a few times now in different situations the splendid idea of the Bible Soc possibly sending her abroad I mean further than the Channel Islands, even to you, and how such experience could so add to her already excellent speaking work & opportunities…we continue to live in hope for this too! Of course nothing is near definite yet but I tell you this to help keep your courage up for it! Now my dear love you will be living in my heart this whole week & beyond and I need hardly say surrounded with my special thoughts & prayers for the 4th even more than usual with all the love I can send for a really happy birthday, ever your own Mother.

SUM Jos

Nov 9TH '55

My Darlings here's just another quick note to assure you all is well & I'm doing fine, but simply unable to write as I've so often longed to. The week away in Kulere was most useful but very busy – as is every week it seems at present – and the Convention went well even with fewer people wanting to get right with God, though of course each one is most precious. We have done a lot with the Women's Groups (6 now!) & they are all growing & when they were all together Kay spoke to them & did well. At the main Church Communion we received 120 new members, and the end of month accountings for Sept & Oct went off well. On Sunday Oct 29th I spent a Quiet Day down by the river where it was so lovely & peacefully quiet I really was able to use the time to pray & think & decide about staffing issues & some unresolved palavas & generally get a bit rested. This had become a priority & I'm glad I did it & the following Thursday I got David to do the same. I had a lovely birthday & your dear letters arrived on the day! And your book Mother just before, so thank you all so very much for all your love, prayers & kindnesses; and all the Christmas cards have arrived safely too. While I'm here, for meetings and stocking up on essentials as usual, the car is in dock yet again with further trouble with the back wheels & brakes. Yesterday's committee did not finish until this morning, it is a huge & colossal responsibility making these plans & changes to general and school staffing that affect so many people's lives. At present our own staff will remain; Joan Onions is a very nice girl, sensible, quiet hard-working sort but I fear we won't have her with us for long; Frances will come to Mongu but not much before next spring; Dafwash is going to Abwor and Katya to Munpun and Yadang to Chip & now my dearest love to you all, Chris.

31 Queens Rd, Immingham

13.11.55

Darling Chris I do so hope you had a very happy birthday; you were much in my thoughts throughout that day. The CSSM has sent off the new book on The Acts by J.B. Phillips & I really hope it will arrive by Christmas – it comes with our very dearest love & with every good wish. It will I believe be good reading & you will find much pleasure, profit & enjoyment from it. Nothing of interest has happened here. Erik still awaits word from Sweden. I have now had 2 iron injections out of the prescribed 12 and cannot report any marked difference and the Dr tells me it is only the anaemia still causing the breathlessness, pain & swimmy head upon walking or any slight exertion. Tomorrow DV we are going down to Brookfield I am so looking forward to seeing them all again. In Ant's letter last week he said he's to be moved to Bentong to train the new troops but so hoping he'd not have to do that for the rest of his Malaya tour; I am thankful to think of him out of the jungle. Poor Mouse struggles on with 'O' levels but I have not much hope of his passing them. I have been trying to read & study the book you gave me by Dr Scroggie, but there are so many differences aren't there, on minor points anyway, with what the PBs think or the Jehovah Witnesses. Our postman is a JW and has been here a couple of evenings discussing the Second Coming and getting most indignant & angry at what Erik says; dear love from Rene.

Panyam

Nov 19th 1955

Darlings, just back yesterday from another trek to find letters from Mother & May which fills me with delight! I do so regret the falling off in my letters to you but I've had to attend more planning committees and go out visiting more school districts & new buildings urgently before the end of the school yr Dec 9th & note each building needing repairs – too many of them. I long to be able to share the little details – amusing & otherwise – of all of these things as in previous years, I'm so sorry for the lack of time. Tomorrow I must start out again to visit an outstation not seen before, Koyilum, overnight there then to Mupun on Monday, then Abwor & back Tuesday for the usual Daffo day. All this traipsing around is tiring but oh so well worth the effort & I love getting out there amongst the dear people who so appreciate a visit! And you would have been so proud with me when I popped into a class where Katya was teaching English & was delighted at his excellent pronunciation & clear way of doing things. At Koyilum I found 70 folk all waiting Sunday school for us so I had to speak there too; and after dark we gave them a – new to them – projector showing, to their great delight.

Later: just had to go out to measure up for foundations for a new house for our new Bookshop Assistant, Kefas Dokbish, training at Maiduguri to start here in the New Yr. I have been invited to go with Mary Craven to Kaduna for the 4dys of the Queen's visit there & 12

GLB girls will be paid for by the Govt to go as well – how ever will I choose from all our girls?!

Now it's the 22nd & I'm back from Daffo & revelling in letters from Rene & you Mother plus the parcel with the dress, thank you so very much, & I finished 'Good Morning Miss Dove' what an interesting read! Now about the enthralling prospect of May's visit!!!! It is awfully hard to suggest which weeks or months have the best weather; April should be drier for visiting other places, but right through into June is also lovely. No need to bring a mosquito net, just boots, & I'll buy them from you after, & ordinary summer outfits. Nakam left a sun helmet which could be yours for any trekking we do; you must have Yellow Fever injections (negligible) & recent vaccinations. I'm wondering if my next rounds of schools visiting will be with you darling May – how utterly wizard that would be!! Now goodnight and dearest love as ever, Chris.

Panyam

Nov 29th '55

Darlings you know what a joy it is to me to think & plan for May's visit – can it really be? It seems like a dream! And it's like a dream too to think of the Queen & the Duke coming even unto Jos, as we heard from London this morning, & who knows what she might do on her informal weekend here?! I feel sure the Panyam new road will be an attraction with its beautiful scenery! David of course has been told that he will be among others spending the 4 days with her at Kaduna – just think of that! By the way Mother the river where I spent the quiet day is on our compound, only a stone's throw away from the house, but so sheltered & peaceful down in the far corner of our compound. It is lovely to know you were praying for us on the Daffo day, especially this time as David had to go to a Govt meeting at Mongu which meant I had to cope quite alone with chairing the mtg and steering the discussions plus writing the minutes too. I felt greatly helped through it all so your prayers were well answered. I'm everso thankful to be able to tell you that Kay seems generally much better now & is working hard in the Dispensary. Along with Aristarkus to help, she will take one of the 6wk Bible Schools here in Jan-Feb next year. Joan Onions is so very nice and is working hard with Kay on Hausa lessons. Today I found out that Joan has skipped with a GLB team in the Albert Hall so from now on I've handed over all my skipping squads to her! David is facing more difficulties within party politics; he was voted in as President of a new group of non-Moslem peoples. Certain men of position in this party whom David does not trust have been doing strange things & organising meetings without telling him. In today's local paper it says they have expelled Pastor D Lot plus his secretary, but when talking with me about it David appears quite unperturbed, saying everybody knows these men and the trouble they like to make. He intends to make a full statement of the true facts to the paper. Goodbye my darlings, as ever yours Chris.

Panyam

Dec 8th '55

My Darlings it was 25yrs ago today that I first arrived here in Panyam & I remember most of it as if it were yesterday, especially the crowd of horsemen – David among them – that galloped in ahead of the car, all in eager welcome. Well, a lot has happened since then & today has been considerably fuller of activity & interest than even Dec 8th 1930. I might not have remembered the occasion if it hadn't been for May's dear letter in which she mentioned the 25th anniversary of my sailing, I thought I ought to commemorate it in some way so last Saturday Dec 3rd the day I first set foot in Nigeria I invited 3 married couples who were here then & are still going strong, to come & spend the evening. They were David & Christiana, Bitrus Bishtu & Unaisi Anwet (she is David's sister) Eliya Tokan & Victoria Nasik; they came at 7.30 & we had a simple meal of curry of venison which David had shot the previous evening & rice & mashed potato eaten with spoons & fruit salad & custard then cups of tea. They all seemed to enjoy it & most asked for second helpings then we looked at my old photo album & the old faces & scenes brought much happy chatting & laughter which felt like it could have gone on all night, but I played some gramophone then David led us in prayer & they left about 10pm. Dorothy, Kay & Joan enjoyed it nearly as much as I did! Rene writes that she found you Mother & Father quietly confident and not as burdened as on previous occasions which of course rejoiced me – so you see we all share in the Help provided in spite of difficulties. Two of my girls, now ex GLB, Grace & Damaris are going off together to run their first Camp, how I should dearly love to go & see them at it but that won't be possible, nor I think very wise anyway. We have to discipline Christopher, David's son; this would be most difficult & awkward except that David is even stronger on this than I am; but I do feel so sorry for Joanna & their 3 darling little ones. Now about my poor watch: it had a sad accident when the strap broke I put it in my pocket & it got left there during the wash & not noticed till our cook came to iron it. Strange to say it did still work for a day or two after that but has completely stopped now, George Williams at Gindiri opened it & gave it a good oiling, but advises me to send it home to you. With that packet will come my most loving greetings for Christmas to each one of you, wherever you will be spending the Day. I have written & sent off all the cards you sent to me but there aren't enough – did I only ask for

50? Please would you give my warm greetings to Ted & Carrie, Steve & Bessie, Edie, Kathleen Willis and her mother, as I usually send to them also but cannot do so now this yr. And a lovely card has arrived from the Clyro family with a letter from Barbara – my thanks to her please. I will send this to Immingham in the hope that the lovely plan will come to pass with you all there together. So dears we will rejoice together though 'sundered far' and here we shall just be three, Joan, Kay and me, and as always with my dearest love, Chris.

Kwangwhamoon Bible Society, Seoul, Korea

December 23 1955

Dear Miss May Cheal I thank you for your nice letter it reminded me of the hours I spent at your home. It seems that the fact I was at your home and had a swell dinner and looked around the fine Nursery Farm was a dream, a dream very very pleasant. The life I am living now is a reality and it is a very very cold and confused reality. The new Bible House would be completed next spring. It is very cold to do any cement work now water is frozen so work is stopped during winter. It seems that we will use new house sometime in May 1956. I am so anxious to be in it because our present office house is so small our work cannot be carried out efficiently. I am glad that your sister has gone back to work in Africa. The days I sojourned in Isle of Wight were also a dream too. Now I cannot discriminate the faces of those whom I met over there. My family is alright. Our Bible Society is having a great Christmas sale. We are sending 4000 or 5000 copies of Korean Scriptures to districts every day; the space for packing is just 4' by 5' but 3 packers are packing 100 or 300 packages every day. We have a half ton pick-up truck it is very busy to bring Scriptures from warehouse and take packages to station. We keep almost all our stock in rented warehouse which is 2miles from office, office is 32' by 27' with best wishes I am yours sincerely Young Bim Im.

Panyam

January 16th 1956

My darling May what a day this has been with supervising paint mixing for the 2 boys distempering the house in preparation for your visit & in case the Queen should pop in! So moving out of then back into my room & bathroom for all that while raising salaries for this month for Baron & Kulere staff & sorting out yet another palaver about a couple of school children from Abwor & Gu that has upset the Chiefs, plus too many interruptions for supplies, small troubles, and Christians refusing to help other Christians or otherwise evade responsibilities. A day heavy with disappointments so I'm feeling rather browned off; just the sort of day when one needs to spend some hours in prayer, running to the Great Shepherd remembering they, and we, are all the sheep of His pasture. A sweet letter has come from Nakam rejoicing over your coming & Kay & I spent the afternoon getting the GLB girls into shape & into new uniforms; never have they been better at Drill, all so keen to be selected for the march through town & lining the road for the Royal arrival. Thank you for sending the proposed itinerary for your trip, it is all so wonderfully exciting, but oh I do so hope you will feel you can come back here after Lagos. Don't you think that for once a Cheal could take their full due – that fortnight's holiday owing to you from 1955 surely means you could be here the full 6 wks? And the week of Bible Society business in Lagos surely means you could take that on top of your six? That seems reasonable to me & I know it is backed up by my deep desire to have you here for an unhurried visit; it is such a priceless, wonderful opportunity – one we could hardly expect to be repeated, so darling do just take a header into it and for once throw duty to the winds! To spend so much money on fares & then have anything less than your absolute limit is a thought that grieves my economic, & selfish soul! I know the worry of Father & Mother being alone that long is a reason for your quick return so we'll pray that someone might be given to be with them. I long too that you will be able to share my life here as far as is possible so that if it's His will that we should share our later years together, we might have this blessed experience to look back to & enjoy. My prayer is that you will be rightly guided in all your plans & preparations. Don't bring mosquito boots for I have decided to order a new pair from Griffiths McAlister the tropical outfitters for you, with a couple of other items I need from them – we are both size 6½ aren't we – and for hats, travel in a felt that will be some protection from sun & also bring a summer straw for Sundays & dress occasions. I do not intend that you should walk anywhere in the full heat of sun time but I have the spare sun helmet for you when we are trekking. Cotton washing frocks are most useful & seersucker is a boon because of no ironing when travelling; bring 2 better ones for evening & in Lagos you might even need evening dress, but a black skirt & bright blouse would do instead, oh and a cardi, and indeed a mack you'll most certainly need when we get a storm! Strong walking shoes with rubber soles are the best for walking over rocky paths, and an old really comfy pair for trek, & a couple of prs of tennis socks, plus sandals & maybe a pr of white suede slip-ins but most types of sandals are available here. Take care of yourself darling, ever yours with dearest love Chris.

Panyam

12.2.56

My Darlings now that the Queen's visit to our area is over I can begin to look forward to May's with great zest! It was a most exciting weekend and all planning went off well, even to the pre-arranged transport arriving promptly & with plenty of space for all our girls plus two fellows to help with luggage, & the 3 of us. The entrance to Jos was gay with flags, bunting & banners, plus a great banner made by the BB so we decided we'd better get one made also; we already had posters for the car. That evening Mr Bristow & others just back from Kaduna told of the Garden Party where Mr B was introduced to the Duke of Edinburgh & had a chat with him! Later on I had a phone-call from David still in Kaduna to confirm some details & he just happened to mention he'd spoken to the Queen 3 times, sat with them on the Weds eve dinner, and been photographed with her!! Not much sleep for any of us with noisy girls in one room and noisy boys in another. We left at 8.30 after breakfast, all our girls in good formation; it was rather wonderful to be the Officer in Command of such a big parade, with Marjorie beside me of course: 6 Company Colour Parties plus our Band of 4 Drummers all marched through thick crowds either side of the road, for about a mile to our allocated place to 'stand guard' just next to the BB place so we saluted each other in passing! Our Sura boys looked so proudly official at the head of their Companies – Moses Nerle, Katya, Datilik & Bibwahat, & David Daika. Then the waiting began and it was a bit tedious until 11am when SHE came along in an open Rolls Royce car. She wore a pink dress & a small white hat & everyone was of the opinion she looked ill, very white with a marble set face, barely a smile. She held up her hand but it looked as if she was holding herself in from being sick or something. She went by so quickly that one only got a fleeting glimpse & many Africans missed it. It got terribly hot waiting for the Duke after his visit to the tin mines but he warmed all hearts by waving & smiling with his head out of the window of his closed car. We then had to ladle tins of water out of buckets for the poor girls were too hot & thirsty to march back again for a while. We could not get near St Pirans Church where the Queen & Duke went on Sunday morning so we paraded with our girls to the overcrowded & very hot SIM Church; it was a good service. We had our own drumhead outdoor service with the BB in the afternoon to which the Chief of Jos came & prayed beautifully. We'd heard the Duke would come but he did not. I'm getting quite used to driving about town in the dark now; my dear love, C.

Panyam

Feb 22nd 1956

My Darlings I am thinking so much of you all in this bitter weather you are struggling with, hoping you don't have to be out much on snowy icy roads; I'm trying to write this in the 80 degrees of the coolest part of the house! We're also struggling with a shock – Damaris our lovely & talented girl teacher was taken very ill with what we think was meningitis but the speedy treatment given by Kay saved her life. Two days later one of our new little boarders from Kulere came down with similar symptoms but with the same treatment he was dead within 24 hrs. He is one of the first 5 ever to come here to Senior Primary school from heathen parents & I knew this would cause a terrific upset so went straight off to take the news to them. Taking 2 of the remaining 4 with me I motored the 42 miles then walked the last two miles & returned remarkably quickly with the boy's father & brothers who immediately fell to the ground & started wailing. The father hadn't a stitch of clothing on except a straw hat which he threw off. Some nearby women & children heard the noise & ran to join in – you never could imagine such a commotion. Nakam also wrote of the dreadful cold & 12"-14" of snow, I do hope you are all keeping warm and safe but I grieve with you over the final Esso disappointment – let us pray something better might be for you. Mother, Kay & I have chuckled about your Shrove Tues pancakes & you actually tossing them! Today we hear the Govt really is to give a 50% building grant on new Jr & Sr Primary schools so I have visions of the 3 new ones we so badly need getting built now. Forgive scrappiness now for I must stop this one, C.

Panyam

March 13th 56

My dearest darling May my heart beats quicker when I think of 6wks today but I do so understand that in the midst of your dreadful weather, family illnesses and heavy work burdens of course doubts are going to assail you as to the wisdom of leaving Mother & Father for so long but let us together pray that the right person will be given to be with them. Just as my furloughs are always times of huge rest & blessing in every way for me, so I am sure this trip will be for you. 'Rest in the Lord & wait patiently for Him' can you not just hear Uncle Alex reading that out at Ifield Meeting; I believe the Lord who has led you thus far will make possible the glad fulfilment of this hope & dream. As if in honour of you the big new bridge across to Chip is at last open. My mind is full of plans for while you're here but I am trying not to put them to paper or overwhelm you until I hear that you are as sure as I am about the rightness of your trip but perhaps you could be thinking about this one thing? Would you be willing to talk to my Bible classes and Women's Fellowships about the influence of the Bible in other lands? Just the simplest stories would delight them, & of course I'd interpret; nearly all our Christians contribute every Christmas Day to the Bible Soc and so to see and hear you would be most interesting for them & I believe you would enjoy it as much as they! And it gives me the greatest delight just to plan our days here together & trips out. There are warm invitations for you to come to all the people I visit for they are so pleased to think of welcoming another member of our family! Much prayer already has gone up for you & Victoria Nasik refers to you by a Sura name 'Na-me' i.e. Na-May and I expect you'll be that from the first! I'm back now from a long day of meetings etc in Gindiri and find your dear letter waiting for me – so now we really can say DV 6weeks today?! How utterly wizard! Kay has lent her camp bed for our treks & I've just popped a mouse-trap into our trek box! Could you please bring some Porosan caps for 1lb jars; economy labels; my watch currently being repaired; & a small bottle of that stuff for cleaning suede shoes? Thank you for telling me about Father being so trustfully calm in spite of the awful Business troubles, that is marvellous, what an example he is to us all. So now poor old Aunt Grace is out of her suffering & weaknesses – a mercy for her but please give my love & sympathy to Barbara; she will miss her. Dear love I must go to sleep, in happy anticipation of seeing you soon, as ever Chris.

Panyam

April 5th '56

Time is flying on May & it will soon be 2 wks today, then next week and then that lovely moment DV of the 'renewal of the fellowship of hand & voice!' Knowing how you appreciate your room to yourself at home I was glad to get your last letter saying you will be happy to share mine but you shall move into Kay's the minute she has left or be most welcome to share mine all the time; I want you to be free to say and do what you would most like in all these sorts of things. If you can get the morning plane from Kano we could leave a little earlier but if not till the afternoon flight we'd leave directly to get to Panyam before dark as I do want your first impressions of the compound to be in daylight; and if Dr B can take you round Kano early morning you should be able to see as much as by staying a few hours more. Don't be tempted to buy anything there as prices are always higher there than most other places. Mother writes so happily of your coming, bless her dear soul, and of her hope & prayer that she & Father might keep well & not cause any hindrance of mind to your leaving. It was lovely to be able to go by car right through to Longkat & back yesterday, Frances & I both enjoyed the day very much. She has written out some ideas she has about means of widening Bible distribution in Bornu particularly & in all our Mission areas generally and I hope to be able to discuss this with you. I do wish you could meet her yourself & hear more details. It might be possible because she has to fly to Lagos soon for a Leprosy Conference so perhaps you could meet there. Maybe you'll get another line from me but if not darling may our dear Lord wrap you round with lovingkindness & tender mercy every step of the way and bring us to a glad meeting on April 24th with dearest love as always, Chris.

In the plane to Kano

23rd-24th April

My darlings I trust you have all slept rather better through the night; we had a 4hr wait at Tripoli while they repaired a propeller which, they said, was not damaged when the lightning struck us but later developed a fault. Great care is taken over inspection & repair which is comforting. I am thankful we had not to make a forced landing here; we did pass over a rocky part of this desert with some form of trees but here it is just limitless stretches of bare sand. Poor Chris will have a long wait in Jos. The pilots came around to assure us that all is well even though it was an unexpected sudden storm; but for me it was a little worse than that Sunday afternoon I flew to Ireland with lightning all around us. When the big bang came we thought it was thunder but the brilliant flash seemed inside the plane then we bumped & rose & fell for 40minutes. It was most comforting to think of all the friends who were praying, & remember that 'God's got you & me & the whole world in His hands.' Once it became steady I have moved about the plane without any sensation of upsetting the balance! We've just had orange juice followed by fruit salad, bacon, egg, kidney, rolls, butter & marmalade & coffee – I've done well! One very thrilling thing is that this aircraft is the Atlanta, the one in which Princess Elizabeth & the Duke went in to Kenya in 1952 and in which she returned as Queen on Feb 6th! And my seating area is in the part that was converted from her bedroom! Now darlings thank you all again each one for your loving thoughts & prayers for me; I am so thankful Rene is there with you & trust you all slept well; goodbye for this time, take great care of your dear selves & give Nona my special love, I do hope she is getting better, ever yours May.

Panyam

April 22nd '56

Darling Mother & Father you can imagine my thoughts & excitement as the time draws near for our dear May's departure & arrival! I want to assure you that I intend to do all I can to make her visit here a real rest & happiness for her, getting her to relax certainly during the first 2 weeks while we mostly stay around here. Our outings I think will be Fri 27th to Kabwir, 28th & May 4th to Gindiri. The one thing I fear is that she'll be inundated with kindly folk who want to greet her! David gave it out in Church today that she comes to represent the Bible Society & it "will be our mutual joy to meet her & for her to meet us!" Mwantet & Dafwash have written to say they are coming up specially to see her. Our compound looks simply gorgeous & I should have her back here by 6pm in the best evening light!

The 23rd now & here I am in Jos & our dear one is probably at Tripoli Airport – it's about 10pm. I came in today bec the car need a new battery & a service at garage and I picked up your letter Mother at B.Ladi & was so glad to have it & to know that all is well.

Tues 3.45: Here we are after a joyful meeting!! Their plane was late at Kano so both Frances and May came on aft one & now we've had a cup a cup of tea & we're off! Dearest love Chris…and…yes we are actually together & of course we've just laughed & laughed! I had such a nice time in Kano, and Chris is looking very well, her hair is only a bit grey round her forehead; all our love May!!

Panyam

April 25th

My dearest family I cannot promise very frequent letters throughout my stay but I know you'll want some first impressions. The flight from Kano to Jos yest took just an hour, in a Heron, slightly bigger than the Dove, with an English pilot & African wireless operator or 2nd pilot – which does sort of symbolise Africa today. I am so struck by the eager alert look on the faces of the young people, their upright bearing and interest in everything. No restrictions at Jos Airport means that friends are allowed as close as they can get so as we taxied up to the 'terminal building' there was Chris in her blue popper dress & shining smile trying to wave and get her camera positioned at the same time! I think she is thinner than I am but she says that's rubbish! We had a most welcome cup of tea at the SUM HQ before setting off & the whole drive was through beautiful country with always the blue hills in the distance. We stopped at Mongu market for a moment as Haruna Chinman was there to greet us & for the 8 miles from there people along the road were waving & smiling. When we actually drew up at the house we were surrounded in a second by scores of happy laughing people all wanting to shake hands – what a welcome! All so sweetly friendly & all asking how are you M & F! Chris is so marvellous with them all & they just love her & I simply came in for the overflow! David came in as we finished supper, he'd been away doing weddings, with such a dear & warm welcome & a few minutes later Old Father Lot appeared who had made a special night walk up to greet me which was most touching. He kept looking at us both saying 'Kai' over & over, they all think we both look very alike.

Now it's the 26th & this morning C took me to School Assembly & after Readings & Prayers the Headmaster Nehemiah welcomed me

& I had to unwrap the Nakam Cup & hand it over before being shown into classes. In the Dispensary hospital I saw the smallest living human I've ever seen: a baby girl who at 2 months still only weighs 5lbs but is making progress; then a short visit to the Bookroom. The compound is simply beautiful how I wish you could all see it & all the flowers & vividly flowering trees, everything is clean & tidy and the hills around are lovely. The house is 'home' immediately, so comfortable & cool; the rooms all much higher than I'd imagined – much higher than ours so you have a sense of space. I had imagined swarms of insects as soon as the lamps were lit but there were none last night although windows & doors wide open. The light from the lamps is good. I haven't honestly missed running water, or even the chain that pulls, for everything is arranged so well & cleanly. I'm sure it cannot be so at every Station but certainly is here, and I slept well! Yes I wore the mosquito boots last evening and took Paludrine & have no bites. I enjoy the food, which is much like we have at home, and feel generally thrilled to the marrow to be here! Dear old Andreaus Karkiyes came round with his greeting, you just feel their kind friendliness flows out of them like a warm spring. This evening the Teachers have been in here for their weekly meeting to discuss any problems then pray together; one of them prayed so sweetly for you Mother with your 2 daughters away, and gave thanks for all your prayers. Now it's a beautiful Thursday morning, I think of you all & hope you had a good night after that meeting in Crawley. Mrs Reed should be with you by now & I do trust she will settle in quickly & be of real help to you; Chris joins me in sending masses of love to you each one, always yours May.

Panyam

April 30th

Darling Mummie I have an idea you may be thinking of me this evening remembering that one week ago we said goodbye & 47 yrs ago I had almost arrived! I don't think I realised that the people & things & places that we've heard about for so long would come alive in such a vivid way when actually seeing it all. Both Dafwash & Mwantet have been in with their warm greetings, both eager to know how you were & to tell me of their gratitude for all that you & your prayers mean to them; how I wish you could see them & all the Teachers & boys too & hear their deep gratitude for your prayers and truly know what you prayer is achieving here; and how much they need you to continue praying for them all. It really is an exciting time in the development of this country but also an awfully dangerous time for these youngsters who've had the advantages of Gindiri education but still face enormous temptations. Yadang & Moses Nerle have both come in for talks with Chris, both splendid chaps & so bright & cheery. It is staggering to see all that's going on & available in the secondary school against the background of the home life of many if not most of the boys & girls. Yesterday in Church I was picturing you picturing us; Pastor David spoke and Chris took the afternoon SS classes. After tea we went visiting in one or two other compounds, finishing up with Old Father Lot who told us again how he became a Christian. Next week, after the end of month business meetings, we are going on trek, all wonderful experiences for me & I'm enjoying it all tremendously, sleeping, eating & walking well as well as relaxing quite often on the verandah. You would be so thrilled to see the love these people have for Chris & the way she talks & works with them all. Now darling I trust you & Father are taking good care and not getting up till after breakfast; blessings on you both & my dearest love May. And now I take over on this last page to tell you how lovely it is to have May here to see & share my life; nearly everyone we meet says we are so alike! May is wonderful the way she chats away to folk, in English to those who understand it & by interpretation to those who don't. All are so deeply interested to meet her & hear more about you both & dear Dafwash so generously brought us a leg of lamb from a feast his family had for his brother's wedding, we had it for supper when the Barndens & Kay were here & it was delicious. I'm very thankful that May seems so well and able to enjoy everything, specially our food – including mangoes she says! Mother thank you for the lovely dress, it is a perfect fit & so nice; and the nightie from Rene is just what I needed also, many thanks to her too please, as ever yours C.

Panyam

May 3rd '56

Darlings this is Chris to start, to tell you May is quite a part of this place now & makes her way about with her smile & handshakes & her little bits of Sura; you would love to see her with these people & when Mwantet came he was nearly incoherent with delight! Tomorrow DV we go to Gindiri for the day & back with a stop at the Mongu Leper Colony & next Weds we hope to start on trek & be away 5 nights. May seems really fit, only with a bit of prickly heat on her hands – but it is pretty hot & we've had no rain yet to cool things down. Dearest love as ever from me…here she is: Darlings I think of you so often & wonder if you are alright & have had the result of Father's Xray. It is so very interesting for me to see Chris at work, in her office most of yesterday with the month-end accounts, as all the men come in to pay in their monies from the schools & be paid their salaries. Many of them in the flesh are the ones whose names are so familiar to us & for whom you have prayed so faithfully. They love to laugh & what a blessing it is that laughter is the same in all languages; my faltering few words of Sura cause gales of mirth and Barnabus Kohop very carefully brought out for me a sentence in English before bursting into peals! This morning there was a lovely communion service & I was glad to stay on in church afterwards as David gave the Reports & dealt with all the questions & problems & Chris gave me whispered interpretations. I couldn't help wondering how much of what we owe to our Christian background we simply take for granted. It is only when you hear the difficulties these men are up against, working in places where there has been no Christian witness at all before, that you realise how greatly privileged we are. They took a short break at 3.30pm having been in session since 10am after early church, & Chris said they will probably go on till 8pm. This month she won't spend all day there but she usually does, & David of course has to, on top of taking the communion service first, and when he's away Chris has to do it all. It is tiring of course but her energy in the heat amazes me. David asked if I would speak in Church on Sunday morning, mainly about the Bible Society so I feel I can't refuse. It is a great responsibility and a great privilege too. Goodbye darlings with my dearest love to you all May.

1st Bn Royal Lincolnshire Regiment, Rompin, Sembilau

May 5th '56

Dear Auntie Chris & Auntie May the opportunity of reaching you both is too good to miss, it is just wizard to think of you both in Panyam & I'm sure it's being a wonderful time. I heard your plane had been struck by lightning – how thankful we all are that you were brought safely through that storm. Now one can assume that the inter-aunt link-up has been successfully carried out! It is splendid to think of you both 'cracking' round the Mission Field & even visiting the Chief of Chip etc! After four weeks here of ambushes, getting soaked, then sleeping outdoors, I'm glad to report we were relieved by another platoon last Tuesday. We've been in camp several days now in between operations but by no means idle. All rice is cooked centrally & strictly rationed & my chaps have already discovered and stopped several irregularities. Tomorrow is a big Moslem feast so we are relieving as many of them as possible as they did for us at Christmas. Next week we'll probably be back in the jungle watching for bandits but it will be pleasant when we can stop thinking of, as Nanny would put it, 'wars and rumours of wars.' I'm sure after being out here I shall value far more the blessings of safety and peace and home – and a bed to sleep in. Even if the things we have to do out here never seem like adventures at the time, they most certainly will when surveyed from the comfort of the sitting room at Brookfield! I must go to sleep a bit before my batman brings my shaving water at 7am. Only 149 days left in the Army. This brings all my dearest to you both, Anthony.

Panyam

May 7th '56

My darlings this is May & it is after 10pm but no chance of sleep on account of a thunderstorm. Tomorrow we go to Vom to take Kay who is going back on staff there, I think she is very sorry to be leaving. Still nothing from you in today's mail so I am really hoping you are all well. Now Chris: last week we had a school visit from the Minister of Education, an African Moslem, who came with his European Secretary & the European DO; they gave us a superficial glance & left again in 15 minutes. Then May & I went off to Butura to check the building of houses for Teachers which should have been finished, but was not. So I had to do as I'd said & sent Datilik's two classes to their homes & brought him back with us hoping this will spur these incredibly lazy folks into action. If they cannot build a house for their Teacher they do not deserve to keep him. May has done wonders in speaking to the women & they have asked her to repeat her stories to the fellowship meeting next Tues so I'm sure she will. The closing Display of the BB & GLB seemed disappointingly ragged to me & so many were away, but David Daika asked May to be the Inspecting Officer which she did with wonderful efficiency & grace. That evening we went for a walk to a lovely quiet valley. On Sunday morning May preached in Church & David interpreted for her, it was special & they all listened well & for afternoon SS class I took M to our nearest outstation Niyes & we had such a happy time. Now I've had a spot of fever so Frances is taking Kay to Vom tomorrow & May has elected to stay here with me, so it will be a rest day, so goodbye my darlings, ever most lovingly C…and blessings on you all darlings with such dear love as always from May.

Chip

May 9th 1956

Darlings, here is another from us both & how glad we were to get yours which took 10dys to reach us!! I long to know how Mrs Reed is looking after you, & Mother don't <u>you</u> go doing things – if she doesn't do them they can easily wait till I get back which will be DV three weeks today. It's an absolutely lovely day & we got going early this morn on our 5dy trek with all the loads plus 2 people & 2 bags of cement in the back of the car & Chris, Frances & me in the front. The views are magnificent & I wish you could see it all. Chip has its own Church Council, meeting for the very first time today, so I'm writing during that going on while Chris takes the reports etc. Chris has not quite decided where we spend tonight, either Longkat or the next village, we want to see Katya but he has not been well. After the Women's Fellowship meeting yesterday Chris encouraged some of them to tell how they first heard the Lord & it was so lovely to hear how one heard then helped her friend and so on as they led each other into faith. When saying goodbye one of them returned shortly at 2pm with a huge cock as a present for me; it wasn't killed till 4.30 and we ate the poor bird at 7 for supper & I knew how horrified you would be Mother but all was well though it was not exactly tender! Chris needed to see to something out at the Fish Farm then we came back to pack up for today. She always has a tremendous lot to see to & there are so many interruptions. But now we are out together & it is lovely – I still can hardly believe it's me! As we left this morning we felt as we used to do when we left home at 5.30am all packed into the old Ford en route for the West and our holidays! I do hope preparations for Chelsea are going ahead satisfactorily; please give our love to Wilfrid & Barbara & we both send masses to you two & of course R&E also, ever yours May.

Mupun May 14th: In a little free time Darlings, though I cannot think where this will be posted. How often your names have been mentioned with enquiries as to your health etc & when Showul came to greet me I felt I was in your place and receiving from him all he has in his heart for you. We walked down to the same river where Katya was baptised & it was wonderful to see it & remove socks & shoes to wade in a bit & get cool. A group was waiting for us in the Church & seemed so glad to hear C's interpreting of my Bible Society related stories. After dark some chaps brought over the battery from the car & Chris rigged up the projector & crowds gathered to enjoy the pictures of themselves, local places then Elsie Anna Wood's slides of the life of Jesus. Next morning after 6am prayers at which Chris spoke, we walked on to Minting to such a lovely welcome from the Evangelist there; it is hard for him with very few adults coming to anything he tries to do but Chris chatted with a group of little children who quickly surrounded us. Chris had our camp-beds set up outside in the open space between the Church & Evangelist's compound as the earlier storm had badly damaged most roofs. Next stop after N'Jak was Jing where Istafanus Jakden welcomed us effusively & there we could use the fine new school building. I have never eaten so many chickens in so short a space of time nor been blessed with so many eggs! Plus so many kind enquiries about you! School inspection followed, then tea and a rest before we walked to Jibam down & up a gorge at the bottom of which there is a lovely river washing over great rocks – on which we crossed, but that's impossible when the rains come. Many folk had gathered & listened so well to my BS stories again. A lot of wind damage there too & nowhere really for us to stay so we returned to Jing in time to visit the old man, sort of father to the people- he's a Moslem but very friendly to Chris. On Friday we went on to Abwor which is in such a lovely position & has a good feeling of progress & well-being. Nathan Benle is Headmaster & Dafwash teaches in English & Hausa & I did so enjoy his class & noting the really lovely looking & bright children in it. Another thunderstorm in the aft then Chris showed the pictures and the filmstrip of Mary Jones to a very big crowd. We had a good night there & left by 6am to walk back to Mupun; delightfully fresh for the first hour & even then I did not find it too terribly hot, and there were 2 rivers to wade – so refreshing. Katya was back from hospital & it was so very good to meet him & Dafwash specially, they are dear boys and one feels there is hope for Africa if God gives leaders like these two. Katya told me he feels your prayers are like a wall between Satan & him; he has given me a bag of rice just for you. We got some washing done & rested well before the afternoon GLB Display & in the evening I spoke & C interpreted & after that 3 teachers came in to talk for they are very interested in the BS stories. On Sunday we walked to Asa which used to be a completely heathen area & all trees considered sacred but today even the few remaining heathens cut down the trees to use for firewood as they see nothing bad happened to the Christians for doing so. The church was packed & Chris spoke first then I gave a few BS stories; it has been inspiring and most moving to meet so many warm-hearted folk.

It's Tuesday now, safely back at Panyam; Chris was going to finish this but found, as usual, so many things she had to see to right away; so many problems to which she is expected to find solution. Many of the dear people we met walked parts of our way home with us; I really hate to say goodbye & it has been difficult, as it is most likely I'll not meet any of them again in this life. Your dear letter was waiting here for us & we're both so thankful all is well & that Mrs R is managing beautifully for you and you've enjoyed that good visit from the nice American woman. Now dears we send all our combined love, M and C.

May 16th: Gracious me Darlings, 2 letters from you today & one from Rene, how lovely to sit & read them & know Father's Xray is clear & he is feeling better & that NonaJane is over her operation, I did not know she was to have it so soon. Also the wonderful Simnal cake which arrived in perfect condition, it was lovely & we all enjoyed it, thank you so much. You are quite wonderful how you enter into all our doings out here & keep lifting us up with your prayers. The work here is developing so fast it is necessary to plan for at least 2yrs ahead for schools to be adequately staffed, provision made for the increasing numbers of children, as well as new outstations & churches. And then come days, additional, unexpected times, like yesterday which was rather amazingly wonderful. Returning from Kerang we stopped at the crowded Mongu market for photos of Joseph at his stall of Gospel literature & as we walked back with the Evangelist such a big crowd followed so he suggested we all went into the church for us to talk to them. C & I quickly discussed what we should say then she spoke to them all. 98% of them had never been inside a church before or heard the Gospel so it was such a great & wonderful privilege to pass on the Good News! Ever yours May & of course C too.

Brookfield

May 18th '56

My darling girls how we have enjoyed your letters & hope for several more yet, thank you so much for writing so fully and for the new batch of Kodachromes most of which are truly excellent! Beautiful ones of both of you looking very fine & May so relaxed, as though she was quite at home! We will borrow the projector from Mr Compton again to marvel in greater detail at you both & the beautiful scenery & views. Miss Reed has just gone to tea next door so I said she could take the pictures to show them; and Ted has just asked how Miss May is getting on so I must show him the lovely one of you two together. Father & I feel that now the houses & trees all down the Charlwood road have been demolished making way to expand Gatwick 'drome, giving new opened views to the blue hills beyond, it looks so similar to some of your views. He wants to add a line now: The pills are stopped so I am getting better; Mother is not pleased with the Doctor. Your pictures of Panyam gardens are certainly fine. Our Bramleys are a mass of flowers but we had 8* of frost tho' I hope we may still get some apples. Chelsea is practically ready for the Opening on Tuesday; I've not seen the final design. We pray the remainder of your visit is a blessing to all and Wilfrid has had May's car out to keep it in good order for her return; from your loving Father.

Our meeting at Ifield yesterday was full & very good & with so many asking after you two & saying May would never want to leave. Nakam was there & told me she had heard from May of the great times you both were having. Miss Riley had a flannelgraph display which was quite artistic and effective. Many others wished to be remembered to you: the Suffils, Miss Noakes and the Maxwells & Dawsons. It is a lovely Whitsun except for the NE wind still rather bitter. I pray much for both you girls that the message of Pentecost may come home to you with deeper richer meaning – All Power is given…go ye therefore…they went everywhere, the Lord working with them & confirming the Word with signs following. 'My Spirit remaineth amongst you, fear ye not'… he that believeth, out of him shall flow rivers of living water. These are just some of the Truths that have been swirling in my thoughts this day & turned into prayer for you two in your very useful lives. May the dear Lord bless you with His fullness as He keeps us all safely to our next happy meeting together. We are so looking forward to seeing May again tho' for her sake & yours Chris I could wish her visit to be longer; very dear love from Mother.

Panyam

May 23rd '56

Our Darlings, this will probably be the last joint letter from us after what has been a lovely experience for us both, knowing your prayers & love surrounding us every day everywhere we've been. Our last night on trek was very good in Ambul of Kulere area; May has stood up to it all amazingly well, leaping about on rocks like a goat, particularly around Pasa Kai and Tof and she has spoken a few words in nearly every place &

in several has given a message. We've walked miles without any difficulty, been rewarded with breathtaking views after steep climbs plus many very touching welcomes, greetings & visits. Perhaps more than all else these days have given May glimpses into the darkness of heathenism: hundreds of little double-sided huts packed closely between the huge steep rocks, all filthy dirty – huts and people – stark nude men, women & children sitting around on the rocks, reasonably friendly but doing absolutely nothing. And in the midst of that is the Evangelist Filibbus telling them the stories of Jesus and the changes He can bring. Filibbus himself was born near Tof, into that dark life, a thorough going heathen along with the rest of them until 20 years ago. Back now after a Daffo day I've been totting up the miles & after Jos tomorrow it will be 600 by car, almost 40 on foot & she did a further 20 with Pastor David plus 2 other villages on top of the 21 she & I went to. I can hardly believe that she will so soon be gone. Ishaku our dear houseboy spoke for all of us really when he said goodbye to her with, "Tell her Nakris that we don't want her to go, it isn't sweet to us to think of her leaving." Now this brings our very dearest love to you both & all the rest of the family from both of us Chris & May.

Palm Grove, Lagos

May 24th

Dear darling Chris I seem to be still living along side you from here at 'the Residency'. I feel I can never cease to be sufficiently grateful for all the experiences of the past month & for the blessedness of being with you. I can never thank you properly for all the care & thought you gave to the planning of it all & the way you acted as such a perfect guide

& hostess the whole way through. Also for all the time you gave to me & my concerns, and your patience in translating both ways and really for all you did and thought and simply were. I do thank you from my heart. Although the event in time is now passed, the total experience is one we shall have for always & it will be a special bond between us for which we shall always give thanks. I believe I shall remember the story about Bishop Smith forever: how that man from Baron had heard of the Way of Christ from his brothers but rejected it, then met the old Bishop who "took hold of my hand & that changed my heart; I was in a dirty old blanket and he was clean and yet he came and took my hand; it was a bishop who led me to Christ." I hope you have written that letter to Bshp S by now Chris?! Mr Hunter's new house here is very comfortable & the room I'm in has a verandah on two sides & a bathroom attached. There is no-one else staying at present so I'm glad to be in a sort of private apartment tho' I think I would be happier if there were others around. I have seen a lot of how the Youth work is managed here, what clubs are available & the work of dedicated Probation Officers dealing with the effects of broken homes, and lack of delinquent education; a boys' remand home & approved school for girls, but oh such overwhelmingly difficult work without the strength Christ can supply & the backing of a Mission & Christian fellowship. At the newspaper office later I was able to have a great talk with one of the editors about encouraging Bible reading and similar articles.

Now it's the 26th and there was a grand evening dinner with the Colonial Chaplain, the head of the Lagos YWCA, and an ex-Crusader Leader whose sister – died in the War – was the wife of Norman James who subsequently married Linda Mellows that was, & they now live in Sanderstead! Sunday morning I am to be taken to the Cathedral, then several more appointments before flying home on Tuesday. All my love darling & so many thoughts & prayers...Palung Zum...ever yours May.

Enugu

May 24th '56

Darling Mummie & Father too this will probably be my last letter from this amazing country, I'll post in Lagos. Chris & I had a little time together in Jos, visiting many dear people she knows there, the Muirs, the Smiths & Evelyn Goldstein. They sent warm greetings to you & the S's specially remember Father's talks at the Annual Meeting. I left Chris where I first saw her, smiling & waving; we really have had a wonderful time together & we feel that goodness & mercy have followed us all the days. There's a 45min stop at this aerodrome which is just out in the bush with no sign of a town anywhere. We are travelling in a Bristol aircraft seating about 30, & have had a smooth & comfortable flight from Jos; coming over dense forest & the Benin River & due to land again at Benin I think before going on to Lagos…55 mins later: no it's Port Harcourt & we've just landed here in pouring rain. This waiting room is little more than a covered shed, there's a bar but they don't even serve tea or coffee! However Mrs Muir kindly made sandwiches for me as they make no provision for meals on the plane. Again the airstrip seems set in a clearing of palm trees…now it is 4.10 and we've landed at Benin for 20mins, it's a rather more civilised spot where I've had a cup of tea! A number of R.C. Fathers got in & now there is only one other woman besides me on board. I'm hoping the next stop will be Lagos we were due there at 4.50.

Well now it's 6.30am on the 25th: we had a good flight though an hour late, Mr Hunter was here waiting for me & we were soon out as his very nice house in the new European quarter of Lagos. He has arranged a full programme for me and a lady is taking me round Juvenile Court Centres & this afternoon staff – some of whom have met Chris at Miango – at the big Christian newspaper with very wide circulation, 'African Challenge' invited us to tea, & tomorrow I'm to meet the

Headmistresses of the Meth and Bap Girls Schools and Sunday to Morning Service in the Cathedral plus an SIM service in the afternoon; then on Monday we go to Ibadan & Tues to the Orthopaedic Hospital where the Queen visited, then I fly home! It will be so lovely if you can come to the Airport on Wednesday morning, the flight number should be 272 due in at 9.50 but do ring up BOAC to see if we're on time. My heart's love always darlings, May.

Panyam

July 11th 1956

Darlings I do thank you so much for all your dear letters and oh how I have sensed your prayers. I've wanted ever more details of the impressions that still linger, May, and how you are able to use all your experiences here in your continuing Bible Society work & meetings at home; and there is not the time to tell you of all the comments and impact you have had here but I trust you have enjoyed the descriptions I was able to write in June. Mother your prayers are of vital support to us all & it is our earnest hope that you may be spared to continue this ministry for a while yet although I have a strong feeling that such service is carried out on the Other Side, even maybe enhanced. I am quite sure that your intercessions have had a considerable part in what the Lord has done through Dafwash & you can share in the joy of harvest & victory in that little home in Milet in these sad days. There is another brother in the family, Tatu, who in his callous & uncaring way, did attend the funeral, so now Mother please add your prayers to ours for this fellow that his eyes might be opened. Each day seems to be full of travelling & writing notes to tell all our Districts of what happened just 4 days ago, and much fixing of things as best one can to fill the gap left by our dear Dafwash. I went to Tahas to fetch Salau the only extra Teacher anywhere, to keep things going at Abwor through until the end of term exams are finished. He is good but he is not Dafwash or anything like him spiritually; we are praying that this experience will be a very great blessing to him. The schoolboys certainly gave us a warm welcome with gratitude for a new malam (Teacher) & an opportunity to talk. I went to visit Mwantet who was with Daskiyes the one who was also struck by the lightning but who recovered. He is much better but we gave him 2 days off school so he could get re-adjusted & recover somewhat. We met Barnaba Kohop going for the same purpose so we walked through the bush together. It was a blessing to pay that visit, a great ability to praise within the grief and Mwantet was wonderful with his quiet humble acceptance of God's will & yet with thanksgiving for all his son has been & has done. We were invited inside and we all talked together for about an hour; I was able to tell them of the 25 Abwor boys who recently gave their hearts to Jesus as a result of Dafwash's teaching & personal example. Mwantet had not heard about that but he was most touched by those boys offering to come & do a days farming for him. We had a comforting time of prayer then went outside to find Dafwash's mother sitting there with some other women. It was only a month ago Dafwash told me joyfully his mother had stopped drinking so I was able to encourage her to press on in the right way that had made her son so happy. Mwantet brought out the things Dafwash had had with him on his bicycle when he was struck down & among them was the copy of 'The Spirit's Sword' which I had just given him from you the day before. I'd given another copy to the Abwor boys so I passed this copy to his friend Daskiyes. Mwantet has given me all Dafwash's school textbooks & notebooks for the use of someone else one day; in one I found the essay he'd written about our trip to Jos in 1952 finishing with, "we all went there in Miss Cheal's sister's bag and we thank her for her help to us, may God bless her & us Amen" (that phrase in her bag means 'out of her own purse') & for that help I thank you again May. I also found tucked into his Hausa Bible a scrap of paper on which he had scribbled, 'promises of God – Psalm 55:22 & Luke 12:22-32' I think they must have been the last he read & noted, so I looked them up as a kind of final message to my own soul, and indeed they were a blessing, promises I too need to lean on. This aft I went to Mongu to welcome Frances; now with dearest love as ever, C.

Panyam

Sunday July 22nd 1956

My Darlings my heart is still glowing in the warmth of your loving letters so full of sympathies I cannot thank you enough May and Mother, and a dear one from Nakam too, and your beautiful one for Mwantet's mother. A group of us including Frances, Rahaba – Dafwash's little sister here because she had been cooking for him in the Dowaki, & Daskiyes, decided to return to Milet for the service this morning to be with them & hand your, now translated, note in person. It was a lovely day & I took several photos, & felt honoured to be asked to speak even though they did not know we were coming; it had to be on John 3 & the need for new birth, in memory of Dafwash about whom I talked a bit at the end. Afterwards they were all most touched as I read out your letter Mother & the messages from Nakam & you dear May. The miracle for me was that I could gladly share such messages with his mother who has a new light about her face & there's no doubt God's grace is working in her heart, setting her free from the essence of dirtiness, slackness & general imperviousness to the Gospel for which she used to be known. Daskiyes similarly comes from a ghastly home, only about 300yds from here, a hotbed of heathenism, drink & vice; it is no wonder he prefers to stay in the Dowaki. Frances & I went there yesterday evening to see if we could find his parents sufficiently unintoxicated so that we could have a word with them. In the entrance hut there was a 44gallon drum of beer around which his mother & several other women were dancing prior to serving it to the crowd of men already partly intoxicated. We moved on, sick at heart. I remembered one year Daskiyes had been home very ill with pneumonia and I had to fight my way through that milling drunken crowd to get to his poor hovel of a room. Is it not a shining miracle that a boy can grow up in a place like that & become a Christian at all, and progress to being a teacher?! He faithfully prays for his parents, on his own or with us & knows his mother has really quite a bit of intelligence if she wasn't so befogged with drink. The evening I walked to Niyes there was a marvellous sunset turning the rocks rose pink when a little chap no more than 12 came charging up from the fields leaving his friends for a while to walk with me. We got to the spot where Dafwash fell & this boy started talking about him & how he had preached to his class & many of them had written their names down because they had taken Jesus as their Saviour. So I asked if he had & he said with the sweetest smile, "Oh yes, about 7 yrs ago!" He could hardly have been off his mother's back by then! Following Malam Dafwash's fine example, he too is learning that whenever there are difficulties, it is wise to pray first about it; now dearest love to you all as always, Chris.

Jos

August 5th 1956

Darlings I am on a short & very welcome holiday here, so grateful for your recent letters especially one from Rene, and writing this brief note to go with Mwantet's lovely letter to you, herewith translated.

My Mother in England I am writing this little greeting to you with sweet thoughts that can't be expressed. For these three years you have joined with my friend Nakris and with Dafwash who has gone ahead of us and is now at the right hand of Christ; and so I am one of your children even for ever & ever unto Heaven. I have looked at all these texts of yours, and that Nakam sent me too, and I have nailed up your letter on the wall of my house so that it may remain as a precious symbal always. I want to tell you about Nakris and Miss Barnden and all the trouble that they took over us, and Pastor too, they used up alot of petrol to come and see us and we are very grateful to them. I want to tell you about our Church at Milet we have made it very nice now and Nakris came & spent Sunday with us. I believe you will be able to see the building by the hand of Nakris her pictures. Please now greet my Father for me very well. I see you as holy people, as if you were beside me day by day; there is nothing I want more than to be one with you forever, your son at Milet.

I reassured him that this is true even now in spite of mileage, race & customs and that in Glory it will be altogether so. I am really sure that your love & sympathies to him & his family at this time has been a very great help & strength. He has written a perfectly sweet letter to Rene also, who wrote her sympathies to him; he said, "*I know that you knew sorrow during the war and as you put yourself into the Hands of our Lord & He helped you, so I am putting myself into His Hands also.*" Now I am sending my dearest love to you all as always your Chris.

SIM Miango

Aug 12th '56

My Darlings, now I'm comfortably settled here in the Rest House for the GLB Training Camp, and have loved receiving all your letters thank you so much; but I do feel so sorry & sad about the troubles swamping dear Uncle E & Auntie E in their declining years it does seem so very hard. My room, all to myself, is delightfully peaceful & the meals are delicious. While revelling in quiet luxury I have managed to get much planning done, and even had a game of chess with the man responsible for Gospel Broadcasting and to my great surprise I beat him easily! Then I played a new game to me – Scrabble, something like Lexicon. Good spiritual food has been provided for us too with some good short talks on Bible readings. While still in Jos I was able to arm myself with DT newspapers & here have found time to read them, finding some helpful clarity on the Suez Canal, but oh what a ghastly coal mine accident in Belgium! Huge log fires are lighted in the lounge for the weather is cold & damp, very different from when you were here May!

19th now and Mother a letter you wrote on the 14th got here on the 16th – amazingly fast! I'm so glad you had such a very pleasant Irish holiday & were able to see so many dear relatives & friends. Ah May, thank you for writing on the 16th which just arrived, telling me of our dear Auntie Edie's funeral service at Ifield. Yes a blessed relief for her to be free of the bodily limitations, but as you rightly say, the first of many such gaps that will inevitably occur if our Lord does not come back soon. The thought of such losses within our nearest & dearest is painful, but as the Suras philosophically say, 'it is nothing new' and now having been brought so suddenly face to face with death & bereavement over Dafwash, it seems to me rather less grim that one would expect, both for those who go & those who remain. I do hope that our dear Uncle Edward has been & is being borne up by the loving kindness of those near him; I'm sure Father, Uncle P & the 2 aunts feel most thankful for the strong help that you & Wilfrid & Mollie can give in such a time. Darling May it is indeed grieving about these apparently lost photos; I have just commended them to the Lord as I'm sure you have already done; He knows where they are & if it is in His will He can most certainly bring them to us even yet. We've had a good week with some classes able to be held outside though many not due to rain & we've had to fetch the girls from their Mission compound over a mile away. Joan Onions is a simply splendid instructor & all in her classes are progressing very well indeed. She excels in skipping & you would have loved to see the precision of all her girls' ropes turning at speed in perfect timing. I've been deeply enjoying 'When Iron Gates Yield' by Geoffrey Bull of his time in Tibet & as a Communist prisoner who was able to circulate many New Testaments before his capture. A Belfast woman, Kathleen Spence, is staying here too, a very nice person; we have just been for a lovely moonlight walk with another girl also. My holiday here will be over in a week but it has been most relaxing & a real blessing, but now I must go to bed so goodbye my dears all with dearest love as ever, Chris.

Panyam

Sept 23rd '56

My Darling May, here are just some snippets for you: when I was talking with Old Father Lot he said, "The love that your sister has for us is quite extraordinary!" I was up at Niyes this afternoon, my first time back there since we went together, and as I cycled I thought you simply must come again in a September, the deep radiant green and yellow of the daisies just blooming now are so very beautiful, and the superb light on those lovely hills as I returned! Do you remember old father Pofi the nice old man who offered to find a husband for you? He asked warmly after you but I told him I had no faith in his sort of talk, just talk & no action. He queried what I meant so I added, "Didn't you offer to find a husband for her? There we were watching the road for the newcomer but he never came – that's all your offers mean!" Then of course there were howls of laughter from them all! Returning from Jos the other day I had more trouble with the car – smoke pouring from the steering wheel this time; 'fixed' at a garage, it got me home but today it did it again. Pastor's driver worked on it to no avail & now Ernest Killer has disconnected the offending cable & replaced it with another. Moses Nerle has been off colour for days then last night became violently ill & Frances was called out 3 times, finally sure it is cerebro-spinal meningitis so gave him 10cc M&B. Early this morning we sent for the Ambulance & he was taken up to Pankshin. I do hope & pray he is spared. Tonight I'm on the verandah getting 'chawed' by mosquitoes, even through Nanny's rug over my knees they are most voracious so I think I'd better give up & go to bed. But first I'd like to share a paragraph from this short letter I've translated for you, written to you by 'your faithful one, Renje Amyit': *I do thank God & always remember you in my prayers. I was not aware it is you are the one helping my brother for Gindiri School until I was told by your Miss Cheal sister. My mouth cannot express the thanks, only God knows it. I pray God's blessing enrich you & we will meet again at the Last Day and me seeing you getting the reward of what you have done for me likewise your sister Miss Cheal, we do thank her greatly as she undertake this great task in upbringing this country into a spiritual life as she spend her whole time for that. Only God can reward that. My father & mother all very pleased to hear me writing to you and send you their excellent greetings & to your Mother. My last word is to say may the peace of God be on you all.*

There's no time for more darling, dearest love & prayers, yours always Chris.

Panyam

Sept 30th '56

My Darlings yesterday brought me May's letter with the lovely news of the big family gathering planned for next week so the next best thing to being there with you is to send my special love & greetings. I shall be eager to hear of Ant's safe return & of this happy meeting at dear Brookfield. I wonder if it will be possible to have another complete gathering when I arrive next year?! Let me remind you that our Field comm. meetings are to be October 30-31st & the question of staffing during my furlough is to be discussed & also my flight dates. The urgent need is for someone to supervise new building here plus the new SP School at Jing and someone who can be School Manager; there is food for much prayerful thought about it. This past week I've had 3 days in Gindiri at meetings, and they arrange for our meals in different peoples' homes so I've seen a lot of folk, especially Pat Cummins, Mother, so I've heard a lot more of her visit to you. On my way home yest. I went by way of Mongu to have tea with Frances which was so pleasant. I ran out of petrol, maybe the gauge was not quite right; however I got a cyclist to take a note to Senlat & Bibwahat back at Mongu & they tore off on their bikes to Frances & she brought 4galls herself after a while. I used the waiting time to write an article asked for by the GLB. I told you about moses Nerle's illness; today Dr Wilkins came down just after we got out of Church to tell me she is worried about him for he does not seem to make any real improvement & seems to have some serious trouble in the brain. Katya does seem to be improving; we are much in prayer for them both & I hope to get to Pankshin on Tues & will see them both then. Pastor D brought Jephthah back from Vom after his poor wee Elisabatu died on Monday; we grieve for them & with them for this second loss in four months. There is a move on here to revive an old custom of a regular routine of visiting all heathen compounds & holding short services on Sunday evenings & we are compiling a list of all compounds and of volunteers in couples willing to do this; now dearest love as ever, C.

SUM Abwor Sunday

Oct 7th '56

Darling May I'm sitting in the Church here that you know quite well from having slept & fed & prayed & talked & laughed in it. We called the people to come for 8am for the day's Gathering & it's now 9.25 & the bell has just been rung to spur on those lingering along the road. I've been having a good quiet time in the room where Dafwash used to teach & where the Lord first spoke to those boys then chatting with Fwanchin the first Abwor man I taught to read many years ago. The Church became packed & the first session lasted an hr & a half after we brought in extra planks for seating. We sang, we prayed, Pastor D read Acts 2 then in his honest & fearless way he invited an orderly presentation of all grievances; nearly every remark was prefaced with some form of, 'we are very pleased our leaders have come here today to put us right' etc etc. In the afternoon session David began summing up everything, carefully showing how mountains have grown out of molehills & I added a word on the devil's strategy to knock down the Church & tarnish its witness among non-believers but how the Lord had spoken to the hearts of 25 Abwor boys through Dafwash's teaching in this very room; and He was perfectly able to do the same again today. David read Rom 8:12-17 & opened the meeting for prayer & there followed a steady flow of it for nearly an hr then David closed at 3.30 as many had long distances to walk home. Truly it felt as if there was a very happy, very different spirit from the start of the day; I felt throughout that you, Nakam & Frances were praying for all of them & us & that God was answering right in the midst of the trouble really being far more serious than we realised. Our Convention is in less than a month & I've been busy going through all the Log Books from 1907 to compile 'The History of the Christian Church in the Panyam District' to be read out during the Service of Rededication held in recognition of our part in the growth & development of the Federation of Churches in the Sudan. Well we have a new worker here, Joyce McQuone of Leicester, a fully trained nurse from a Missionary family. She's been very glad to make a start in the Dispensary today by examining a young girl and giving a penicillin injection to a baby with severe bronchitis. The news from Pankshin is that poor Moses Nerle might be just slightly better but still cannot talk much for his throat is still very sore. And we have had 2 weeks of the new Sunday evening visiting out into heathen compounds, & our people are becoming rather more enthusiastic; with dear love, Chris.

SUM Jos

Oct 31st 56

Because I know you'll all be waiting to hear darlings, I'm writing though there is little I can say after the Field committee as there will be another in Jan & possibly March too, they are loathe to make staffing plans this early. It looks like I may not be free to take furlough until June as the Killers want to take theirs in Nov '57 & there is really no-one else to relieve me. I shall have to be prepared & ready to go in March but June seems far more likely. I am sorry for I know it makes it hard for you to plan anything but it is impossible to say more at present. But there is better news of Moses Nerle: the specialist thinks it is a cyst on the brain, probably TB in origin, & wants him in Kano hospital for radio-therapy which should give at least partial recovery from the paralysis. So I've arranged for Moses to be transported by air this Sat in the SIM plane & by Ambulance both ends of the journey; I think Joyce McQ will go with him. We have a new African ADO at Pankshin now – he is a Moslem with 2 wives. May, you will want to know that Joseph Waltu is back again at his Market Bookshop work & doing well; in 2 ½ weeks he's sold £7 worth of books, mostly the 6d or 9d little ones. Since your visit there has been no further consignment of Hausa Bibles from England; I'm sure he could have sold dozens if he'd had them; what about the large type Gospels? Whatever does the News this evening portend now? It's absolutely horrid to think that we are bombing again – oh I do hope it doesn't end in war on a large scale; dearest love to you all, Chris.

Panyam

Dec 5th '56

My Darlings I continue to be so grateful for each one of your dear letters and especially for all your loving greetings & cards for my birthday plus those most interesting books. What dears you are and how enriching our correspondence has been all these years! There may be only a few moments to write but as I'm sitting on the verandah thinking of you all I want to make a start; old Father Lot has just passed by having tethered his horse near the river & all is quiet & peaceful. Cows are lowing, birds chirping happily in the trees along the river, & our boarders are bathing before Church; so what do I make of the turmoil in the world outside? The wireless seems to be saying the threat of war in the Middle East is receding, but what about Jordan breaking alliance with Britain; how I'd love to talk with you all & hear your own views and I feel sure that, apart from the Lord's grace & favour, the Business outlook must be even more difficult now with petrol rationing to add to the other problems, and May, how will this affect your work, surely you can't mean you must now cycle to the station in icy weather with your heavy loads of books? I long to hear that Rene & Erik have made the decision to move south again to be near you & also Mother that your unpleasant pains to not keep affecting you like this. I will continue praying about this and indeed for this wretched duodenal trouble that is bothering poor old Wilfrid – he does have such heavy burdens to bear and the duodenum does seem to be the spot where mental worry tends to react. Last evening I listened to a lovely programme of music which cheered me so, in fact it sent me quite off till I danced around the room, to Joyce's & the boys' utter astonishment! Another 2 matters for praise is that I do believe the agricultural training is moving along a bit; Peter Batchelor has agreed to take on 2 more boys to add to the 2 already caring for the Gindiri cattle so that in 1958 DV they can go home to Chip to start new farming ventures there. The Chip Ch Council heartily agreed to the need for securing suitable bush land probably beside the road to N'Jak and David will find sponsors to obtain more cattle and two ploughs! The other matter is that in less than a month now we can start to say 'This year!' even though I still do not know the month I can come home. My days are so busy with school doings, setting & marking exams, preparing to close for this year but deciding and putting new suggestions to the School Committee for the next years to come, accepting new children, arranging fees and new quarters for additional boarders, and of course who will teach which classes requires much re-shuffling of Teachers & probationers. We are putting up another double classroom here but the builders need to buck up to get it finished in time for re-opening in January. I feel we also ought to have a new bigger Dispensary as the current one is quite inadequate when so often over-full; this could happen by turning the bigger guesthouse into a new Dispensary then build a new guest house under the mango trees near our house; or maybe using the current one as a midwifery block. The medical funds are well up for this plan to be paid for. The other day when in Jing I walked to Jibilik for a couple of hours, the first time back there since your visit with me May, & in the Log Book I saw Ishaya Jakden had written, 'Chirstine H Cheal our manager came to see us. Miaery K Cheal her sister came and saw us too!' I think we shall have a new girl with us just for Christmas, Joan Rhors, and also Pat C which will be nice but it does mean I cannot go to visit Frances P as it would not be right to leave 2 new ones here alone but I might be able to get away for a few days the week before; must stop now darlings with dearest love as always Chris.

Panyam

Dec 18th '56

An exciting packet has just come containing the most beautiful nightie – Darlings you are too sweetly kind, but it's almost too posh to wear, certainly for the likes of me, but it will be lovely when it gets hot again for right now I'm wearing the wooly pyjamas you gave me when I was home last time! You will like to hear the good news that Moses is a lot better & has actually walked a few paces and they expect to discharge him quite soon. At the other extreme I know you will share my sorrow over poor Jephthah & his wife Tarifainu; this time it's their eldest girl just home for the holidays from Gindiri was smitten with virulent meningitis and died that same night. It was so terribly sudden they are simply numb with grief. Tomorrow we are to have another school committee to face the fresh problem of staffing here now that Christopher Lot has resigned. He wanted the Senior Primary & was peeved to be put to teach in the JuniorP but also was complaining bitterly about me but I refused to accept his resignation telling to go home & re-think it. This gave me time to pray for wisdom & guidance, asking the Lord what or where I needed to change & why I have found him to be so difficult. But he soon sent over a chit with his final decision to leave teaching altogether. Although I am personally relieved I don't know what his father will say & I grieve for Joanna & their dear little boys. I believe we shall put Nathan Benle in his place and bring in Dinatu – Mrs Polycarp Fian, for Class2 but until the new school is ready we shall have to hold some classes in the afternoons – that should hustle up the building! I have been terrifically busy lately so am really looking forward to getting off to Mongu from Friday tea time till Christmas morning if I can get everything ready for the girls here in my absence. How I thank the Lord for Jonathan who is such a capable hard worker, cheerful & energetic, buying in sufficient grass to roof the big school building and coping with all the women paid to weave it; and Shadrack Davem is working in my office patching & sewing up all the torn school books ready for next term. Nelson Renje wrote me a letter saying that 15 Jibam boys have now accepted Christ after a particular Scripture lesson they had up on the hilltop – isn't that just glorious news! As is my visit this evening to Jephthah & Tarifainu who are quite marvellous in their calm bravery & quiet faith; it was a blessing to be there; for really these ones so victorious in bereavement are wonderful to witness; now ever & always yours Chris.

Panyam

Christmas Day 1956

Darlings it is one of those days when I know our thoughts & love & prayers have been meeting & I do so hope you have as happy & peaceful a day as I have. My weekend in Mongu with Frances was lovely & restful & today she brought me tea in bed at 6am & I had such a nice time of quiet & remembering my dear ones then at 8 we had a very lovely English Communion service in the little church May will recall, with just a dozen of us as the early morning sun streamed in. I don't know when I've enjoyed an Anglican service quite so much. Ernest K took it beautifully & read from Gal 4 which I'd been reading myself earlier and I was re-struck with 'God sent forth His Son' and then 'God sent forth the Spirit of His Son' thus connecting Christmas with Pentecost. We got back here in time for our Morning Bible Day Service, including several new testimonies, and during the afternoon usual feasting & dancing we listened to the Queen's very good message. Our dinner was delicious, well topped off with Christmas pud and mince pies!

<u>26th now</u> & we've just been eating a present meant for you! Mwantet sent a boy to us with a leg of mutton & a basket of potatoes a gift from him to you, but asking us to 'inherit' it for you which we were glad to do & it was very very tasty! No newer news of Moses but I hear Victoria wrote to their eldest son Oneisimus saying it would be 2 weeks before he's discharged. May you would have loved to be with us at Mongun as we got out of the car all the little girls came rushing to take my hand with "Mwanle Nakris" & escort me into the dancers' circle; some of the bolder ones did the same for Joyce. The Chief insisted I accept a huge duck or 'little hen' as he called it, for my visitors, as well as the chicken from Yusufu Dakahap. And Mother you would have been amused to see Joseph Konshik with just a Sura skin bag on his back with a leather apron

thing tied on behind, with a big rattle in his hand, dancing round like David with all his might! Now I must stop and go to bed, with dearest love darlings & lovingest best wishes for the New Year from Chris.

31 Queens Rd, Immingham

Jan 1st 57

Happy New Year Darling! Thank you so much for the lovely bag you sent me, I shall be so pleased to use it for it is such a nice size. Your dear Christmas letter arrived on Christmas Morning which was very nice & we felt so near to you & sent you many loving thoughts. As I expect you've already heard we had hoped & planned to go to Brookfield for it seemed there were to be no boats but then on the Thursday before we heard that one was coming in on the 25th instead of the 28th so we had to phone home & cancel our visit and then pack up & post off all our presents & for the Clyro folk also. Then on Monday we heard the boat had broken down with engine trouble. We debated whether or not to go then but decided against it as it was so late & Erik does not like night driving. So we stayed here & had a very quiet but happy Day. That boat came in on the 28th after all when we had a small party for the 16 men & another on Sunday when 34 came. The Committee in Sweden have again postponed making any decision about Erik so he still thinks of going to Pulborough to do what he can for the Business through the week, returning here for weekends, for 6mths at any rate. He wants to take a further course at the Swedish University but I would stay in this country. Both boys are well & go back on the 18th & we plan to go to Brookfield on the 14th. I'm really hoping to see you SOON so till then dearest & best love from us all with every blessing for 1957 ever your loving Rene.

Panyam

Jan 6th '57

Special Birthday Greetings my Dear Mother & hope this will reach you in time to bring my dearest & very best wishes for a most happy day. I've written to The Ancient Bookshop & ordered a lovely book to you & Father for your joint birthdays – I do hope you haven't got it already, & I trust you will love it as much as I do, I think you will. There is good news from here in that Moses has been brought back home, wonderfully bright, walking with a stick – Hallelujah! He came to church today but his speech is very slow & vocabulary confined to about a dozen words. Frances gives his hand & arm daily massage & trying to help him with sentences. It is unlikely he'll ever be able to work again. The GLB Display in Mongun went off really well, organised & presented excellently by Damaris – it was lovely for me to be able to sit & watch it but I did march with them to the Market where we sang 3 hymns & Yusufu & I spoke & we had a huge audience; yours as ever C.

Panyam

Jan 7th '57

May my darling dear your last 2 letters have made my heart reach right out to you; I am asking for you the patience that I know you saw I badly need too day by day – we can both sympathise & pray for each other along this line. I can only too well imagine the little causes of friction & disquiet at home & I pray for grace for you to bear it all

& be the cheer & light that I know you are, even though you might not always feel like it. With so many demands on one's time, energy and emotions as I know you have, as I do, sometimes I wonder if my life will ever have any leisure again – I'm sure you understand. Do you remember the Saturday afternoons when we used to curl up with a story book & one or two large apples, Russett, or Lane's Prince Albert, and have a good long read?! I have some lovely books here now but not much chance of reading them. This is a critical time of year here for so many folk: end of school frustrations to those who don't pass their exams & New Yr likewise for those who don't secure jobs. It's always good to find a scapegoat for your bitterness & who better than the manager of the schools? It seems to have been my lot to bear the brunt of angry thoughts & words from a great many just lately. Christiana stormed in raving at me like a madwoman on behalf of her whole family, Haruna made similar rages for his daughter failed for Maiduguri Training, and all this on top of work pressures such as I've never known and so I do get ratty & bad tempered & certainly I have never felt the need of patience more than recently. And yet on the other hand the S.U. daily readings lately have been so wonderfully appropriate, & I have been given glorious opportunities for preaching in some heathen compounds. Darling I do so hope that you too have been truly conscious of help and compensations. I had gorgeous letters at Christmas from Wilfrid and Barbara, full of interest & news – how I long to hear of a lifting of burdens there; I do feel more certain now that it's likely I will be free to come home in the spring but getting ready for it & the handing over is rather daunting; special blessings on you darling one, Chris.

Brookfield

Jan 7th '57

My darling Chris I am especially thinking of you today so want to try to get this note off to you – I do hope you are alright? Do you remember, not really so very long ago, when we were embracing you half way up the path & throwing your hat over the hedge in welcome?! Would that it might be sooner than expected this year; I had a note from Nakam yesterday saying she can't understand Gordon Muir's casualness over furlough arrangements. She doesn't think he considers it nearly seriously enough & she hopes you are coming soon! Darling dear I know well some of the frustrations you must cope with in your work, currently over Naki, and the huge staffing responsibilities to name but two. It is a comfort to know that you know some of mine too – how wonderful that we can meet at the Throne of Grace to receive pardon & patience about in equal measure. Mother has had a better week but poor Father has been again upset in his stomach and struggling through another night of nasty palpitations. It must be the inevitable physical reaction to the severe strain under which he's living these days; still there is nothing pointing to any Business relief and I do not know how much longer we can go on like this. I am really hoping to be able to go to our Staff Conference at High Leigh from Tues to Friday but I don't like leaving Mummie alone to look after him while he has to be in bed. You have heard I expect that Rene had a fall & has broken a bone in her foot & now has foot & leg in plaster for a month poor darling; all my love May.

Brookfield

Jan 7th 1957

My beloved Chris this day I am particularly thinking of you & May perhaps even more than usual & of course of poor Rene too with her leg & foot all bandaged up in Plaster of Paris after slipping on the last stair. I pray that this New Year might be for all of us one of increasing knowledge & love of God and thinking of & praying more for others. We remembered you darling at Camp & so glad all seemed to enjoy it. May wanted me to include this photo of Senlat's dear baby so here it is. Yesterday morning I went to Meeting for the first time in 8 weeks though May was dubious thinking it a risk, just before she is to be away at HL for 3 nights, but I am thankful to be feeling better & stronger so I 'put my foot down with a firm hand' and all was fine! Oh how wonderful if you will really be home again soon, perhaps even this spring, may it be so indeed. I try to be consistent in prayer for all your 'children' for it is good of the Lord to have blessed you with so many, but I feel most burdened at present with Naki, Christopher and Mwantet, & hope for news of improvement in both cases. I do try not to worry about Father when his pulse races so very fast then his stomach becomes upset; now he tells me he is better enough to keep the appointment at Hellingly if I will accompany him so I must stop this – & hope to post it while we are out, your loving Mother.

10 Harewood Rd., S Croydon

Jan 13th '57

Dearest Chris you really are very good to write so fully to me & so often & I do hugely appreciate it, thank you so much. Yesterday I saw Cicely Radley – a lovely meeting – she got home from Egypt with only one suitcase as everything else had to be left behind. She told of the last service she attended there which was a beautiful baptism of an Egyptian girl whose parents are Jews so they are giving her a bad time & she too will probably be expelled from her country; do pray for her, her name is Vivianne. I'm so pleased you were able to have that lovely European Communion Service at Christmastime and that you feel able to tell me some of the less pleasant parts of your responsibilities; you are certainly having your share of 'more kicks than a halfpence' just as I did before you. I am thinking these days that the sooner everything is in African hands the better then they can slang their fellow countrymen! When you get to doing the Jan Reports with all the staffing changes would you send them to SUM via me then I can make an extra copy. I try to keep pace with all the changes but with so many alterations I am muddled as to who is where now. As for the new man who was to leave shortly he has now withdrawn from the Mission entirely because his date of sailing was changed. He wrote me an awful letter about it claiming he's been deliberately deceived to which I replied that he was evidently not answering any Call from God but his own self will & I hoped he would be given the needed spiritual readjustment, so he got no change out of me! Dick Perfect is coming to see me next week though Eve can't leave her mother, now very frail; now with much love to you and all, Nakam.

31 Queens Rd, Immingham

Jan 13th '57

Darling Chris the holidays seem to be over & we are going down to Brookfield tomorrow DV. Ant left yesterday & now it is quiet for he is so gay & full of fun & wit. Mouse, or should I now say Christopher, is very helpful in the house & very kind but I know he is still smoking; I have not questioned him about anything as I feel it is probably better to leave it for the present. When I had my 'home accident' the pain was agonising and last Monday I had to have the plaster off – they must have put in on too tight for my foot swelled ever so much & my toes went all black & blue. Now the swelling is right up to well above my knee but the crepe bandage gives little support. There is still no result from the Swedish Committee so Erik has made his own decision, to ask for leave of absence for a year so he can help Wilfrid until September then go to Sweden for further University study. He might go there next week to sign up for classes & there is a boat leaving from here on Friday that he could take. Mouse will be called-up in Sept so he registered here last week & he wants to do some farming in Sweden after Easter; with very dear love, yours ever Rene.

Brookfield

Jan 13th '57

My darling Chris it was so lovely to find your letter waiting when I got back late on Friday after our Conf at HL. Thank you darling for all your loving understanding & prayers; I feel a beast adding to your own burdens but it is so good to know that you do understand. Just as Mother is having good days now & feeling much stronger again the forecast is for more very cold weather & snow likely everywhere. That fills me with horror & apprehension for I dread intense cold & the additional horror of frozen pipes & then bursts of course, but it hasn't come yet so perhaps we shall be spared. I just hope nothing prevents Rene & E from coming here tomorrow & we shall revel together in the simply wonderful thinking of you coming home soon which will also be such cheer for M&F in these drab & difficult winter months. There were many good talks at HL & I was most interested to hear Wilfred Bradnock speak on East & West Africa where in spite of the welcome given to Union versions of Bible translations, the demand is moving back to the vernacular languages. He emphasized that it is always BS policy to fit in with the lead given by the church in local situations but he considers that the production of the Union versions has had the effect of sending native people back to their own particular language in a sort of tribal nationalism. Also, Dr Cockburn gave an interesting review of the resurgence of other religions like Buddhism & Hinduism showing vitality likely to continue & grow. There were several enquiries after you & a Welshman gave me a copy of the Gindiri School Magazine & asked if I knew of it?! A woman home on furlough from Gindiri lives in Wales but he could not recall her name. I am so very glad to know Moses is home again & I believe that even if he is to remain physically so limited he will walk so closely with the Lord that his influence & presence anywhere will be a benediction & a challenge to the whole of Panyam. Please greet him warmly for me. I send you all my love & much thought & prayer as ever M.

31 Queens Rd, Immingham

Jan 20th '57

My darling Chris thank you very much for your letter but my, what a busy life you lead these days, no wonder you have a 'spent look' we must get you back here, permed and rested as soon as possible! I have no doubt at all that your spirit is as youthful as ever. Thanks for asking about my leg which is improving slowly but still I cannot get any shoe on. Erik cut out several thicknesses of cardboard for me so I wear a sock next to the bandage then the cardboard then another sock so I manage to get about a bit, even in London the other day with Mouse for his interview. Down at home M&F seemed fairly well but Father went to bed in the afternoons, but I do feel anxious for May having to travel by trains & buses – and bicycle – carrying such bags of her books & literature. It is difficult after she has been able to use the car for so long; and you know she finds the Danish girl very trying indeed for she seems incapable of doing anything properly. I think Erik wants to go back to Sweden as soon as he can. He has not been able to sell the shop yet & does not want to be responsible for closing the Mission here but there is still nothing forthcoming from the Committee & no help for the church either so possibly it will mean a rented house or flat in Crawley, it must be somewhere the boys can come also. We do so long to hear of your home-coming darling, how lovely it will be; yours as ever Rene.

Christ Church, Oxford

Jan 23rd 1957

Dear Auntie Chris the presence of this rather ancient airletter form in my desk drawer causes me prickings of conscience which I hope to assuage by writing on it. I was sorry to see in one letter you actually admitted to being run down – I mean I'm sorry you're so tired but glad that you admit it; so please don't reply to this, especially if you're coming home in March. How lovely that will be! We've been up for 5 days of this Hilary(!) Term – as always Oxford is hilarious (!!) and terrific fun; we had our first game of rugger this afternoon which we won 6-3. I got thumped in the jaw but have avoided stiffness by eating large meals. Work is going reasonably well I suppose, the benefit comes in all the reading one has to do for exams and the enormous amount of general stuff, to the imbibing of which the atmosphere is ideally suited. Many people here think this new Prime Minister will abolish National Service so perhaps Mouse may not have to do it, which could be a pity in a way. Crumbs, I nearly forgot! Richard (cousin) has just been commissioned into the R. Sussex Regt and seconded at very short notice to the 2nd Bn Nigeria Regt in Lagos & he leaves (presumably by air) Feb 1st for a year or so. I gave him your address & assured him of a warm welcome if he can get there. Now I must read some Virgil and sleep; with my dearest love, Ant.

Brookfield

Jan 27th 1957

In your dear letter to Father for his birthday you said you are probably coming in April – what a blessed prospect but darling I do realise how much you will have to accomplish before leaving. My prayer is that you will be kept in peace with your mind stayed on God & that He will bring to your remembrance all the things that require your attention, yet keep you from worrying over the things for which others can take responsibility. I'm sure that sounds like a big request, but it's not too big is it?! If you could be here by April 15th it would be great as at present I have no meetings that week – Holy Week, or the following Easter week either so maybe we could go with M&F for a week to Eastbourne or Brighton to enjoy each others company in a restful seaside atmosphere. And perhaps a week for us two up at Keswick & the Lake District, or would you prefer Ireland where we might be able to borrow relatives' caravans – oh I do hope the petrol crisis is over by then. It is so nice having Rene with us this week but I am not clear what her plans might be and truly I'm not sure she can even know poor love, while Erik still has nothing definite in either Lund or Upsala. If he is to take further training again I think it is surely wise as soon as possible while his brain can still take in & remember all that he learns. After a recent Southampton meeting I took another train to Bournemouth to visit Uncle Edward. He was warm & comfortable but still so bothered because he is quite sure Auntie Edie is still in the room with him all the time; it is so sadly pathetic to hear him talk. Although he says he accepts my word that she is not there, he says he can't find an explanation in his mind for the constant certainty he has that she is there with him for he can see her so plainly. I do hope the Lord will take him Home soon so he can really be with her again. It takes so much longer having to do all these journeys by train, waiting for connections, or just missing them because you can't hurry away from meetings where perhaps important work is happening in personal conversations continuing on from the meeting proper. I was so glad to hear that Mr Herbert had arrived safely, it was so very stormy & rough just at the time he left that we feared he would have a bad tossing about in that plane. Blessings on you my dear love, please take good care of yourself, we all send heaps of dearest love as ever, May.

Brookfield

Jan 29th '57

My beloved Chris I do thank you so much for your welcome letters especially this last one telling of the almost definite plan of your furlough in April! Today Rene & I went into Crawley, the first time for me since November; we looked at a coat but I am not prepared to spend 14 guineas, preferring to wait now for a spring garment to welcome you home. There is a little more money coming now but of course it has to go out again on wages & accounts so very quickly, but we are thankful for all blessings from the Hand of the Lord: for example a gentleman Wilfrid recently met asking if we had the space & would we grow a new kind of barley for his company. The book you kindly ordered for us has not come yet but I'm sure it will very soon. Rene has made some lovely looking wholemeal bread this morning, we have found a 'quicker' mode of doing it and are trying it out. When Christopher rolled in unexpectedly last week we had a cup of tea together. The strong smell of tobacco made me beg of him (for the first time in words) not to let this habit get such a hold of him for if the Lord called on him to give it up, he would find it most difficult. He knows how we feel about such things & I told him it is not for me to do other than lovingly advise him; and there we must leave it except for prayer. He is a very nice lad & has such a winning way with him. Another day I took a little walk to fetch two eggs to poor Mrs Brooks who has been in bed with more leg troubles. First the mosquito bites turned septic then the powder that the Dr sprinkled over them caused her to come out in large spots all over her whole body! So much for some new powders! May left for Kingston taking your Kodachromes to illustrate her talk on her visit to you last year, and then she goes to the Isle of Wight again. Goodbye my darling love, you can think how much I dwell on the thought of your coming home & pray daily that I might be spared to see you again, but all shall be well, we will not fear, ever your loving Mother.

Gibralter Cottage, The Common, Tunbridge Wells

Jan 29th 1957

My Dearest Chris this comes to bring you my best wishes for the New Year and to thank you & Pastor David, Haruna Cinman Lot & Barnaba Kohop for your very kind thought to ask me to come out to Panyam for a visit towards the end of this year 1957, the 50th year of the arrival of the first missionaries of the Gospel – I myself arriving with Mr & Mrs Hayward (their 3rd term) in January 1913. How I wish I could accept this loving invitation but I fear I am altogether too old for such a journey now. I should love to meet again some of the friends I knew and to see Panyam Compound again, and the journey from Jos so very different in those days. And one part I should specially rejoice to see would be the Companies of Boys & Girls Brigades – I have so enjoyed seeing the photos. But I shall be able to somewhat picture all that will be happening especially as their Nakam hopes to join you all there. Please give them all NaJen's love & grateful thanks; this year I become 79 and have so much in every way to praise the Lord for. I do pray that this year may be a very blessed one and I rejoice indeed to hear that there will be DV three new Pastors ordained at this Jubilee Celebration. God bless you dear Chris; with much love and again so many thanks from your loving Carfax Sister, DML Barrett.

Maresfield Rectory, Uckfield, Sussex

Feb 1st 1957

My Dear Friend your kind letter of September last reached me some weeks ago and gave me very great joy. It is now 46 years since the Lord's call sent me to Panyam in His service & I have never ceased to thank Him for the joy of bearing witness to Him there. I have followed with deep interest, and abundant thanksgiving, the growth of Christ's Church among you & all around; it was a great joy to meet & talk with Pastor David when he came to England two years ago & I hope he may come over again soon. It would give me great joy to visit you for your Jubilee Celebrations but at present I do not see that it would be possible. I am an old man now & not able to do very much without getting very tired although I am still on full-time work in charge of a Church. However, I will ask my Doctor about it & will find out what the cost would be to come by air if he agreed. Then I will give you a reply. I hope that Nakam will be able to be with you. May God bless you all, your friend forever, E Hayward – I can still say "Darang-me-Kat" and add to it "A deng" do I spell it right?

31 Queens Rd Immingham

Feb 10th '57

Darling Chris, it's Sunday morning, damp & foggy after a week of gales; Erik didn't get back till Tuesday night after all, due to fog. He found out he cannot do University as the short courses are no longer available – it's the full 4 yrs or nothing. There is still no decision about this place but the secretary thought of asking if E would be interested in Aberdeen where there is a vacant church. E says he has always been interested, well, lately anyway, in Aberdeen so has applied to be sent there. Of course there a lot of problems, from my point at least, the worst being the long distance from Brookfield and from the boys just when I did feel I'd be able to get nearer to them and relieve May a bit; and if we go I suppose we shall see practically nothing of you this furlough. The accommodation is a newish English house I don't know where in connection to the church & E is sure it will be furnished which makes it rather difficult about our own furniture. Erik is now going down to Brookfield tomorrow to discuss it with them as Wilfrid may feel it's not worthwhile for E to go to work at Pulborough for such a short time. Oh dearie me may God lead & show us what is right to do. Dearest & best love & I should be glad of any comments from you on all this if you have the time, ever your loving Rene.

Panyam

Feb 11th 1957

My dears all, apologies for bad typing but it is so cold here still & my hands are very rough making any kind of writing difficult. Last Thurs Frances & I had to go to Longkat & Jing so we took Moses Nerle with us for the ride! His first ride since coming home & he'd never been over the new Randa Bridge – I don't know who enjoyed it most, he or we! He was a little upset going down the big hill & was sick at the bottom but he wouldn't hear of stopping off at Abwor & was perfectly alright after that. We stopped at the Bridge so that he could get out to walk over it, Frances holding his arm; he was of course amazed, then we stopped for a cup of tea under a tree near Longkat & he enjoyed that too. I realised he had not seen Adamu since his illness, and really the meeting between them was most moving; Adamu coming out led by Enoch Dajan & his face just beamed with delight when he heard who it was. He came and groped for Moses' hand and just held him and I think others beside him were nearly in tears; then crowds of folk came to greet him, Alisabatu was quite speechless with joy (Moses had saved her life after her asphyxiation). It was a good while before we got away & almost dark by the time we got back. The next day was hectic & Frances was a real brick doing the Inspections for me as I wrestled with accounts, wrote business letters & tried to get ready for a short weekend trek to Baron country; finally I left by 2.15 minus my sponge-bag, getting to Daffo in time to see the Evangelists at their Bible School before they scattered off for their weekend. Meeting with the Teachers I was relieved to see they had collected all the school fees; then I went on to Butura for the night & gave them a showing of Kodachromes plus Bible pictures. It was bitterly cold with a howling wind all night & next am nobody showed up bec of the cold so I had a leisurely breakfast before going to see the Chief. I had to read a bit of the riot act to him for so few children for the now three new Teachers in place there – he assured me they would be forthcoming. Leaving my stuff at Maikatako I went on to Murish by a road made by the mines, to see Haruna but they have done nothing at all about starting their new Class 1 so told them what I thought of that. Back to Maikatako for a peaceful afternoon and an evening of showing pictures to a large crowd before another really cold windy night on that bleak bare plain; thankful I had a Beatrice stove with me & had the chance to do all my own work – quite nice for a change! After a talk & prayer with little Eliya Malan I pushed on to Maiyanga for morning service where I found lots of well dressed folk but a not very reverent atmosphere. For afternoon SS I went back past Maikatako along a bush road to Kunet & found over 100 children waiting! On the way home I called in at Mile7 on the new road to greet Daniel Wuliyang & his wife who lost a baby son last week; and found Joseph Waltu's sister ill with pneumonia so brought her in with me, and so ended my full & interesting weekend – the last 4 villages were ones I'd never visited before. Tomorrow the plan is to leave here at 4am & try to get to Bambur by nightfall. Much love to each of you, Chris.

Brookfield

Feb 18th 1957

My beloved Chris I am listening to the Queen's reception in Portugal & such enthusiastic shouting & cheering, perhaps because I believe she is the first British Royal to visit there since King Edward VII her great grandfather in 1903 – dearie me I hope I have that right. Now the commentator Audrey Russell is telling us of the hot sunshine there & the delight of the Portuguese people to see the Queen and the Duke looking so happy together after those awful suggestions of a rift between them (made by an American but also in our British papers) I shall continue to believe it was not so. Now I have just taken three lovely looking loaves of bread out of the oven but I do not want you to worry, it was not strenuous work and Rita was here to help with the mixing. We have been specially remembering you for your time at Bambur, may it be a happy & fruitful experience for you, though it sounds a very long way away please do tell me exactly where it is. Today we expect Erik who will stay here travelling to Pulborough each day; he was unhappy at the guest house because he said they kept asking him too many questions about why he was here & how long he would stay & so on. If he & Rene do go to Aberdeen we might perhaps take our summer holiday up there, but in any case it surely holds more possibilities for them then Immingham and I do feel Rene would be able to lead a more normal sort of life. Our prayers must be constant for them that the will of God shall be made clear for as we know that is the only way of peace & blessing. Rene fears she will see nothing of you if she's up there but I reminded her there is an Airport nearby. Sending you my fondest & best love as ever, your loving Mother.

Panyam

Feb 21st '57

Darlings once again there is so much to say but simply no time so I'm enclosing with this note a list of special prayer requests so that you can join in with your support; and please be extra patient & Nakam will send on to you the detailed log of the time at Bambur. I do feel the time there was a real oasis of refreshment, physically & mentally & spiritually; it was such a complete change, and I feel much less tired and sort of stimulated by all the discussions & fellowship. I seemed to be unattached to any special European companion therefore free to enjoy the company of African & European alike especially now that I'm more used to Hausa – quicker at hearing it and speaking it too. We had a jolly journey home, sharing our meals with much enjoyment. David remained intrigued with the riddle about the desert…nobody needing to be hungry because of the sand which is there…na-he-ha ha! May darling, I've had to write a strong reproof to your friend Filibus because he was called by the new Moslem ADO to return to Tof and he went even though he was down to speak at the Sunday meeting. I feel terribly disappointed by his action, for if a Moslem was called to do anything on a Friday he wouldn't dream of agreeing. I fear some of our Christians would rather obey a Govt Officer than put God's claims first. This was to do with the Chieftan-ship & I suppose he thought he stood a chance of being chosen again. I will bring this up at the next District Church Council; dearest love to you each one Chris.

31 Queens Rd Immimgham

Feb 24th '57

Darling Chris I wonder how you are this Sunday evening? We've not heard when you're coming but Mother thought April 14th? How lovely if it really is so! I'm writing at the Mission, not at the house, as we are on duty although there is only one boat in & no men in here at all. But these days are rather strange altogether with Erik down at home Monday-Friday going back & forth to Pulborough having a great 'outdoor' life; I do not like being here alone but Ruth is coming next week which will be so nice. Still we wait, this time to hear if Aberdeen is open to us, and now E has heard from the Swedish comm. & they seem sad he is now planning to leave. Mouse/Christopher will not be here for he's off to Sweden to live with a family & work on their farm for at least 5mths; I think it will do him a lot of good but I do hope he behaves himself. Then in Sept he'll have to do Nat'l Service. Ant writes happily from Oxford but I do wonder if he actually does any work, he always seems to be entertaining or visiting and girls are coming into his letters quite a lot now. Perhaps we shall see you soon, I hope you are well, dearest love from Rene.

Panyam

Feb 24th 1957

My Darling May it hardly seems credible that 8wks today is Easter Sunday and DV we should be spending it together! I'm on the verandah & the sun is just dropping to the horizon. Also hardly credible that 10mths ago today you arrived here! What a happy day that was, I'll never forget the lovely welcome they gave you here under the big tree! Your letter & all its suggestions about furlough are utterly delightful. I can't think of anything nicer than going with you 3 to the sea for Easter, then to Ireland & having a caravan in which to do some touring around with you, then room sharing in Ruth Henman's house at Keswick, so do go on with any and all of these arrangements. I should very much like to visit the CIM old people's home in T. Wells to see the Gillies & also the Matron who is Florence L's sister; and I'd like to meet your friend who prays for me. And on a more mundane level, could you make an appointment for me with Brother Cramp? I fear I shall need his attentions as soon as I get home. Do pray with me that in spite of this unexpected run of special events just before my departure, I may be enabled to get through it all without undue pressure. Mr Farrant has asked the Comm that I will be allowed to go in April in order to be back in time for the Panyam Jubilee! I feel sure that if Evelyn Goldstein and Joan Onions are both allowed to come here then my job of handing over will be made easier; EG is Froebel trained & Joan's school admin skills are better than most; dearest love from Chris.

Brookfield

Feb 26th 1957

My beloved darling two wonderful letters from you this week, how I thank you, and the one sent on from Nakam about your great time at Bambur. What a programme is set before you now to accomplish before you leave! And I thought your days were full up already! I have carefully written out all the dates & occasions to keep them in front of us as constant reminders in prayer; I believe it is one of the small bits of service I can still do in these days of physical restrictions. I never find time in my days goes slowly, and give frequent thanks for my sight as I can still knit and read well. Nakam wrote of 2 young missionaries who are sailing now, one of whom is to take Miss Onions' place when she goes back to Panyam while you are away. Last Sunday our morning Meeting at Ifield seemed a better & more living one than many recently. Bryan Reed spoke well but shortly on the need for our daily preparation rather than perhaps only weekly and that we should always live in a state of yieldedness, as exampled by John Woolman's life of obedience (strange that I also had thought of J.W. in my early quiet time, and his 'secret of obedience' throughout his life.) Right after BR Father followed on by reading 2 Pet. 1:1-8 the great & precious promises & for faith to appropriate them. Then Mr Philips, who sits to speak, spoke more on faith & hope, and Jo prayed with allusion to those in the Meeting who have this Living Hope. Then I felt I must give this word, 'Faithful is He who calleth you who also will do it' and told of my earlier thoughts of John Woolman & how yielded he was to God, obedience being the key & which led him to do many things at which we would shudder but perhaps we would not be called to such things as times have altered but God has not. Surely He who in His great love for us wants our love & has a right to our yielded obedience; and as we yield ourselves to Him He will work in us to will & to do of His good pleasure – great and precious promises indeed. Well, Mrs Canfield thought we had had a wonderful Meeting, and certainly it seemed as tho a breath of God's Spirit had passed over us. What a blessing to feel that. My darling I am longing to see you again & now sending you the love I can send, your own Mother.

Brookfield

March 10th '57

Darling what a lovely letter that was, thank you so much; but I do feel it is more than good of you to make time to write anything at all in these final days & I've told Mummie not to expect any more from you till that blessed day when we see you in person – but still she is always hopeful, "Perhaps there will be a letter from Chris tomorrow." I have now booked for us at a very nice Christian place in Eastbourne in Easter week, hoping that Rene, Erik & Ant might be able to join us as they won't probably have other opportunity to see you. Rene rang last evening to say E has been accepted for the Aberdeen position & tho' she did not say it I know she is dreading going so far away so in her heart is very disappointed, she says, "I must believe it is the right place for us." Let us pray she will be led into a richer fuller life up there where she can feel of use, and also hear some larks in Scotland for she fears she will miss their singing. She enjoyed Ruth's company last wk. Did you hear that Erik has bought 12 pigs for the field at Pulborough, hoping they will fetch a good price presently? Now darling it is good to know we both pray for each other as the numbers of meetings, commitments & responsibilities for both of us just seem to keep increasing. The day before you are due I have to be down in Barton-on-Sea for a drawing-room mtg in Dr Kate Ball's home (do you remember she was at W. Wickham?!) she & Vera Lynn are organising it together especially to get new people in as there are so many Naval folk around there. I have a conf in Boscombe on May 3rd & how lovely if you could come too & then we could visit Uncle Edward afterwards perhaps. I saw him last wk & found he is a little brighter & now wants to travel in Mexico & Canada!! We have each had another 22galls of petrol allocated so maybe I will get to the Airport to meet you! A wk tomorrow I go up north for 4 Womens Rallies, then to the I. of. W for 6 mtgs and 2 schools. Blessings on you my darling with all my love and Eph 4:7 in JB Philips, ever yours May.

Panyam

March 26th '57

How wise you were May darling to 'expect no more letters' – it has become a necessity from this end. But I must tell you that my flight is confirmed to Kano then on to London arriving DV 9.30am at Heath Row April 17th! Polycarp is back from Bukuru where he was interpreting for Howard Jones the American Negro Evangelist; he says several hundreds attended all meetings & there were many conversions, and a very good time. Several of our Sura boys were there & among those who stayed behind. One of Dafwash's boys came into my office for the first time and sat & wept when he saw D's photograph – no sign of the acute feelings lessening yet even after 8 mths. We talked & I told him of my furlough, then he looked at your picture on the wall & immediately asked if you'd be coming back with me. Jonah & Filibus send you their warm greetings. I know you'll be remembering us this weekend and again at the Snr Primary Mission next month 7-14th and I'm praying poor Wilfrid's ambulance to hospital will have found the cause & treatment for his leg. Now darlings, God willing – DV indeed – we shall soon be together, all dearest love till then, Chris.

SUM Leprosy Settlement Gudi

April 2 1957

Dear Chris, so much to do…so little time and now another letter… but this one needs no answer. We would like once again to thank you for your hospitality, kindnesses & fellowship of the last few days; it has been a privilege to meet with you & your folk in Panyam. A few great convention days and now the folk have all scattered, and who can tell what is in their minds? With what expectation you planned the Convention, with what jot you saw the people come, and now, what? The Lord Jesus is working in ways we do not understand, using means hid from our sight. I do pray that we may reap in joy where we have sown in weakness unutterable. In the days to come as from across the seas your eyes turn to this land, I do hope He will not leave you without knowledge that your labour is not in vain in the Lord; may He be with you as you go home to Britain & in His time may He bring you back to things He has planned. We trust you will find your folk well, so much the better for seeing you again; with every good wish, Allan.

Panyam

April 5th '57

Darlings, every now & then I take a peep round the corner – what will it be like in 12 days time?! But there's no chance of any more than that as there is still so much to see to. I am so very grateful to have Joan Onions here; she is a splendid girl so efficient & hard working, seems to love it all & in just 4 days has got the hang of things pretty well. I'm sure she will manage everything & she and Frances will get along alright I should say. Our Convention went off really well, with big crowds and Allan was good – just solid Bible study; & already I have heard several say it was of a great help to them. The rain held off until an hour after the last meeting – such a blessing! I believe it is in direct proportion to a fruitful convention that the enemy is working hard to undo a good Christian marriage; John Mark and Grace are not getting on & he has now brought some terrible accusations against her to the Church Council but none of us feel she is guilty of what he claims. And that is just one instance of wrecking & troublesome anger; perhaps God is planning something grand for us with so much opposition from without. Tomorrow the women are starting on their annual, week-long preaching itinerary; and Bob Smith has come to lead our Snr Primary Mission starting with the 7.30am mtg tomorrow, and Frances B has a day in Jos for supplies shopping and I'm hoping for a day of packing; now goodnight darlings, my dear love until our joy-filled meeting on the 17th. C.

Brookfield – no, I'm in Tonbridge today

Ap. 7th '57

My dearest darling I hope the Mission went off well with some specific answers to prayer & encouragements – I'm longing to hear about rather than read about it! The days & even nights aren't long enough to get done all I have to do & to plan so I'm quite sure it's even more the case with all your final preparations now. May your heart & mind be kept in peace & may you find the grace to know the important things to do & the less important to leave; and may the Lord bless your going out & coming in & give you safe journeying with the blessed joy of reunion! I am very much hoping to be at the Airport, but if you do not see Mummie with me do not be alarmed, I might persuade her to stay in bed & welcome you at home! If there's no sign of me then get the bus to London and one of us will be at the Terminal to meet you there but I want to be a Heath Row; always yours, May.

Panyam, N. Nigeria BWA

April 16th '57

Dear Mr & Mrs Cheal, just a few lines here for salutation. It is time for Nakris to leave us and go and see you although we need her with us; but it is good for her and for you to live together during her holiday. I know that Nakris will show the pictures of Panyam and tell you all the news more than she used to write to you. We do pray that the Lord will keep her on the journey by Air. My wife and family join their greetings to you we are always remember Mrs Cheal in our prayers for her illness although we know that she is old but God will give her strength and we praise the Lord because Nakris will see her, with love from Pastor David O V Lot.

~ ~ ~ ~ ~

SUM Mupun

Aug 17th '57

My dear Mother Nakris I hope you will be very glad to hear the wonderful thing that happened between Christians & the heathen people of Mupun where there had been no peace between. In July there was no rain, crops were almost dry the weather was just like dry season, people were suffering with hunger. The heathen people were trying to do their safi-dance which they thought would bring rain for them. But it was not so. On 21st July the Christians decided to gather to pray especially for the rain. On 23rd July they all gathered together at the Church at 6am and first of all we prayed for forgiveness secondly we remembered God's promise in Matthew 7:7-8. Thirdly we prayed that He may answer our prayers so that the heathen people will know that there is only one true God. Fourthly we prayed that we must have confidence and believe that we have received what we asked Him. Before that prayer was ended we heard the sounds of rain and before we reached our homes it was raining. People were very amazed and one heathen woman praised God when she saw us leaving the Church. I hope you are well with your family and happy for your holidays with my love to you all your son in Christ, Katya.

28 Abbotshall Drive, Cults, Aberdeen

Sept 3rd '57

My Darlings all how I wish I were still down in Sussex with you all, but it was good to get your letter Chris with its news – sad & grim though it is I would much rather know it all the same. I do think Wilfrid & Barbara are marvellous in their faith, and may God help & come to the aid of us all as we continually cry out to Him. He can still work miracles & perhaps we are going to be allowed to see something in the Business beyond our imagining. In reading Psalm 42 again this morning, I was struck again & took courage – and claimed it for all of you too darlings, in spite of the problems. Here we have 2 boats in and I think 10 of the men came to the Communion service at which Erik spoke in Swedish first for them [Ed: only this first page of Rene's letter remains.]

Maresfield Rectory, Uckfield, Sussex

October 3rd '57

Dear Miss Cheal, very many thanks for the book about Mwantet which I much enjoyed reading although I did not know he accompanied me to the railhead when I last came home 38 yrs ago! I did not know it was to be my final parting for I fully expected to return after a six-month furlough. I would love to have visited Panyam again but I fear it is impossible; I am not strong enough to undertake the strain of the journey. A friend who sought my financial help years ago has sadly let me down very badly and I am committed to a very large sum which is likely to involve all my savings. So, reluctantly I must refuse your kind invitation. May your return to Africa be very joyous & your next tour abundantly blessed. We continue to remember Panyam very specially in our prayers, now with kind remembrances, sincerely E Hayward.

Orchard End, Waterstock Oxford

Oct 20th '57

My dearest Chris today I am setting aside to live with you & yours throughout the day. I do love you all so much at Brookfield and know the cost as it comes to the last days before another separation. May the Lord be fully 'in the midst' of you all & His strength unto each one of you in this great crisis. This time your going is made harder with the future so uncertain for your dear ones; I was touched by your sweet trust that these things are all in His care. The way must seem dark & lonely for darling May when she turns away from the Airport and I pray that she will feel as never before the presence of our Dear Master. For ourselves, we are so grateful for that opportunity to see you at High Leigh & hear your wonderful talk with its back picture making the harvest of today a real miracle – now your work is much clearer to me. May you all be surrounded with God's love, Margaret joined with Cyril.

Greygarth, Altringham, Cheshire

Oct 23rd '57

Dearest Chris, before you left I pray some assurances were yours of the shadows lifting…if not, I know that every step of these days of trial is indeed undergirded. I pictured you all being upheld as you went forth again into the service of Panyam that each would release you with gladness to this job of God's appointing. Yet of course there would be the tug of the heart as well. I think of all your African friends & some of the problems we discussed; it does seem that the wayward heart finds difficulty in keeping close to God, whether it be brown, black or white, and our job is constant upholding as we travel toward Home. I hope you had a good journey back; I can picture the welcome pouring out from many hearts & the light on your dear face as you greeted friends from far & wide. I'm sure you found everything in apple-pie order & I wonder was the flaming tree in bloom? My heart goes out to you in prayer about my Cheals every day – what a wonderful thing prayer is whether the the spoken word or the silent worship, we are pulled in to the heart of God. May He surround you with His power, with quietness of heart, and in the service of each day give you the touch of Himself on all you do; Daisy.

Christ Church, Oxford

Dear Auntie Chris, just a note to assure you of our thoughts & prayers now that you have to go – not that they're only just starting now, nor will they cease when you get safely back to Panyam. I think it is encouraging for us all to realise our 'spiritual togetherness' when we are physically separated. I do hope you'll have a good journey & find everything going well when you get there. It's been wizard having you! Do you remember how you were volleying 'with the prodigality of genius' one evening?! Also, I do thank you for laughing at my feeblest jokes; now with all my dearest love, Anthony. PS Nanny asked me to tuck in her little note when I wrote to you: My beloved Chris, I will say again how thankful I am for this lovely furlough. We will look forward with hope, love is of God Eternal and our love is centred in Him so all is well your loving Mother.

Rome

Oct. 23rd '57

Darlings here I am in the great ancient city thinking of Romulus & Remus, Horatius, Paul, Peter, Nero, Aquila, Priscilla, Phoebe and others. Now I do hope you didn't wait to see the plane off? We were all strapped in, sucking sweets as went taxi-ing along but soon slowed, 'a slight technical hitch' (temperature gauge wasn't working) so back to the Airport for a nice lunch & a long wait till 3.27. Very cloudy till a magnificent sunset then tea served as we approached Geneva, then we had to fasten seatbelts as there was a lot of lightning all around but all was fine. We came down here for a 45min stop with more tea & biscuits!

Tripoli: another lap of the journey over and another meal and oh how I have been thinking of you all & pray you got home safely & are fast asleep now, kept in peace, not lying awake. I'd love to have some glowing word to express all that's in my heart, but I know we all feel the same over that. Thank you each one more than I can say therefore for all the kindness, love, care & fellowship of the last 6 mths – another bright milestone on my way, and I am glad of all the experiences we have shared together, the burdens as well as the pleasures.

Panyam: I posted to you from Kano, and Frances was at Jos & she drove to Barakin Ladi where I took over, slipping back into it quite easily, we passed precisely 3 vehicles in the 28 miles from BL to here! Such a wonderful crowd lined the road waiting for us with a gay banner between the trees, so I left F & Joan to unload while I walked back to greet them; there must've been 150 handshakes & so many loving enquiries after you all & Nakam also. By the time I finally got in to the house a brewing headache intensified until I was sick – what a way to begin! A Veganin & some soda & a cup of tea then a good hour's sleep restored me wonderfully. Frances has a bad chest & asked me to give her a penicillin injection before bed, she's still cheerful but looks thin & worn & I think has found it heavy going; Joan seems to have done splendidly & continues calm throughout, I am so thankful she is to stay on here until next March at least, I hope longer.

25th now, Moses & Victoria have a 3rd son! They are very happy although he'll probably not be able to work again. Frances P came through on her way to the Leper Clinic at Longkat; she stayed to lunch & tea, seeing some patients for me plus Frances B who feels a little better. FP looks well & was asking so warmly after you all & she was v pleased with the Peace rose and the apple. This eve at our usual PM so many prayed beautifully for those I had left behind me…to whom I now send so much dearest love before I go to bed, Chris.

Panyam

Oct 27th '57

Darling May this one is just for you for I must tell you how I marvelled at your courage & fortitude during the last week. I think you were strengthened by the prayers & love of so many but nevertheless it amazed me to see the effect. I shall never forget your prayer of last Wed morning and I've just now been praying that you might be spared a reaction – the sort of physical & mental reaction of gloom & heaviness that so often happens naturally after a period of strain taken victoriously. I have asked this for all the family but especially for you. Here there have been many loving enquiries after you, one specifically from Abednego Jar, the gardener at the Fish Farm, & he also asked after the sister who lost husband to the War. At the Teachers PM earlier I was telling them about how you are using the experiences of your visit here to illustrate your talks at the Bible Society mtgs all over England. Now the bell is being rung up on the rocks so I must go & greet the folk as they come in to church & as F is still in bed I shall have to play the organ.

9.15pm just as David began his sermon this morning a heavy storm came on & beat on the aluminium roof with such vehemence that he gave up & simply stood & waited for it to stop. So we adapted to a wordless Friends Meeting style until David could resume & he began by thanking God for the rain and that never before had it interrupted thus. What a truly African way of accepting the inevitable & turning it into cause for thanksgiving!

Tuesday now: yesterday was almost all taken up with long talks with Ernest K over developments during my furlough, and plans for staffing changes and dates for Conventions & our priority must be Bible teaching. Scripture Union Daily Bread notes in Hausa will be ready for 1958,

200 copies ordered. Likewise today, long talks with David planning our Jubilee & he agrees that our Market Bookshop work needs to grow & should be a priority. We shall plan Bible courses to be taken by the new Pastors, & I should like to plan a few B. studies to take in outstations when I'm only there on short treks & perhaps only stay for one night, or within a day visit. On the verandah at noon with a lovely breeze the temp is 85 and I see 'Peace' has five healthy buds & 'Christopher Stone' has four! Word has come in the mail today that Datilik has passed for the SIM Evan.Training course at Kagaro for the next 2 yrs but poor Kafas/Katya did not though he was top of the list of those who didn't. I do pray he won't feel too terribly disappointed.

Weds: Frances P has advised that tomorrow Frances B should go in to Jos for a chest Xray as she is still croaky as a rook; she will post this to you. Tell Mummy I've been having a lovely time with Aristarkus translating her special verses into Sura ready for Sunday. He has loved the Bible course at Gindiri & wishes he could go at once out into B teaching work but knows he will really stay on here for the final year. Patrobas Yilhi told me this morning of 2 of his schoolboys at Jing who are deeply in love with the Bible; Scripture lessons are their great delight & what they most want to do is go to the Gindiri Bible School as soon as they are able. Oh and Haggai Jatau has got 30 girls at Jibilik who want to join GLB! Let me not forget another special thank you for the chocolate which I did share with Frances & Joan who were both so pleased; now darling it is goodbye for this time with all my dearest love & constant prayer for you as ever, Chris.

Brookfield

Nov 3rd '57

My darling I'm sure you know my thoughts & prayers are with you all the time. It was so good to have your journeying letter though I'm so sorry about the h.ache & sickness (shades of the Winchester road!) and what a welcome you had! You really are back home again aren't you; and I do hope you've been alright getting back into the heat & the press of duties. There seems such a gap & a blank here now that you've gone; I've been more conscious of it this time than ever before which just shows how much you mean to us all present or absent. By the time you get this your Birthday will have passed but you'll know our love undergirding & surrounding you as we think & pray & praise for you. There is still nothing to report & the strain of that, plus your departure has of course required Mummie to take a few days in bed. Wilfrid thinks the Reigate client must be off, so he did ring the agents to ask for our plan of the Nurseries back, & he & Father are going together tomorrow to talk to Woodson. Being once again actually in the Office I am conscious more than before of the really desperate position we are in and unless something happens very soon I don't think we can possibly carry on. I have managed this week but there is not much I can do & I do not want to stop BS work altogether especially if we really do have to close the Business in the next few months. Darling I do so appreciate and need your prayer support throughout all this. I must seek the time to have a serious talk with W in spite of no chance this week; and I only got away for 2 afternoon BS meetings which were good but not well attended. Kathleen Arnold was asking warmly after you, so glad to have met you. Mother will write tomorrow, but I must stop now, all love May.

Panyam

Nov 7th '57

Mother darling thank you very much for all your birthday rememberings – I'd not even registered the day until noticing the date in Daily Light, & then at tea the girls produced some little parcels which was so sweet of them. Lovely letters also came from Rene, May & Nakam and the GLB HQ plus several local ones. Yes I can well understand the strain, especially at Ifield, of the continuing lack of decision for the Business; my heart goes out to you & my prayers surround you & Father & Wilfrid particularly. I long for all sakes to hear of a settlement but it is good to know the Braeside folks approve the idea of selling up. I had a feeling this morning as I read Daily Light that today's words of quiet triumph & delight in the Lord's deliverance would be ours in a special way this very day so I am recording that feeling & hope soon to hear that something has happened. Some good news from here is that Frances' Xray was negative for TB so we are all thankful. We had quite a party here – the Dearsley family came with 30 Secondary school boys to give their BB Display to our boys, then their Enrollment service followed by a football match! I didn't get back till 5pm & by the time I'd had a wash & changed my dress Frances P, Helen Templeman & her mother & sister Betty all arrived. Joan had got a nice tea ready with the baking we had managed early that morning. We all had a great time except for the boy who got a crack in the face from another footballer's head; Frances P thought it was a small fracture just above his nose so the 2 men took him through to Vom at once. Damaris who was received into Church membership last Sunday, got a nasty septic foot so she went by ambulance to Pankshin Hospital. Now darling I must close with best of blessings & all my love to you & Father, yours as ever Chris.

Panyam

Nov 15TH '57

Darlings it is exactly 50yrs ago today that that Rev Lloyd arrived here to settle – the first Missionary of the Gospel! We have been remembering and speaking of it today & at this evening's PMs both the men & the women took the theme most warmly. Joan said old Father Lot's voice sounded so young that she had to open her eyes to see if it really was him! He remembered Mr Lloyd coming & the spot where he first pitched his tent and the then old men refusing to allow the women to go out & look at him. Here is part of what we wrote for the occasion, with deep thankfulness to Messrs Alvarez and Hayward: *'Panyam, the central village of the Sura tribe, and the surrounding areas were, 50 yrs ago, entirely unevangelised and under the superstition & ignorance of paganism. If you come today to visit this area you will find 120 villages where services are held each Sunday where the young Church is growing rapidly under the care of the Sudan United Mission which in 1930 took over the work begun by the CMS. The Evangelists & Teachers who are responsible for the care of the Christian groups in these villages are men from the Sura, Baron, Kulere, Fiyam and Chip tribes who have been brought out of the darkness of heathenism into the light of Christ through the witness begun 50yrs ago. There are 15 Junior Primary Schools in the District & a second Senior Primary School is about to be opened. A central Bookshop provides for the needs of an increasing number of literate people and two of the Bookshop staff travel around the markets selling the Scriptures & other helpful books. In 9 villages there are medical clinics where leprosy patients are treated, Panyam being the centre from which they are supervised. How is it that this great development has come from such a tiny beginning? Surely the answer is that the Builder and Maker is God (Heb.11:10) It was He who called those young men to go forth into the unknown 50yrs ago – three of whom finally laid down their lives in this land; it was He who called forth the faith & devotion of hundreds from these tribes who are now sharing in the progress of Christ's cause among their brethren near & far. Evangelists, Pastors, Teachers, Missionaries, Dispensary Attendants, Boys' Brigade & Girls' Life Brigade Officers, Women's Fellowship Leaders- all are having their part in the practical working out of God's plan & purpose that we should all be part of the Household of God. There are now 5 Churches in the District, each with its own Elders & supporting its own Evangelists. These Elders are planning a celebration at the end of this year to mark the Jubilee of the Gospel in the District. Our hope & our prayer is that this 50th year may be one of setting free many more of Satan's captives & a year in which much glory shall be brought to the name of our Lord Jesus Christ.'*

On Monday night I was up with a midder case but it was a stillbirth, these are always so sad; now with much dear love to you all as ever, Chris.

Brookfield

Nov 25th '57

My beloved Chris in a note from Rene today she is now not to have that major op. This fills us with thankfulness & we live in hope that it may never be needed. I wrote back at once urging her to be extra careful, not getting over tired & certainly not lifting heavy weights. You will put this down to 'Mother's worry & fussiness' but instead you should allow for wisdom gained by hard experience, and I hope when you write to R you will back up what I have said. After 2 months or more of complete rest one of my black hens has laid an egg! Paice was nearly as overjoyed as we are; and I do wonder if the day – begun so nicely – will bring us news of the Grove Field being settled; we have waited long to hear of this and for news of Ifield Park possibly buying more land. These decisions seem to take such a long time to materialise and our need is patience. Several times in my morning readings recently I've come across this word and it always bears its own implication. One of the men who knows Father came and spoke to me, saying he was sorry to hear F was not too good and went on to say they were speaking of Father at the Thursday eve meeting. There, he said, was a gathering of hard-headed business-men, a vicar or two, and others, and when we really got down to rock bottom over things in relation to business etc Mr Cheal's name came up & they asked what is it that Mr Cheal has got that we have not? I told him I'd go home & tell him & I knew it would be an encouragement to him. Did I tell you of Auntie Lizzie's wonderful gift to me of £100, a love gift she said! I hoped so much in telling her a little of the anxieties we are passing through I had not made her think I wanted money because that never entered my head. She wrote that they had never received even a hint of any such a thing & they're just very pleased to send it. So for you darling I have chosen a beautiful Scotch calendar which should reach you by Christmas with lovely reminders of our happy summer days up there, from your ever loving Mother.

Panyam

Nov 27th '57

Darling May at the unusual time of 8.30am I am writing to you and I'm still in bed! Yesterday was wearying and I do have a spot of fever so shall rest sensibly today. I'm sure you'll want to hear the result of the mtg with the Prov Educ Officer about the Snr Primary at Jing. I believe we shall soon have the permission to open the school and also the buildings grant! I was in that office over an hour having gone in feeling like Esther for Mr Bristow was pretty sure we would not get it until they were better satisfied with Panyam SP but he did suggest that perhaps a woman could do more with the PEC than he could. So I even wore my pink nylon dress! The verse that came to me the night before was 2 Chron. 20:17 stand ye still and see…and when I got there I found he had already actually sent in a request to Kaduna for permission to be granted, & he thinks we should get it in about two weeks! Changes seem to have taken place for the better & I think I can assume that our staffing for next year is good. Also yesterday I had to see the dentist – so ridiculous after Cramp had so recently assured me that all was well – but that tooth will require a second appointment in 2 wks. Don't worry about me, its nothing serious. I took Daraprim which ordinarily clears me up at once, but it didn't quite this time. Frances B kindly came into Jos with me yesterday & did all the driving & shopping. My prayers for you all are for patience & faith to be continually granted. C.

Panyam

Dec 3rd '57

Darlings a quick note to say I hope all is going on well with you as I heard nothing in the last 2 mails & I long to hear any better things in the Business developments & of course how dear Rene is. And to assure you I am alright though still not quite shaking off this mild fever, & getting lots of headaches, so Frances gave me a course of Nivaquine a new malaria remedy. Yes I am resting & leading a really quiet life & taking Iron & Glucose pills. Joan has been off colour for some days too with a high temp & blinding head & now Frances P has diagnosed Dengue fever so she'll be in bed awhile poor girl. Frances B has her hands full but is quite fit herself & will go tomorrow to assist Frances P with a major op – a leg amputation. One beautiful bit of cheer is the first bloom of my Christopher Stone rose which I cut & took in to Joan – oh such a glorious scent!

The 5th now: just a wee line to say I'm much more myself today, loads better & working normally again. And my case of personal goods has finally arrived & is such fun to unpack; thank you again for all the lovely gifts for my b.day & for Christmas, & now I can have my morning tea in a Keswick mug once again! The picture of Balmoral has taken up position of honour on the sitting room mantlepiece, with David & Nakam on one side & you all with me on the other! What a ghastly train crash last evening the wireless told us, in S.E. London, such a dense fog must have been awful – I feel thankful that you probably have not had to be out in it; dearest love to you each one, ever thine, Chris.

Brookfield

Dec 6th '57

My darling, F&M are safely tucked up in bed & I'm sitting by the kitchen fire praying for your health & praising for your great mtg with the PEduc Officer who I hope has sent you written confirmation by now? Isn't it incredible to think of Christmas just 3wks away – I do hope your great Day at Panyam will be as wonderful as usual & yet just as the first service 50yrs ago has borne such harvest so on your 25th may hearts be prepared & open to receive the Good News! You must have heard on your news of the dreadful train crash which continues to dominate all our thoughts as the whole combination of circumstances was so ghastly it makes the tragedy worse. Many of the victims were young office workers or Christmas shoppers going home after a day in town. The horror of these things is hard to understand. Now I think Mother has written but did she tell you that word came from Horley Dist Council that the whole matter of the Grove Field has been postponed until discussion with the Crawley DC so, we seem to be back to right where we were before you came home. We are paying a little on account to some of the most pressing creditors & while we can keep doing this I suppose nothing too drastic will happen. The next fortnight ought to see the majority of the orders sent out but after that I don't know. Is it right to say we'll just carry on a day at a time trusting the Lord will make a way, or should we be exploring other ways, it is all very bewildering & even if we do adopt the day at a time attitude the situation is just as wrong as it was 6mths ago. I've been reading Philippians again with the reiterated injunction to rejoice in the Lord. Can one really do that & expect Him to work something out at the last minute when the Business just goes on about as it has been for the last 8 years? It's hard when actually working in the Office again to see where changes could be made. Darling, don't feel you must answer all this as there's really no more to be said than we've said before. We either go through the worst or the Lord works deliverance for us. Now goodbye my dear love, my heart is with you always, ever yours, May.

Southways (another family home on the Nurseries), Lowfield Heath

8.12.57

My dear Sis, "You've only got to turn your 'ead and Christmas is come – and gorn!" old Parsons would say. It certainly seems as though you're hardly out of the country & here I am starting the annual festive letter. But there's very little to say so it will not be lengthy. It leaves us as we hope it finds you – in rude health other than a completed round of winter colds of course. I have just collected at Brookfield and read your summary of the last 50yrs which is most interesting & illuminating – especially to us in a way, with vivid childhood memories of Tom Alvarez & later on Mr Hayward. The mantle of Ezra seems to have fallen upon you as if made to measure. At Great Walstead David's housemaster Mr Park has been complimentary about his writing, "That son of yours is going to be a journalist!" Let's hope it would be more lucrative than horticulture anyway. So turning to more pressing matters here, you have probably been told the little we know. It did not seem possible when you were here that we should still be carrying on by now without some major developments, yet here we are with none of the possibilities envisaged actually taken place. It has not been easy or pleasant but we may be thankful it has not been distinctly worse. We have had fairly good responses to offers of surplus stock to the trade, and a few quite encouraging orders for private gardens. One urgent problem is disposal of other stock for planting and budding and of course diminishing labour and still no decision on our land at Pulborough. Without forfeiting considerable stock we could not clear out from here in less than 2 yrs. There is so far no talk of intention to close down the farm so we cannot make any reasonable plans for 1958. I am finishing this while having lunch in Brighton – less than ideal conditions-Barbara intended to add a line but she is not with me so you'll have to take the word for the deed. But it brings beaucoup d'amour from all of us & we hope that you'll have a very happy Christmas. We are holding on, thankful for mercies so far, but feeling slightly nonplussed about the future, with much love from Wilfrid.

Brookfield

Dec 13th '57

My darling it is a relief to hear that you are quite well again. You will know how much my thoughts & prayers have surrounded you, and of course still will be as we all approach this Great Day, and for you especially as its your Bible Day too and the Ordination Day – a lot to pack into one Christmas so we'll pray together that its impact on all who prepare, present and attend will be deeply enriching. We go on just the same here – truly cast upon the Lord for if there is to be any change He must work it. A letter has come from the Dist. Council saying the question of the land & where it borders two counties needs to be reviewed again 'sometime in April' and if we do not agree to this postponement the application is refused. So, humanly speaking, there is no way out, and what the Bank's reaction will be I do not know. Our immediate position depends on that. Ant is coming for the weekend it will be good to see him again.

15th now: Ant sends his love & best greetings to you & asks if you remember George MacLeod doubled up in Aberdeen – he was on TV tonight! I went to see Auntie Jo in hospital where she's having a wonderful times acting as honourary Chaplain to the whole ward; & I'm thankful to say, she never once mentioned Jack the parrot or Sam the cat. You would be amazed to see me stroking Jack's feathers treating him as a beloved pet; he must not die in her absence. Now darling will you please tell Joel, Ishaku & Manasseh that I pray regularly for them & all our prayers will be especially undergirding them on Christmas Day & afterwards. And for David too as his mind goes back to his own Ordination & Commissioning & all that has happened since, that this service might be a most special time for him also & the blessing may spill over onto the 3 and further afield too perhaps even to John Mark &

Daskiyes. Ant & I have had some good talks & this time I didn't smell smoke on him or his clothes. J.B. Philips has a new booklet out about Christmas, urging us to get beneath all the trimmings & trappings to grasp afresh the utter marvel of what it really means; one of his points is that God came so quietly that no-one recognised Him. Perhaps He will choose a similarly unobtrusive way to help us now – we must be patient. Darling you have a lovely Day & I hope the wonder of what God has done there during the past 50yrs might inspire new faith in all of us for the future. All my dearest love to you, ever yours May.

28 Abbotshall Dr, Cults, Aberdeen

Dec 15th '57

My darling Chris very dearest love & the best of Christmas good wishes goes from all (both boys will here) of us to you, may you have peace of heart & much joy too even in this a most busy time for you. Of course I'll be wishing we could be together but also knowing that we are united by deeper love & sympathy than perhaps ever before. Tonight is the 'Lucia' or Festival of Light when we have a candle parade & the children and girls all sing carols; we expect a full church. Two women, one an ex Crusader, I have met are making plans to start a class so please remember on the 3rd Sunday January the Aberdeen Girl Crusader Class! We are buying chorus books for them & a room in a church has been lent for the purpose without charge. I am keeping quite alright on the whole & Erik seems to be too; so with our love darling, ever yours Rene.

Panyam

Dec 16th '57

Darling May after re-reading yours of Dec 6th as you sat by the fire, all I can say is how dearly I would have loved to have been sitting with you, talking through the things you raised, specifically the rights & wrongs of living 'a day at a time.' Reading this morning in Matt 6 these words seem to have fresh meaning: Take no thought, no anxious thought, for your life...consider the lilies...if God so clothes them...how much more you – surely this is His own pattern, and I do not think you can say, or even feel, that it is escapism or failure to be prudent, to live in that day to day dependence upon His willingness & His power to supply all our need. Now darling have you been able to talk with Barbara lately? I feel it would be a kindness if you did for you know her cry to me was that she didn't know much about what is happening in the Business. And do you know how they are financially after their move from Clyro into Southways, and if W has been able to draw cheques for their family needs? When I heard from our dear Rene earlier this month of her Doctor's positive verdict, and that 'Erik is his usual dear self again' well, at that the joybells just tumbled tumultuously over each other for that news is so blessed to hear. Has she written any of this to you also I wonder? Dr Barnden is coming to the Ordination service on Christmas morning then after lunch he is to take Frances away & that will be her goodbye to Panyam. Frances P will also join us but for the whole day, & when she has gone then Joan & I will be on our own. When the GLB Camp is over we reopen all schools on Jan 13th & on the 16th Joan goes for her well-deserved holiday to Miango & I've asked Pat to come & stay for awhile, at least until Joyce arrives at the end of Jan. Darling May, I pray that the Lord's presence will be vivid to you on Christmas Day. Oh I forgot to say that Prof. Ken Cragg is staying here & lectured on Islam & Christianity last night, he spoke excellently – very erudite & clever, but so deeply sympathetic with the Moslem outlook too. It was a privilege to be there to hear him. This brings such dear love & longings to you, and to everyone with very best wishes for a time of happiness & blessing, & that others will be blessed through being with you. It has been a strange year of testing & trial but surely we have seen God's lovingkindness too and we will continue to trust to see greater things than these in the New Year; so goodbye my darlings all, from Chris.

10 Harewood Rd, S. Croydon

Dec 16th '57

My dearest Chris I think the cold has frozen my brain for I thought I'd already posted this rather lengthy list of requests & suggestions re the Christmas Day service & New Year doings, but clearly I did not, so will enclose it now with this brief note telling you one amusing & one serious thing. It is freezing hard & about 4pm I went to my flat roof to fetch my washing that I hung up there to dry but lo & behold it was all frozen stiff. I unpegged my thick woollen combinations and they stood on the roof- upright- by themselves. I roared with laughter at them till their feelings seemed to be hurt for they flopped over & leant against me in a helpless sort of way! I had quite a job to bend them enough to get through the door & inside again with them & the same with the other items. Now the important matter, really important: if either of them (you know of whom I speak) continues unwilling to forgive I do implore you to <u>make</u> the time & opportunity to talk openly & honestly with them and find out the real truth behind it, because forgiveness is such a basic thing – you know this. If he is really not forgiving he will debar himself and everyone else from all blessing – he cannot be a channel of blessing to others. Especially in view of what is taking place for them this Christmas Day – a leading part in the Ordination service? This is wrong & cannot be allowed; do please get it all made right; get it right do not delay longer. You know how much my thoughts & prayers will be with you throughout Christmas (in spite of cooking pheasant & plum pudding for my guests!) so goodbye with much love, Nakam.

2 Rockleaze Ave, Snyed Park, Bristol 9

Dec 18th '57

Dear Miss Cheal, many years ago I was a Girl Crusader at West Bridgford & I was always interested in the Lord's work in Africa. On your furlough once, about 1942 or 3, you came to speak & I was delighted that you came home to tea. After leaving school I went to Oxford to read for an English degree, then taught at Wortly for 2 yrs before marrying Michael Farrer the then Curate at St Ebbe's. Last yr we moved here with our son David. In spite of my failures the Lord has wonderfully given grace to keep following Him & I continue to pray for the work of the SUM. Now I am getting your prayer letters and trying to uphold you in prayer; I see from the Lightbearer that Christmas Day this year is going to be tremendously important in Panyam. God bless you in your own soul & in all your work for Him & God bless His work through you, with love, yours very sincerely Annette Gelson Farrer.

Brookfield

Dec 20th '57

My beloved Chris this brings our very best wishes – as you well know & of which you need no assurance – for a truly happy Christmas & New Year full of the Lord's blessing…must stop a moment & get some feeling back into my cold hands…or you won't be able to read any of this. It is very cold & frosty today. Your letter as always brought warmth to my heart, especially now for that girl Joan, I think she is a really good missionary & anyone who is a help to you is my friend! Thank you for the wonderful account of the 50 years – what amazing things our God hath wrought, such wonderful changes & growth. Cousin Jimmy commented to me that the life of a missionary is about the finest there is, with so much evil & destruction in the world, Chrissie's service of helpfulness & building up makes a grand contribution, or something like that. My mind is dwelling on your Christmas celebrations & the most special Ordinations & all the thought & preparations you put into these things; I shall be with you in spirit, may you be blessed seeing the Holy Spirit working in so many lives. My heart overflows with thankful praise for the blessings of my family, May is constantly selflessly busy day & night for the Bible Soc & here at home cooking & cleaning for us & again in the Office helping Father; and Rene is growing in grace so manifestly of late, and Wilfrid keeps steadfastly on. Father will write a bit next time I hope tho' he hates writing. Uncle Ernest sent Father a £5 cheque which is most kind but I fear Tim gave a poor report of Father's suit which I had had to patch at both elbows & which I think was noticed. We did have our party after all & it went well; Anthony came early & is such a help tho' the Thomases hardly need entertaining. The Bridgemans – only he came, she was too busy ironing – he said it was lovely to have such fellowship; W&B came for coffee about 8 and all left before 10o'c which was good. It was the Carol svce at Horley Church in which the girls' school Kingsley takes part – Alison reading one of the lessons, Nona singing in the choir; and did you hear Jonathan got 100% for his Latin exam – to think of it, that child – Latin! B says he loves it; well it is something to be the grandmere of clever children, I hope he will continue loving his work. Anthony feels the nearness of his exams in March so perhaps there will be less gallivanting around Oxford & a little more work, tho' perhaps he does more than I think; all the love I can send, as ever Mother.

Brookfield

Dec 22nd 1957

My darling I wonder if you will get this letter before the year closes – I shall not be sorry to see it close although perhaps later when we see it in retrospect it will not seem as bad. I confess to feeling very oppressed by the sense of failure to accept circumstances, or to triumph over them. But we do know it is wiser to forget the things that are behind & to press forward; but I'm increasingly conscious of the contra-indication in terms which my life presents. Might you get the broadcast of the Watchnight Service? It is from St Richard's Church this year with the address by the Bishop of Chichester. Thank you darling for all the kindnesses you wrote into your last letter, but no, I haven't talked much with Barbara, partly for lack of time but mostly because my own thoughts of the Business are so depressing I don't feel it would do anyone any good to share them. I think W must have drawn <u>some</u> money for B has been on at least 2 Christmas shopping expeditions to Croydon & Alison came over the other evening on her way to the sixth form party to show us her very nice new frock she really looked beautiful. Yes I am indeed thankful for what you wrote about Rene for all I heard was that when she returned from here Erik did seem quite pleased to see her. Perhaps her health scare has worried him somewhat. It is 10.30pm & I've just listened to 'Scrapbook for 1914' which has left me with an aching heart for all the accumulated sorrows of our world & a mind bewildered that in spite of it all we do seem to be rushing into a third war. Unfortunately I have lost the cards Auntie Jo wrote & asked me to give out for her – so you can imagine what I'm in for! I did tell her last eve when visiting her in hospital – she was not amused. I fetch her home tomorrow, and so far the parrot is still alive & even becoming more vocal but I shall not be sorry to hand him back. It is not right to keep birds in captivity; blessings on you, M.

Panyam

Christmas Day 1957

My darling dears all, how I wished you could have seen the activity around here before the big Day! Good numbers gathered for the onslaught of weeding, rubbish removal, cutting down cactus & other overgrown bushes, then the women swept the whole place and girls brought dozens of headpans of sand to cover the rocks around the Church walls washed bare by the rains. Joan, Huldah & I polished the furniture inside, & cleaned the windows. Frances has been hectically busy with her packing and getting medicines made up for when I shall be alone, during her last full days in the Dispensary. After our usual early wake up for carols this morning Joan was doing the flowers in the Church & I was on last minute prep and the bell started ringing at 8am & people began filling every seat inside & many outside. The service went from 8.45-11.0 but didn't seem at all too long. As the 3 new Pastors were given their new Bibles by Dr Barnden, he said to Ishaya, "This Book is Light & will be a light to you and to those to whom you minister." To Joel he said, "This Book is a Sword and will be your armour to fight against evil." And to Manasseh he said, "This Book is the Word of God to feed your own soul and the food you will give to your people." Pastor Damina's very good address was on 1 Tim. 6:11 the graces seen in our Lord, only possible for us when Christ is living in our hearts. He then urged the people to support their new Pastors. David then gave out the long awaited notice of the new Theological College entrance exam in July and the requirements of study levels for both the Certificate & Diploma courses. Then it was time for Communion with David using the Hausa prayer book and the new Pastors distributing the bread and wine. A wonderful day altogether, but now my darlings it is dark & I need my bed; it has been so good to feel the prayers of so many surrounding us today & I can only add mine in longing that God's purposes might have been fully carried out & fulfilled here this day; very much love, Chris.

PS on the 26th: Special thanks for the wonderful feast of dear letters from each of you with cards & extras too & the glorious calendar as well – I am blessed! Do you remember those brightly coloured shirts I bought in Crawley? Ishaku, Ali, Joseph Waltu, Jonathan Abwam and Gochin were so very pleased & excited to receive them! And May dear I gave your messages to David & Joel but didn't have a moment with Ishaya or Manasseh to speak but certainly will tell them later. This morning Joan & I went down to Jing to mark out the ground for another Snr P Teacher's house which an Abwor Christian has agreed to build on contract for £26. We were kept waiting because they had not cleared the grass from the site as I'd asked them to do so I had to get them to burn all the grass first and then we fumbled about in the ashes measuring and putting in marker pegs! I slept this afternoon – after washing off the ash – and we've worked hard this evening preparing equipment & messages for the GLB Camp Dec 30-Jan 6th so now it's goodnight again dears all, Chris.

Panyam

Dec 30th 1957

Darlings I didn't expect to have the time to write again this year but I do so with joy for there is good news to tell! David has told me that God is answering our prayers & the prayers of our people in England…John Mark asked him to call the family together so that he JM could repent of the wrong he has done & he now wants to take Grace back. This is lovely, but David's happiness in telling me was almost greater because as you know I've had a suspicion he himself has long been harbouring hard unforgiving thoughts against JM. And now Grace is willing to make a full public repentance in Church also. It is a blessed relief to feel the wind of the Holy Spirit is blowing freely again, bringing the balm of forgiveness where it has been so badly needed. Nakam has known about this & has been praying faithfully, and Father, David asked me to thank you specifically for your prayers for him; and all of you for your interest & support; all best love, Chris.

Brookfield

Dec 31st 1957

My beloved Chris what a happy & joyful morn with both yours & Rene's letters so longed for & welcome. We have thought so much of you & pictured the scenes in the Church on Christmas morning – but I think it must have been even grander than we thought! Oh what blessing will surely come through the faithful lives & ministry of these 3 new men, only Eternity will show it, may God bless them all, keeping them safely faithful to Him to use them greatly to advance His Kingdom here on earth. Now darling I send you my best love & all best wishes for a wonderful God-honouring year of fruitfulness & spiritual blessing, constantly seeking first His Kingdom then all else being added unto you. We had a very quiet Christmas and the TV helped us quite a lot, so we thank you once again so warmly for such a thoughtful gift. Father really enjoyed many things & of course we saw the Queen & heard her good message. May had decorated the tea table on the 25th so very beautifully & all 13 who sat down did justice to our baking. How thankful to be able to keep Christmas in our own home, no other place could ever feel quite the same; and yet I am prepared to go anywhere if that way is best. Gladstone Moore has been again to the Office talking with Agents – there has been a very rude letter, but I know nothing further. Now Mrs Crowhurst is here, she is a good soul but does love chatting with coffee; I am glad to have her, talk and all. May has been wonderfully generous but I am not allowed to say anything of it, perhaps only that it is something you will rejoice over; as ever with my love to you my precious Chris, Mother.

Brookfield

January 5th 1958

My dearest darling there can't have been many years when I haven't written to you on NY's Eve; during the past week I've had to write over 60 letters – all but 3 by hand – & all different so you'll understand how addled my brain feels & unwilling my hand. It was lovely to get yours & hear all about your marvellous sounding Christmas Day, I'm so glad it went so smoothly, at least, you made it sound as though it did. I hope the people gave Frances a nice farewell send-off. Around here everyone seems to be really poorly and want me at their beck & call: you'd weep if you saw Edie trying to do for herself when she can hardly take a step her legs are so creaky; Auntie Jo's diet sheet from the hospital has a list of forbidden foods but she insists a little of some of those when she wants will do no harm – how can one help such an attitude? Father wants me to continue for him in the Office but there is absolutely nothing for me to do now except answer the telephone & I could not think of asking for leave of absence just to do that; but I'm still not sure about the thing that is essentially wrong. More & more meetings seem to require my presence & usually my voice too & it is increasingly difficult to fit them all in. I don't think I've ever felt as down-hearted as in these past weeks. Did Mother tell you of poor Eddie's disaster? He had to kill over 1000 of his pigs for they caught some infectious disease – swine fever I think, it's only a pig illness but I don't remember the name. They are not allowed to start rearing again for 6 clear months. Rene should arrive tomorrow for a week's visit which will be a great cheer I'm sure to us all. Please take good care of yourself darling, with my dearest love as ever, May.

Panyam

Jan 6th 1958

Darlings all there a few minutes this evening to chat to you now that I'm mostly unpacked from our Camp at Jibilik & before starting on the 1001 things needing to be seen to for the upcoming challenges. We welcomed all the expected girls plus about 30 new ones keen to become part of GLB, even though some of our Panyam girls were a bad example to begin with but they did improve & there was I believe much benefit to all. The NCOs really have learned how to lead & take responsibility very well, their competence was a pleasure to witness. Two girls came up at the end, very much wanting to talk & get reassurance so we read together John 10 & one of them prayed most fervently, asking the Lord to hold her in His hand. You know the staffing issues are a permanent headache for so many changes and moves have to be suggested, encouraged and finalised but then a teacher or probationary decides to get engaged or married, request a season off to farm or a number of other reasons all requiring further re-arrangement. But for the start of this new school year & new term it does seem at last that everyone is where they need to be & not unhappy with the pay. Tomorrow the mail should bring the permission for Jing SP so we can go ahead there; and we expect Kefas Katya to start as Headmaster at Jibam on Monday 13th & he'll have an Assist. Teacher plus 2 probationers with him – I know you'll be remembering his especially. Now Mother dearest this brings my best love to you for your birthday & I trust that Saturday 11th will be a lovely day for you; dear love to Father too of course & to May to whom I owe a letter, Chris.

Brookfield

Jan 13th '58

My beloved Chris you timed your birthday letter just right, it came & was so welcome on Sat morn thank you my dear love for your prayers & love with which I felt surrounded all day. It was a really Golden Day, of all birthdays I do think you can count on your 80th being the very best, I found it so – such surprise in both letters & presents & cards & 3 greetings telegrams from Ireland-New Orchard, Eglantine & Isabel & Jimmy; and a lovely bunch of daffodils & anaemones from Gertrude & Ruth H with a 10/- note to buy a small luxury; and Kathleen L sent a most beautiful Clydella nightdress. Father presented me with a large box of sweets, and May took us both to Brighton for a picnic on the Front (in the car) watching the rollers breaking, then a short fresh walk – the sea air was delicious. Home for tea, my heart so full of gratitude to God for all His rich blessings to us, rich in the love of my beloved family & friends & relations, also that I feel so much better physically & can manage so much more. If earthly joys are such, what will Heaven be like!! Darling in my last letter I fear I did not comment on your Camp doings so please forgive my over-lookings and forgetful mistakes for you know I carry every word you write in my heart. Perhaps it is good that 80th birthdays come only once in a lifetime. Rene & I had a lovely quiet restful week; she left on the 8.26 this morn from Horley & May felt she'd probably have had to stand until London the train was so crowded. Father returned from taking the car to the Crawley garage for the last time & he has returned to bed, I think he really feels the parting from it; we have had many delightful rides in it together & I tell him we do not give up the memories of those happy times. He would feel it less I am sure if there was better news from the Business, if we could pay off some of these accounts & perhaps he could enjoy some of life a little more. May God bless us all & keep us near to Him, & now I thank you again darling for your lovely card as I gaze on such nice soft colours, your own Mother.

Panyam

Jan 26th 1958

Well darlings here's just another hurried note I'm afraid, hoping so much dear Father that your 80th celebration today is as delightful for you as Mother's was for her & that you can sense my loving prayer surrounding you. Of course I know you long, F, as we do with you, for some relief from the heavy burdens carried mainly by you & Wilfrid, some blessed answers to Business prayers. It is strange that things seem the same as last summer however we know we are in God's hands then, now and always forever. It must have been such a cheer to have Rene with you & I'm sure she & May had some good talks. On radio newsreel I heard of the dreadful snowstorms in Scotland – how I'd love to be able to send you some of our sunshine & heat! Please dears would you pass on my thanks to B & W for the lovely Times Calendar they sent. And 2 more prayer requests Mother: poor Kefas Katya did not pass his Mubi Entrance Exam which makes him the only one of 'my' boys not to get in the the ETC course; and Yilbiyak who has passed it, from a Govt Training College, has now been told they will not accept him because he came from a Mission School. This is very hard to understand, & both boys need much prayer support.

28th at last the permission for the SP at Jing has come! I'm sure the long wait for it has been all to the good for it has focussed our prayer and given time for them to complete all the outdoor work in preparation for the building to begin. Did you know that Mr Grindley, Headmaster of St Margaret's school in Ifield, recently sent a nice letter to Polycarp Fian which he was most pleased to get & to which he has already replied! Mother, please could you send off a card to Nakam about Jing, many thanks & my love to all, Chris.

Brookfield

Jan 28th 1958

My beloved Chris yes I am starting this but Father will continue writing it: Many thanks Chris Dear for your kind letter & card and so very much also for the cheque transferred to my account, and more than all that for your prayers for us all in these difficult times – this is such a strength to us. Miss Willis came into me on Friday last bringing a splendid gift from the Staff for me, a Parker set of pen and pencil, most useful & I am using the pen now. She says that she thinks she now has the longest service record of anyone on the place. You do seem to have a very busy life from details you give us & we do our best to uphold you. My life is now very different since giving up the car, most of the time is spent at the Office desk doing various books which I have taken on but I am there for reference by all. Goodbye and every good wish for you & David also, your loving Father.

Panyam

Feb 8th '58

Good news Darlings – Jing Snr Primary School is opened & I had the pleasure of attending the first Morning Assembly & taking Prayers! 52 of the expected 55 children were present at 7.45am and it was a wonderful day. Joan & I used the time well & visited Chip where I saw something of the opposition the Evangelist Obadiah Kumlat faces from the unfriendly heathen Chief & his followers. We inspected each school & stopped at Abwor also before finally turning for home. About 6 miles from here Joan, who has a learner's licence, took over the driving, going sensibly slowly, but on a bad corner very near home a big saloon car appeared and I knew we were for it. The right front wheels & mudguards crashed & locked together. Mercifully no-one was hurt. The other driver was a German doctor from the R.C. Hospital & he had his wife & baby with him. Eventually help came & surprisingly both cars were drivable though mine was stuck in 3rd gear. This is the first accident to any car in the 27yrs I've been out here, I've been amazed that it has worried me so little but I'll have to get to Gindiri & put in an insurance claim. Which makes me think of poor Eddie, will he get any insurance or compensation for all those poor pigs? I feel awfully sorry for Joan because she is terribly cut up about our car even though our folk keep crowding to offer sympathies & see if we are alright. It must be time for us to have a new car – you know we have had considerable troubles with this one, including the wheel nuts cracking causing an occasional 'wobble' but this has been fixed a few times now. So I must decide if it is best to get it repaired: the garage quoted 3 wks and £100 or to sell it as is, best price, I'm told, £80. I am altogether unwilling to accept any loan, however kind, when there is no realistic hope of repaying – surely our Business troubles have taught all of us that lesson. There is some money in our 'European Gifts' account so I'm writing to Nakam for her views on putting that towards a new car. There is a Morris Kitcar, and a Standard Pick-up available almost at once but they are each over £700. Joan is going on trek next week, using her bicycle or walking, as I did so often in our pre-car days (or I should say before I was allowed to drive!) She'll visit Jibilik, Mupun, Abwor, & Katul. Goodbye darlings for now blessings on you all, Chris.

Brookfield

Feb 16th '58

My darling I want to thank you again for your dear sweet understanding reply to my letter of miserable woes last month. That you longed to fly over for a good talk and to bring me strong cheer was virtually all the medicine I needed, thank you from deep in my heart. How lovely that you had that note from Katya, sorry Kefas, that his heart had not perished from disappointment over his unsatisfactory exam result. Now I am so truly thankful that everybody was alright in that horrid motor accident and I do feel so for poor Joan, and trust that your insurance will be able to help. My thought would be the car does not warrent the expenditure of those repairs & a new(er) one would be wiser but I do see especially with Nakam coming that you need one pretty soon. I'd like to think of the Mission financing it for you but I do realise they may argue that what they do for one Station they'd have to do for all & that would be impossible. I would love to take out some of the money Susan left me and put it straight into your account to solve your trouble right away – and darling you know nothing would give me greater delight, but, as I'm sure you can see, in all probability this whole amount will be needed to keep Mother & Father for as long as it or they last. I'm with you in prayer over it all & as soon as you have clear guidance on the best way, just let me know. The Queen & the Duke are coming to Bible House on Wednesday aft, how I should love to be there, but will be on my way back from 2 mtgs in Peterborough. There is simply too much paperwork connected to every mtg and I'm getting behind in writing up reports etc from last year before even starting on this yr's schedules. I have told Mrs Slater very strongly that I feel all this needs serious reviewing as I'm quite certain a great deal of it is entirely unnecessary. She is very sympathetic but whether anything can actually be done I'm not sure. With my dearest love darling C, as ever May.

Brookfield

Feb 22nd 58

My beloved Chris we are thinking so much of you at Chip this weekend & praying it may be a time of real blessing for you as well as all those others there. I look forward to hearing about it in due course; we are so grateful for you being so good about writing to us whenever you are able. Now it is so very nice for me to be the bearer of good news: this morning letters came for each of you 4 from Uncle E's solicitors who are settling up Auntie Edie's property and had pleasure in sending you £308.6.8. All the same & I imagine all the other nephews & nieces likewise & May thought it best to open yours to let you know as quickly as possible then I imagine you'd want it put into your W. Africa Bank in London. Surely this is an answer to prayer about your car?! But I do hope the Mission will see its responsibility in the matter despite this wonderful kindness on Uncle E's part. Now I will enclose the form you must sign & send back to the solicitors, meanwhile we rejoice with you and give God thanks for every good gift is from above & I will close so May might add a line or two, sharing in your joy over this unexpected gift, your loving Mother.

PS 'Tis me now darling wanting to share rejoicings with you tinged with sadness for I think dear Uncle E has only days left, possibly hours, he is very very weak, but we can't wish him to stay on here when his reward in Glory is so close! After the service in East Grinstead yesterday I was able to visit Elizabeth Hinson the woman who asked me all those questions at the Coffee Morning. She is such a sweet girl with 2 dear children & she was so impressed when I told her some of what you are doing, & why, & the Lord's power in the lives of so many in Panyam. She had told me she's not a bit religious but curious, quite happy so not looking for anything, just wanting to know how she could find peace. I tried to help, inadequately I fear, using Rev 3:20 and John 14:18. She has talked further with Ann Batten – who brought me to her – and now I believe she has come right through to Jesus!! Bible House put on a marvellous Tea, as I can well imagine, & Mrs Slater was presented to the Queen & they sat together at the same table; she told me that Her Majesty asked very intelligent questions & was most interested, so that's lovely isn't it?! Darling I am going first thing tomorrow to see our dear Uncle E, even though I can only be in with him a few minutes, if I get there in time; I just feel I must go and say a personal thank you from us all for his wonderful gifts to each of us and more for all that he has meant to us, you & me especially, over the years; always yours with all my love, May.

Panyam

March 4th '58

Darlings I really feel rather overwhelmed by the surprises in today's mail: a £10 cheque from Kathleen Priestman towards a new car – Frances had told her of the need; an old age pensioner in Crawley, Mrs A. Wood of 5 Princes Rd, West. Green sent five £1notes with a 3d stamp for my reply, bless her dear heart; then this wonderful legacy! I have written immediately to dear Uncle Edward in hope that it may reach him before his HomeCall comes. What a great blessing the careful saving & generous giving of dear ones can be. I've also sent back the signed receipt to the Solicitors. And let me also say such a thank you to you for your welcome letters; I rejoice to think of each of the others being recipients of such a welcome sum & I believe we shall all be given wisdom as to investment or sensible spending. Frances P has been a brick the way she's put herself & her car at our disposal, so we have be able to take down more furniture for Jing School plus some extra stuff to Chip where I 'camped' in the schoolroom, May, that you will remember! The old fallen down place is rebuilt & awaiting its new roof then it too can be another school room. I took no boy with me but had my Beatrice stove & did my own small cooking but could not keep enough water boiled & cooled for drinking as it was terrifically hot there so I had to drink a lot of it overly warm. We had some good meetings for prayer & for business matters; and some were not good due to poor attendance & the afternoon for the BB & GLB Displays & Inspections I nearly expired for you recall my uniform is rather uncomfortably thick! Pastor Joel spoke excellently at the evening mtg & again on the Sunday morning & he led the Communion service so nicely. I took the Women's Fellowship mtgs & was much encouraged firstly by so many – we overflowed all the available buildings, & then to hear Lidiya, Pastor Ishaya's wife, speaking very well indeed, encouraging them in their desire to adopt a new outstation of Bongmut, and to have annual preaching treks like the Panyam women! At the final PM led most capably by Kefas with a good choice of hymns, he then called out the 2 new Evangelists & they were publicly dedicated for their work. Frances returned by 8am Monday to drive me back & since arriving there has been a constant stream of people and jobs needing attention & I've just started a Station labourer on to paint the outside of our house with yellow whitewash, but this must be all for now dears with my best love to you all as ever, Chris.

Panyam

Mar 11th '58

My darlings another amazing thing has happened! In Jos today with Frances P I was met by Gordon Muir saying he had a cable for me; cables always give me a bit of a shake but his eyes were twinkling…it read, 'News received Webster £500 gift now available here Panyam car requested Cheal go ahead please advance when required writing Herbert.' You can imagine that 'lost in wonder love & praise' just about described my condition! So I went along to the SCOA the French company with whom I deal, and ordered a new Peugeot Kitcar & signed a new insurance (comprehensive) policy for it, and all will be ready for delivery to me next Thursday when I'm in again for the Field committee. I closed with an offer of £70 for the old car Phoebe & went to say goodbye to her. I think I shall have to call this new one Fibi Nanchin which means God-given or God gave; the full cost of FN is £807 including insurance, licence & rail charges from Lagos, all of which has come in during March 4th-11th and that includes an anonymous gift of £250 which means I shall not have to use Uncle E's legacy after all. Of course Frances is just about as thrilled as me over this wonderful provision & as she says it is such a stimulus to faith, it shows that when God's time comes He can provide everything in the most remarkable way; whereas when I prayed last year that gifts might come in for a car, they didn't. It must have been that He had something of value to teach us through the accident – perhaps especially for Joan, certainly there has been a feeling of peace in my heart from the beginning that He had got the matter in hand. So dears let us all take this as an encouragement to our faith for our other great need, He can surely provide for that just as surely as He has done for this car <u>when His time is ripe</u>. I do believe His bringing of Uncle E & Auntie E's money out of Cylon just now – when the Authorities were saying it had been permanently confiscated – is another equally remarkable part of this amazement, and surely shows His absolute control over our affairs, great and small. Now darlings I think you M&F might be on the I. of W. with M this week but wherever you all are this brings my very dearest love to each & of course R&E and W&B too, Chris.

Panyam

Mar 25th '58

Darlings just another few words on the great blessing in that after everything was paid there was still enough for me to purchase a new kitchen stove and a comfortable canvas & aluminium chair – mainly for Nakam's use. And 2 bicycles, one for our second Market Bookshop colporteur & the other for Pastor Manasseh who has no transport. Our new car is much bigger than the little Austin we had before, it is grey with a long bonnet and a removable khaki canvas canopy at the back, it can take a load of 17cwt & does 30 mls to the gall & we set off home, Ishaku with me in the large front seat, easily room for 3, singing 'Praise God from Whom all blessings Flow!' Two other good things came out of the Field comm. that day: in future we shall do away with monthly statistics and retain only the yearly return which will save so much work. Also that definite progress has been made towards some sort of agricultural training for ex-schoolboys which is I believe a vital step in a very necessary development. Joan is to be sent to Maiduguri to help out there from mid April-mid May but I shall not be bereft for Nakam will be here. She is due in at Jos on Thursday. Pastor David & I will each take cars as there are so many folk who want to come out to meet her. At all the mtgs during the Convention we have arranged one representative from each of the 5 tribes & Churches in our District to speak briefly on the conditions before the Gospel arrived, of how they each individually were converted, and the growth since. We plan a good Exhibition of some of the old apparel & implements that are rarely seen or worn nowadays. As you can imagine I have been thinking much of our family needs, and asking that news of this great amazing provision for us out here, will not bring feelings of despair to any of you who continue to wait for the answer at home. Oh may this here be a foretaste & pledge of what will surely come to meet your great need. We are all equally helpless to find out own solution but He is just as able to provide for you there as us here.

Later on, 28th. Nakam is safely here, looking fine & happily none the worse for the journey. Thank you Mother for the letters & invaluable little book she delivered from you. Crowds of people lined the roads near home, many holding up welcome banners in English & Sura, & Frances B had cycled down with iced fruit drink which was so thoughtful of her & most acceptable. The day before Joan & I had to appear in Pankshin Court where it was decided the accident was our fault as Joan was in the middle of the road. She was cautioned and fined £1 but it also means we are responsible for their repairs, or our insurance will be. It is rather a plague but will no doubt be salutary to us all. As we sat on the verandah for a late tea this evening the temp was 100 and Nakam speedily forgot the biting east wind she'd left back in England! But then I heard the wireless say you are now having warmer days, almost spring time, and I am so thankful about that for you; blessings on you all as ever, Chris.

Brookfield

April 7th '58

My beloved Chris how very kind it was of Nakam to send us such a splendid report of the recent Convention – please thank her from us all & for those verses she spoke from too which really helped us visualise the scene; & tell her it did our hearts good, what a wonderful time it must have been & with so many attending! And you were able to have use of an amplifier?! We are praying that the work will continue to grow & develop and that the victory & glory will be the Lord's own. We have thought so much of Nakam settling back in, remembering all her Sura language, and enjoying the peoples' delight. I am glad she likes your new car and darling I have been praying, as I know May has also, that N's return has not brought any of the old difficulties with it, that you & she might discover renewed fellowship. Dear May has begun the spring cleaning so faithfully but today has gone to E. Grinstead to see the young lady whom she led to Christ after that Coffee Meeting; they are going for a drive & talk then back for tea & then to another meeting in Haywards Heath so she will not be home till late. Mrs Brooks was operated on this morning for some internal trouble the uterus was taken away but surely that cannot be the same as is pending for R for Mrs B looks so much older. Now with all the love it is possible to send you, your loving Mother.

SUM Panyam, N Nigeria

April 16th '58

To the Artist & Staff of Wykeham Studios, Victoria St, SW1

Dear Friends you may remember last year that you made a portrait from a small Kodachrome photo of a young Nigerian man. I brought this framed portrait back to Nigeria with me last October and I want to let you know what we have done with it. A new Senior Primary School has just been opened and a number of boys who were taught by Dafwash, the Teacher in the portrait, have now passed up into this school so we thought it appropriate that the picture should be hung there in his memory. The English Missionary in this District for 35 years is back here on a visit and officially opened the school as the Guest of Honour. Also present was Dafwash's father who spontaneously stood to his feet to confirm the truth of the Guest of Honour's talk describing his son's exemplary Christian character and that besides helping many of his pupils into the Christian way, he also led his father to Christ. Now we hope and pray that this portrait will bring loving remembrances and a strong challenge to those who look at it every day. Your splendid artistic ability is helping to perpetuate the influence of that fine young African life and we thank you, yours sincerely Christine H Cheal.

Brookfield

April 23rd '58

My beloved Chris I think May wants to add a line or two in a moment but I want to say I thought your letter to the Art people was beautiful, & so lovely to hear of Dafwash' picture there in the new school and dear Mwantet's little word of testimony. What wonderful times you are having and all out on this same round of places that you took May to & now Nakam can see them again without arduous trekking. We are still full of praise over the provision of your car just in perfect time for N's visit – I hope she's enjoying her special chair also? All that you have written about God's timing and generosity have encouraged us in our prayers for the Business. A man came last week enquiring about land, raising our hopes; he said he would send his surveyor at once but has not done so. Father is rather low with little energy for anything except resting in bed but still we must keep up our hearts remembering from whence cometh our help, we continue by His grace & loving-kindness. Now I will hand the pen & paper to May…

23rd: Darling Chris my heart is with you through these days – I've been climbing with you that last steep ascent to Tof and marvelling at that rocky stronghold so high up there, & tomorrow you'll be going down again to Ambul & I'm sure you'll take Nakam to see the huge stone! I'm certain your visits will bring cheer to the Christians in each place, and amazement to Nakam to see all the fruit from her initial labours. Just to think two years ago today I was just airborne & my marvellous experience had begun! This last weekend we had such a good conf. at Elfinsward, Rev Ronald Orchard was one of the speakers & so very good indeed. Mrs Guillebaud was there with me & she said it was years since she'd heard talks like this & wanted to persuade him to get them printed. Many dear folk there were asking after you. Tomorrow I must leave early morn to be at New Milton for the Coffee Morning mtg, then to the New Forest Area Comm at 3pm, then I've promised to look in for half an hr only to the Ringwood mtg but must not be late back for the next morning off early for the Canterbury Day Conf. in the lovely new Friends Mtg Hse there for which I'm chairing the first session. Father has been in bed all day, not ill, just weary & with no energy to get up or even eat much. I think it must be a form of escapism and my heart simply yearns for relief from the crushing Business burdens & that he may know of it before it's too late; with all my love as ever, May.

Tof

April 23rd 1958

Darling May In this place of memories & on this day of memories I want to share my thoughts with you & I expect you're on the same lines! Two yrs ago today you were flying towards us & now I'm sitting outside our little house here in Tof. There is a thick mist everywhere just as there was when you were here. Nakam & I have been around visiting & yes we did see Awnshun & his wife as they just came home from a day's work. He's not forgotten that word we spoke to him Sunday eve 2yrs ago, & he is still struggling with the desire for beer – the only last thing holding him back so we urged him again to commit himself fully to the Lord & proving the His power is able to do what he cannot do for himself. Nakam urged him to take action now not keep putting it off & we invited his dear wife to pray with us for him; she is very keen. From that home we went into Joshua Ajis & his eldest daughter is Bilhatu who sat on your knees at Ambul, they presented us each with an outsize banana! The next girl below her is called Nakris & there's now a baby boy called Elisha. Ishaku is with us & he is getting supper ready in the tiny kitchen; we slept last night at Bangesh & got here early at 7.45am; Nakam managed the walk quite well, so did Moses – yes, he came with us too & I only had to help him down one steep slope near Ambul! We met a nude man on the way who looked at Moses & greeted him with "Sanu Nerle!" remembering him from when he was here with the Spencers in about 1933!

Friday: safely back at Panyam with no untoward incidents. At Ambul we found the second school building in use & Simon Adigi the first Kulere ETC was giving his class exams and I was so pleased with his work & theirs! Do you remember Rebeka, Malachi Zumpan's wife? She has another baby daughter a perfectly lovely baby so clean & sweet. Rebeka is lovely & so friendly with the Ambul women & is busy helping Shakan, the girl on whom the rock fell, who is married now to a Christian who has lost his way & Rebeka is being such strength to her friend. One of the Baron Evangelists has taken up Market Bookshop work & I took him his first box of supplies on Tues, Pastor Manasseh is very pleased & encouraging him; by Friday he came in for more! I am making enquiries re permission to get a small American print works to re-print the Gospels in bulk at a far lower price. Niger Press will be moving to Lagos anyway. Mother kindly asked about the Exhibition we put up for the Convention of old garments & implements etc, even some old fetish ornaments. Crowds kept coming in to see & wonder, so afterwards I took them in to the Jos Museum with a writeup on each article carefully prepared by Polycarp. Mr Bernard Fagg the Curator was quite charmed with everything and paid handsomely for them all, which made the donors extremely happy, & then he gave me £3 travelling expenses for bringing them all in! Darling this brings my dearest birthday love & good wishes & all the love it is possible to send as Mother would say, C.

Brookfield

May 11th 1958

Darling Chris I'm sitting by the Garden House in glorious Sunday sunshine, such a wonderful change from the bitter cold winds & prolonged wintery days – in the weather you understand, no such welcome improvements in the Business. Everything's shooting into growth & bursting into flower but it is a bit strange to have primroses in their full beauty along with daffodils and pheasant-eye carlesii and the flowering crab too. And as for the birds, there is that marvellous quality about their singing which seems to hold it all up into the hopes of youth & spring as it has been from time immemorial. My birthday was a lovely day with Mummie coming with me to a Coffee Mtg in Tonbridge Wells which she enjoyed, & the lovely drive. Also that week I had to be at meetings of various sorts in Bible Hse in London on two different days, Guildford, Littlehampton, and Godalming & Eastbourne. Before I forget, since I last wrote to you, we've heard from BH HQ of the official appointment of CS to the Staff; he is to train colporteurs for work in Islam areas in addition to his ongoing translation work. This morning at Meeting Wilfrid spoke so well on, 'The Lord knoweth how…' and I felt his faith is as firm and serene as ever despite of his physical – or more likely emotional ailments, and Father being laid so low also. If something doesn't transpire by August I simply do not know how we can continue. But I must remember W's word & the testimony given at the E'bourne mtg of a Chinese Christian professor working under the communist regime; he always thought that 'the peace of God which passes all understanding' was just a beautiful phrase with the words chosen for their lovely rhythm. But now, after being kept alive, and sane, through that heavy & difficult time, he knows that phrase does mean exactly what it says. For us right here right now, we need this experience of Truth for things are very hard & difficult and the crash of voluntary (though unwilling) liquidation looms louder & closer. It feels impossible in the midst of so many meetings, for me to make any sort of plan, perhaps to take M&F away somewhere but F will not leave & I cannot take M and leave him; so we wait. On Thurs I went very early to Southampton, then Brockenhurst then Bournemouth for Coffee meetings, then in for a few minutes to see poor dear Uncle Edward. He is mostly confused now with rare clear intervals, in bed all the time – except when stumbling about his room on his own. How one longs that the Lord would release him and take him Home. Perhaps you've heard already that Daisy's mother died at the end of April. Mother has given me all her own & Father's old silver wedding presents to polish before taking them to the jeweller but I doubt he will give more than 10/- or £1 for the whole lot. My heart's love darling & blessings to you as always whatever happens May.

2 Rockleaze Ave, Sneyd Park, Bristol 9

May 25th '58

Dear Miss Cheal it was so good to have your letter written in February, thank you for that & for your Prayer Letter. How wonderful to hear of all the answers to prayer, not least for the new car. In thinking especially about that my husband & I now find that we have a small sum of money: £7.10 which we want to give to your work in Panyam for the expenses of the car or for some more urgent need. Do I send it to you direct or through the SUM in London? It must be splendid to have Miss Webster back with you & to take her to the new S.P. School in Jing. I am sorry to say I have lost touch with the two people you asked me about. But two of our Clifton students here, Edmund & Ruth Drew with their baby are coming out to you, to start at Gindiri. We have known them for years, they are a splendid couple. This week I am in Bognor for a bit of a rest, with my mother & sister, for my husband & I are praising God for the promise of another baby in October; I'll write again, with love & prayer, Annette Farrer.

At Brookfield

June 1st 1958

Darling Chris you'll be surprised perhaps that I'm down at home again, partly for dear old Mrs Henman's funeral, & lately there have been such 'cries from the heart' in both Mother's & May's letters, I just had to come & be with them a wee while, I took the Tues night train. I am glad to be here as W&B are now not coming up to us for it really does seem that the dreaded end of the Nursery is in sight. Wilfrid is going to see Sir Gordon Touche in case there is anything more he can do to get the local Council to allow us to sell off this land. Poor dear Father is still saying he is confident the Lord will somehow intervene, and Wilfrid is outwardly calm but one can sense the deep concern & weariness of the dear boy – he has tried so very hard & been so full of faith. I have now cancelled our holiday in Oban, for neither May nor I would feel happy being so far away when anything could have happened by then. But darling our dear Mipsie carries such a dreadfully heavy load of responsibilities; I do worry about her & feel she simply must get right away for a complete change & a rest this summer but she will not leave M&F with things as they are. I have told her I will come to look after them but she is not keen to go alone. And of course she feels she cannot give up her BS work because she has to practically keep the family. I give her a little towards this as & when I can but it's not much. I cannot see how Wilfrid is managing to feed his family but I expect Uncle C must help them. I plan to be here again for August to do what I can, after the departure of the Swedish girl coming to us for July. I did give your message to Mrs Bell for Mrs Wink who replied that Mrs Wink has had all her bottom teeth out. I am so sorry about this dreary letter, but I know you'll understand & accept all my dearest & best love as ever, Rene.

Panyam

June 6th '58

My Darlings it has been so good to get your dear letters, I do thank you for continuing to write when things are so difficult. It gives me the feeling you are all facing the issues squarely & still not giving in to dismay. My prayer is for daily courage & faith; somehow when one reaches the end, as this seems to be, there is nothing left to do but cling to God's promises, watching to see what He will do. Alison has written twice to me lately, the second letter tells of Jonathan's delight at going to Great Walstead, and Wilfrid now in the choir at St Mary's & each Sunday evening he wears a russet coloured cassock & white surplice making him look like Gladys Aylward or a Chinese Mandarin! Also she writes about the plans for the Queen's visit. A few days ago when I went to Jos to collect Nakam back from the heat of Maiduguri, I took Unaisi Anwet in to the hospital at Vom because she was far from well, looking to me as though she has active TB she is so tired with a dreadful cough. Untreated I fear she'll not be with us long. At the Sura end of month gatherings it became clear that too many of our young girls are being seized by men & taken off as wives or often second wives. A heathen chap came in to Enquirers Class & seized the leader; she managed to escape but her mother was furious she had done so, so she has opposition from all quarters & now the other 6 girls have been prevented by their parents from attending further classes or Sunday services. The 12 yr old daughter of Istifanus Jakden has had 2 letters from a horrid man trying to seduce her to run away with him. Mercifully the girl is sensible & showed the letters to her mother who took swift & furious action. I spoke to all the Evangelists & begged them to keep a careful watch over their daughters & all the young girls. Much love to you each one, as ever your C.

Brookfield

June 10th '58

My beloved Chris yesterday was the Queen's visit to open Gatwick Airport & we saw it all on TV with Auntie Jo in here & Edie Parsons too. Then we went down to the gate, each with a lovely red, white & blue posy of flowers, and waited 15 minutes by the road. As the cars went past us the Queen turned to us & smiled, bowed her head, raised her hand, and we got a grand view. Everyone remarked how nice she looked. Soon they reached Queen's Square in Crawley where Father was waiting, he was introduced – and there was a grand picture in the paper today, close to her as she planted the tree. She asked him how was the other tree she planted, & he told her "Very well indeed and I hope this one will do as well." W&B and all the children were invited to see them when they arrived at Southgate Church, the children sitting up on the Bridgeman's flat study roof with the Bp of Chichester's 2 children also. Barbara was very thrilled to have got some close up photos. As I write this to you important matters are being discussed in the Office with Wilfrid, Mr C Brooks & the District Planning Officer for Surrey Co Council, and Wood Son & Gardiner also…houses are needed for those with new jobs at Gatwick, and our land is in the right location. Father has left them and is home now so I'll not write more now. We are given grace to wait patiently. I suppose Nakam's visit will soon be over – how I wish you were coming back with her; all love, Mother.

Brookfield

June 18th '58

My darling this has been the most glorious summer day & now I'm sitting at my bedroom window, the sun has just set in a fiery ball and all the evening scents are breathing out their fragrance while the birds are singing vespers. The week began with the excitement of the Queen's visit & you'll have had details from Mother; we did so enjoy her waving her royal hand at us as we waved the posies I'd made for the occasion. She really looked lovely with such a gentle face, not that rather bored look that the newspaper photographs sometimes show. Barbara was so excited with her wonderful views at St Mary's Church. A day or two later Uncle Compton went to see the Bank Manager who suggested we go into Voluntary Liquidation & then he tried to get an appointment with the Solicitor. Father had 24hrs of his worst palpitations requiring Dr Knight to call in the specialist Dr Hunter (who was born in Coleraine, N. I!) and they warned Mother that anything could happen at any time. At the end of the week F felt a lot better and the Solicitor advised against Vol. L so there we are, still stuck in uncertainty. I feel it is not possible to pray in words about all this, but just to be before the Lord in quiet humility. Darling I do hope you are well – and not too bothered with those hot turns; all my love to you as ever, May. PS a little extra message from Mother: 'Take care of your dear self my darling, you are precious to me, my hope & confidence for your safekeeping is in God, again I commit you to Him and pray for His rich blessing to be over & upon all you do.'

Panyam

June 25th 1958

My darlings Nakam must have posted this to you from London so you will know she's landed safely & that I am quite well but wishing I could have returned with her to come home & share with you in person all the heavy burdens you are bearing these days. Your latest letters have filled me with longing & concern for you each one in the anxiety of this critical state of things. There is not time for me to write a great deal so I'll just give you the verse that has recurred to my mind several times in the last 24hrs: That the trial of your faith, being much more precious than gold…might be found unto praise & honour & glory at the appearing of Jesus Christ.

Surely in His sight the most important thing in this situation is your perfected faith 'much more precious than gold,' & whether that perfecting will be through the very dark experience of liquidation which we dread, or whether in His mercy He will spare us that, is in His hands alone. You know how my love & prayers & deep concern is round about you all. Today Nakam gave her final message to the 295 men & women gathered for Communion here at 8.30 she gave a very good word & it was a lovely service. We are taking two car loads of folk to see her off. Now goodbye my darling dears with special love to you Father & of course to each one of you as ever, Chris.

Kano

June 26th '58

My dearest Chris we are here, safely so far & an easy flight & the steward brought us sweets then a little later iced drinks, WAAC (West African Air Corp) is coming on! It was so very sweet of you to give me that dear card & message, thank you. As before, it was just awful to see you receding and it swept over me in full force. It was so awfully sweet of those dear souls to come to see me off, it was a great comfort to have them there. Please give them my love & tell them so. I sort of feel at the moment as if the end of all things has come – after these wonderful 3 months, but perhaps I'll get a saner outlook after some sleep. I can never thank you enough for all your goodness to me & loving kindness & thoughtfulness in such countless 101 ways; very much love & again many thanks, Nakam.

Brookfield

June 8th '58

My darling Chris there is nothing new to tell you but I do have some questions: if one is completely overwhelmed by the heaviness of burdens & numbers of people, and situations to pray for, and one takes endless hours speaking out wordy pleas for each, to the point of exhaustion, is that prayer? Or, what about simply listing quietly the name of each, just one word for each person or problem, is that prayer? Or being silent before the Lord throughout the day, and night, every waking hour, at all times consciously aware of Him but trusting He knows everyone & everything in one's heart, & that He knows, far better than I ever could, exactly what each person & problem needs, even me – is that prayer? Father still clings to his sincere hope that even one large cheque we are owed for work done will come in, or the Council giving permission to sell this land for building to a buyer, is that faith? Mother continues in trusting faith that we shall never have to leave here, is that faith? Wilfrid & Barbara have cancelled their holiday for he will not leave; he looks grey & more unwell than Father. Yes I know there is nothing too hard for the Lord & it is His property to have mercy, but we all know of so many Christians having to go through deep deep trials without seeing deliverance, and yes, whether we live or die we are the Lord's. That's a better note to end on darling, I'm sorry for the gloom, and I know we have your continual support – as you have ours for your daily round of difficult trails to plough through over there, blessings on you as ever May.

Southways

15/7/58

My dear Chris I felt quite overwhelmed when your letter arrived & I saw what you had sacrificed in order that we might have something more. You know how impossible it is to find expression for one's true thoughts at such times & this is no exception. How much I wish that the flow could be in the other direction, and please God it may be some day; may you be rewarded a thousand-fold in the meantime. I have not yet had time to discuss this with Barbara to what use it should be put, but possibly for day outings with the children during their holidays which are almost upon us. As you will realise we cannot think of holidays in any larger sense than that this year I'm afraid or as far as one can see. It is also impossible to give you any concise summary of the present Business position. It is just a matter of living from day to day, concentrating on stocktaking & making comprehensive plans to realise as much of it as possible this coming autumn in order to keep fluid & reduce our commitment for use of land and labour. We have unmistakably been helped in ways which are not manifest at the moment.

21st: You probably heard that I went up to Town with Uncle to see the Genl Secy of the Hort Trades Assoc who was pleasant & seemed anxious to help, suggesting I contact a man well-known in the trade. This resulted in him asking for detailed lists of our stock, acreage and houses; sending his manager down to inspect, and possibly offering to buy if a mutually acceptable amount can be agreed upon. He is even prepared to make a substantial payment in advance. This all sounds most hopeful but we must wait & see. We have received 20 replies from the 90 creditors to whom I wrote explaining out position & asking for further time to 'put our house in order'; most responses have so far been favourable with agreement to wait until autumn. What upheavals have occurred in the world since I began this letter; it would seem that no-one is to be allowed to settle down for long at a time in these Last Days, I mean on the international plane certainly. Although news travels so much faster today there is no guarantee that what one hears is true, or the whole truth; and the same events can be reported in completely different ways according to the outlook or nationality of the reporter. As has been the case over Iraq, the initial news was most unpleasant, but then later it was suggested that we might have been misled by what we thought was the position before the revolution. Who can or will tell the whole truth, if anyone? I suppose if there is any increase in Nigerian nationalism or anti-European feeling, it would not become noticeable on the Plateau until it was very manifest in your towns; and being self-governing now you may be spared some extremes although no doubt foreign propaganda is growing, possibly also Nasserism in the north. Here the family is complete again now the boys are both home but Alison has come out with chicken pox today – a cheerful start! David had it at school but not the others; he finished quite well but narrowly missed a scholarship to St Lawrence. Barbara is organising a camping holiday with all four on the Nursery at Pulborough while we still have that land. The crops there have done well, certainly barley, sugar-beet & broad beans nearly 34tons from 9acres. Once again, very many thanks to you with much love from all of us, Wilfrid.

Panyam

July 29th 1958

Darlings I'm thinking of you all on Rene's birthday – I expect she is with you, may it be a happy day for you all. Thank you for your latest letters & how I long now for further news of a real transaction completed successfully and real money paid in. Mother your letter made me see again what a wonderful example of faith & courage you are to us all, and your dear words too Wilfrid, and May your heart-searching questions also (to which, darling, I trust you've received my response by now) then Rene's letter saying the same thing; how very precious it is that we have this deep fellowship together that neither distance nor outlook can alter. And today I was everso pleased to receive a letter from Nakam written the day after she'd been to see you, she too made my heart warm by writing, 'Your Mother seemed marvellously well & bright & on the spot; she is wonderful the way she follows every detail of your work, & the people by name. Despite your current troubles, of which she told me very little, she remains calm & peaceful – how she shames me!' N also really enjoyed the raspberries you provided. Last Friday at Pat Cummins' invitation, I went away for the weekend and it was a lovely little holiday which I really enjoyed & more than made up all areas of sleep! I was able to combine it with the monthly inspections at Fiyam; & three different people asked Pat & me out to meals. The Dearsleys gave us such a pleasant time & told of their brief visit to you; even their little Christine remembers seeing Auntie Chris' mother & daddy! When last in Gindiri there was time for Joyce & me to see many of our boys & their wives & J examined Naki & thinks she's a breach (i.e. the baby's feet will come first) so has advised her to get to Pankshin hospital in good time for the birth where a doctor can look after her. Now it must be goodbye darlings for this time with my dearest love to each one of you, as always Chris.

Sandalls, Mayfield, Sussex.

Aug 3rd '58

My dearest Chris it is high time you had a letter, though I suspect this will be no more than a mere note even though you are so often in my thoughts & prayers. I pray you will be daily strengthened guided & blessed in spite of all the difficulties & the burdens of responsibilities which rest upon you. On Weds it was lovely to see your mother & Rene & May at the Bible Society Meeting, there was a good number there and May spoke very well indeed; the response was good too so I do hope she felt it was worthwhile. My family holiday in Scotland was unspoiled by cloudy grey drizzly days; the lochs are beautiful in any light, and the flowers! Masses of foxgloves, rhododendrons and dark pink wild roses & yellow irises – oh how lovely it all was, a truly memorable time. I had a week after that in London with friends, getting new glasses, and one wonderful evening at the International Horse Show – we'd been given super tickets! Just being at home without any specific responsibilities at present is so very nice, enjoying each precious minute, for next month deputation work begins & I don't yet know how heavy that will be. On Sept 2nd we hope to go DV to Brookfield again to visit your dear family. Now Mother sends her love to you & to Joan & Joyce & all Panyam friends, much love to you from Frances.

Ocean View, Boscombe

Aug 4th '58

Darling I know Rene has written telling you she & I managed to get here for this Bank Hol weekend; our room is small & cramped but has a balcony where I'm currently sitting, gazing out over it seems the whole sea whose waves we hear all night, and the afternoon sun is perfecting all. It is lovely & we've no need to go down to the extraordinarily crowded beach but can breathe in the fine air from up here. We have been for walks & yesterday R & I went to St John's where Gordon Guiness took the service & preached in such a practical, down-to-earth manner on 'Ye are not your own.' Giving 3 reasons for this a) because we belong to one another…drawing attention to the thoughtlessness of many, that more people would be killed on English roads this weekend that altogether in Cyprus; b) because we belong to our country, speaking of the debt we owe to all those who have gone before, reminding that it is the anniversary of the outbreak of the first W. War, quoting those beautiful lines by Rupert Brooks about England; c) because we belong to God, on which of course he spoke beautifully

& clearly leaving no listener in any doubt. He took the whole service in such a satisfying way, with all the prayers coming straight from his heart, the readings with such deep expression, and even announcing the hymns, 'There is a Name I love to hear.' We went back for the evening service too. Now goodbye my darling please take good care of your dear self, ever yours with all my love May.

Miango

Aug 7th '58

Darlings this will have to be briefer than usual as we are here for a lovely tea-party to say farewell to the Muirs; and to lead the GLB Course with a new responsibility this time: there are two groups African & European, from the DRCM area and the CBM area about 800 miles apart from each other, but both wanting to learn all GLB basics in short order to go back to their distant homes and start Companies, so we must teach fast! And I know you will want to hear this newspaper testimonial in the 'Nigerian Citizen' of David written by a Moslem who is suggesting David as a suitable person for Leader of the Opposition: 'the quiet-voiced, God-fearing Pastor David Lot, the gentleman of the House…he may not be a brilliant politician but he will never sacrifice principles for expediency.' That I felt is a splendid tribute even if he doesn't get chosen as opposition leader – which I rather hope he doesn't. In the car now hence scribbles, with all love as ever C.

Brookfield

Sept 5th 1958

Mother wants me to write about the apparent easement from the Horley council but really there is nothing definite and so we go on, until their next mtg Oct 3rd but of course it becomes more difficult to find wages each week. We can but trust that we will somehow be brought through. About 6pm Friday the sky got dark as night & the most awful storm we have ever known broke & lasted for 2hrs with almost continuous lightning & loud thunder and then a tornado of wind & rain for 15 mins brought terrific noise of trees cracking & splitting. A limb from the red chestnut crashed into the pergola bringing that to the ground with all the climbers in a tangled mess across the rose garden; a large poplar fell across the tennis lawn, another right across Ted's shed and the Stirling Castle apple tree fully fruit-laden. Our electric light & power was cut but mercifully not the telephone. We are thankful for no structural damage to any of our houses and no-one was hurt. Now Mother will continue, your loving Father.

My beloved Chris as we went to Meeting this morning the damage is considerably worse all along Bonnetts Lane and dear old Masey Cottage has a tarpaulin over the roof. The good from that storm is that the dining room is much lighter – as May has always wanted – now the pergola is down. Father did not mention the one offer we have had: £20,000 for the Nurseries <u>and</u> our houses but of course we hope for more so must wait for settling of one other scheme which may be possible. May is not hopeful but she is away at several meetings & not expecting to be back till late. So I will close now with my very dearest love, knowing that your prayers mingle with ours – ask that we may not fail the Lord through any want of faith for HE IS ABLE, He is willing, so doubt no more. He has promised never to forsake us – I lean hard upon such words, and give thanks for the many blessings of love in our family, a good measure of health; we do have a living HOPE in our Living Saviour, a God whose ear is open to our cry, and so we will praise His name forever & believe that all things are working together for our best good; with all the love I can send you darling, your loving Mother.

Brookfield

Oct 2nd '58

My beloved Chris, here we are, another month slipped into Eternity; how quickly the time passes. I can say Father is much better, perhaps quite well since giving up – with Dr B's consent, the Nutradonna pills though he still sleeps and rests a lot. He does walk to the Office some days but prefers his chair by the fire with the newspaper crossword. There was the usual Autumn Show in London yesterday and he just read out to me our name mentioned for our Purple leaf Maple! The only other Business thing to tell you is that a man who deals in plants, trees & flowering shrubs in pots at Covent Garden came yesterday in a very grand car. He looked around then said he could take a lorry load each week starting mid Oct; but we need a frost first. It's not a great order but it is something, as long as we can start lifting soon. And the Horley Council should be giving us their answer this week or perhaps next. Meanwhile the only one sure thing is that all things work together for good to those who love God so we trust Him who knoweth the way that we take, we will trust and not be afraid. Rene came down last night again for another fortnight which is such a comfort as May must be away tomorrow for the week. This was enclosed in a card we received the other day & I copy out now to share with you, from Luke

17:5 for it seemed so real & true to me; as ever Mother. "Faith came singing into my room, the other guests took flight; fear, anxiety, grief & gloom fled out into the night; I wondered that such Peace could be but Faith said gently 'Don't you see, they really could not live with me."

The Waiting Tea-room at Gatwick

Oct 3rd '58

Darling Chris forgive so little from me but these days are terribly full with such a lot of writing that has to be done after every meeting. We have a long delay due to crosswinds over the Guernsey airfield. I feel I have failed you in not praying more about the multitude of difficulties – in people and places you have to deal with & I am so sorry; but how good it is to read of dear Pastor Manasseh & his developing gift of wisdom, may he be kept walking humbly with the Lord. I have not thanked you properly for the two dear letters you wrote so full of strong comfort & encouragement to my faith. I think it is wonderful when you are so far away & so deeply involved in all the work of the Mission with care of all the churches, that you make the time to pray & think & care & write as you do and I am deeply grateful. At home we are still going on a day at a time & it is a recurring miracle that we are able to do this. In just a word with Wilfrid the other evening he said it is as though the lions' mouths have been stopped. It is not as yet the deliverance we long to see, but so far the worst hasn't happened. It is a great help when I'm away to know Rene is at home; we had a brief talk last night. Both her boys were here on Saturday bringing much happy laughter as they worked on cutting down the poor old stump of the red chestnut and picking masses of apples.

Later, safely on the Island after a bumpy flight, very comfortably settled in with the Area Secy & his wife & their 2 dear little girls; it's a heavy programme with 15 mtgs this week plus a 40min opportunity at the Ladies College. But now these kindly folk want to take me out to show me the Island – a pleasant break from preparations; blessings on you my dearest darling for your refreshment & quickening, with all my love as ever, May.

Forum

Oct 5th '58

My darlings here I be...on the first stage of holiday, staying with Frances Barnden, going on to Jos then Miango tomorrow. I'm sitting out on the little square verandah of F's house with a quiet lawn & trees before a great expanse of open ground further off, so all is quietly peaceful under blue, blue skies, birds, butterflies & bees also enjoying the lovely sunshine. Of all the hard work & necessary busyness before finally being able to leave it behind, the one thing I'll tell you is that we have acquired a new orphan baby boy, a dear fat little chap brought in to us the day after his mother died birthing him. Joyce is happy to look after him until we find a couple to adopt him. Thank you so much for your last letter (Sept 23rd) Mummy, your steadfast courage always strengthens me; perhaps there'll be another waiting for me at Jos.

Later at Miango: well, two were here for me thank you so much! I kept this open to tell you the address where I'll be as from Friday in Garkida, or I'll be back DV in Jos on the 25th. Never have I been that way, it is on the far eastern border of Nigeria. Do you remember the Liberty soft white & green lawn material that I found in Croydon? Now I am making a new dress out of it for my travels. I've found Amy Carmichael's notes these last few days to be so very helpful & lovely & I'm glad you have the book also so I do not need to copy the encouragements out for you. I do feel Mother that your calm courage & faith must surely please the Lord. If Rene is still with you which I do suppose her to be, please give her my much love, and much to you all each one, and trusting to hear DV some solid good Business news before too long, ever yours as always Chris.

Brookfield

Oct 8th '58

My beloved Chris I'm sending this to Miango for I do think you are there & I trust it will be a real rest for you and also refreshment of spirit, you need and deserve a very good holiday. How very much we all need wisdom from Above, for life seems more difficult not just generally but especially for young people – I must turn my anxieties over Rene's boys into prayer for them. About Business affairs, well, I thought the H. Council was to meet on the 3rd & we should've had an answer by now but Wilfrid thinks it is only today, so we must still keep on patiently waiting for some days yet. The man in the grand car has not re-appeared; we have only had a very slight frost so cannot sensibly begin lifting trees yet. Our flowers are being sent to some shops in Crawley & a new one, Queensway Stores had 300 bunches of dahlias last Sat at 9d a bunch selling for 1/- and a standing order at Sainsburys all year pays £3 per week. I suppose every little helps. Apples are so plentiful this year that no-one seems to want them.

13th now but no point is running to post for this as all BOAC planes are grounded because of the airport workers' strike. What a pity, and just as they hoped to get the Comets into service before the American Boeings; dear oh dear what are English workmen coming to? I do hope we shan't have to resort to ocean mail once again. The Horley council people still have nothing definite to say to us but they did ask some silly questions such as were we joining in with any others in the district with our request & petition. Of course we are not but possibly they have at least been considering our situation. May has had a good week in Guernsey & now is in Jersey, Tom Rees is to speak there tonight – he is having a mission to every county in England. Now my dear love I will send this with all the love possible to send with it, you know you are in our hearts always, & assuring you of the reality of my peace of heart even though there is nothing rosy to report...except the last verses in Habakkuk – although...yet! your loving Mother.

In the air, en route for Gatwick

Oct 17th '58

My darling love another fortnight gone since I last wrote from the airport tea room & now I am thankful to be on the homeward journey, and you'll be starting out on your long journey to Garkida, I do hope it won't be too terribly wearisome & hot, but really nice to be going somewhere quite new. Do you remember Joyce Walker who's in charge of all GLB work in Jersey? She took me to see their lovely new HQ in what was a Mission Hall & introduced me to a Warrant Officer from New Zealand who seems to be on a world tour, both send you their regards. I had 29 meetings altogether, 2 were committees at which I didn't have to say much & one was a coffee morning where I had just 5 mins but all the rest were hard work and I trust profitable to some degree. The Guernsey people are so very friendly & hospitable; they're nearly all growers (tomatoes & flowers) right now they're sterilising the soil in the glasshouses for bulb planting. The Jersey folk seem far more reserved & polite, and not so easy to talk to, but there was one small group in a very rural spot with a keen Vicar & there was an Officer of Mariners (or some such title) from Lagos but he said he'd not ever been up in the north but is shortly going back for his last tour so maybe…

Sunday 19th: sorry darling it was too bumpy to continue, I was very glad & thankful to be down safely, and to find both M&F in a good way; but I must get to meetings every day this week & there is so much writing in connection with them all plus what had to be written up from the Ch Islands also. I had really thought something would have transpired with the Business in my absence but they are STILL waiting to hear from the councils; the barley crop was not spoiled too badly in the awful rain & the sugar-beet is being harvested now & looks like being a fair crop. Darling just think, its a year this week since you left us so we must wait two more till we can plan to welcome you back again; now the Lord keep you close & pour blessings upon you, ever yours May.

Jos, Waka, Marama, Garkida, Jos, Panyam

Oct 25th '58

Darlings I will try to jot down just highlights of a very full & interesting trip for all details would simply take too long! We started out at 6.30am – that's Mr & Mrs Mark Keeney, their small daughter & their African boy & me – in style in their fine Opel car & as the roads were tarmac most of the way we made excellent time. Mrs K (Swedish) also drives so they took turns but they showed no signs of stopping so I had to nibble on a banana & a biscuit to keep me going till we did stop for our good picnic meal at 12.30. We picked Afiniki who was waiting at the appointed place. Waka is a fairly new Station & is the education centre like Gindiri is for us; they have 16 hard-working Americans on staff plus many Africans, of two large triple-stream schools with a fine GLB Company who were so keen to learn the new skills Afiniki came to teach them; an older European couple and a nurse. My Kodachromes seemed greatly appreciated. We spent several days there then on to a smaller place Marama a further 25 miles where A interpreted for us into the local language. One overnight there then on to Shafa, a small Station, for breakfast & further GLB demonstrations for which A & I both wore our uniforms. Eventually we arrived at Garkida the big central Station of the CBM area; here they have a good Hospital, Leprosarium, another huge triple stream JP and SP School, Business dept and a Mechanic Shop. So many girls in school here, not just the boys, there is a great demand for education throughout this area. Mrs Michael arranged a big meeting for all interested girls, to which the boys asked to come as well! A vast crowd gathered & I spoke in Hausa telling them all I could about GLB and of course Jesus too then Afiniki spoke & it was translated after which she & I gave a little Display on the stage & this received huge applause! Many of the girls sang for us and later I showed the Kodachromes but it had become rather an unruly mob – in a temperature of 100 degrees, so not very satisfactory. We had to take A to the Hospital with a sick fever & then next morning I was asked to speak at 7.30am School Assembly so I told them the story of Dafwash. On the Sunday I met up with Linus Tembe (well known to Frances Priestman) a fine Christian who worked years ago at Maiduguri, he was cured of leprosy but then got TB so for many years now has been unable to work. He lives with his dear wife quietly at home, exercising a most gracious ministry to the many who come to visit him to discuss their problems. We had a lovely time of fellowship & I told him Dafwash's story which seemed to move him greatly. Then he asked me to ask you Mother to include him in your prayers with also his eldest daughter Mary who married a man they thought to be alright but who has proved most unsatisfactory. I went a second time to the Leprosarium to show the Kodachromes & to discuss their desire to start a GLB Co – though rather large it was a pleasantly orderly & quiet group there. To my surprise the Nursing Sister at the Hospital asked me to drive her & some others back to the Lepers – in the Opel car as she was not experienced enough to try it; I'd never driven one before either but it wasn't too difficult at all. So to the final day & very early start; it is 413 miles from Garkida to Jos & with shared driving & several stops we got in at 1.30am where I found lots of lovely letters from you but kept them till the morning; then at last back to Panyam to start back to work; dearest love from Chris.

28 Abbotshall Dr, Cults, Aberdeen

Oct 27th '58

Darling its October end again & time to wish you dear love and every best wish for your Birthday & many happy returns of the day, may God bless you & give you His Presence & Peace. Now darling I am not sending any parcel but hope to put a little something into your bank for Nov 4th and for Christmas too. I left Brookfield a week ago, and Mother was fairly well & keeping marvellously cheerful & patient although I know her heart is often fearful over the Business. Father I think is not at all well & seems to be failing quite quickly, his voice is thin & high & weak & he walks so slowly and sits doing nothing for long periods of time. Oh how one longs to ease their heavy burdens. Prayer seems to be very urgent & unceasing these days & it is of the Lord's mercy alone that the Nurseries continue at all; the ongoing delays & dreadful disappointments plus the awful weather problems are more than enough to shake anyone's faith. Here we've had a few more coming in to the Service but this is the last Sunday Mrs L will play the piano – but she doesn't know it yet. Erik is going to give her 2mths pay tomorrow as she has been so chronic lately that he feels he cannot stick her any longer. The wife of the painter is an excellent musician & she's willing to take over. Ever yours, Rene…and I also send you my best wishes & pray that the Lord will undertake for you in all your work, Erik.

Brookfield

Oct 27th '58

My beloved Chris on your Birthday – let this bring you all the love I can possibly send to wish you many happy returns of the day! Darling may God bless you in a special way, revealing Himself to you filling your heart with Himself HE is infinitely more than even His own blessings tho' that is rather hard to write and understand. I think of it as the Bridegroom is more to the Bride than even all his choicest gifts; that is my desire for you that God may be All in all to you for then I know you will be happy, joyful & filled with Peace. This is our gift to you this year tho' I grieve there will be no parcel but you do know how much you mean to us & how large a place you hold in our hearts – so please take the will for the deed. We have only 2 white hens left & last night the fox got one; the last remaining one looks so frightened & mopey but she has managed one egg today. I fear it is my carelessness for I did not shut the <u>little</u> door as well. I will be sure to do so this night. Business doings seem at a standstill except that the offer of £20,000 has been raised to £22,500 but Wilfrid could not close with that it will not meet our need.

W does not want to talk & Father does not know. The Lord knoweth however and is enabling us to go from day to day week by week. Darling you know our thoughts & prayers will surround you not only on your birthday but every day & I'm sure Father adds his love even in sleep, your ever loving Mother.

Sandalls, Mayfield, Sussex

28.10.58

My dear Chris a very Happy Birthday to you for next Tuesday, I shall be thinking of you especially then. This really is a grand furlough despite heavy deputation work & a lot of travelling since end of Sept, with a meeting in Haywards Heath on Monday & a local Women's group but its lovely seeing so many kindly folk, friends of the Mission, people who make you feel warmly welcome. Hildenborough was a very happy time, & I did see Nakam there; my parents came, & Aunt Ruth & they all agreed it was the friendliest conference they'd ever been to, with excellent speakers. Here are some titbits, you may have heard them:

'Your life depends on your estimate of Christ,' (the quality of your spiritual life)

Je–Ho–Vah = the One Who was–Who is–Who is to come.

They – the Jews, intended for Him a grave with the wicked (they meant to throw His body out onto the rubbish heap) but God gave Him a place with the rich (Joseph of Aramathea's tomb)

No doubt Nakam will have written you at length about her thoughts on your Gindiri/Panyam staffing, as well as her new flat where she seems to have settled nicely. My mother, still delighting in our rain-soaked garden, is cutting some chrysanths for the table & asks me to send you her best wishes for your birthday. I think of you often and pray daily grace may be given you for the daily needs, and a sense of joy in His near Presence, with much love from Frances.

Brookfield

Oct 30th '58

My darling I am ashamed that neither this letter nor anything else from me will reach you in time but I should think you expect by now some such opening sentence to my birthday wishes to you! You know my love & thoughts & prayers are with you always & I do hope you will have a truly happy day with some special blessing of the Lord's love & care for you. We both must hold onto His love and know that nothing can separate us from it ever. Please do get something for you that you'd really like with this enclosure – perhaps nice dress material, or frames for the photos – which I'd love to send but postage would be heavy; my heart's love always May.

Panyam

Nov 4th '58

My darlings I am rich in lovingkindness, what a happy state! Thank you all so very much for every one of your dear letters & cards, generosities & remembrances, and several wee surprises found their way to my place at the breakfast table this morning! Filimon Katya was 5yrs old on the 2nd and is rather too sturdy for one of those wonderful vests you knitted Mother, but two of them will be perfect for Nelson & Naki's little twins, thank you; and thank you especially Mother for your lovely gift in words in your letter of the 27th. I shall treasure it! The photos of Father with the Queen are splendid, quite lovely I'm only sorry you had to pay 2/6 postage for them but the cardboard kept them nice & flat. I am so grateful for them; they have already been taken by Joan to show to classes in school, as well as David & Christiana & others in their compound. In the last two weeks 140 people have been accepted into membership between Sura, Fiyam & Daffo churches and next Sunday another 25 will be in Chip so altogether that's many more than in any previous year, and the new Pastors did so very well in all services; dearest love as always, Chris.

Brookfield

Nov 4th '58

My beloved Chris on this glad day which 53 years ago brought you to our happy home I must begin my letter. You know something of what your arrival meant to us! Already this morning I have been giving thanks for all you mean to us then and all the years since & now I want to thank you again darling for all the love & thought you have given us so freely & I pray for some special token of God's love to be your happy experience today. In the midst of your busy life may you have His Peace filling your heart, His joy, which no man can take from you, His love shed abroad in your life that all may see something of its marvellous grace. Bless you my dear love no words of mine can half express my feelings. I wonder if the photos have come, certainly our letters should have reached you – it seems so little to send but I know you understand how things are this year. Maybe in the happy future things might be different. Your letter of your long travels was such a joy & so full of interest – we too would have applauded & enjoyed seeing you perform on that stage, did you skip also?! Well I suppose it is that keeps you supple & your heart & mind young as well but how tired you must have been after it all. Mr Compton & Wilfrid have responded to an advt.in the Times: wanted to purchase a Nursery. Well, Park Farm is already to be sold as we have just heard from the horrid agent, but maybe the rest of our Pulborough land? Wilfrid says we can only continue to be patiently waiting. I shall take this into the sitting room where Father is awake now...I heartily endorse Mother's thoughts on this day & in looking back over so many years we have been blessed as a happy family. I have been praying this morning for you & your work. I am sorry now that I cannot give Wilfrid all the help in Business matters as I used to. There are some good orders on hand so we have started lifting once again, this should help financially. These are very anxious days & Wilfrid has a lot of matters to face up to & we pray strength & guidance for him in them all. Pray something might come from the seed grower's enquiry. I see that David Norris is to join the staff of All Nations Bible College next yr as Pastor. Well goodbye again & every blessing, you loving Father.

Brookfield

Nov 10th '58

My darling don't think I've ceased to care about you or lost interest in your work for not asking about it or commenting upon your lovely letters, tho' you might well think it. You know that awful overloaded feeling in the mind when you can't keep up, try as you might, with the essential side of work-related correspondence – I cannot let the B Soc down; but nor can I somehow catch up with the extreme pressures of other work with all the meetings…and Auntie Jo has just asked if I would speak at Ifield next Sunday night – one week in advance! There is a new woman there who types well so I have asked if she might have a day or even half a day spare to help me with letters; & I'm going to the Labour Exchange to see if we can get someone to help me in the house (up to Mother's standards of course!) Wilfrid has had this big agent from London here but does not think our land is suitable for his needs, & W continues trying for planner permission to build – even an American type of motel – one estate agent was rude enough to laugh. Until that I thought poor W looked a little more encouraged but he seems back to where he was & I've never seen him so low, so down, almost bitter. I've never known that in him before & it rather frightened me. The London man talked of at least "a life tenancy of the house your father built & is occupying" just what W has clung on for, but the other man laughed at that idea also. I do not think I have grown sufficiently, or even at all, through these trials & tribulations as one is surely meant to, but darling I send my love to you anyway knowing you'll understand, May.

Panyam

Nov 18th '58

Darlings all just a brief note to accompany this letter for you Mother from Kefas Katya. I spent a nice weekend with them all at Jibam and Mary strutted around in her vest from you Mother, and would not hear of it being taken off. She is a fascinating little person, tearing around & into everything & always getting filthy. On Sunday I found her sitting outside Church with the skirt of her minute dress full of sand which she was trying so hard to winnow like her mother does with their grain. You can imagine the state she was in when she toddled in a few moments later. On Sat Joan, Joyce & I all went down to Chip, Joyce had 3 expectant mothers to examine & Joan & I had GLB uniforms to fit but it was disappointing that some Chip girls, so near by, didn't turn up till the Enrolment svc was almost over while 18 other girls had walked the 7 mls from Jibam & were all there in good time. Afterwards I took a load of the girls back to the Jibam turning where the schoolboys had cleared a track for the car so that I could take it off the main road well out of sight and there I left it and crossed the river that May will remember, & walked the mile or so into Jibam. The hut built for Bibwahat & his wife has not yet been occupied so that was where I stayed, just a big round hut with no door or windows, just spaces, so my old curtain did duty once again as a door. After tea I went out visiting with Kefas & saw all those he wanted me to talk with, & we met a most interesting old man, well known to them, wearing a dirty blue cap with a long tail in which he stored 'biscuits & other things' as he told me. He listened well & enjoyed the pictures as I told him the story of Naaman; then the next evening he came to visit me clad this time in a most gorgeous robe & a scarlet fez on his head. Obviously thrilled with the impression he was making, he then re-told me the story of Namaan before asking for English lessons, offering 2 eggs as a gift. Back in the little round hut preparing my simple supper, Ruda the very nice probationary teacher, brought a small dish of food she'd prepared for me, then Nishe sent her in again with a second dish of 'visitor food' so I insisted they came in to join me at my meal. Their contributions were really tasty though rather too hot for my liking with the red pepper without which they think food frightfully insipid. They had a bit of my stew, and fruit & custard and thought it nice too. At evening prayers Kefas & the others spoke in the Chip language so I couldn't follow but then we sat out under the stars & numbers of folk dropped by & we chatted partly in Sura, partly English & partly Chip. Next morning Ruda & her friend escorted me to Girong about 2½ miles away, where the Evangelist was killed by a snakebite. Malam Adamu was already there with a newly baptised schoolboy from Chip as his guide, & he interpreted for me into Chip. The church was very full and it was very, very hot. A good talk with Nanay who has not been in Church at all for several yrs, under a big tree, showed me she could still remember how to read the Bible which was encouraging. 'Mad dogs & Englishmen walk out in the midday sun' I believe but there was nothing for it but to walk back to my little round hut and lie down, wondering if I'd ever be able to take the SS classes. After an hour's rest a good wash & a dry dress I felt quite alright again to speak to Ruda's 35 tiny ones sitting under an enormous olive tree, they sang so sweetly! The evening brought more supper offerings, without pepper this time, really very delicious, but no chance of an early night as the school children had prepared a 'Play' for me – the story of Naaman no less! Then I was surprised again as they sang a Negro Spiritual in English for me – it was beautiful. Many of them had to walk home as far as Girong and in the dark for the moon had set by then, but they were all in school 8am Monday! There is talk of new rules coming in soon from the Education Dept, now refusing to let a child repeat a class which will mean a number of 11 & 12 yr olds being turned out of school altogether which can only mean deep resentment from parents. I shall have to go into Jos and face them about this. Goodbye my dear darling ones, with so much love to you each one, Chris.

'Therese', Parkhurst Rd, Horley

Nov 18th '58

My dear Miss Christine, just a few scratchy lines to wish you a very Happy Christmas & New year. I do hope you are keeping well and all your people at your Mission Station too. How very interested I am in all your work, when you can get a little time I should be so happy to hear from you. I am sending you this small gift which I hope will help you in your work in some way. I am thankful to report I keep very well but my legs are a trouble, they don't like walking but there is a bus which runs about; now dear, with my love & all kind thoughts & also prayers from yours sincerely Elizabeth S Brown.

Brookfield

Nov 25th '58

My dearest darling how I have thanked God for you & your love & thought & care & help; I've felt again how rich we are in the things money can't buy & I'm sure the Lord has been answering your prayers for our upholding, so surely then will He answer for our deliverance too. Maybe there is a tiny flicker of hope in that some money is coming in as we continue with the lifting of trees etc and another Council mtg is scheduled for the 2nd and the Planning Officer here on the 3rd. I have pictured you on these recent walks you described, getting so dripping hot, inspecting, talking & helping so many dear folk and I'm sure laughing a lot too! I am praying that Kefas really can go right through into Theological Training. I showed all the pictures at rather a select group in a Dorking home & they seemed deeply moved as well as impressed; and then again at a most extraordinary mtg in Eastbourne when the young 'leader' told me he had offered for SUM but Mr F had told him to get a job for 2 yrs then re-apply if he still felt called. I should say in the circs. that was very wise advice! After the Women's mtg that afternoon then there was the Youth mtg at 6pm as well as the 7.30 mtg. I did think they would have made some arrangement for a meal for me with all that long day's programme, but the Secy came to me after the Womens saying "I expect you have got friends to go to now for food haven't you!" I was so taken aback that all I could muster was "Er... yes" and went out & had a poached egg on toast at Plummers. It really shocked me, and to see how irreverently the mtgs were conducted; I think they'd be equally shocked to know what I thought about them. What patience the Lord has with us all! Please greet the friends for me specially Kefas, Ishaku, Joel, David and Istifanus, and for you darling my heart's love as always, May.

252 Selsdon Rd, S. Croydon

Nov 29th '58

My dearest Chris I do thank you for your very welcome letter with all its news & for all your time & trouble spared out of your very full days to write it, thank you, I devoured every word. A long letter came to me from Bitrus Gwanya saying he wants to get married now before starting the Training so that his wife could get training too – will that work? Does that mean he has given up H? Oh I do pray he gets the right wife – who will make such a difference for his whole future. How good to hear of the Jibam folk doing so much for you & even putting on the play! It must've been lovely there in the warmth & under the stars & moonlight – rather different from our fog & damp & drizzle & perpetual cloudy dark days! I am so glad to know Thompsons & Turners have both had their babies safely. Do give my love to Joan & best wishes for her journey home, I'll write to her once she's back here. Now Chris I must urge you, do get all the rest you can and don't try to pack quite so much into your days & nights. You must keep fit yourself, physically, mentally and spiritually – it is amazing how the Lord strengthens you for so much heavy work & responsibility; our next SUM PM is here on the 8th & I do hope the Perfects will be joining us at it, would be a real help; much love & much prayer, Nakam.

As from Sandalls, Mayfield, Sussex

Dec 9th '58

My dear Chris, thank you so much for your letter & the Kodachromes & I'm glad you had such a great time on the Garkida trek. I am sorry, though not at all surprised, that you are getting rather tired! A slow pulse isn't anything to worry about of itself it is just an indication of physical weariness & a warning that you really ought to take more rest somehow; more time on your bed in the afternoon & earlier to bed at night if at all possible. I think too you should have a course of Multivite tablets, 1 lds after meals for 4-6 weeks at least. There is no doubt that the quality of the food in Nigeria, grown on poorish soil, is not all it should be – one can't help noticing the different flavour of meat & veg etc here at home – so it is very well worth while to supplement from time to time. When I get back I hope you'll be able to come over to me for a quiet weekend. It's just a little more than 3 wks till I travel DV I should land in Jos on Jan 8th in time for tea! I don't expect to write again before I see you, please take care of yourself & a very happy Christmas to you all there with love from Frances.

Brookfield

Dec 9th '58

My beloved Chris I must thank you for your prayers darling on our behalf for I often feel lifted & I know someone has been interceding for me, and perhaps the dear Lord Himself 'who ever liveth to make intercession for us,' be assured all is well here, we are happy & peaceful and so very thankful for our own comfortable house. Some things of course we would have liked different viz that planning man never came because something very important in Guildford had hindered him. These things are an enigma to us but not to the Lord, and we can only wait His time. Meanwhile some tree money has come in and men have been paid. Last Sunday at Ifield Meeting after a long time of silent worship Josie brought a good word on John 3:15&16 when God wants to emphasize anything He repeats it: whosoever believeth and then Father read most of John 14 with those beautiful words falling as a benediction & stressing the need for belief in God if our hearts are to be kept untroubled. Then I had a word given me on belief itself – so often used & a word we all know but intellectual assent is not enough; as a child I recalled a preacher telling us to turn that word belief around, into live by: if our faith is real – & in God alone, nothing else – it must be transformed into daily living, for faith without works is dead. Then Wilfrid prayed beautifully to close. Arthur Worthy was there & invited us to look round his new school & oh my there were books everywhere, a treasure house of learning & delight (what that would have meant to me when young!) He told us his belief was that one of the main objects every teacher should hold before him was putting each child in touch with sources of information which he could then discover for himself; not meaning there should be no teaching in class but acknowledging so much of that is in one ear out the other. Now goodbye my darling with all the love it is possible to send you, Mother.

252 Selsdon Rd, S. Croydon

Dec 9th '58

Dearest Chris it is too absurd for you to speak of all the things I gave you; have you forgotten all those many weeks you fed & watered me freely & refused to take my board money? Also all that you forked out for my parcels on my way home, when I had not enough Nigerian money? My! It is I who feel you have given me too much, not vice versa! But after such a passionate plea for me not to send you anything more for Christmas, I shall respect your wishes but my greetings & prayers are none the less sincere even tho' unaccompanied by anything tangible. I do hope your Christmas will be happy & harmonious and not too rushed for you with all your visitors. Next week I am to be taken first to the GCU (Girl Crusader Union) Carol service at All Soul's, then for a drive round London to see the lights & decorations, then to a meal out & finally to the Albert Hall for Bach's Christmas Oratorio with carols – won't that be a treat! But a great sadness – I read recently that in 1957 in Great Britain 1in4 babies born out of wedlock, oh dear me isn't that wretched. And I know it is not only in this country. may you be given all the wisdom & strength you need for teaching all your young women. Your last letter left me breathless! How can you keep going at such a pace? I am sure you ought to try and reduce the amount of running about you have been doing for you cannot expect to last long at such a pace! It makes me thankful that I retired when I did for if I had stayed on I surely would have ruined the work for I never could have done half of what you do. God's timing is always perfect! So please do try not to pack too much into your days – sanctified common sense, with very much love, prayer & the best of good wishes, Nakam.

Southways

Dec 10th '58

My dear Chris I fear I am rapidly losing any faculty I may ever have had for family letter writing, it is certainly decaying through lack of use. It is a sobering thought to reflect that you have now spent more than half your days on earth in Africa. I seem to be very out of date with news of Panyam & its inhabitants but we did see the one you wrote rather recently to Brookfield. I have not seen Barbara's effort to you but I'm sure it was filled with the children' doings; they do seem to be making progress along their own particular routes & it is very interesting watching their individual development. I think you will have heard by now that we have received the official refusal from the Council to our application for the 'motel' but they say not a word about the sports ground which we also applied for. Not altogether a surprise judging by recent rumours but nonetheless infuriating & frustrating after keeping us waiting 11 weeks out of a limit of 13 allowed. Thro' the regular weekly bulletins from Mother of all the Business developments you will have sensed the strain under which we have all been living. It is of course humanly speaking purely a miracle that we have been enabled to reach another lifting season & got half way through it and we've been able to reduce trade commitments which is some relief – the crops at Pulborough contributed to this. The farm there has been bought to be turned into a fruit orchard and we may now stay on for 3 yrs on 13 acres, some comfort after long months of uncertainty. The sale of our land has been worrying & it seemed right to turn down the slightly increased offer, certainly until we heard from the planning people. More creditors have agreed to accept trees etc instead which is a help. We are carefully considering whether to lodge an appeal against the land decision but of course there may soon be some special local development hitherto unguessed. I have just been reading Numbers 9 again & find vs 8 & 22 rather pointed in present circumstances. It is very difficult to continue patient & trustful & to present a confident attitude to one's staff & customers, and naturally the enemy is very busy at times. I am sorry this epistle is so full of business but there is little room for anything else. Give our united greetings to any interested Africans and take all you can absorb for yourself, with much love Wilfrid.

Brookfield

Dec 14th 1958

My dearest darling you know that I shall be constantly with you in spirit & pray that for you Christmas Day will be a blessed & happy time with a precious sense of the love & nearness of the Lord to warm your heart & overflow to all you meet & speak with. You have been having such a very hectic time lately; I do pray that those who are coming onto your Station to help will perhaps be already there, or are due soon. I'd like to get for you a copy of Lyman MacCallum's 'Call to Istanbul' it has been described as: 'One of the very important frontiers of life in our times where the Christian world and the world of Islam are in contact…LM's behaviour is without surrender or concealment of his fully Christian belief he yet lived a life of identification in love with those beyond the gulf.' The challenge for me was to see the way in which this man met those of other faiths with such Christlike love & because of his contact with them he found it necessary to be absolutely sure of his own ground as a Christian. He also wrote, 'What is it we possess which makes the remark 'all religions are the same' sound as far from the Truth as a child's uncomprehending remark about the size & distance of the stars? The uniqueness of Christianity begins at Bethlehem, is completed at Calvary & realized in the Resurrection. Through the ages men have tried to explain & understand Jesus on purely human terms; some are willing to accept Him as one of the inspired prophets; but those who know Him best are compelled to cry out along with doubting Thomas, 'my Lord and my God!' Darling I feel it would be so good for all Friends, as well as friends too of course, to read this book and receive thereby rich blessing. I continue to be surprised and oh so thankful for the impressions made by all your pictures & Kodachromes as I show them & speak about them so often at so many of my meetings; and for you in your crowded days up to Christmas and beyond, I pray you will be very sure of the Lord's peace & power garrisoning your heart in all you say & think & do & plan; with all my dearest love now my darling, ever yours May.

Panyam

Dec 17th '58

My darlings this comes with so much dear love & my very best of Christmas greetings to you each one. I long to hear that you will have had a happy & peaceful time; I know that much love will be streaming towards you from many different hearts & homes just as will flow from you to us each one, and that will make us all rich in the things that matter most. So may our dear home be the centre of blessings given & received this Christmastime, as has so often happened in the past. I'm pleased to tell you that the orphan baby Joyce McQ was caring for has now been adopted by Pastor Ishaya of Chip & his dear wife Lidiya. She came up on Monday eve and was going to walk back the same 27miles with the baby on her back but I said I would take her if there was no lorry. She started off in the early morn saying I could catch her up when I was ready – so I was practically forced to go after her as soon as possible! But Kefas was on his way back from preaching in Kulere & gave her a lift on his bike. I can hardly think what his strength must be to cycle with a woman plus a baby and quite a big bundle of their loads on the back of the bike! I overtook them on the very steep escarpment near Abwor so added them to the 2 other men & their loads from Panyam already on board. A bit after that I ran over a goat. It just ran out from some tall grass and straight into the car, the poor thing. The Ishaya home is thrilled with the baby – he certainly is a dear wee chap of about 3mths old. Naki's twins – Rose & Robert are lovely fat babies & growing so quickly. Tomorrow is Joan's birthday & her departure so we are having a little party feast tonight, we take her at 7am & she flies from Jos at 11.30am. Thank you for all your dear letters, each one a cheer to me, but I do pray you will be given some cheer in the Business even over Christmas time, with my dearest of dear love to each one of you, Chris.

PS Mother I particularly treasure & agree with your sentence, 'this does not convey by half all I think & feel and the love I have for you, I hope you will be greatly blessed & have a happy jolly (?) time – it was your question mark after jolly which amused me, & then this: the Lord will watch between us while we are separated one from the other.'

6 Winchendon Rd, Teddington, Middx

Dec 22nd 1958

Dear Chris we had a lovely smooth flight although late from Kano but neither Pam, nor Jean nor I objected at all for the delicious food just kept being served to us! It is lovely being home & as you said, one does slip easily back into the routines of home life. My father & brothers seem determined to help me rest, not allowing me downstairs before 8 and that's after they bring me tea in bed at 7am! Such a change in my brothers who are now most thoughtful; obviously having to look after themselves has done them no harm. I am glad I can give them a little 'mothering' for the next few months. I've not forgotten your Prorsan tops but when I noted W&F at the Airport & found they had none, I went all over Toddington today without success so will try Richmond tomorrow & then will try to get them to Frances P to bring back for you. Please give Joyce my love & I hope you all have a very happy Christmas, with much love, Joan.

At Rustington!

Jan 1st 1959

My beloved Chris my prayer for you is that you will be given all the strength & wisdom you need for all you must do, your many & varied tasks. I loved the thoughts you wrote of waves of love passing between us over Christmas for I am quite sure it is true & I have been blessed, greatly blessed by it. The evening party at Southways was nice all the children were on duty so to speak – they certainly are well brought up. Our Day was quiet the only guest poor Auntie Jo who could only talk of the fox taking 2 of her hens & leaving the last one without its head; Sam her beloved cat was missing for several days, and the parrot died. Oh dear oh dear. Sometimes it feels as though we are being brought to the end of many things. And now dear-heart we have to contemplate leaving our beloved home, Wilfrid says the HDC is adamant on no changes, so he must now re-contact the man who did make the slightly raised offer. We must continue to remember God is not restricted in His ways, He knows the way we should take, and His plans are good. W felt inspired to talk to the land owner at Tilgate forest who seemed most agreeable to some ideas but I can only tell you more if anything developes. Dear May helped us prepare for our little holiday here, we left at 1o'c (before the News!) & now she should be on the train to Aberdeen; we have a lovely bedroom overlooking the Eastbourne sea, once again thanks to our beloved May. She is so very good to us & I'm so thankful she's now on the way to Rene for what I do hope will be a week of rest. Now darling our very dear love & wishing you God's best, Father also sends his love, Mother.

Panyam

Jan 1st 1959

My darlings how I wish we could really talk instead of just writing 'Happy New Year.' We had a pleasant time & I think all our 4 visitors enjoyed their short stay here, but the same cannot be said for poor Yusufu Dakahap & family. Fire completely gutted the Mission compound at Mongun in the early morning before Christmas Eve & they barely escaped with their lives & one box of clothes, hens & dogs were all lost. Yusufu's wife was scared by a big snake & put fire down its hole. Later they poured 2 garwas of water down too but probably didn't extinguish it completely because at 4am they were awakened in the middle of an inferno. What a mercy their lives were spared. The Sura Church has made generous gifts to help them. I must say, we thought last year was the peak of staffing issues but now we are facing one horrid palava after another, having to take them to be fully discussed at the Church Council. I really am feeling a bit battered by all these complicated wheels within wheels, finding some we trusted to be lying and some shouted at & railed against & brought to tears publicly, are found perfectly innocent of all charges. Such ongoing – and even increasing – disappointments & perplexities with these folk; it feels like groping along a treacherous way in thick fog. You can hardly see the next step & have to take it extremely carefully. What comfort to know the battle is the Lord's, Psalm 119:105 was written for this, He will not let His Name be disgraced forever. I know you will be even more in prayer once you read these things. Lilian Blenko has come for a few days to help me with school supplies etc; I met her off the Gindiri lorry, & she has been the greatest help.

Now it is the 4th: we had a long day at Chip yesterday and at last some further school fees have been paid. In this morning's Communion service David preached very well, speaking 'straight from the shoulder' about those who gladly call themselves Christian but do things in secret that are dishonouring to Christ. As I came out from SS later on some of our boys with Joseph Waltu were waiting for me to tell me that Maryamu Waltu is very ill. With no prospect of getting a lorry of course I had to go & took Joyce with me; we found poor M had given birth to a stillborn baby about an hr before & was indeed very ill. Joyce did not want to move her but as we had no medicines with us we gently bundled her into the car with Joseph holding her. That seemed to revive her slightly tho' she still had a high temp & pulse of 140 or so, so then Joyce gave her at once 2cc Penicillin plus a sedative. Goodbye for now darlings with so much love, Chris.

28 Abbotshall Drive, Cults, Aberdeen

Jan 4th 1959

Dearest darling you can read my apologies for another long gap between letters in between these lines & I'll go right on to wish you a truly blessed 1959 I find it such a comfort to think next year DV Chris will be home! Did you manage to get any rest at all over Christmas – I don't like to think of you being so very bad & having these bad heads, which are so horrid aren't they. We know poor Wilfrid would agree with that. When Frances P gets back could you ask her to prescribe something for you? Although our Christmas itself was very quiet the preparations beforehand seem to get more numerous as the years pass. It troubled me very much that what should surely be one of the loveliest, holiest times of the whole year is becoming increasingly hectic. Cards start arriving so early & you're swept up into a whirlwind of preparations so there's no time or inclination to be still & ponder the real meaning. It is not right, yet I'd hate to have all the gifts bought & parcelled and all the cards bought, written in & addressed by October; it will never happen that way for I just couldn't! Poor Auntie Jo really is a problem, it is not right that she should be living there on her own. On top of all her Christmas bereavements, on Sunday after evening Meeting the bus carried her right past the gate & on towards Gatwick so she had to walk all the way back & cross the road with heavy traffic both ways. You can imagine what she felt, especially after only 4 people bothered to turn out; I suspect the difficult question of that service might soon be settled for us. It does seem certain now that the Nursery will be sold this year and we shall have to move, or certainly by next yr. Wilfrid is intending to close on the offer tho' it will still leave us short, but there is still stock to sell, & he is slightly brighter since talking with the Tilgate man; this seems to me to be the only way. For now my darling there is another thing as well as where we shall live & A Jo also; the doctor noticed my neck is bigger the last time he came to see Father. It has been troublesome, with the old strangled feeling some days, so now I must see the specialist at Bart's. Doctor thinks another operation is necessary but I feel that with treatment that could be avoided especially if anxiety is relieved all round. You know an op does not worry me but the complications of it & what to do for M&F (who do not know any of this yet) is a worry; I know Rene would do what she can, but I dread them getting in a flap & Mother thinking she must do more than she is able for. Mrs Crowhurst is quite unable to come again & the Labour Exchange was not able to help. It is lovely to be up here & the house looks wonderful in all its new decoration. I feel the atmosphere is happier but R & I have not spoken on this matter yet. I go back on Thurs & our Conf. at High Leigh is from 13-16th & I see the specialist after that; all my love dearest, May.

28 Abbotshall Drive, Cults

Jan 4th '59

Darling love how nice it would be if you were here with Mipsie & me this afternoon, then we could talk instead of having to scratch away on paper. It is so lovely to have dear M here & I'm so thankful she could come even if only for a week. When she told me of her visit to Dr K & next to the specialist, I am more than glad to be able to give her a rest first. Already she looks better & she's taking the iodine regularly & so far her heart is not troubling her. The future of course is unknown, a little more so now with her news, but of course I will do all I can, either having them all up here or going back down to Brookfield myself; may we all always remember that God is on the Throne & He knows the future. Dear old Mouse is really hoping for a change from London soon, he was attacked again on Wednesday night by 4 wretched teddy-boys who gave him a badly scratched & bruised face; it is such a worry to me. We sent a wee bit of paper to your Bank darling with our dearest love and every blessing in 1959, ever yours, Rene.

Rustington, Eastbourne

Jan 6th 1959

My beloved Chris we have been here almost a week living in the lap of luxury & enjoying it all very much. I would like Father to write a bit but it is difficult to get him to do anything, he says his head is dizzy but I think it is the hot room central heating to which of course we are not accustomed. I have come down to the sun lounge where there are tables for writing but no sun; it has been raining rather a lot. I rejoice that dear May & Rene are together, M say the house is so improved since we were there. It was a sorrow to me that we could not arrange a visit with the Priestmans before we came away, with Frances leaving tomorrow, I am about to write to Mrs P. Perhaps we have all this year and maybe next also, but May feels if we must move then it should be sooner rather than later. I cannot visualise leaving this home where we have spent all our married life & been so very happy & where you were all born & brought us so much happiness, but the Lord knows, and we must pray for His will to be done in this as in all things then indeed shall all be well. Now with my dearest & best love & wishing you great blessing in your work & in your own soul, you are more precious to God, your love & devotion to Him personally than even the share in the great work He has given you; may He bless you continually with His joy & peace, your Mother.

252 Selsdon Rd, S. Croydon

Jan 10th '59

My dearest Chris, oh my dear my heart aches for you for I know so well how all these sad palavers weigh one down. Surely whenever the devil gets as active as he has been around you lately it is a sign that he realises that there is a worthwhile work of God in our District, or he would not make such efforts to upset it. So we must take courage & thank God for all He has been doing, for all the souls saved & built up in Him, and not allow these wretched happenings to cast us down. I am sure you do rightly feel battered & bruised & I do sympathise deeply with you but God is still on the Throne & the work is His, & it was He who said the gates of hell cannot prevail against His Church. Keep clinging to 2 Cor.9:8 & keep looking UP. I was also distressed to hear that Peter B did not come to help you after all the talk & plans; you are the Senior District Superintendent & I think you must make it clear to him that he must come to assist while Joan is away; surely he would have felt ashamed to know Lilian had to come from Gindiri – because he had not. And please tell me about Maryamu, I do so hope she has recovered. Here it is bitterly cold with ice making walking & motoring dangerous. May our God bless & encourage you, with much love and understanding and sympathy, Nakam.

Panyam

Jan 11th '59

Darling Mother I have been already wishing you a very Happy Birthday many times today but just putting it on paper now before I go to bed; I expect you may be still in Eastbourne but not too badly 'gripped' by the ice & snow the wireless news tells me is gripping Britain, and that you & Father remain safe, well & warm indoors. May is probably still in Aberdeen & the cold must be even more intense up there; I do hope she has been having a happy time of change & rest. It was lovely to be able to greet Frances P once more, thank you for writing to her & her mother she really appreciated that – as I do, bless you. Although I spared you many of the details of our recent palavers you will want to know that the girl who witnessed against Jeremiah Konshik came to me with her mother & brother to confess that her story was a lie. She had been bribed by 2 of our young teachers plus 2 other Christians from

Kerang. It was good to have poor Jeremiah K cleared of what I felt all along was false accusation, but I was aghast that anyone calling himself a Christian – & 2 of them were baptised last yr – should stoop to the crime of bribing a non-Christian girl in their efforts to dislodge a senior Teacher they happen to dislike. Now Kefas has written saying his pains are back, may he come up for the hospital, so a lorry brought him & the Pankshin Doctor will examine him tomorrow.

Tuesday: your dear letters have arrived today, from E'bourne & Aberdeen, many thanks. And your lovely book also, many thanks indeed for that, I shall delight in it I know. My heart goes out to you all, including Wilfrid, Barbara & A. Jo, as these big decisions must be made. May God bless you & guide with such clear assurance that peace might reign in your hearts, & May darling I'm thinking so specially for you. The Doctor saw Kefas and put him on heavy doses of Aspirin for his heart muscles, confining him here for at least a week. Peter B has come to do some school inspections for me to check up on ages of the children and so on, and he will go to Jibam tomorrow to arrange one of the Prob Teachers to take over Kefas' class; this is a big help to me. C.

Brookfield

Jan 12th '59

My beloved Chris, Father thinks I should come up to bed as he's been there all day but I want to write to you as my first opportunity today, after an unexpected visit from Joan Onions who stayed for 3 hrs as she was feeling quite at home, we had such a pleasant time. She helped me get the tea & carried up the tray for me and had a little chat with Father – quite to his liking! After we had ours in the sitting room by the fire she went up again for his tray then washed up the things. I think she thoroughly enjoyed her visit & got the 6.15 bus. Now darling to the serious matters in your letter of Jan 1st such problems call for much prayer & I have been especially asking for wisdom for you to know how best to deal with one at a time. And our serious matters continue on with some glimpses of hope but nothing definite to tell you and Wilfrid is to London today for a POCA meeting so will have no more to say until tomorrow. May will post this for me, you will know how much I feel for her over this goitre trouble but do we not all know how the Lord has so often and will continue to undertake for us all in all these trials & concerns, ever your loving Mother.

Panyam

Jan 18th 59

Dearest Mother & Father, first another thank you or even many more thanks for the book 'To Live Again,' it is a work of art in ideas expressed so beautifully & satisfyingly & I am thankful to be taken out of the rut of my own work & thoughts into spiritual literature of this kind. And secondly, I shall be in Miango for our Prayer Conf. over your birthday Father so this brings you a special line of loving greeting to wish you every blessing on that day. I hope your week in Eastbourne was a happy time of change & meeting new friends as you two invariably do wherever you go. If the offer is closed and the Nurseries are sold, surely we must be confident that something better will unfold and if it should be that you need to move to a different house I fully expect you'll be given the resilience to take even that in your stride! I await further news with deep & prayerful longing. Two of our weightiest palavas have been sorted out after a great deal of time and talk but we are quite sure that much prayer has been answered and we were guided through all the perplexities step by step. David has been magnificent throughout and his final prayer is one I hope I never forget: "Lord we were all born in sin and the wages of sin is death," then he continued by praying for forgiveness for all those present who had done wrong in any way; now my dear love to you both ever yours Chris.

Brookfield

Jan 20th 1959

My beloved Chris you will want to know that dear Uncle Edward died on Friday aft & very peacefully according to Capt Staines. There seemed no sadness around his passing & we have just come back from Ifield where his body was laid beside Edie's. One can't help wondering who in our family might be next. Wilfrid conducted the funeral & read a passage, Capt S gave a message written by E himself, there were two hymns, Father prayed at the grave & May prayed indoors after. It was a good service and we had 10 back here to tea. Tomorrow May goes to St Bart's for the specialist. The offer to sell has been accepted by the London man and the HDC has said it must stay as greenbelt and we have some months yet before we must move, and W is arranging a sale on the premesis of as many trees as possible. Father is rather up & down and felt the palps were coming back but I think it is just nerves. I am keeping well and was able to make a pie yesterday and scones for tea. Goodbye my precious love & thank you for our birthday greetings, Mother.

Brookfield

Jan 22nd '59

My darling I'm really leaving for Purley but must scribble this to you first to tell you I saw the specialist yest. at Bart's – Mr John Horsford – and found him to be a competent, kind & understanding man. He asked various questions, examined my neck & said yes it is growing again & now pressing on the windpipe so I will have to have the op. They can treat some forms of goitre now with rays but unfortunately not my kind. I told him a little about home circumstances & work pressures so he agreed to leave it until June, he will do the op himself & I'll get 2 wk's notice of exact date for it. I'm so thankful I haven't to write telling a whole lot of people why I can't attend their meetings & making alternative arrangements for them. I'm sure I've written nearly 100 letters already this year but I never seem to get through them all. Now darling I'm not unaware, nor ignoring, all the heart suffering & disappointment you've been going through & having to deal with recently & I pray for strength for you & fresh wisdom – may the Lord make Himself wisdom to you; all my dearest love as ever, your May.

Panyam

Feb 2nd '59

Darlings what momentous news your letters have been bringing me: dear Uncle Edward's been released, imagine the joy he must be in now, a true return of the youthful strength & 'joie de vivre' he always used to have; and dear May needing the op; and what can I say about the Business? Only this, that after all the prayer & faith offered up to God for so long, we must believe that this is according to to His will & guidance and in that fact is our peace. So dears whatever this year brings of change I know you will be led into & through it with a deep sense of His protection & care. Almost as soon as I read your letter I thought of Jacob & the Lord's vision granted to him as he removed from Canaan to Egypt in his old age. Please pass on to May that Ruda & her husband Jotham had twin babies on Jan 27th as we went to Kirang at 4am to be with them, & then brought her & the one surviving twin back with us for Joyce to look after, but early today that baby also died (there is a family tendency to TB) it is so very hard for them. And please tell Father that David was thrilled to get his letter which came just as he was setting off to Gindiri for yet another gruelling palaver between 2 Fiyam elders; now with my dearest love & constant remembrances, Chris.

Brookfield

Feb 3rd '59

My beloved Chris on this cold frosty morn with Father in bed I can have a little time with you. His routine eye appt yesterday morn in H. Heath meant he had to hurry to dress (hosp car was very early) then when he returned he brought the driver & wife in for coffee at 1o'c just as May & I were sitting down to dinner in the kitchen! With a bit of a scramble we managed to get them tea – oh it was a lovely pot too they had 2 cups each & several biscuits! When they left we ate our cold meal & Father went up to bed, still, what is life for if not to entertain strangers and perhaps find angels unawares?! I was so glad to hear of the lovely time you had at the Miango Conference with the refreshing spirit about after the difficult experiences you have had to deal with recently, and that you are sleeping so well. But darling I do think there are things I forget to comment upon, I am so sorry tho' several things I am forgetting these days; Uncle Robt was 79 yesterday, we are all growing old but never mind the Best is yet before us. Mr. Lawrence who has bought the Nurseries – if all goes according to plan – it must be signed by all before the thing is certain, different prices for different plots & houses & I see ours is set at £4,750. Father already leans towards some place not too far from Crawley & altho' May can fix on nothing of course until after her op we were surprised to note Crawley is just about the centre of her 'parish' for work. Rene has said she will come to us anytime and E has agreed to this plan; with my heart's full love darling, your Mother.

4 Woodbury Close Croydon

7th Feb 1959

Dear Chris I feel very ashamed it has taken me so long to thank you for letter of Christmas good wishes, we both much appreciated your kind thoughts. As for some years now we spent a very happy Christmastime with Barbara, Wilfrid & the children. I still try to help Wilfrid in this most difficult position in which he is placed; you will have heard of the latest developments which naturally centre our thoughts on the future. I feel so particularly sad at the prospect for your Mother & Father at their time of life having to move. Still, I do not doubt that they and we all will be guided aright; you know, I am sure, that I shall ever do what in my small way I can to help the position. May God bless you in your work is our earnest prayer with our love and every good wish from us both, yours, Herbert Compton.

252 Selsdon Rd, Croydon

Feb 16th '59

Dear Miss Cheal you will be sorry to hear that Miss Webster is in bed with a very bad dose of the 'flu, quite unable to write. She went to help the Talbots for the whole family came down with it at once & she thinks she caught it there. This winter is so horribly cold, raw & wet there seems to be an epidemic of this flu and I am to tell you that half the staff & 200 girls at the school here are down with it. I am to thank you for your recent letter with all the news & assure you of a reply soon. Please accept regards to Pastor David and all your staff; I have seen many of Miss Webster's beautiful pictures I am most interested, you are doing a great work out in Panyam. With Miss Webster's love and I wish you every blessing, sincerely Mary L Turner.

Brookfield

Feb 17th '59

My beloved Chris many thanks for your always welcome letter and since I last wrote to you I have been in bed too alongside Father, he is mostly giddy now & so tired, and I have a bad throat & a cough not unlike whooping. Rene came down on the Thursday train & I could not rise to welcome her; it is strange how these trying circumstances come about, and so often one after another. Lizzie writes of poor Willie, 'death is drawing very near;' and another loud Home Call has come to us this week dear 'Uncle' Compton passed away in his sleep on Friday night, Mrs

C found him when she had no response to her call to breakfast (they did not sleep together) Barbara is very low indeed & grieves outwardly much more than anyone tho' I think Wilfrid feels it greatly too. The funeral is tomorrow at Croydon crematorium. W&B were only up with them a few days before & he told them he had just written to you. Darling the thought of how we can ever move out of here, especially when May is not too strong at all, baffles me at times. Under any circumstances would you ever feel it right to ask for an extension of leave from the SUM has it ever occurred to you it might be possible? Perhaps you would send me a private note about this. Whatever happens here or with you we know there is the Glory beyond but for now I send this with very dear & tender love to you my precious Chris & love to dear Frances P too please, your ever loving Mother.

Panyam

Feb 18th 59

My dearest darlings, three letters yesterday!! From Mother, May & Rene thank you each one so very much. How I wish it were possible to slip home in times of emergency! I was ever so sorry to hear this morning of the bad air crash at Newdigate in which the PM of Turkey was involved – was it due to fog? Now, the signing of the deed of sale (has it actually happened?) gives one many thoughts. If the Lord does not intervene in some other way & the sale really goes through then we will trust & not be afraid; I am quite sure that 'the trial by faith shall be found unto praise.' In fact I think it is now for I'm sure we all are impressed by the calm faith & courage you have shown. We can only give thanks and pray that this all may somehow turn out to be a means of blessing to all concerned. Regarding the move, as it seems to be coming to that, I should be glad to think it were possible to postpone it as long as can be so that DV I could be with you at that time. It is almost more than I can bear to think of you having to go through that upheaval & me not there to help. Since writing the above, I've had a lovely long weekend with Frances P in Mongu; as usual she insisted on bringing me breakfast in bed & I enjoyed sleepy afternoons with evenings of much happy talk. On Sat she went off to the leprosy clinic taking Joyce so I had a pleasantly quiet morning before we all went to Gindiri for the opening of the Theological College & saw 3 of our boys Bitrus Yamden, John Masheru & Ezekiel Panchin with all the other students with their fine rooms, Library etc. Back again I found another dear letter from you Mother in which you ask a question: the answer is 'yes' I have thought along those lines, but so far it is only my own thoughts and yours. I also received word that the Duke & Duchess of Gloucester are coming to N. Nigeria for the Self Govt celebrations; she is also the Patroness of GLB and has asked to meet those of us connected with it here! May dear you kindly asked about Maryamu Waltu, she made a good recovery & is back home again, Joseph brought in a lot of eggs as a thank-you. Goodbye darlings with much dear love to you all each one with many, many thoughts, longings and prayers Chris.

Brookfield Crawley, England

Feb 22 1959

From The Hon Pastor David QV Lot MHA to Mr Ernest Cheal

Dear Mr Cheal many thanks for your comfortable & encouragement letter on 26.1.59 and for your assistant in prayer for the work in

Panyam especially for my families and difficulties within the Church. We thank God because He leads us & guides us to see what is right for His glory. I know that Nakris have wroten to you & explained everything, we are always remembering you & your wife through illness for your both old age. I always see the view of your house in Crawly & the garden I went round with you since I was in England, I am glad to hear about the grown of the town but sorry that so many are not go to any Church. We are preparing for our Convention in Panyam 20-22nd March & please do remember us in your prayers that we should see true repentence and blessing of the Lord. Today I am in Kaduna 229miles from Panyam for the Budget Session of the Northern House of Assembly we hope will adjourn sine die on Thursday & I will be going home but to come back again on March 13th for celebration of the Norths Self government. Give my love to Mrs Cheal & all the families I heard about what is troubling your daughter May from Nakris & I am remembering her that God will protect her in the operation when it time comes, with love from your son David.

Out in the garden!!!!

March 1st '59

Darling sister how I wish you were here too enjoying this most glorious afternoon, I'm out by the dining room window with no coat on & it's perfect! If you remember that lovely week we had one March just after you'd arrived home it's like that. Last Sun I took Rene to see Ruth & Gertrude in their very nice new home; for the life of me I cannot imagine why they are out of heart with it thinking it small. I know that if we had anything comparable to go into I should be very happy. They paid £3,900 for it which will give you an idea of how prices go for a house with 2 living rms, small kitchen, small pantry, 2 bedrms, one tiny room, a bathrm & lav and a coal shed which could be turned into a downstairs lav. Finding somewhere similar for M&F I would very much like a bungalow to save all the going up & down stairs with trays & hot water-bottles etc. But anything we might get will have to be with what little Lsd I have & it will not be easy to find something to suit us and my pocket! I have been invited by Joyce to stay in her house in Frinton in July or August or whenever I want; she hopes to hire a beach hut so I could be down there all day if the weather is good. It sounds lovely & is very kind of her. Quite a few people in Bible House often ask about you & are faithful in prayer for you; you'll be busy preparing for the next conf but could you tell me which of our books you think would be useful for the new College Library? Wilfrid & Barbara & the girls have gone down to Ramsgate to see David now that they're all over the 'flu. B is missing Uncle very much indeed & finding it v hard to get over the shock & grief. She said she had a letter from you yesterday; now she is sure you must never have rec'd the proper photo of the children posted in time for Christmas as you have still not mentioned it. Goodbye my dear love, you know that my love is always with you, May.

252 Selsdon Rd, Croydon

March 4th '59

My dear Chris your letter was a joy to get, thank you so much. I told Mrs Turner that you had appreciated her letter; she was just kindness itself when I was ill, I really don't know what I should have done without her. I've not been ill like that in England since before I first went out to Nigeria 40 yrs ago – not bad going! I find that the after effects of the flu are far worse than Malaria & I'm not fully right yet, finding it irksome to feel so utterly disinclined to do anything! My thoughts are constantly living over again this time last yr & my thrilling excitement in preparing to visit you all. Thank you for telling me of your home troubles & of course it shall remain confidential. Do you think it possible perhaps even likely that your parents' unwellnesses could be largely the abominable stress they're living under? And this wretched set back in dear May's health seems not unconnected. It is so terribly sad to think of the probable sale of the Nurseries and Brookfield too, I do sympathise most deeply and pray that the Lord will give them – and you – the strength and His Peace to see you through. Will Wilfrid have to move his family also? This is a big burden for you to be sharing with them, and from so far away, how you must long to be home with them all. I am praying the Lord will enable & sustain you & guide you step by step as you comfort them on paper while you have to be dealing with so much else in and around Panyam. I shall be keeping the 15-16th as days of prayer here right alongside you in Nigeria & for the stirring of those Tahas women to bear much fruit. It is lovely to think of you getting out into the Kiper district after all these years, I hope you were able to visit all the places you wanted to; I have such clear memories of my treks there & of the people in those days – how different I think things are now. But how good to hear of Polycarp chairing that meeting so well! I will remember your Field Committee next wk & especially the fresh troubles at Vom. Much love dear & God bless, guide & use you always, Nakam.

Pankshin General Hospital, Ward 2 Bed 4

March 5th 1959

My dear Mother I hope you are well. I am here again for treatment, my illness is this: my eyes are yellow I feelt very weak & cold. The doctor observed me and wrote 7 injections & I have just taken the 5th today. It is a bad disease called Shawara in Hausa or we may say Discusting in English. I am very sorry for myself & the school this year, the school fees is still with me I have not been able to make up the total. Will you please send my greetings to Nayen; your son in Jesus, Kefas Katya.

28 Abbotshall Drive Cults

6.3.59

Darling Chris it is a week since I left Brookfield & very hard it was to leave them. Mummie is terribly concerned – as I was – about our Mipsie who really is doing far too much just killing herself by all her tearing around for everyone & declining to go to Rustington or somewhere like it over Easter. I am to write to Mrs Slater to ask her to persuade May to ease up before her operation or she'll be in such a poor way for it. But I don't feel I can do this for I don't know MrsS at all and I do know May would be terribly upset; but Mummy is insisting. Would you write to her for me? I would certainly go down again over Easter or have M&F up here but I don't think F could stand the long journey now. I am very sorry to burden you with this problem darling, & I will try to write the letter if you think I should, but you always have such wise judgement & it is such a relief to have your opinion, help & advice. We do not forget your own troubles which I know to be difficult ones just now. God is indeed taking us through strange ways at present; we will all be brought through in His time and our times are in His hands. My heart aches for poor Wilfrid in all the decisions he has to make on his own now without Father's help or Uncle's; but we are blessed in our united love & thought for each other, ever your loving Rene.

Panyam

Mar 7th '59

My darlings thank you for your dear letters; I just wish so often especially these days that I could be there with you to cheer you a bit and help you. Perhaps by sharing some of my life here I can give you different things to dwell on even for a short while, and be a help in that way. After a pleasant night at Mongun with greetings to May from Yusufu Dakahap & Joseph Jwander, I left at 5.40am accompanied by 6 stalwart boys from Kiper who had come just to help me and carry my 4 loads containing essentials such as my bed bag, food box plus saucepans, Beatrice stove, medical supplies, and of course the gramophone & records. You walk for about 6 mls to the top of the world then drop down a sheer escarpment for about half a mile then another 5 miles or so to Kiper. I had 2 rests of 15mins each & got in at 10.30 to be met by the Evangelist Jidauna & some of the Christians out to escort me in their nice way, keen to show me the school they have built, although the money to pay a teacher is very slow coming in. I rested well in the afternoon then held a meeting and gave them gramophone & delivered special messages from old Father Lot who was their first evangelist.

A crowd of women gathered round with such warm greetings, some remembered me from 1941 when I was last there but some had never seen a European. A chicken given by the Chief was prepared & cooked & we shared it together then sat in the starlight & chatted; that sort of thing is one of the best reasons for going on trek especially places where we can go so rarely; you can really listen to their troubles and try to help. Next morn we left at 6.30 for the village of Bul, 'near' they told me, but what a path! The first mile was through farms & trees then another precipitous slope down & down to a river bed then up & up the other side. These villages are perched on the top of hills with the most terrific ravines between them. The work at Bul has been slowly growing & now they have quite a number of Christians tho' none has been baptised yet. Upon arrival I was sweetly greeted by Ishaya Dabwap & his little flock, given a deckchair to sit in inside the little Church & soon the gramophone was going again with Harry Lauder & Laughing Gas still as unfailingly attractive as they were 15 yrs ago! Followed by Hausa hymns & Scripture verses & the new Hausa Gospel recordings plus a few Bev Shea & the Harringay Choir! I met a blind woman who has followed Jesus for years & her great desire is to get baptised this year. Some Christians from Mahlay & Jwahal appeared after my rest & I thought that would save me from going out to those 2 new outstations but this made them terribly upset saying, "We are new, our people have never seen you, they have been preparing for your visit for several days, and the way back to Mongun from us is much easier!" So they persuaded me! The final meeting at Bul was well attended & all the Christians put on a 'dance,' blowing on huge reed pipes making a terrific noise, all expressions of their joyful hospitality. They are so unsophisticated & this sort of 'do' is just like David's dancing before the Lord with all his might. We had more of the gramophone & I treated some sick children & was preparing to leave when another cooked chicken was presented so of course had to be shared. The visiting Christians felt personally responsible & walked one in front of me & one behind & hauled me up the steep slopes and I let them for they were truly strong & I was truly tired by then. We arrived after dark & I was glad of an early night. After morning prayers I went on the 2 miles to Jwahal with no gorge to climb, & was met by a Christian boy with such a bright face called Danan. He gets about on hands & knees with his poor bits of feet dragging behind. The usual greetings and programme of welcome & then came requests for gramophone, & gales of laughter and repeated handshakes all round plus chicken sharing too! Our home bread is not keeping well at present due to a bad batch of flour, & mine had turned so horrid I could not eat it and the Fulani cattle folk I'd expected were not there so my one tin of milk did not last long. However here's what I had or was given: eggs galore, chicken every day, plenty of tea & coffee without milk, rice crispies, buns & biscuits, butter & marmalade, a tomato or two, & rice with the chicken. During the 'dancing' I was amazed to find Danan taking his place in the circle & taking a turn on the drums keeping the rhythm well. He is quite a part of the community and respected by all. He came & talked with me in the evening saying he really wants to be allowed to take the test for baptism this year. Yohanna the Evangelist told me he is always crawling around to visit the compounds and preach the Gospel, he can read well and do a lot of crafts. Many heathen folk began crowding in for medicine but I found most of them were old & had advanced VD and/or sleeping sickness for which I had nothing that would do them any good. Sadly many of the older Christians who wanted medicine for similar symptoms – I am afraid the old life of sinful habits has left many of these new believers with damaged bodies. The Jwahal Church is so crowded with seats that I had to sleep outside and it was lovely. My carriers came & slept on the ground near by & we were up at 4.15 & away by 5am for the 6mile walk to the bottom of the steep ascent where my faithful attendants, the 2 Yohannas, hauled me up so we got to the top by 8.15 for a rest and some food. I think it was another 7 miles to Mongun where I was thankful to be & to find Fibi Nanchin just as I'd left her & I was soon into her & away &

back here soon after noon. I don't know which was more acceptable, a long cold drink, a nice meal or a hot bath but I had them all & then a good rest and Joyce brought tea to my bedroom too. My eyes were a bit sore, probably from wind & dust, but not wanting conjunctivitis I bathed them in Optrex & Joyce administered some Penicillin cream. Now today I should have gone to Gindiri but asked David to go instead with Joyce so I am free to write this epistle to you. I came back from that trek with 4doz eggs, 4 chickens, sore legs and another lot of happy memories of warm hearts and a growing work for the Lord in these distant villages, many opportunities, and a better idea of the needs of these places & others still further away & in need of an Evangelist. Of course I wish they could get a new motor road to Kiper, but that would be a huge undertaking. Yes I did indeed get the lovely photo of the children at Christmas & wrote fully of it to B so it would seem it is my letter to her that was never delivered. Now my time, and paper, is finished, dearest love from Chris.

Anna Valley, Andover, Hants

Mar 15th '59

My darling your last letter was thrillingly full of trek details – I almost could feel the rough terrain, the heat & the thirst. I've used parts of what you wrote at two or three meetings & the folk have been so interested. I do hope your eyes have fully recovered now that you've had some chance to get rested. Mother has told me of her requests to Rene & you to contact Mrs S to persuade me into hospital sooner; darling I hope you know that is the very last thing I want & I am perfectly well able to speak with Mrs S myself should I need to. I am confidently hoping

I'll get through till June. It is still not possible to make any plans but if we have to move before you can come I shall attempt to get M&F to E'bourne perhaps & Rene will come down to help me clear the house. I don't think we can reckon on any money for ourselves which means I can only put down a deposit of less than £1000 on a house if I can see my way clear to meet the subsequent payments & keep us 3 going. Even more reason for me to continue working as much as possible. We may not reach that point & 'some other way' may yet be opened to us but from a purely human point of view the outlook is not rosy. I hardly think leave of absence is feasible & you'd only ask for it towards the end of a furlough if it was imperative for you to stay longer. I know that if time should mark the end of the journey for me, you would come as soon as possible to be with M&F for as long as needed, but you know dear it wouldn't be at all easy for you to gear yourself down to being here with things as they are, it would be very frustrating at times. For myself it is just the daily life at home that constantly makes me feel what a hopeless sort of Christian I am, not worthy of the name. In spite of prayer & determination to be patient & understanding & gentle, I am just the opposite & often must surely make life miserable for them. Perhaps that's one of the reasons you should come & tho' I'm not suggesting you would fail as I do but it is one of the factors you need to take into account. Any one of these increasing almost daily attacks of palpitations Father has could be the last & he really cannot be left alone any more. We must trust that we will know what is right when the time comes, goodbye darling dearest love as ever, May.

As from: 6 Winchendon Rd Teddington

23.3.59

Dearest Chris how thrilled I was to receive your letter & one from Bill telling me that I'm to come back to Panyam DV – I can't get back soon enough! I don't yet know the date of my return but have written to Mr Herbert to get something moving. It sounds as it there are at least 2 nurses ready to come out before Sept providing they're accepted & passages booked. So we are to have the TEKAS meeting at Panyam next year: it will be a busy weekend but we shall enjoy it I'm quite sure. I'm so glad you were able to go on trek to Jipal country for I know you've wanted to go for some time; & how lovely that you met the blind woman & the crippled boy who are preaching the Gospel! It was an arduous week for you but so worth it for I can just imagine how encouraged the folk were to see you. I'm already thinking of my next trek! I hope you Chris, & Joyce, are doing well & that your news from home is good; I'll leave it until just before I go to visit your parents so that I can bring you up to date news. Please greet Ishaku & all the other folk; I'm praying much for you all & looking forward to seeing you soon, with much love Joan.

Panyam

March 31st '59

Darlings, there is no time now for another epistle but I know you will want to hear of the special Girls' School meetings in Gindiri. I spoke to Class 7 & 6 in English & Dorothy Somerville spoke in Hausa to

Class 5 & 4. Nothing could have been more ordinary than the messages at least mine & I think D's too, but the Lord was certainly working & many responded. We both gave appeals for those who wanted to get right with God, whether to accept Christ for the first time or to talk over difficulties, to stay behind after class. 12 out of our lot stayed to accept Christ and 26 out of Dorothy's. She dealt with hers en masse but the next day we saw them individually, I spent over 2 hours counselling on the Sat afternoon. All the Suras came to me & it was a great joy to find that 2 had already taken Christ the previous day & were quite sure about it & that He had received them. Two others wanted a bit more explanation one was Timothawus Kwarshak & the other Rauta's little Mutnas who is only about 10 & very bright. She didn't quite know what 'faith' meant but when I explained a bit she said she saw and proceeded to pray the sweetest prayer asking the Lord to accept her, cleanse her from sin & make her His. Several others who knew they were saved came to talk about such sins as anger, lying, unforgiving spirit & to ask prayer for unconverted relatives. It was really a very great privilege to help them. Several of the Europeans around here have been asking after you & assuring of their frequent prayer for you. Best & dearest love, Chris.

Brookfield

April 14th '59

My darling Chris your thoughts will often have turned towards us knowing that Joan is here in the spare room! It is a great help for she seems willing to do anything for us, she has gone just now on the bus to Crawley to buy meat & bread etc. May did a lot of cooking /baking on Sat before leaving so we are well provided for & as you know we live as simply as possible. I think she is glad to be here in the quiet, I think her home has TV/Radio blaring away all the time. Yesterday was like summer & we sat outside in the garden & had tea in front of the dining rm west window. Your ears might often burn we talk of you so much I rejoice in the esteem & love which Joan has towards you & I'm so glad she's going back to Panyam. I am thinking of asking if she would come back to stay another week before June to relieve May a bit (M is in I. of W. again this week) Last eve I took Joan over to call on Auntie Jo and then Wilfrid's family at Southways. No further news but W has signed the papers & is going about preparations for Chelsea again this year; I would think that is not necessary but no doubt he has his reasons. Joan hopes we shall never have to leave this lovely home – so do I – but it can be done if necessary. Father's palps are bad again & he complains much of giddiness which I think is the pills (Ephidrene) in some measure making him thus but he thinks I am entirely mistaken! He wishes Dr Hunter would come back again to see us. Joan is taking awhile she must be having a good look around the town she is to assist in the making of curry for dinner today. Miss Wightman wrote of having to come back home because of her sister's serious illness but how she was torn in two over leaving her AIM work in Africa wondering if she could ever return to it. I feel her position would be very similar to yours – if you had to come home now; very dear love & constant remembrances my darling, ever your loving Mother.

206 Grt Falls St, Falls Church, Virginia, USA

15 April 1959

Dear Christine, your Mother, at my request, sent us your address because we have so often re-lived the wonderful day we spent with you in Crawley, and wished to send you greetings. We have read with pleasure your book 'For Light & Truth' about Dafwash, a true inspiration for all. Josephine & I have been at home all winter which passed all too quickly with many anticipated jobs still awaiting attention. I have enjoyed weaving – the Nadeave loom is fascinating and easy of operation. We also knit baby sets for friends' new arrivals and have just sent one to Sicily. The three acres across the street from us will soon have 6-8 storey apartments on it; the bulldozer is working to cut & remove 20 beautiful tall stately maples. Sometime if there should be a need in which we could help in your great service in Nigeria we'd be grateful if you would tell us. Josephine joins me in sending good wishes and love to you, Anna May.

En route from Ryde to Portsmouth on the car-ferry

April 16th '59

My darling I don't often write while on the sea but I can spend this calm half hr with you. Nor do I often take the car over to the Island but I had some meetings at the Freshwater end meaning 3hrs there & back by bus. Also this year I really didn't want too much walking about or carrying bags of literature. It's been a real treat with the car & on the two good days the Island was looking absolutely lovely! I stayed with Dr Matthias who has retired here from London & has this house right on the side of the Downs above Sandown. She is so very kind & has a most efficient housekeeper maid who brought me breakfast in bed every morning & generally spoiled me. Meetings on the whole were good & well attended & last night Miss Alexander (you met her at High Leigh) invited friends in to see your pictures then she prayed so very sweetly for you & all your co-workers. It really is awfully good of Joan Onions to have stayed with M&F & she may still be there when I get home tonight. I think they've enjoyed having her & I hear she's been wonderfully helpful – I hope she got some rest. Today I showed the pictures again, to two schools & there was much interest in spite of the new 'rear projector' they laid on (which seemed unsatisfactory to me & nowhere as good as the other type) but having spoken for nearly 2hrs this morn plus half an hr this aft I am thankful to be quiet now. Tomorrow there is a Coffee Morning in Sanderstead then an afternoon mtg in Purley so the pictures will be aired again.

It's Fri now in Purley & I keep thinking darling that it's three yrs next week since we met in Jos!! I'm constantly amazed at people's responses to your pics and I really think that that visit & all the planning you did for it had a special Divine ordering, something that spills over every time people see them & hear the stories. Now I must say goodbye for this time, sending my dearest love as always, May.

10 Cleveland Rd, Gosport Hants

April 16th '59

Dear Miss Cheal greetings in the precious Name of Jesus. This short letter is to tell you we have sent a £15 cheque to you at SUM London for your ministry in Panyam to be used to bring souls to Christ. It is from my 'Children's Farthing Fund' in the Sunday school and I would very much like to hear from you that I might read your letter to the boys & girls. May God multiply the amount to bring many to Christ, for I feel we are coming to the close of this Dispensation & Jesus will return very soon. There is much to do & it is very hard in England, people are so full of pleasure and what this world can offer; we need a mighty outpouring of the Holy Spirit, may God grant it. We pray for you every Sunday afternoon may the Lord Jesus continue to bless you with strength to carry out His work; Mrs Burt sends her greetings, God bless you, yours in His love and service, FM Munday.

Brookfield

26.4.59

Darling when I wrote to you last week from Cults I had no idea I'd be down here at home today! On Tues Dr Hunter came to see Father, gave him some new pills but did not stay long. Later that evening May went upstairs & found F collapsed, very poorly & distressed however an hour later was improved & ready for his supper. Then on Friday eve I was very surprised when F himself rang me up to say poor dear Mummy had had a bad fall up in the buildings yard & had broken her wrist & needed 3 stitches by her left eye. She'd apparently been playing 'tennis' with Alison, hitting the ball alternatively against the wall & she slipped. Poor Alison was frightened, couldn't lift M up so ran home for B&W who took her to Crawley hosp. May was in Canterbury. The hosp would only do the stitches saying she'd have to go to Redhill for the setting so W brought her home just as poor May arrived home. May then immediately drove M to Redhill although she'd had no tea, and Mother was put to bed, so May came home. Mother finally got home at 11.45 pm in a hospital car. I felt dear May had had enough so I got the night train getting here 10.15 this morning. Mother is of course sore & weary with the pain in arm and face (very black eye) but otherwise quite fine, & F seems quite fine too. May is off to an eve service in Tun. Wells, I don't know how she does keep going; dearest & best love as always, Rene.

Brookfield

3rd May 1959

Dearest darling your birthday letter reached me in good time & I was so grateful for it and the lovely nosegay of Panyam flowers. Thank you for all your loving thoughts & prayers for me. Friday was a beautiful May morning, we had a good coffee Mtg in Wimbledon & made £24.6d; then Gertrude & Ruth came over for tea & short tour of the New Town & Airport and Rene had of course made a lovely three tier cake & everyone was so loving & kind. You will have heard by now of all the goings on here lately – I really thought Father was going that night, slumped across the bed looking like death & gasping for air. Of course he would not allow me to take off his trousers, not would he rest in or on the bed. I am thankful Mother was not the one to find him like that. Dr Collyer told me he'd seen the recent Xray of F's heart & has a very poor opinion of his condition, warning again that he could just go anytime. I am so very thankful to have Rene here for I should have had to cancel all the meetings or get alternative speakers, which is so very hard at such short notice. Mother is somewhat better today & actually managed to dress herself (without bra or corsets!) but as soon as she can knit again the days won't seem so long to her. Always yours May.

Panyam

5·5·59

Darlings I was so grieved to hear of all the anxiety & pain you had last week with Father's bad turn after the new pills & Mother's fracture. It certainly eased the news for me to hear in the same letter that F had been out to Meeting – I think Barbara drove you & A. Jo – and then to have a letter written by you Mother so it's your left wrist that was hurt & as you so wisely say, 'no more ball games!' I'm sure the comfort of Rene is a great cheer & help to you all. You can imagine my surprise when I heard that I would soon be contacted by Lady Bell (the Governor's wife) & probably invited to an official luncheon party in Kaduna when the Duchess is there. All I had asked for was a section of the road for 100 of my GLB girls to parade in welcome for her on May 20th so that I should not have to go into Kaduna's heat wearing the thick brigade uniform! We shall see. It is the time of year when several of the big heathen festivals are held & several of our small schoolboys in Jibam have been already taken off by their heathen fathers to take part. Wailing at deaths has suddenly increased – with some Christians drawn back into this & the killing of a goat & sharing in the meat 'to help the departed' another entirely heathen custom. Sadly one Evangelist went up in smoke about all this, making a dreadful scene & upsetting so many folk. More difficult days full of difficult palavers, here & further afield, all rather wearying. Some Gindiri students went on an educational trip to Lagos & the member of staff with them was booked to stay in a transit house for missionaries but when they saw he was African they refused to take him in – we were so very grieved & ashamed to hear this. That same man has since been my guest for we are determined to treat all people just the same as any European visitors. But there is some good news too: Nelson & Naki & their twins plus Nehemiah & Christiana & their 4 children plus a nurse girl all left to go to Banchi for a year's Rural Science Course, and Yabal an ETC teacher from Kerang has gone happily to Chip to replace Nelson! And 2 weeks ago three of our leading women came for tea with me: Victoria, Eunice, & Keziah Ningis to share their happiness at their preaching itinerations, 79 of them went out together in wonderful fellowship preaching in every home in the villages & found only one heathen chief who would not let them speak to him. They took the gramophone & some Gospel records which were all well received & a great attraction. So goodbye my darlings may the Lord help you all through these days & give strength & patience & every blessing. I want so much to write to Wilfrid & Barbara for their birthdays but it's rather too late now; dear love to each of you as ever, Chris.

252 Selsdon Rd, S Croydon

May 7th '59

My dearest Chris many thanks for your most welcome letter yesterday. I'm wondering if you remember May 7th 1938, it was the day of our Beer Purge! (& also in '41 Ishaku Toma's death) What agonies that Beer Purge caused us, but time has shown has it not, that it was a right & necessary step for it has only been since then that the work has got really established & has grown & developed so much! Today's Daily Light is so appropriate & also the SU portion in Ezek 2; a missionary's life & work has so many heartaches yet it is all so well worth it, and yes, we do see the 'nevertheless' afterwards. Joan is coming to see me next Friday & I'm giving her to bring back 2 colour films and a lot of knitted baby vests, blankets & bags all done by our Fellowship women. I am sorry to hear Joyce is still losing weight in spite of Miango's big meals. Has she still got worms do you think? Also it's so sad about your Mother's fall & broken wrist, such a shock at her age; what a mercy Rene could go to them. Troubles do seem to mount up for your saintly parents just now! Anyway the Lord knows He can trust them with it all & that their testimony will help & strengthen others I'm quite sure. It has been so bitterly cold here I still have a fire & have been wearing all my winter clothes but suddenly yesterday it turned very warm with no wind & today everyone has emerged in summer frocks & even I have discarded a few layers of winter woollies! Long may this last! Very much love, thoughts & prayers, Nakam.

SUM Jibam

May 9th 1959

My dear Mother thank you very much for sending me the application form for Kagoro Bridge Course, I have finished filling the form. I think you will be interested to know that Hajaratu Nishe has got a new baby boy on the 6th May, she went to Longkat on Monday, there she borned her new child. Will you pray that he may grow well & know the Lord Jesus as his Saviour? I am taking the jumper which you gave me some wool to kneet it for him to Longkat today. Thank you for the wool and for the £2 for sport on Celebration Day. I should like to know from you before we ask builder to start the foundation of the new school perhaps it will need siment. Will you please remember Dashi in your prayers he is coming to the back of the Church with his Bible, perhaps his mind is changing to remember the Lord Jesus. I hope you are well how are your parents with best wishes from your son in Him Kefas Katya.

Brookfield

May 12th '59

My beloved Chris as you will remember it is dear Wilfrid's birthday today & how I hope he will have some token of the Lord's blessing & favour this day. More & more I come to realise, that is all that really matters most in this life & how much we all need HIM is of supreme importance to me. The way Wilfrid has so consistently lived out his faith in God has helped me so often; I tried to write of this to him in a little note last night – may it encourage him today. The weather is pleasantly warm, the wisteria on the house over our bedroom window is a lovely sight & in the garden clematis, lilac, tulips, bluebells & still a few narcissi, primroses, forget-me-nots etc all bringing their own delight & joy. Your dear letter came on Saturday I'm afraid it was a shock about my fall, you may be sure I hope never to do it again! May went off to Kingston some time ago so Father & I are both so thankful to have Rene here. I know you will continue to pray for them as only the Lord can meet the need. Some Aberdeen people have just called in at the Office to leave R's summer clothes sent by E but they did not call in here. May still has had no reply from the surgeon giving a June date for her op; I shall be so thankful when this is all over safely. She must go to E'bourne tomorrow & asked R & me to go along but I have the feeling resting here in the garden is perhaps just as good for me. My hair is getting very thin on top so I have been in to fetch the old cream parasol (now you will be able to picture me!) to keep this lovely hot sun off my head; only 2 more weeks until this hard bandage can come off – hurrah! Darling I wish you could hear the blackbird out on an apple branch singing for glory, it is beautiful, now blessings on you darling love roll on next year when we hope we might see you again, ever your loving Mother.

Brookfield

Whit Sunday, 17th May '59

My darling I wonder if you're off visiting outstations today, and are you getting excited about going to Kaduna for your meeting with the Royals this week?! Soon you'll be making preparations to welcome Joan back again – I know she is eager to return. Mouse & I went to the evening Annual SUM Mtg but I'm afraid I did not find it inspiring, Joan was really the only speaker who gave any idea of what is actually happening on the Mission Field today. So I don't think my hopes of getting Mouse inspired came to very much. After that I had to be in Town for more meetings all week but did get back in time to take Mother & Rene motoring over to Leith Hill to see the bluebells; they were absolutely heavenly – that wonderful blue, intensely blue carpet defies description. I wish I could send you the exquisite scent of them. We've had the most marvellous weather & several evenings I have taken the others out; Father was quite bucked when we went to Hever, especially when one of the estate men just happened to be walking out & had a good talk with F. We all went to Brighton on Friday & while R & I did shopping M&F sat on the sea Front then we all had a picnic on the cliffs towards Rottingdean & it was lovely. I have just longed that there might be some outward obvious demonstration of the Lord's power so we personally could prove His power & that His promises may not be only words to which we cling but facts in which we rejoice. I do know that very many are called to go on in faith these days but it seems to have been such a very long time as far as we're concerned. There is still no word on the Business sale & I feel now he's just not intending to go through with it. Last week at the Day Conf. we had Rev Cleverley Ford for the first Devotional & he was SO good on Matt. 10 the messengers of the King; he went through the disciples as their names are given &

showed how many ordinary men there were, those about whom we hear so little afterwards but they were all needed, and chosen, by the Lord. Thomas with his honest doubts was needed; Simon the Zealot whom we would never have put on a committee was needed, & so on. It was most refreshing to hear someone of his quality & scholarship give a real Bible reading. Goodbye my dearest darling take care of yourself & may you be blessed & helped, ever yours May.

Panyam

May 22 1959

Darlings you will have realised by now that I didn't go to Kaduna, never having heard another word from anybody about it. However it was just as well because I was in bed with one of my rare bouts of fever – quite alright now. Joyce has been in the wars though she was taken with bad sharp pain on Sunday eve last, during a difficult midder case but at 10pm we decided we'd have to take her to Pankshin where they diagnosed gall bladder infection/inflammation & gave her an injection of Pethedine & at midnight we were drinking tea in the Doctor's house at the top of the hill. It was well after 1am before we got home to bed. On Monday Frances P came & took Joyce off to Mongu for a few days rest & further treatment & I know to relieve me of the necessity of nursing J on top of everything else. Today I went there to collect her, thankful she is much better tho' still on a fat free diet. I had thought it would be nice to write a letter of greeting to the Duchess as we hadn't been able to see her so I wrote it, Winnie approved it & we both signed it. We also wanted to send her a small gift but no-one had any ideas & all I could think of was a sample of embroidery by Namuret – 'a girl who has had no education except in the GLB,' and a new skipping rope 'made of locally grown hemp and used widely by GLB Companies in the North,' so we parcelled up these two things in my best Mornay soapbox then wrapped in purple crepe paper! When we got to Jos I took it & the letter to Tudun Wada where they were to be staying but had an awful time getting anyone willing to take it in. All the gates were barred & guarded & no-one seemed able to cope with this purple parcel; finally one very grand African official said he would deliver it. We did accumulate 100 girls to line the road, I think the Panyam & Jos girls were certainly the smartest; our site on the route was under shade trees so we were happy and the banner we'd made was the only one so the Duchess most likely did see it. Of course when they came past it was all over in a second or two but she did smile at us very sweetly! This evening I received a letter from Barbara Holland, Lady in Waiting saying, "The Duchess of Gloucester desires me to write and thank you all for your kind telegram of welcome...and to tell you how pleased she was to see so many lining the route...and to congratulate all concerned on how smart they looked. Her Royal highness sends you all her warmest good wishes." So that is nice but I have a strong suspicion that the official at the gate never gave her the purple parcel, for it & the letter were not mentioned. David got back from Kaduna on Tuesday, and all our girls, and everyone seems to have enjoyed it but there is disappointment in that there was practically no acknowledgement of the part the Christian Missions have played in any progress in N Nigeria's development. Bill & Mollie Tett were furious that the lack even extended to the survey of leprosy work. Our compound looks simply lovely, I have taken 4 good photos; much dear love C.

Somewhere in Haslemere

May 25th '59

My beloved Chris I have come along here with May as it gives a little opportunity for talk, and seeing as the signed agreement has finally come back I suppose I can say that the Nurseries are sold. We have had little time to discuss things yet, hope to do so soon but it is Chelsea week & Wilfrid will be up there a good deal. I hear that the new owner of Hyders is very interested; he's now done the old place up & turned it into an Inn to be opened shortly and wants more stuff for his garden in the autumn. Dear Rene went home on Tuesday last & now on Thurs it is Erik's birthday & their wedding anniversary. She says he does not seem well, rather downcast, he has got a tonic from the doctor. I am not happy about them and can only pray that God will undertake for them & work a mighty change. I am asking Father who knows nothing of their situation to write a birthday greeting to E, it will be better that way. Queen & Prince P were round at Chelsea last evening & George Miller was honoured by a word from P about a huge cone on top of the Monkey Puzzle tree, who remarked "Hello what have you got there?" I wonder what Geo M said in response! We now keep looking at pictures of bungalows & May would like a room above – chalet style I think they are called but we might have to be satisfied with less and with people close rather than lovely quiet gardens. I hope for some view of sky & a green field or two; if it's a new house there will be the interest of making a garden, but it is all so uncertain still. Father sends his love & I add mine of course and longing to see you as soon as might be possible, Mother.

Brookfield

May 31st '59

My darling your letter was a joy thank you for all its love & prayers. I wish I could tell you when I'm going into Barts but I still haven't heard; I shall be thankful to know the date & that there is no delay or it will be awkward when it comes to September workload again. We were so thankful to have Rene's letter on Friday just saying prayers are being answered & they've talked a lot and reached peace & better understanding of each other. I understand them not wanting anymore said than that at least for now. Also I am thankful because lately it has seemed to my faithlessness that the only answer we can expect to any of our prayer has to be no. Now I have to alter what Mother wrote to you because apparently the sale papers are not fully signed (or correctly signed?) so nothing is settled which makes me most uneasy. I see no prospect at present of Father ever living to see all the liabilities cleared & unless Wilfrid sells the stock much better than at present seems likely, there will be nothing coming to us at the end of it all. W is so vague about his intentions; I fear his plans for Tilgate or Pulborough will bring the same old difficulties. Darling I am sorry for writing such a moan, I don't mean it that way & am sure we shall be brought through somehow, all best love May.

Panyam

June 7th '59

My darlings we are in the news again, in a way nobody would choose: yesterday morning, Saturday, I went to get the car from the garage but found the padlock hanging on the open door, to my utter amazement it wasn't there – Fibi stolen in the night, and our 8gall drum of petrol gone with it! David went directly to the Pankshin Police who sent an African Sergeant to take all particulars & send them everywhere with police watching all over the country roads. They & we feel there is already an obvious suspect, newly released from prison for car theft. None of our folk have ever heard of such a thing and all are feeling quite stunned. David was sweet in church this morning, reminding that God had given the car to us – as her name implies: Fibi Nanchin – so God had some thought in allowing this to happen, & we must all be in prayer about it, we have been as you can well imagine. One of the Christians who led in prayer prayed for you Mother & Father by name, and Nakam also, I hadn't heard them do this by name before!

I'm in Jos now to see the Police Supt who had not yet heard of our theft, & to complete an insurance claim form, and collected your dear letters in B. Ladi – so very welcome, thank you. Darlings as you are now precipitated into the matter of thinking about somewhere else to live I will give you the verse I gave Nakam when she left here in '54 & didn't know where she would go, the promise was remarkably fulfilled for her: Num. 10:33 The Ark of the Lord went before them…to search out a resting place for them; constant love as ever C.

Miango

June 9th '59

Dearest Chris just a word of loving greeting & cheer over this disturbing event & hoping you'll soon have news of Fibi. I thought your acceptance of it & trust through it all on Sat was a real witness & must have given many who came to see you cause for thought – may it be used to strengthen the faith of many in the District. Would you like to come to tea on 20th & pick cizaki berries? There are masses of red ones & some black ripening nicely; with much love my dear, Frances P. Of course I'll come for you if you still have no car.

June 12th

My dearest darling I am still at home but ought to be leaving for Swanwick, waiting for two more of my passengers Mrs Gregory, & Mrs Lomas (from the Congregationals) we are going to be hearing Dr & Mrs Niemoller again so I'm sure it will be a really great time. You will have already had Mother's letter telling you that I have to go into Barts on the 21st before noon; they don't say exactly when it will be done but I expect either Monday or Tuesday. I am not at all anxious over it so I hope you will not be either, 'God's got you & me in His hand.' I'm so thankful that I haven't to wait any longer & can now reckon on July/ August to recuperate & plan to start work again in Sept. I've just had a note from Joan in which she refers to the loss of your car! Darling, I am so sorry – there's a letter from you for Mummy so we shall soon have details – but you know I'll be specially praying that the answer might be given soon. Also she tells me she has passed her test so that's good. Blessings on you my darling and now may the Lord hold you in His peace, ever yours, May.

Redhill Hospital

June 16th '59

My darling Chris, no, no more 'tennis' games, I have just come up here for p. therapy which is already half an hr late. Your letter with news of your car having been stolen came as a shock & we have been remembering you very often, I hope you have it back safely...I believe you have by now, we shall be so very glad to hear it is so. Now it is 3.45 I have had the therapy treatment: heat first & exercises after, it looks as though it will be some time before my fingers are straight. We've had a quiet & happy weekend on our own – May is in Swanwick, and Mouse (oh dear, Christopher) was a cheer & stayed until Monday morn. 8.15pm now, he told us of the accident he was in last Tues eve I think he was late out at some party & to get to his flat quickly he jumped into a taxi. Almost as soon as it had started up again he moved his seat to the further corner & almost at once a bus turned a corner & crashed right into this taxi which then skidded across the street & into something else then I think must have overturned as it took several people to get M/Christopher out. The side from which he had moved was quite smashed in. I do believe he felt thankful for it was indeed a merciful deliverance; he only had one day off work & a slight cut on his forehead. Anthony's letters continue to be full of parties etc may the dear Lord keep His loving hand over them both & bring them right though into His service. I think I didn't tell you that Barbara & I went to Lottie Miller's funeral last week & as we passed down the aisle to our seats a man close to me at the end of a pew lay back with a slight moan, I thought it was a fit or a faint. B had to step back as 2 men came to get him lying down & B pushed a sort footstool under his head. The poor man was Cyrus Yetman and he was dead, such a shock. Mercifully the funeral was late so these sorrowful happenings did not quite coincide. All the love I can send you darling your loving Mother.

Panyam

June 16th '59

Darlings it has been a mercy to have Peter Batchelor only 8mls away with his Land Rover, we're planning to go with him into Jos on Saturday to meet Joan & welcome her back. We are getting ready for her return by having the little round guest house repaired & altered a bit. May will remember it as a rather ratty, dusty place altho' very picturesque; we're having 3 rows of bricks added to the walls and a ceiling of cornstalks put in, plastered over above & below with mud like we have in our house, then the roof put on again over top. This should be done in a week & a half & shouldn't cost more than £10 so it will be well worth it to have a clean house & be free from the noise & droppings of mice from the roof. Peter B has been doing quite a bit of school inspection & he is very good at it, producing full & useful criticism of all he finds. After a day at Jing he came straight up here to tell me of a very disturbing discovery. The Jr Primary under Luther Dabirong is much improved but on the desk of the probationary teacher, a Kulere boy who finished SP last year, there were 2 typed sheets of paper with the most awful pornographic filth. He claimed it had been given to him by Istifanus Jakden's son on holiday from the Govt Training College. Peter spoke to both boys & tore up the papers & burned them in front of them; he also wrote directly to the principal of the College. The boy responsible did not seem to think anything was shameful or wrong in it, but oh the infinite harm it could do in the hands & minds of these young susceptible boys who all think anything in English is clever & desirable. It is the first time I have ever heard of anything like this being circulated as literature. You may not know but tomorrow is the Prophet Mohammed's birthday! As we are now a self-governing state & largely Moslem we are all forced to keep Moslem as well as Christian holidays, so the schools and all public works are on holiday. We are going to Frances P to help her pick ci-zaki fruit & make lots of jam & jelly. We have just heard & greatly enjoyed the broadcast from Australia of Billy Graham Campaign & also Eric Hutchings. I'll be prayerfully remembering May of course as she prepares to start her sojourn into Barts Hosp I'll write to her there, blessings upon you all each one with my dearest love as ever, Chris.

June 18th: Hallelujah!! Fibi Nanchin is found!! At a place called Mamfe in the Cameroons, a young policeman thought of the all alerts message when he saw a Peugeot getting petrol, asked the driver for his licence which of course he didn't have, so arrested him on the spot. The engine number corresponded so the Jos Police have gone to collect her from Mamfe, about 1000 miles by road I believe!! We are so very thrilled & thankful, & now I'm sure we should concentrate on praying for the thieves, 2 Panyam boys. Goodnight darlings & let this answer to our prayers be an encouragement to us all to keep on trusting even in the most difficult of situations, your Chris.

252 Selsdon Rd, S. Croydon

June 25th '59

Oh Hallelujah indeed how thankful I am Chris to get your news today – what a mercy your car was caught before it crossed over into French Territory! I do hope they have not done it any harm by driving so far & that the necessary overhaul won't take too long & will be fully covered by insurance. I presume that silly boy Job C & his pal will go to prison – we will be praying for him while in there to see the Light. As to the other evil matter in your letter, oh what a lot some Europeans have to answer for, in taking filthy pornography to such primitive people. I am reliably informed it is on the rise here at home too. We must remember God is at work even through this sort of thing. I am quite certain you are clinging to that fact in the midst of all the difficulties you face & must deal with each day; and however awkward and frustrating, it is always a comfort & encouragement when sin is exposed, tho' it is usually so painful; I pray that all hidden sin will be brought into light & so be dealt with; and I pray daily for Godly wisdom for you in all your dealings. A card from Rene today tells me poor May's op has been postponed for the surgeon is ill?! We will know one day why this has been allowed to happen & His wisdom behind it. Be at peace & take courage. I am sitting out in a deckchair in Turner's garden watching young Susie enact the police capture of your car thief & then its joyful return – priceless entertainment!! And we are all rejoicing with you & I send much love as well, yours Nakam.

Panyam

July 1st '59

My darlings it was indeed an anticlimax to hear May's news of postponement – what perplexity it must have given you; I am praying you will be kept well, and calm, in the waiting. Here our main troubles have been around the making, drinking & selling of the forbidden gruel (not beer, but if left long enough becomes equally or more intoxicating) The makers & users hotly claim innocence and those in authority seem only able to turn a blind eye for the sake of peace. Some Pastors & Evangelists have tried to deal with it in their own ways without consulting others, making a dreadful muddle & ignoring therefore the unitedly accepted ruling of 1956. This last weekend David had to be away but to my great joy Pastor Joel spoke out in Church fearlessly & definitely about this gruel, & that it is each Evangelists responsibility to tell his people and see to it that all the Christians do keep the rule. He prayed beautifully, & on Monday Joyce continued that prayer & I'm certain that really calmed the tensions & helped the situation and we ourselves, for things had not been too easy between us during the previous week. Yesterday we were in the middle of the Tues pm School Comm when Bill Tett arrived, bringing Daphne Fletcher & Joan Onions who'd got back much earlier than expected from Mkar! So we were suddenly most busy getting beds ready & our meal for two enlarged to feed 5! It is lovely to have Joan back, & this morn she gave me the cellophane parcel of perfectly lovely things, how can I thank you for such kindness?! May darling I see the dress is from you & it is simply lovely & Mother, so are the breeks(underwear), a thousand thanks for al!! The alterations to our round guest house are now complete & Joan is so happy to be moving in there; and we have just been given £150 to build another guest house next dry season! I'm going in to Jos tomorrow with David for meetings & to see what news there is of our Fibi; the men sent to collect her left 8 days ago with orders to stop at Enugu for a preliminary overhaul & then drive up to Jos. Now I really must sleep so goodnight with my dearest love to each, with renewed thanks for all your dear letters, and much prayer that you may all know peace and happiness together, yours as ever, Chris.

28 Abbotshall Dr Cults, Aberdeen

2.7.59

My darling Chris we are so very glad to know your car is safely found, & hope it will soon be back with you. Erik has a new car, a Vauxhall Victor Deluxe which he likes and I hope we are to go down home DV in it next Thursday. We do seem to go from one crisis to another these days! You know that Mouse had been in a taxi which crashed & he got away with a cut forehead only; he later went to see the driver in hospital & was told that the poor man never regained consciousness & died from his injuries. And it could so easily have been Mouse too if he had not decided to change seats as soon as he got in! And this morning May rang me to say she'd had to get him to Dorking Hospital where he had an emergency operation for appendix only just in time. He had had a sleepless night with severe pain but it was seen to in time – it was very inflamed but not broken. How thankful I am, that he is alright, recovering well, & that both Anthony & May were able to visit him this evening. And my own trouble is back, as bad as ever, the Dr said there is no disease, but it may well have to be the hysterectomy after I get back up here from my next stay down home at Brookfield. I do hope you are keeping well, with best love from Rene.

Redhill Hospital

July 7th '59

My beloved Chris I am biding my time waiting for the last P. Therapy for my arm & hand tho' it's a shame to be indoors in this glorious weather. I'm ashamed I did not bring you last letter with me although it is of course in my heart. I've been praying for Rene's boys that they might each find and dwell on the things that really matter, the vital realities, especially after Christopher's two escapes from death within one month so recently – surely he must see his life has been spared for a purpose. My heart yearns for The Best for these very dear boys, as for all my beloved grandchildren; the girlfriends and parties seem to take priority, oh dear at times I do feel like a very old fashioned & out of date woman…and there I must leave it. Last week on a very hot day when my kind driver brought me home from here I asked if I could bring him a plate of raspberries. He declined most politely saying he should get on to his next patient, but hesitated & said, "There is one thing, will you pray for me?" Of course I gladly consented! Now perhaps he will be on duty to drive me home today. We shall see; as ever your own loving Mother.

Brookfield

July 9th '59

My darling our weather is the nearest to your particular brand that I've ever known, on those treks we did together 3 yrs ago when I was so very hot…now a shower has just passed through and the smell of it on the hot ground is heavenly…surely I am in Africa again?! At once the sun has come out again, making it even more like Panyam conditions than ever! We've been rejoicing with you over your car recovery & now longing to hear 'Fibi' is safely back with you and in a good condition, proving the Lord really can make good out of evil. Mother has told you of the appendix – right after the taxi crash – & now I can tell you I've just heard again from Barts that they can take me in on the 19th as Mr Hosford is better sooner than expected! That is the very week I'd arranged to take M&F & Rene to Broadstairs but I'll still take them on the 18th & trust Rene will consent, as she needs a holiday as much as anyone, & it was such a miracle that rooms were available at this v. nice Christian place. And, Father is keen to go there (!) for he's convinced we laid out the garden there many years ago. When you next see dear Frances P please do thank her for the lovely card full of her thoughts & prayers for me. I shall be in Paget Ward & I think the op will be on the 21st & I won't be in more than a fortnight; such dear love as ever, May.

Panyam

July 19th '59

My darlings I am wearing today for the first time the lovely gay dress you sent back with Joan; our 2 houseboys were so genuinely pleased when I showed them, telling them it is a gift from May, Yilmak the newer one said, "You have gone back to be like a young girl in it!" Last Sunday we heard such a good word from Keswick – L.F.E. Wilkinson's talk on 'No bucket & the well is deep' I expect you heard it too & I was thinking of dear Ant up there in the audience, as I was 2 yrs previously. After that we heard Billy Graham speaking about Youth. Thank you for your dear & most welcome letters last week, I was so interested to hear of your contact with the ambulance driver Mother, and so sorry to hear of the smash to Evelyn Giles' car & the shock to her and W's girls, but so glad to hear that Christopher is back home & recovering well. We have had visitors all week, some just in for meals, some staying; also much work around the school entrance and leavers' exams and College entrance & nursing training exams & all the necessary reshuffling for that. One girl I'm sure will pass is Toklong, Kefas' little girl – I was very surprised to hear that he had been married as a very young boy before coming to school here in 1950! Most girls are extremely unwilling to go in for Midwifery training thinking it is inferior to Nursing because the general attitude of all young Nigerians now is to aim as high as you possibly can whether or not you have any chance of success! After SS last Sunday afternoon everyone gathered on the playground & we had a praise & re-dedication prayer over Fibi Nanlap (God answered!) she is back in service with us & going splendidly. On Monday we all went down to Chip, had a picnic by the Jibam gorge, then on to Jing for the first football match between Panyam & Jing SP Schools – Jing SP will always be in my mind connected with Dafwash. It was a draw, both teams played very well; now goodbye dear loves, Chris.

Paget Ward, St Bartholomew's Hospital, London

July 24th '59

My dearest darling your dear letter reached me at exactly the right time & it's been wonderful to feel the cushion of love & prayer all around me. Just as I was getting drowsy with the first injection there came these words, "He shall gather the lambs in His arms,' so I was able to rest quietly even tho' it had felt that all the loving support must leave me at the Theatre door & I must go through alone. Right then the Lord assured me I was not alone, He was revealing Life to me, His Eternal Life at that. Sinking into that 'gathering' I lost consciousness. It was dark when I woke, with much more pain & sickness than last time, but they were all so wonderfully kind & helpful; Sister provided a fan which I had on constantly for 48 hrs till my temp came down, I felt greatly blessed. I've been up & walked a bit, washed, & had the stitches out today & expect to be home early next week. There are such nice nurses, not even one hard or nasty one, & I've had so many letters, cards & beautiful flowers. Rene popped in one evening & now it's lovely to think of her with M&F down in Broadstairs in that lovely place. Please thank Joan & Frances for their dear letters, & all who have & are praying. I'm not forgetting your problems darling, always praying your people might choose Life, always May.

Brookfield

Aug 2nd '59

My dearest darling isn't it wonderful that I can write to you again from home, fully dressed & lying out in this lovely sun by the garden house when it was only a fortnight ago today that I went in to Barts! Surely my progress is a gracious answer to the many prayers offered up on my behalf. I feel so much better than I remember feeling after the last one & this op was bigger. The scar is healing beautifully and journey home by train didn't tire me in the least. On Thursday I'm planning to go to Frinton, hoping it might be possible for Rene to join me there for the 2nd week as both her boys will be here then, with Erik expected. My going will help to relieve the congestion here which tends to be a bit overpowering at times especially for R doing all the washing, ironing & cooking. I've been pondering the words: 'The weapons of our warfare are not carnal but mighty through God to the pulling down of strongholds;' I just long for skill & wisdom in the use of these weapons. J.B. Phillips' translation refers to 'deceptive fantasy' & I think that so exactly describes E's condition; I know you join me in prayer for these beloved ones within the family. Thank you, darling for your dear letters & the good news that you're going on holiday with Frances. Did I tell you I had the <u>loveliest</u> flowers from my motor garage, and the Bible Soc. Women's Advisory Council, Sydney & Margaret, and so very many cards & more letters so you'll know how grateful I feel for such blessings, & now with dearest love to you as always May.

Panyam

Aug 6th '59

Darlings there seems just time to scribble my loving greeting once more before my holiday and to thank you Mother for your faithful weekly letters, and to send especially loving greetings to you May dear, I do so hope the pain isn't bothering you so much now & you really are healing up well. How wonderful that you're having this marvellous summer weather! When Fibi was handed over back to me I found the thief had removed the photo from my driving licence so Joan took another of me for the purpose. The more dreadful fact by far is that I had forgotten to re-licence the car at the beginning of this year & never thought of it until filling the form for the new licence to replace the stolen one. I was then sure I'd have to pay a fine but when Peter went to get me the new one in Jos they said nothing. Of course I paid for the full year, being unwilling to 'defraud the public purse'! We are waiting for Joan's new licence – she did pass her test before leaving home, then we shall be all set. Mother I asked Joan if you still listened to Calypso news on TV but the only rhyme I could remember you crooning was, 'Oh I'm an unlucky fellow – I didn't bet on Crepello!' and the one about the Duke of Norfolk but I cannot recall more than 'blues & dues' – can you help?! Joan was charmed to find the 2 solitaire boards, heirlooms from Nakam or the very first missionary here, but neither of us can play it properly finishing in style with just the one marble, preferably in the very centre! You can see I'm planning a little light diversion of the mind for my holiday; with dearest love, Chris.

Allways, Pole Barn Lane, Frinton

Aug 17th '59

My darling I do hope you are having as wonderful a rest on your holiday as I'm having here: breakfast in bed, and supper too if I want it, and motored down to the sea front & collected again at meal times! My hostess is being so very kind & thoughtful & I'm feeling stronger every day & as soon as the stiffness in my neck subsides I shall be quite alright. The only drawback is the Station right opposite with considerable noise from trains etc, but the back garden is charming and much quieter. As I rest, this line of an old hymn keeps going through my mind, 'Make me a captive Lord and then I shall be free' I think it's a G. Mattheson one; such a true paradox of real Christian experience.

Sunday Aug 23rd at home again, well darling that wasn't much of a letter to you was it, but here I am safely back, re-reading your letters. I'm so glad to hear of Nishe's baby Jason thriving so nicely; and how good it is for you to have Joan back again and your good plan for the Quiet Day for Pastors on Sept 10th. Rene & I got back on Thurs after a lovely sunny week of sunshine & sea air, fearing perhaps that dear Joyce who cared for us so well will now be in need of a holiday herself! I am feeling heaps better but the Dr insists I must have at least another fortnight completely off work. I had the dearest letter from Margaret Clark saying she'd heard that a new hat always makes a woman feel better so please would I use the enclosed for that purpose – & my dear, the enclosed was a cheque for £25!!! I felt overwhelmed but I know she only does such things in obedience to what she feels is the Lord's word to her, so I think I should accept it. The Irish trip is quite off, Father deciding he is unable to go anywhere, not even Broadstairs again, unless it is to Rustington once again. I haven't had the chance of a proper talk with Wilfrid which I really feel must happen soon & I know you will want to know what is really happening; as I do. We must make wise plans, and soon, but that continues to be impossible for everything has to be done through solicitors and seems to take an interminable time. I do hope to have more to tell you next time but for now I can only send you my very dearest love as always, your May.

At: Panyam

Sept 21st '59

My dear Chris thank you very much for wonderful hospitality & revival of friendship after so many years; having had this contact with you I'll be able to picture you carrying out such vital work for God.

Your parents would be so proud of you if they could have seen what I have seen & I know you will be blessed and given strength until your work is completed here. Please buy some little luxury <u>for yourself</u> with the enclosed gift. I gave May something for her work and I must equalise the sisters! As you know Govt Officers are well paid & I have no special responsibilities at the moment so life is comparatively easy for me. Don't forget there is a warm welcome for you in Zaria and I do hope you'll be able to fit this in; yours affectionately & gratefully, Margaret.

Brookfield

Sept 22nd '59

My beloved Chris, this week I asked Father if he would sign this when I am finished but he answered, "I think you are better able," you'll remember he has never been fond of letter writing tho' he still loves getting yours & re-reading them. Your news is as always most interesting and it is indeed a fine thing that your Polycarp has been chosen to interpret for Dr Billy Graham in his English speaking Missions in Nigeria in early Feb. Did I read aright that he is to spend some days/weeks in Lagos with Dr G to get the full sense of his messages before the Crusade? What a very fine idea that seems. Might Polycarp's wonderful invitation mean you could go to some of the Meetings? And if your Pastors' Prayer Day had to be postponed for that, I am still quite sure that both will bring much blessing. May has gone off to her first mtg since the op, she is quite fairly well now I am sure; and we have Mrs Waller thanks darling to your kindness, she is a fine worker. We've had Emily S here for a weekend – she has grown <u>very</u> stout – May took her and me to a concert in Horsham to hear Mr W. Brown sing his

German songs with great fervour & beauty. His German pianist played most beautifully, she was middle-aged and fat but no piano playing ever impressed me like hers did, & May was relieved of E's talk while she also sat entranced; it was a very worthwhile occasion. We had a lovely afternoon in Tonbridge at Henry & Peggy's nice bungalow with a sumptuous 5.30pm tea Irish style with bread & butter on the table with a grand lemon tart, & an apple tart, cheese & tomatoes, jam & cake with a big pot of good tea. Here it is, September's almost over but I'm sorry to say we still know no more about this place & what we are to do. It certainly is cheaper for us to continue here while we can for house mortgages do seem very expensive. Mr & Mrs Brooks came to dinner yesterday as they were packing up to leave. I will close now with all the love I can send you, & committing you as always into our Heavenly Father's care, your loving Mother.

Her Majesty's Prison, Mamfe

5.10.59

Dear Miss Chill, Ma, I have the intention of letting you receive my best greetings. I thank God for having let me have the time to write for you should know it was Satan the daivel made me did such a bad act by taking away your car. I have read all the containse of the two books you sent me, warmly received. I have seen all the bad things I have been doing during the passed time so I have come to regret myself upon these wrong doings. I have to beg you Ma, to forgive me of all that I have done for I know that I have sin against God & you Mother I am not worthy to be called your child again please forgive me. Due to your perhaps prayers my sentence has been taken down to 6 month instead of one year, at ending of October I shall be discharging. Please tell my sister that my heart & my mine is now changed and to send some money for transport and some clothes for the clothes I brought in here are all turn. Best Greetings to all people of yours, ever your child Habu Lafia.

[Ed: Chris added 2 notes to the bottom of this letter a) Alias Job Chanding, later in Jos Prison, visited there by me. He did a Bible Study course there. b) After release he was involved in a further robbery in Panyam, attacked, and then died.]

Brookfield

Oct 6th '59

My darling, I want to write now of something very much in my heart. I am wondering if you could possibly consider asking for an early furlough & coming home as soon as possible, November or December. I have delayed asking you, feeling perhaps it was just selfish of me but when I got in last night I found Father had had another of those really bad turns & that Mother had had to cope all on her own till she was able to phone Wilfrid. I do realise that it may seem to you that the very fact that she could eventually get W surely is a case for our carrying on as we are. But I feel M&F will never need you more than they do at this moment & for these coming winter months. I tell you quite honestly if we could manage without my salary I would feel I should resign at once but the hard fact is we cannot live without some money coming in regularly. The other fact, though secondary to M&F's need is that I'm not yet back to where I was before the op & to have all this work to do knowing all the time I should be at home & always wondering what I'm going to find when I do get home is causing additional strain which is hard to bear. It does feel as if these next months are going to be the time of our greatest need. Rene would come down like a shot anytime but I feel strongly that at all costs we must avoid asking her. It just won't do for her to be away from her home for any weeks at a time – unless we want more trouble up there. Darling it is only since I started in to work that I've realised our joint need has so much increased. I know you will think & pray over this & I will also that if it is not the Lord's will for you to come now we will be given some other solution. I haven't mentioned Auntie Jo but she also comes into the picture because somehow I've got to try & persuade her to go to Tim on a definite date in Nov having decided what she wants to take & what she wants done with the rest & generally try to help her over this most difficult step for her. All these circs together do add up to the fact we shall never need you more than we do now; with all my very dearest love & as you know always yours, May.

Panyam

Oct 15th '59

My darlings, this might well reach you at the same time as the one I wrote to May & posted just 2 days ago but I want to let you know that all to whom I have spoken so far: Joan, Joyce, the Batchelors, Pastor David, the Wilmshursts, all agree that I ought to go home to you as soon as possible. So I am going on in faith & making preparations & asking that if this is not the Lord's will then He will show some other way. I have written to Bill Tett asking him to get an air booking for me as soon after Nov 4th as possible; so it may be that we will be seeing each other in about 3 wks time! Yesterday I went to Mongu & had tea with

Frances & a time of prayer over the whole matter; I wish you could've heard the loving way she prayed round you all & the problems especially lifting May up. Going on to Gindiri – my first visit in over 3 mths – & met Brenda Moore our new Nursing Sister. After the necessary Comm mtg etc I was invited to the Wilmshursts for supper & we had a pleasant time. By 6.30 this morning I was at the house where Brenda was staying to collect her & the car & we got back here for breakfast since which she's been in Joyce's hands being shown the ropes; she is a student of Redcliffe Bible College & a keen nurse & midwife and seems really nice. This afternoon I got a distress message from the Canadian Doctor at Pankshin who had his wife & young daughter with him in a car that just broke down out on the road to Chip. That's the first time I've ever driven towing another car & the rope broke 3 times but we fixed it & managed quite well; such a nice family & so grateful for the help. Now Father I pray you'll be kept till we meet DV and darlings all it's time for my bed as I must be up betimes tomorrow & breakfast by 5.15 so goodnight and blessings on you each one as ever yours lovingly, Chris.

28 Abbotshall Dr. Cults, Aberdeen

17.10.59

Darling Chris I think so much of you & pray constantly that you will have clear light upon your way after receiving May's letter; it won't be easy for you. Mouse was at home last week & told me he thought I should go back down there and May, who says they are managing, is to ring me this evening with her decision. If she really does want me then of course I shall put off Dorothy S and the Camerons due here next week & weekend, & get the next available train down. The enclosed is a tiny remembrance for your birthday darling, sorry it is so small. We are struggling along here but there seem to be 'many adversaries' at least in my own life just now but God is a very present help. My dearest love & hoping you are keeping well & that all will work out for the best, ever & always yours, Rene.

Brookfield

Oct 18th '59

My darling thank you from my heart for your letter yesterday & for all it meant to me. In the meantime it seemed Elizabeth the Danish nurse currently with A Jo might be willing to stay on till March but no, she is not. Oh darling may it be God's will to get you home soon. Father is weakening, for now when the palps finish he is left with pain in his chest. However, we all know what the Cheals are for willpower & recovering quickly after bad attacks of anything really! Mother has aged since she was alone with him during the last bad attack and I do know that for them to see you come home next month & thus see them through the winter would be the sweetest blessing they could receive from the Lord's hand, the lifting of a heavy burden from Mother. But darling I do know it will be hard for you, and not your own choice to leave at this time. For me it would be just wonderful to have your help & advice about everything in connection with the move as well as all other things. I don't think it's any good trying to get a foreign girl to come & live in for it's only the young ones who want to & they are all nervous of illness; an older more capable woman would expect £3 or £4 per week. I shall be thinking of you on the 21st as you talk with Joyce & perhaps with Bill Tett too; and I am so glad Frances is nearer to you now & you can talk with her, please give my love to her, & Joan & Brenda & I pray that you'll all have the gift of peace in whatever decision you make; my hearts love darling, ever yours, May.

Brookfield

Oct 24th '59

My beloved Chris you really are coming – I can scarcely take it in but you will know how thankful we are that all seems to have gone so smoothly with goodwill from all your fellow workers. Just after receiving your precious letter we had visitors to tea so I had to try to appear quiet while underneath my thoughts were going, 'Chris really is coming home DV & in only about 2 weeks!' I think almost more for May's sake than anyone I am truly thankful for she has plunged back into such hard work & I can't help wondering if she's going to get through with it she looks so weary & spent at the end of each day. It is a joyful thought that you will soon be here to help. We shall pray much my darling love in your very busy time of preparations ahead for all needed strength & wisdom to be yours that you may leave with a quiet mind, & may the Lord in His great mercy grant you a safe journey & bring you to us in peace. Now, in spite of our advising Rene to stay in Aberdeen she has written saying she will come at any time and as often as necessary because it is alright with Erik as he knows of our need here, and a card today says she'll be here on Weds. One more most unexpected happening this week, although not of course unexpected to the Lord, a man came to visit Wilfrid as he'd heard there was Nursery land or plant stocks for sale...and if it was already sold could he buy it back...etc...W said he should know that we do not do business on

Sunday, to which this man replied, "That's a change, not many say so these days, my client is also a Christian." Cannot write any more now for I do not know more yet; perhaps we can talk it through when you get here, so much dearest love & longing from your Mother.

Brookfield

Oct 29th '59

My very dear darling I do hope this will reach you in time to bring you my most loving thoughts & best wishes for a very happy birthday on the 4th there will be a gift here when you come home. I am most deeply grateful to you darling for believing it right to come home now; I hardly dare think of all it means to you in terms of arrangements for all your work & leaving the people who are your family in God without time for proper farewells, but my heart is with you and my prayers. May you be encouraged and not burdened as you leave them. The few to whom I have spoken here also feel certain it is the right thing for you to be coming home at this juncture & I trust it will prove so as we go on step by step. I am troubled because Rene has come home again although I am thankful beyond words to have her here. If you arrive before 11am on the 11th I'll meet you at the Airport, but if it's later will you catch a bus to Victoria & I'll meet you there before going on to Bible House where I have to report in to a comm. mtg for the afternoon. Thank you my darling with all my heart for coming, I pray you have peace of heart & a safe quiet flight, May.

~ ~ ~ ~ ~

SUM Jos

12 Jan 1960

Dear Chris just a note to thank you for the photos & to say it was charming to be back in Panyam again, Ed Smith & I shared the Garden Hut and Winnie, Joan, Brenda & Isobel cared for all of us white folk lavishly & skilfully. The Africans all got 3 meals a day and were obviously impressed and we all shared tea together. The general effect of the Conference was most encouraging; the Sunday communion service was beautifully conducted by the Sura Pastors. I do hope your father is keeping better, my greetings to your mother & him and your sisters. You would have been proud of Panyam – I was, yours sincerely HG Farrent.

Panyam Senior Primary School

Jan 22nd 1960

Dear Miss Cheal thank you for your interesting letter to me this morning; yes I am preparing to leave for Lagos now and I will send with this a copy of my programme of meetings early next month with Dr Billy Graham at which I am honoured to be Interpreter. My great encouragement is that many people are praying for me and I know the Lord will be with my mouth Ex. 4:12 so I ask Him to be in my brain also to prepare the words in my mind quickly to cope with Dr Graham's speed, & that I will have enough voice to stress what is to be stressed. My Hausa may not be quite as good as the Hausas there but they will understand. Panyam is alright, Panle died outside Church, Yitbak's wife was refused employment for Kabwir, and TEKAS was a great blessing, yours in a hurry Polycarp Fian.

SUM Jos

Feb 15th '60

Dear Chris I know you are on furlough but amongst all the business items I must tell you about I know you will want to hear about last week's meetings at which thousands gathered on the polo grounds in orderly rows on the grass. Lots had come from far away places, one train load of fully 500 travelled several days. Hymn sheets with Hausa & English words were used & a good loudspeaker enabled all to hear well. You will know how biblical, forceful & understandable Billy Graham's messages can be – for nearly 40 minutes he held forth and 'your' SUM Mr Polycarp, a fine Sura Christain, interpreted sentence by sentence and he was excellent. No stumbling, a faithful interpretation and just as forceful as Dr Graham himself. I was greatly blessed to be listening and to be present at this greatest gathering Jos or the North has ever known; such a testimony to all of the firm hold Christianity now has in this country. At the last meeting nearly 500 came forward, a few of them being white people & there was a big organisation of counsellors & follow up teams. It was a most blessed week & I thank God for the privilege of witnessing it & taking part; yours CD.

Panyam SP School

4th October 1960

Dear Miss Cheal we heard the good news that you are looking forward to coming back here & moreover that you might be here soon. Independence is the talk of the day in Nigeria at the moment but I don't feel any difference yet anyway we are grateful to the Lord that it was achieved without bloodshed. The change is that Gwoza is cut off from N Nigeria – perhaps Nigerians would need a passport to go there now! During my stay in Kaduna I observed that the Sardauna himself is a good man, a God-fearer yet a non-Christian but some other Moslems only follow the religion blindly with much beer drinking etc. One of them told me that when the old Moslem men die they would be free to follow any religion they choose. Many of the educated men & women are dissatisfied with Islam, so Freedom of Religion may serve the purpose. Greetings to your parents & other family we pray for them always, Polycarp Fian Datok.

35 The Millbank, Ifield

Nov 2nd 1960

My darling Chris the first time writing to you from this new address, our new home; and your departure day has come, and is bright! Thank you for everything you have done for us this year of furlough – not much rest for you but a lot of happiness for us all, & we will remember Dr B's words about the inward power of nature (which to you & me means God) gives for times of need. Afresh let us again hand over our lives to Him, thanking Him for the joy & peace He gives so abundantly & that we can continue to count on His Everlasting Love. Afresh I commit you into His loving care, continually praying that He will fit you, find you usable for His work in Nigeria, and bless you above all asking. I send you all our dearest love & very best wishes for a happy birthday on the 4th with many happy returns that this coming year might be the most fruitful, bringing the greatest joy & honour to our Lord Jesus. Thank you for the love you have showered upon us, the PATIENCE so needed now in my deafness; you know how much I thank God for the gift of such a loving daughter; I will remember the times we have laughed together, the rides we have taken enjoying all the beauties of His handiwork. Be happy about us here, I think all will go well, and if the Lord wills it we will be here to greet you with joy when you next return. Did He not cause us to triumph throughout our farewells due I'm sure to the prayers of so many dear ones? I know you will go on praying for our dear Rene who writes so sweetly about some church folk up there now talking to her & being so kind. Darling it was very stormy in the night but I knew that might not be your portion; I was awake once or twice so kept committing you afresh to the Lord's care & keeping. I do hope Frances P was there to meet you. We will wait eagerly for your first letter. Forgive the jumble of this letter for my thoughts do keep running up to Aberdeen; but darling my warmest thanks to you for all your wonderful help to us over the packing and move and settling into this new little place & Father joins me adding in his thanks, love & greetings to mine, ever your loving Mother.

28 Abbotshall Dr. Cults Aberdeen

Nov 2nd '60

Darling once again the parting has come I'm sure none of can take it in really yet that you've had to leave; how deeply you will be missed & <u>often</u> longed for; but how wonderful it has been that you have so willingly & gladly been able to stay for this whole year. I pray for you safe journeying, with an abiding sense of God's presence all the way; & my dearest love & prayers will surround you both in the goodbyes and in the welcomes as you arrive back in Panyam & of course especially on the 4th! Ever your loving Rene, Rom 8:35-39 & 2 Cor 13:14.

35 The Millbank, Ifield, Nr Crawley

Nov 2nd 1960

My very dear darling this is to wish you a deeply happy birthday with a year of rich blessing to follow. From the very beginning of this tour I do pray you might have those tokens to confirm you are in the place of God's choice for you. I cannot begin to put into words all that your presence has meant to me in this year & how deeply grateful I am for <u>all</u> you have done. You tackled all the hard things so cheerfully & took the initiative in those difficult first approaches so willingly and I want you to know I shall never cease to remember & give thanks for <u>you</u> and all you are & do. Now may the Lord multiply to you His grace which is sufficient for every need and keep us rejoicing together in His love & care; always yours with all my love, May.

Daffo, Mongu then Panyam

Nov 6-8th '60

My darlings how marvellous to remember last Sunday & all we were doing together & that super supper, & here I am back again as if I'd never been away! However it does feel rather as though I was shot from one world into another with hardly time to think. Such wonderful welcomes from so many, & at Barakin Ladi new Post Office I noticed at once the colour of the Formica counter the same as ours in the Millbank! I gave the rose tree to Frances, was greeted by Mwantet, then here found waiting David, old Father Lot, Yariyep, Bitrus Bishtu, Polycarp & crowds of others all asking warmly about you all. Sadly I had to disappear fast with the inevitable result of a bad head from all the travel & excitement, but after a lie down was soon quite alright again in good time for great welcome/birthday celebrations to which your choc. biscuits Mary made a great addition! I wish you could all have heard the heartfelt praying at the evening PM where every woman prayed for you, especially from Victoria Nasik & Unaisi, 'Be their Protector night and day,' was one I recall. In Daffo I had to speak at the afternoon mtg & chose Sura with Manasseh interpreting, as I felt unable to embark on Hausa right away. Josh. 24:15 'as for me & my house…' about the witness & habits of a Christian home & family, saying quite a lot about you! So thank you Mother & Father for making that possible. The roses are thriving & all sprouting buds in this heat. As I look back on our last days together I marvel that we were all so wonderfully upheld, I thought the calmness & lack of tension was quite remarkable. In past years I have felt it so keenly both for myself & for each of you particularly Mother who this time was magnificent, Father too in his quiet way – 'what wonders prayer hath wrought'! This afternoon I am to give the girls a demonstration of use of the car tools & how to change a tyre; we are all drivers here now but if either of the newest ones found a flat tyre, well, they need to learn! This is all for this time, with so very much love to each of you & a little extra to Mary with your journeyings, speaking & all care of M&F & the house, Chris.

35 The M

Nov 22nd '60

My darling Chris how lovely to have 2 letters & all so interesting, we are very grateful to you for writing as you do. Your letters give me a longing to do something here to interest these women in the work you are doing but I feel it must be done carefully & prayerfully for unless the Lord commands all else will fail. And of course I must think of Mary (it seems to fit that I call her Mary now not May) and not give her any extra anxiety. She keeps well but still looks to me so tired, I wish she could rest, but the Lord has His own way of bringing rest to His children. The Dr has been again to see Father, urging him to stay in his dressing gown but walk about the house a bit more to help his breathing. M insists upon keeping the heating on 'low' for our comfort, oh & she asks me to tell you the Title deeds for this house are complete & now lodged in the Bank so everything is finished up. I am so very glad that all the time & trouble you took over the tape recordings here has been appreciated there & I did enjoy reading about Katya & his family. Our speaker last Sunday read out twice, 'Ye must be born again' but was unconvincing, I must ask him if he means by that the same as we do; much dear love from Mother.

Bornehurst, Bexley

Nov 30th '60

Darling if my writing is more scrawley than usual it's because I'm in the car (inside light gone) under a lampost with 20 mins to spare before going in to a meeting. I've been at Bible House this aft then picked up the car again at Croydon & came on here. I have to speak to the Methodist Young Wives at 8pm but there's a noisy gathering of youth in the Hall at the moment so there'll be a good fug by the time we're finished! It has been so lovely to get these frequent letters from you, thank you darling, Mother is positively lifted be each one & each is such a cheer to Father who is so poorly then much brighter by turns almost every day now. I only have 10 more mtgs until Dec 13th the last until after Christmas I'm thankful to say. Our new little garden has some lovely chrysanths & I picked some for a vase before leaving this morning; and I must get some thick stuff for the bathroom windows for it is draughty these nights in the bath! And I must get Waites back in to see about the water that comes through the lounge wall under the big window whenever it rains. Dear old Uncle E's money has at last come in to the Bank & I am so very thankful for it & will of course check your account too. I've paid Rene hers & now have about £400 left all told so I believe we shall be enabled to get through this winter even with the high bills for the heating on to keep M&F comfortable. Now darling please take good care on these long drives you seem to be doing; always yours with all love, Mary.

35 The M

Dec 6th '60

My beloved Chris how diligent the devil is yet I know you will be given the wisdom to deal with these ongoing disturbances relating to those who make, sell & drink the intoxicating gruel – how you are needed there! We shall seek to be more diligent & better helpers in prayer for I know this all brings sorrow to your heart, as it does to mine, to see those you have raised and taught slipping back into their heathen ways. You have this enormous task in shepherding them & caring for their souls, to speak out clearly the error of their ways as you urge them to seek help from the One Who died for them to bear such burdens. I know you will be helped to do this in the best possible way. Did Mary tell you of the filmstrip she recently showed at one of her mtgs, 'The Modern Miracle in Borneo? The people were so given over to drunken immorality & unhealthiness that the govt called them a dying race. Then 2 missionaries went & today 90% of the people are joyous, clean, witnessing Christians; they have wonderful Bible Schools there to which thousands come & the 4yr course is always full & overflowing. The explanation given is sound teaching, wholehearted following of the Lord Jesus & the church leadership training available. Well my darling may that be of encouragement to you to keep going with all you already do and keep trusting God for His good results. There is much could be written about Father's erratic condition and the Doctor's visits & new pills and urging us to go out a little more on fine days, and this day F does look a quite brighter but we must not dwell too much on his ailments – as we old people are in the habit of doing. Our times are in His hands; but when F is distressed & in pain I trust He will spare him a lengthy lingering on; now with all the love I can send in this short letter & blessings on you that you will be held in peace; ever your loving Mother.

Panyam

Dec 20th '60

My darlings there is just time for a quick note which I hope will reach you to bring so very much love from me to you over Christmas. I shall be thinking of you altogether for Tea at 35 The M. I wish you could hear the recording, made here – I hope you soon will, of the 10min message David was asked to prepare for Broadcasting on Christmas Day; he showed me what he has written & it is beautiful with very few corrections necessary. I have sent a copy of it to Nakam as it also contains greeting to her from the GLB girls & me, and have asked her to send it on to you, it really is so lovely. The lovely calendar from the Ifield Friends has arrived & is so very nice especially with all the signatures, thank you. Please tell them how much I appreciate it. We had a visit from Prof. Spencer & Mrs., from Ibadan University where he lectures in Phonetics, brought to us by one of our Sura fellows, a student there Ayuba Tense. He had told them I am an expert in Sura (!) so they came to ask if I would go to a Conference on African Languages to be held in Ghana about next Easter! I should be very pleased to go but of course it depends whether my Mission would give their permission. A new tape recorder is available in Jos for £21 & I'm wondering about getting it with Uncle Willie's money. Dearest love to you each one as ever your Chris.

35 The M

Dec 21st '60

Darling love it is a tremendous comfort to have Rene here – the Doctor said I should call for her 'at once' last week when Father was really bad (again) and we all thought (again) that it was the end but he has rallied (again) albeit only a little, he sleeps a lot but then rouses himself & wants to hear the News on & even attempts some of the crossword but then usually calls for Mother to bring her Bible & read to him – she remains wonderfully quietly serene. Our Christmas – for which nothing has been prepared – might not be quite like usual, dear R is trying faithfully to be of cheer & certainly looking forward as we all are to Ant's arrival. She was so wise to ask the District Nurse what we'd all been wondering – if she would come at the very end to help us and she said yes & that she could be here within the hour whenever we rang for her. It is so lovely having R and Father was so pleased to see her. We both feel quite sure that whatever happens, you did the right thing in going when you did it was <u>no</u> mistake, because you are so depended upon there especially with all the troubles at Chip. You do not seem far away for our hearts are knit. R sends her dearest love & tells you she is glad to be here & will not leave till after New Year. If the Lord does not take F when R has to go & my meetings start up again then I will trust Him for some other provision for our need. Although I cannot feel at all festive I do know that all shall be well and am sending you my heart's love, with blessings untold upon you my darling, ever your Mary.

Panyam

Dec 24TH '60

Darlings my heart has been with you & lifted up so often for you, my thoughts & love go winging away to you so very often & how I wish it were possible to phone or look in on you; but I know that our times are in His hands and all will be well.

Christmas Day & no doubt our prayerful thoughts have again met today at the Throne of Grace. It is 9.45 & I'm in my room as the others have all gone to bed, I'm picturing Mary & Rene sitting by the fire now & I do trust you have all had a happy day. Ours started as usual with the very early carol-singers, and Church was completely full & we all rejoiced at the marvellous sermon on John 3:16 preached by Bitrus Yamden, as invited by Pastor David. In Jos I did buy the Grundig Cub tape recorder brand new with all accessories for £19 & today have recorded some lovely singing. This eve I took the 2 visiting girls to a Fulani compound just across the river; Anna, being the vet. surgeon was particularly interested in their cattle. The other is Jean Cameron from Cheadle who I met at the Aberlour Crusader Camp; they'll both be at Gindiri when their language studies in Kano are finished.

28th: Francis Naule who has been on holiday here returns to the Eye hospital at Kano; he makes lenses & frames so he is taking my broken pair in for new frames which is such a help & he will post this. On our way to Tahas the girls & I stopped at an outstation by the road to greet them in their Christmas celebrations. I was distressed to find a motley crowd of heathens & beer drinkers mixed up with the Christians but managed to push my way through to speak to the Evangelist Habila about it. He explained that a truculent backslider had brought this rabble along deliberately to wreck the Christians' Christmas party, and he would not go away, so we took Habila on into Tahas to report to the

Senior Teacher there. Now dears please will you write to me even a line or two as often as you possibly can with updates on Father; my special prayer at this time for F & for all of you of course, is that the Lord will wrap you round with His loving kindness and take away any & all fear and distress; so goodbye for now with such very dear love to you all each one from your Chris.

35 The Millbank

Dec 25th '60

My beloved Chris we hope you have had a happy Christmas. Your dear letter came with the news of Ghana; I hope you will go for I feel the Mission will not hinder you. We had a nice card from Mr & Mrs Farrant, the first time he has sent to us. Father came down for half an hour by the fire & we saw & heard the Queen's speech which was good but he is back asleep again now. He saw Wilfrid & family yesterday; of course it is also an unusual Christmas for them now living in Brookfield. We opened our presents in relays today; I am wearing your lovely nightie this evening; Barbara gave Mary a grand wooden 'dryer' (electric) for clothes but so far they can't work it – Wilfrid said Gates had fixed it so that may explain the reason!

26th: the vacuum has just stopped, much work going on in the kitchen, the Brookfield family coming to high tea at 5.30pm with a few quiet games after and the Doctor expected later on he is on duty all day.

31st: Father has just seen in the paper the news of Pastor David receiving the MBE please tell him how glad we are, we send our warm congratulations. We had such a thrill last evening when Rene answered the door ring – a lovely bunch of chrysanthemums delivered for Father

& the card said, 'From the Scandinavian Church Folks' and we felt it showed their love & appreciation for our dear Rene. We will phone but Father says I must also write, he added, "words run off your pen like water" but I tell him it is not so easy as all that. He looks fairly well but is a good deal thinner & frail, still with little appetite. I now sleep very well indeed the pills at night give me sleep which makes all the difference in the day time tho' I hope & pray I may not get an addict! I think I mean addiction; now with very dear love, as always Mother.

Panyam

Jan 6th 1961

My darling ones, my last to you was written while waiting on the road for the GLB girls but after 2 hrs with no sign of them I returned here. The naughty girls didn't leave Kabwir till nearly 7am so didn't get to Pankshin till midday, spent the night there with someone they knew so not back here till the next afternoon. I got into a lot of trouble with their parents for I was at least partially responsible for their safety; it made me feel I would never try to take them out anywhere again. In past years our girls walked from here to Kabwir in the day then back again at the end of Camp, but not now – things are changing! At the end of the earlier Camp a dreadful quarrel broke out between the Kabwir girls & ours; our 13 came up sobbing saying they were going home there & then for the others had called them 'dogs' & cursed them & their mothers. We managed to get them together and after an apology grudgingly given & received, relatively calm dispersal, but what a sad end to such a good time of 'fellowship'! It was lovely for me to get all your dear letters though long delayed perhaps by the Airways strike, & to hear of all the loving gifts & remembrances for your first Christmas at 35. It isn't remarkable really for you are just reaping what you have been sowing all these many years into the hearts & lives of so many folk, but it is lovely all the same! Next week I leave for the TEKaS Conference in Mkar near Makurdi; David & Manasseh, Victoria Nasik & I are the 4 delegates going this year. Joan is having a much needed holiday.

8th now & I'm on the verandah watching the beautiful sun set. The roses I brought out with me have done marvellously well & beside me is a crimson Josephine Bruce, Pres. Hoover was the first to bloom, & Peace is coming on nearly ready. I told you Evelyn Goldstein is staying here writing her book; this aft. I took her out to Pushit for the aft service, Enid is away in Fibi so we cycled, it's only 3 miles. I suggested she might give them a word so she gave her testimony in full & Ishaku Dabiring interpreted into Sura. It was most moving; she was converted from Judaism while at Teacher Training in Roehampton & had such a lot of bitter ostracism to face from her parents. Everyone listened intently & Ishaku added a fine postscript then Jacob prayed beautifully. Yest evening a very young fellow came up from Jibilik with his day old daughter in a small box on his head; his little wife had died in childbirth, her first baby after just one year of marriage. It was so pathetic to see him thus bereaved with this tiny helpless mite & no-one to feed her. Joyce is in her element now looking after her but we need a permanent foster mother & a good supply of milk. All the relatives are heathen & the father cannot trust them as they would leave it out to die, as has happened to many another motherless infant. We have 2 couples desperate to adopt but it seems harsh to ask the poor father just yet; as ever Chris.

35 The M

Jan 11th '61

My darling these are such strange days – we've moved into another year, and a different house and yet without much significance for I find caring for Father day and night sometimes not just wearying but just continuous. I was so thankful it was I who was with him not Mother – who slept through it – when the most recent horrible loss of consciousness happened. He is better since. Thank you for both their birthday messages, always so warmly appreciated from you as you know. The good thing is I have no urgent mtgs for the next 10dys so I can stay in most of the time thus freeing dear Rene who is leaving today, not really knowing how she will find things once she gets to her home, but she will come back at the end of the month DV. Her boys might be able to be here for this weekend. The Dr pops in almost daily & did bring in a specialist to examine Father's throat to see if there was anything (malignant?) in there stopping him swallowing, and causing his significant weight loss, but all is clear he assures us. Your letters continue to cheer us all, thank you so much & the news of Pastor David foregoing his salary so that 5 new outstations can now be opened is simply wonderful!

15th: And how we have talked over you & Victoria N sharing that guest room at the HQ, she who had not ever slept between sheets before nor used a flush toilet – blessings on her what fun you had together, what stories she will have to tell her family! It was so good to hear of the young Jiblik girl related to the grieving father, who has now taken on the care of the newborn in the father's house, we give thanks for that; yours forever and aye darling, Mary.

Panyam

Feb 16th 1961

Darlings there is just time to tell you a little of the trip to Abwor with Joyce, for Mary will be able to picture the school room where we were camping and how the meeting for the morrow was brought forward by Victoria to just right then as their food was not ready! So we talked through all the 'business' matters till after 10pm when I was then invited to go & share their meal but I was no longer hungry so, after a drink of coffee & some bread & butter, I thankfully lay down. Then found that for the first time ever I'd forgotten my mosquito net! I heard no buzzing, only a mouse nibbling something nearby. Several of the women came back & slept in the school room with me on their mats on the bare floor. Next morning it was cold with a strong wind; John Mark's sister Tabita was the main hostess & she had been up since 4am preparing for all the large numbers of visitors. By 9.30 she had a wonderful meal ready: rice cooked beautifully with butter and meat, and their usual porridge with lots of red pepper! The gathering lasted from 10am-2.15pm with much discussion on the committee's suggestions particularly concerning the new Orphans Home. One dear old lady had walked from Niyes to Abwor (about 13mls) praying all along, 'Lord You can help me.' I was able to ease her return with a lift in Fibi & when she got out at Niyes she did a little dance in the middle of the road for joy & gratitude! Tomorrow I hope to go to Jos to fetch iron rods & aluminium roofing and to see about air travel to Ghana & whether my passport is in order for there. I do hope you enjoyed the newest tape & could understand Tony Berry's broad Yorkshire telling of that funny story. I trust you are all doing well especially you Father dear, may every blessing of peace & strength & comfort be given you, with my dearest love, Chris.

Dungate Manor, Reigate Heath

26.2.61

Chris dear your Christmas letter was so good to have, thank you. It was a great joy to have dear Rene with us last Sunday, how we long & pray for an easing of her hard way; it seems such a strange impasse which only our loving Lord can show the way through. I always ask Him to give me a special word for each year as it opens & this year it was clearly just 'Yes, Lord' and I've learned so much from it already for it seems to come into everything as I continue learning that immediate, willing obedience. Especially when I find my initial reaction is 'No!' Isn't He so wonderfully patient in our oft repeated silliness?! Now dear Chris God be with you in all that you do, giving you wise love and loving wisdom as you reach out and touch so many lives – may He fill all our lives with His loving Holy Spirit so much that it overflows; my dear love to you and my prayers, very lovingly, Madge Drake.

35 The M

Feb 26th '61

My dearest darling, no need to apologise for more long gaps for you know my heart well! Besides your photo on the mantelpiece is...what do you think?! About 10 perfectly heavenly primroses which I stopped to pick in my special spot on my way back from Southampton. I fairly shouted a greeting to them as soon as I saw them up along the bank! We've already had one or two such lovely spring days, & on one

I took Father out for a little ride which he really enjoyed. It has been so good having Rene here but she had to go home suddenly on Friday because Mouse developed some sort of horrible poisoning after being pecked by a chicken (Mother thinks it to be Tetanus which used to be considered fatal?) but he seems to have recovered quite quickly.

Wilfrid & Barbara have taken NonaJane to Ramsgate this weekend for David's confirmation by the Archbishop. Poor W has had one of his worst kinds of bad head, perhaps due to the re-selling of the Nurseries by auction now set for March 16th. It is apparently to be sold off divided into several land sections I understand. Darling I hope the plans for your Ghana visit are going well & that the trip will be stimulating & truly beneficial. I've a busy month ahead too so we'll remember each other; blessings on you darling & masses of love as always, Mary.

Panyam

March 12th 1961

My darlings I do enjoy getting all your dear letters, thank you each one so very much. Please pray with me that God will lead the Chip church elders to set a better example to those of the Sura & Munpun churches as I have a strong suspicion they are all somehow involved in the making, selling & consuming the wretched intoxicating gruel. They need to return to His Way of no compromise & a purer dedication in all habits of life. The next thing after our Convention is my trip to Ghana; the plane leaves Jos on Monday afternoon for Lagos but I can't leave there until Tues aft; the return fare is £58.16! My address there will be: c/o Commonwealth Hall, University College of Ghana Legon Ghana. Dr Armstrong has asked me to bring my Sura dictionary with me – what a strange journey it will have from our kitchen table at Brookfield where most of it was typed, all the way to the UC of Ghana! On the way back from Chip with a carful of people we had two punctures & were again blessed to have menfolk on board to help! The second one occurred at a lovely spot near Jing known as Cold Stream; the water was handy for mending the tyre & also for tea. Florence, Joyce, Enid & I gathered sticks & made fire and had coffee ready – there was no tea left – for when the repair was completed. Some things now which might surprise you: four Africans are now members of the Field committee – I hope there will soon be more. And we are to have a single man here from next month on, a veterinary surgeon called Tom Owens, Welsh, at present on language study in Kano. Don't quite know what we'll give him to do but I'm sure he'll be useful. He's a brother of Dilys Cotton at Gindiri and Maurice Cotton is on the Comm & suggested he should come here. Also, we have been asked to start a Leper Colony in NE Bornu on the shores of Lake Chad, supervised from Maiduguri. It will be very close to the new Fisheries programme; Jacob Lot has a good position there & wants others from Chip to help him start a Christian community there. As you can imagine much laughter has come from Fish & Chips! Now from a sore mouth after losing yet another of my few remaining molars, sending as always my dear love Chris.

35 The M

Mar 20th '61

My darling love I'm thinking so much of you on your flights & journeyings, wondering if you're actually there yet, if you have a comfortable bed, & if you've met up with any Ghanaians and University folk yet? I do pray it will prove to be a most worthwhile experience for you. Can you picture all the forsythia that's round the front door here & under the lounge window? The wonderful warm days have turned it from its dead twig state into a laden mass of glorious yellow blooms; the pansies next to it have come out and even a few lily of the valley too. But in all that lovely time I didn't get any gardening done myself. By the time I've cleaned & cooked & written even some of the mountain of BS work letters & played Scrabble with Mother there is nothing of me or time left. There have been so many normal mtgs plus many extra paperwork & responsibilities & mtgs for me since our lovely Regional Secy died in his car of a sudden heart attack. He was the best older Anglican on staff and will be much missed. At a Coffee Morning near Banstead last week the Rev there was so charmingly pleasant to me & seemed avidly interested, clearly thinking I was you. When I explained he visibly lost interest & walked off, so darling if you ever meet him you'll have no need to mind approaching him!! Mother will have told you of F's recent bad turn yet again, tho' not as bad as the awful time; he's stayed in bed looking so poorly for several days now. You have asked me to tell you of the gas bills etc but the quarters for it and the electricity do not coincide so it won't be easy to work out for the year. This warm spell has of course helped, but for Nov-Feb the gas is just over £16. But, it has been wonderful to see the publicity given to the new translation of the NT and the Daily Telegraph's whole page advert giving parallel verses of the AV and the new one. And it's very encouraging that stocks in the ordinary book shops have been sold out within an hour & so on. I think I agree with M who is not so fond of the Lord's Prayer in the new version but feels we must not criticise at all but let the words make their own appeal – perhaps many people who have never bothered to read the Authorised version now will be able to understand better in the new. It is past 11pm now so I'll do as you always tell me & try to get to sleep; take especially good care of yourself there my darling, my heart is ever yours, Mary.

Ghana

March 22nd 1961

Darlings here I am safe & sound, and so cheered to find your letters waiting here for me – thank you! The Mannings were kindness itself & I really enjoyed my stay with them in Lagos en route, it was a really happy time together. They had a copy of the New English NT and I lent them my copy of the Amplified NT in return until I get back. Arriving in Accra I had to go through Customs & change money & so on then got a taxi for the 4miles to this magnificent modern University with beautiful spacious Halls & Residential Buildings with huge gardens with fountains & flowering shrubs, no expense spared & at night lights blazing everywhere. A young American woman met me & showed me to the Women's Hall where I have a lovely room to myself with marble-like floor, whitewashed walls and polished wood furniture. Bathrooms are palatial with baths/ showers & hot & cold water in abundance. Margaret Dykstra of Lupwe is also on this corridor so we see plenty of each other. A tutorial class was just starting when I arrived so I joined them at it; Dr Armstrong the phonetics teacher from Ibadan who is in charge of this course, welcomed me then went right on with his lecture. I was at once out of my depth in a subject I've never touched before; the chapter heading was: 'Classing Allomorphs into Morphemes' and they were discussing such things as a 'voiceless labio-dental slit fricative'!! With the help of a Linguistics volume priced 48/- and a workbook priced 20/- which I was given, I have been trying to tag along and learn something of what they were talking about. Today I've spent much time studying phonetic script, and what morphemes and phonemes really are, then another class this afternoon which left me feeling even more sunk in ignorance. The Ford Foundation is paying all expenses for this Course & Language Congress for the 80 people expected & one professor has just arrived in from the USA.

23rd now the weather here is very warm & humid like Lagos but utterly different from Panyam just now. It is nice to have one's skin soft & hair fluffy again. I hope to get down to the sea sometime. Hurrah, just met up with the Taylors at breakfast who've invited me to join them on a run to Tema the great new harbour that's being developed about 25miles from here. So goodbye for now darlings, take care of your dear selves; I was thinking much about the Nurseries sale yesterday and Nona's birthday, yours Chris.

University of Ghana

March 28th '61

My Darlings, here's a second attempt to let you share in some of this most interesting experience with me. I met Prof Joseph Greenberg from Columbia University USA who concentrates on W. African languages & was keen to see my dictionary. He was intrigued by the Sura proverbs that rhyme in tone pattern & asked me to write an article on them for him to publish in some highbrow American magazine. This I have done, and given him a copy of my dictionary. The Taylors took me to the Methodist Church of Ghana for a lovely (tho' long as it was in English as well as Ga language) Palm Sunday service, where I'd hoped to meet Rev Bannerman, the Ga Meth minister who was in Crawley helping Mrs Galliers, do you recall?! Unfortunately he was in Toma, where I'd been earlier in the week! But I did meet up with Mrs Dagadu who was quite charming. Our first official session was on Sunday at 2pm and discussed papers written on language distribution and grammatical & phonetic similarities & comparisons from wide areas across the Ivory Coast, Togo, Ghana, Nigeria and some even in

French! I do not begin to understand much of the technicalities and yet we are all united, equal members as it were of knowledge & experience in one or more of these African languages. It is great fun to be amongst & meet such variety of students, professors, missionaries, doctors, teachers, administrative workers, Africans, Europeans, Americans, both Protestant and RC. Dr Abraham is also here, the British expert who has published classical dictionaries & grammars in several important languages including Hausa. He told me he knew about 60 languages! He looks as old as Father but is now studying the Ibo tongue. On Sunday eve the Ghana Govt invited us all to a Reception at the Ambassador Hotel in Accra; it was on the roof of this very posh place, from which we got a fine view over the city & 5 ships lit up in the Bay. I met two African Christians, one of whom is from near Mamfe so of course I told the story of Fibi; yours C.

35 The M

April 3rd '61

My darling love we do hope you had a very happy Easter Day yesterday and that perhaps you are back again from Ghana. I still marvel that your very own work of creating that dictionary in the Brookfield kitchen (oh! my attempts to learn a word or two in Sura!) should now be circulating amongst those very grand sounding University people, well done! Our Day was rather quiet but with one item unusual: Wilfrid & David came to fetch all 3 of us to tea at Brookfield, my first time of seeing it since the day you left. It was a treat and the garden looked so lovely with the Viburnum Carleesi out, & many daffodils & flowering shrubs. I do miss these very much, and was disappointed that

B did not offer us any but there was little time & they were hurrying to get to church. As tall as David has grown, W is very stooped, so like Uncle A but also very fat which must be a hindrance to him. We heard nothing of what is happening with Mr Hickmet but there seems an easement of feeling all round so we do not know if he will soon be occupying Southways and Auntie Jo's place for himself or perhaps Clyro or the old house? Yest morn Father's first words to me were, 'The Lord is risen indeed, & His word to Peter, I have prayed for thee, and, He ever liveth to make intercession,' and he wanted me to give those thoughts to the Meeting which I did at the end & then gave thanks for this glad Easter Day and its message still so true today. I wonder often what Mrs M would make of what she heard if she ever did accompany me one Sunday morn, but the Lord has His own ways of dealing with & speaking to souls who have not thought they were hungry, I must simply pray on. Father had a good day today, dressing and going into the garden for a little in the sun; I think he had hoped to speak to Mrs Batchelor about her roses but she had gone in! Now it is dinner time & I feel ready for it having taken no coffee this morning – trying to bring down my weight a bit...have we ever discussed this point before? I rather think so! My special greetings to Enid, Joyce & Joan and dear Frances P of course all my love to your dear self darling, Mother.

35 The M

April 25th '61

My beloved Chris, fifty nine years ago today was our engagement day so we have much for which to give thanks, and the future, obscure on our terms but bright with the promises of God! Glory that excelleth! I try to think more on this and not so much of actual dying, for I am sure there will be grace given for that time when it comes. Meanwhile we have many pleasures, sunshine, and short rides when Mary has a spare moment, & the beauty of this spring seems greater than any before. But you know how much we enjoyed last year – do you remember that barrow full of pansies?! Rene has to leave us on Thurs there seems no betterment in that home for her to return to so far as one can see; we shall miss her dreadfully. Wilfrid's affairs seem more difficult to write about than ever and he more burdened; I think he had to pay highly to work the piece of land from the Office to the road by Southways and that only for a year as a trial. Perhaps he will write to you himself with more details. These things are hard to understand, but I just wanted to tell you of our engagement day and send you all the love in my heart, Mother.

35 The Millbank

30th April '61

Darling Chris it was so lovely to get home on Fri & find your birthday letter to me and your general prayer epistle telling of your wonderful trek to Kadim. It really is inspiring to think of Christ's Church beginning to take root in a place like that, & the Light in the darkness of dear Andarawus & his wife leading by such fine example – I shall specially be praying for them. So often I live over again the experiences I had with you 5 yrs ago; isn't it wonderful that the opportunity came then for it certainly wouldn't be possible for me to go now. From the 5-28th Ap I've had 24 mtgs + 1 conference & travelled 1500 miles so you'll understand why I've not written much to you. How thankful we have been to have Rene for a fortnight. There's been no change in her situation & E still insists on studying for the exams to start at Univ this autumn though with no clear idea of what to do even if he gets a degree & no word from the Swedish Mission if they'll even pay a salary. It is so complex. Darling we can but pray, and constantly. I took her to Hastings the other day & she really enjoyed it and we both took M&F to see the bluebells on Leith Hill & all loved that. This evening David & all the Brookfield family came over & D showed his coloured slides of Switzerland & Rome. Father was incredible, got dressed & came down, giving the names of the lakes & mountains & quite a number of facts about the places! Mummie enjoyed the pictures but was quiet – I know she is pining for Brookfield, and the Irish one, and having an inward struggle with herself which is not good for her blood pressure. She longs for the Brookfield garden flowers, the azaleas, the wisteria etc. now with my heart's dearest love to you darling as ever, Mary.

Panyam

May 19th '61

Darlings our new member of staff, Tom Owens, has arrived & is a nice fellow tho' not as young as we'd thought, he has a confident air & is well settled & charmed with our little round guest hut. He feeds with us but prepares his own tea tray & has that alone, spending a good deal of time on his language study. I was able to sit with him at the Daffo mtg, explaining what was going on. He was deeply impressed with the growth that has taken place there & indeed I was too as I realised that when I first came out there wasn't a single outstation in all the Baron/Kulere tribes and now there are at least 40! The most moving report was from Andarawus of Kadim who told of the great heathen festival & how they demanded that Damulak, the little boy who had accompanied me, should go with them to it. He refused & his father explained he had given his son to school & could not take him back. The heathen leaders ignored that saying if they didn't get the boy they would take all the father's possessions, then they dragged the boy off anyway. They smeared his body all over with oil insisting that he drink beer from the big bowl at the same time as the heathen Chief did so. They said special sacrifices of cows have been made since this child's birth in order to make him their next Chief successor to the 'witchdoctor.' The boy refused to drink so they tried to force him again & again he refused, then suddenly was able to run away & ran sobbing to Andarawus for help and prayer comfort. I have promised that we will pray for him and that I will ask you to do so also; he was so pleased by this for they do all value your prayers & remembrance. He ended his report with, "Do please pray for us very much; but in spite of it all we are not afraid of them for we are looking unto God & we will remember Psalm 27:1&2." Another report was also moving, from James Akibin the Kulere Evangelist, who has found certain things going on which he knows are not right & speaking out about them & incurring displeasure from his flock. His wife, whose baby is due fairly soon, was taken ill with bad fever & her relations came insisting they should do the old heathen rites for her. They refused, but were very frightened, so went to see the senior evang Daniel Ashawat. They were much comforted by praying together & his wife is a little better. It makes you realise what these dear folks have to bear when they are beset with sickness & fears and so far from medical help & under such pressure from heathen relatives as well. Thank you so much for your lovely letters this week & I'm so glad you did get the tape – I am working on making another for both you and Nakam. Where the people are speaking to Nakam & I'm interpreting for you, you can hear the heathen horn blowing in the background and some babies crying! Our dear Pastor David has now had confirmation of his latest award: life membership with the Bronze Medal of the Royal African Society & a cheque for £10 and a nice letter of congratulations from the Governor! It is marvellous to think of all he has accomplished & of how it has been acknowledged. Now with my very dearest love to you each one & my best greetings to all whom I know & who might be interested, yours as ever, Chris.

35 The M

June 4th 1961

My beloved Chris, Nakam was here on Friday & we recorded a little for you tho' it may be a long while before it is finished & you hear it. We so enjoyed hearing the messages on your tapes she brought to us, giving us such a great picture of what you do & how it is growing, and please thank Kefas, Datilik, Jacob & Yilhi for their lovely messages. I am grateful for the encouragement they are to you. I am interested to hear about the Welsh man Tom, I hope he may soon find a good wife if that is the Lord's will for him. Rene's letters don't give us any more news but the women of the church all seem to be standing by her for which I am glad, but how will this end? I pray her health may be preserved. We – yes, Father & I! – sat out in the garden in the nearly finished shelter, it is a pleasant place. F seems in a new lease of life & is up & dressed most days, quite like old times. M went into Crawley with £3 from me to buy a new garden chair as we only have the one brought from Brookfield; B did not think there were any others as May or Chris found they had woodworm & wanted them burned...are you the culprit?! However now we have two nice aluminium light ones with bright green canvas so we are well set up for A. Lizzie's visit next month. She expects to cross with

Isabel & Jimmie & Anna & then wait to meet Mary at Victoria under the clock. I can hardly believe she is truly coming but it does seem likely now, I know you will be praying with us about this visit. The ground here is parched dry like a rock & poor M has not yet managed to get the plants we took up last autumn planted out they are still in the garage but growing well. M took Nakam to Redhill where she got a bus from there & she has promised to come any time when you send tapes, now with dearest love from Mother.

28 Nuthurst Close, Ifield

18.6.61

Dear Christine Cheal I have delayed writing until I can tell you that my mission is accomplished. I have bought second hand a very nice little Grundig Cub for £15 and will repay you the remaining £11 as suggested. Your mother tells me this morning that a new tape has just arrived so it will be played forthwith. I had looked through many advertisements but yesterday in a Radio Shop in Tilgate on quite another matter, I found that a man had just left one with them to sell because he was going abroad. Which is good for it means we now have a Crawley firm behind us. May tried your last tape on it and it was perfect whereas on mine of lesser quality, you sounded rather like a high powered American business executive. I think it is a most kind and Christian action on your part and will greatly enrich the lives of your parents and help them feel much closer to you. I am glad to have been the instrument of such an action. Your mother looks well and bright and I believe your father is doing quite nicely also. Now I shall finish with love and best wishes from all of us at Ifield, yours sincerely Arthur Worthy.

35 The M

June 18 '61

My beloved Chris first we have your dear & welcome letter with the new tape and then the great & very wonderful surprise of the machine to play it now being tried out in the shop & soon to be here with us by the kind hand of Arthur Worthy, and Mary will find out from him the correct way to use it. Darling I am sending you my most loving thanks with the hope that you are not denying yourself of any of life's necessities by sending such a generous gift to us? I will now try to get recordings of people & visits that will bring you pleasure, the ones you specially asked for did make me smile, the milkman's voice, trains passing, and good Ulster crack with Lizzie! We are so very grateful to you. We have Alison here since Thurs as W&B + Swedish girl have gone to Ramsgate for David's half term 'do' and NonaJane is staying with the Curate's family in Crawley. I wish you could see The Millbank in this evening's sunshine, gardens full of roses & other blooms, our 2 trees in full leaf and a very quiet Sabbath calm over all – we are blessed to have this home, ever your loving Mother.

Shell BP Port Harcourt

July 11th '61

Dearest Auntie Chris, thank you so much for the welcome telegram which cheered my arrival tremendously. It is very comfortable here & the air conditioning in bedrooms makes blankets essential. I'm often glad of a thick sweater, which I felt foolish in bringing; some of the Africans are reported to be suffering from frostbite. Initially I shall see around all the departments & then go out into the bush to see the oil wells & rigs. We're about 9 miles out from PH so it will be necessary to get a car. There is a company plane which occasionally flies to Jos & I might be able to get a lift on it to come and see you so I'll be looking forward to that eventuality, with much dear love from Ant.

Rustington, Eastbourne

August 6th '61

My beloved Chris, Mary brought us – Rene & me – down here & left after discovering they do now have another room available so she will fetch Father down also. I did not like leaving him one bit. I'm sure he will benefit from the sea air as I am doing. R had a taxi (!!) this morn, such a lovely surprise, to take us to the Friends Mtg and as we entered a woman greeted me with, "Why surely it must be Annie Cheal!" She was Mrs Sharp who used to live in Crawley & she kindly found someone to take us back after. Two very short words were given at the start then a very, very long silence caused me to ponder upon Hamilton Livingstone's first Quaker mtg as a lad, and then speak on it: not one word was said that morning & he felt the silence throughout the whole place to be awefull, awe-filled, so much so that he began to pray that <u>some</u>one would say or do <u>some</u>thing, but not a word. He then found himself on his knees asking God's forgiveness then hearing His call to follow & serve Him. As you know he responded & became a much loved & honoured Minister & a good servant of Jesus Christ. I added that a silent mtg may be used by God to speak to hearts normally too distracted by other voices, but I wonder if He is not disappointed sometimes that we have so little to say of our own individual experience of His love in our lives. Goodbye for this time & blessings on you darling, Mother.

St Helens Gardens, E'bourne

Aug 8th '61

Darling Chris do you remember our picnic here about 6yrs ago? All we had was mandarin oranges out of a tin & some cream! Today there is a gale blowing & the sea is just covered with white horses, & lovely clouds billowing across the sky, allowing warm sunshine through if rather fitfully. If this paper still looks very creased by the time it reaches you, you'll know it's been buffeted by winds coming around Beachy Head! Presently I plan to take the Cub down onto the beach to record for you the sound of the crashing waves & the wash of the shingle as each recedes; I'd hoped for gulls' cries too but they seem to be quite silent today. Rene is inside with M & F who are much happier reunited again, & R is a little brighter for this brief rest before her busy fortnight cooking for the old dears at Dungate. Darling it was dreadful to see on the front page of the Telegraph that yesterday Dr Niemoller while driving with his wife & housekeeper crashed into a tree and both women were killed. He is injured in hospital but oh how awful he must be feeling for he & his wife were so devoted. It is so hard to understand why, I cannot understand, why such things are allowed. And yet I heard last week yet another story of the mercy of God: Dr Stanley Smith told us that when Rosemary Guillebaud had finished the OT translation she had a (sailing?) passage booked for the start of her furlough but suddenly had a strong sense that she must go at once. She was able to get a seat on a flight just cancelled by someone else & as she got home to Cambridge & walked into her mother's bedroom, found her unconscious & the family gathered around. When Rosemary spoke her mother recognised her & rallied, raised herself in bed to greet & bless R. She lived just 2 more days & then went Home! I do wish you were here with me to share this wildly beautiful day but I'm sending all my love as always ever yours Mary.

Panyam

Aug 20th '61

My darlings what a pleasure it was for me to get your dear letters from Eastbourne & know you were actually all four down there together! I'm grieving with you Mary over the dear Niemollers, and longing for the tape of the windy day at the beach, & now am imagining Rene having a good few laughs with Eileen & Madge & Delia in between her Dungate duties. Here there is such a fresh & growing desire for education & every village wants to be in the forefront of progress so I hope they will be as good as their word & get cracking with their building plans, and expansions, and bringing in the school fees for their children. However, quite often intentions take rather a long time to become realities! Our women are excited about the Maternity Centre & happily agreed to help enlarge the existing building by carrying (with alacrity) two of the heavy mud blocks on their heads every trip back & forth. They are also making pillows of kapok & sewing sheets for more beds. Our male missionary Tom has been ill again; I have told him he needs a thorough overhaul; now he has bought a horse! It is the first time one of those has been resident in our compound, it's a nice black creature.

23rd now: Malam Adamu, Polycarp Fian & Pastor David returned from the Zaria conference saying, "You see how our faces are shining with the joy we have from the wonderful conference!" Nearly 1000 people gathered from all over the North, with speakers from S. Africa, America, Liberia & Kenya; everybody initially conscious of his own denomination or Mission, wanting his own way of worship or his special tenets of faith to be recognised. But after a day or so all that disappeared in a growing sense of their unity in Christ Jesus so that in the end nobody thought about their differences, only about their common faith & love in Him! So many books were sold that a special trip to Jos had to be made to get more supplies to meet the demand!

Thank you Mother for another cheery letter, how amazed I was to hear of Father attending Meeting again and taking part – isn't he really wonderful! Old father Lot's testimony is due to appear in the Lightbearer quite soon despite the concern over possible objections from those who might still be ashamed of the days of cannibalism. David's response to his father's story was, "It is the truth, why should it not be published?" I believe it is necessary & will help to highlight the changes that have taken place over the years. Now goodbye my darlings & God bless you each one, ever yours Chris.

Dungate Manor

Sept 3rd '61

My darling Chris this is my first time of sending you a letter from this lovely restful place; we have a lovely large bedroom with a very lg window looking out over the lawns & gardens, no sound of trains but my there are planes! We'd heard last week from Lena that Jo was poorly then the next morn there was Mary coming in here to tell us of A Jo's passing & the funeral at Ifield on Friday. We could not be sad for dear old Josie but it was a bit of a shock. M of course made all the arrangements & to have everyone back to 35 for tea, with Alison's help & we agreed we should stay quietly here for I don't think Father could have gone & I did not care to leave him. He has not been other than thankful that she was spared further suffering & is now safely Home. Goodnight now my precious girl, God bless you abundantly, Mother.

Panyam

Sept 4th '61

Darlings I do hope you'll soon get the tape I sent off this week & that it'll be reasonably intelligible, for there was not time to re-check if all the speeds were right. It seemed too slow so I got new batteries but that made some parts race, I do hope it is satisfactory. I'm wondering very much about Rene these days and if any progress is being made. I've loved having letters from W and B, David, NonaJane with a bit from Jonathan, Ant, and Alison all in one mail last week! Ruth Batchelor lent us a Sunday paper she'd had sent from home giving a full story of a young Nigerian Communist who was being sent to organise a revolution here after being trained in Russia; but he got cold feet & left all this then gave a full report when he got back here of what he had been ordered to do here. After reading it I passed it on to David & Polycarp & others who were all horrified. I'm told it was reported on the Radio although I did not hear it. Apparently the Prime Minister just laughed when he heard what the Russians were trying to do. Let's hope his optimism about their lack of power to destroy Nigeria's peace is not ill founded.

Now the 8th: Fibi is again out of order & Peter Batchelor's Land-Rover, also hors de combat, had to be towed into Jos, and Tom's horse in a bad way too! On Sat it broke free & ran several miles before falling down some steep rocks into huge cactus plants – it was eventually found & cut free but Tom is not at all sure it will recover, poor thing. This is all for now darlings, with dearest & best love as ever Chris.

Confirmation of telegram from Mary to Chris:

Father safely Home.Mother upheld.Funeral Friday.

From the Crawley Newspaper:

Mr Ernest Cheal, who belonged to one of the oldest families in Crawley, died at his home 35 The Millbank, Ifield on Tues Sept 12th 1961; he had been about as usual & the end came suddenly at 10pm. He was born in 1878 & it was his father Mr Joseph Cheal together with Mr Alexander Cheal who founded the nursery business J Cheal & Sons in 1871. On leaving school in 1894 Mr E Cheal entered the business, later to become Chairman & Managing Director. His speciality was landscape gardening and he designed & laid out gardens all over the country & on the Continent. The Nurseries have a national reputation & Mr Cheal was rightly proud that the firm's annual exhibits at the Chelsea Flower Show had been visited by three generations of the Royal Family & he had photographs of the occasions in his office. A deeply religious man, Mr Cheal responded instinctively & unselfishly whenever he could be of help to others. He was a Recorded Minister of the Society of Friends at Ifield & for more than 50 years was secretary of the Crawley Auxiliary of the British & Foreign Bible Society. He held a clean driving licence from 1904 to 1958 when he gave up driving aged 80 due to failing eyesight. He was the oldest customer at the Westminster Bank at Crawley having opened an account on the first day that the Westminster opened its doors on the High Street 64 years ago. Mr & Mrs Ernest Cheal celebrated their Golden Wedding Anniversary in 1953. The family's association with Crawley goes back to 1750 when Mr E Cheal's great grandfather came from West Hoathly to establish the grocer's business in the High Street which is now Kingham's Stores. It was there that Mr Ernest Cheal's grandfather Mr John Cheal was born in 1800. He lived to be 96. Mr Ernest Cheal leaves a widow, a son & three daughters: Miss Christine Cheal is a missionary in Nigeria; Miss Mary Cheal lives at 35 The Millbank, Ifield & is Area Secretary for the Bible Society; Mrs Irene Forsback has two sons & lives in Aberdeen. Mr Wilfrid Cheal is Director of the Nursery Business & lives at Brookfield, Lowfield Heath, which his parents vacated a year ago to move to Ifield; Mr Wilfrid has a wife & two sons & two daughters. Mr Ernest Cheal's funeral will take place today at the Friends' Meeting House in Ifield, today (Friday) at 2pm.

From the Ifield Friends' Record:

The serenity of Ernest Cheal's life was typified in the ancient serenity of the Meeting House, his spiritual home. One can hear him say, "Yea Lord, Thou knowest that I love Thee," an acknowledgement which meant service, and he lived a full life of service to God whether in business or for family, friends or Quaker Friends. He discharged his duties faithfully & efficiently and would frequently rise during Meeting to give a short & searching message, gathering us all into a united consciousness of the presence of God in our midst. He visited the sick, always with his wife Annie by his side, bringing rest & peace; or by request when a new baby was brought to Meeting for the first time, his message a benediction. He was always the same, unhurried, unhasted, whether digging the first sod for Crawley New Town, burying a Friend, shaking hands with Queen Mary at London's Chelsea Flower Show, or quietly welcoming you to Meeting each Sunday morning.

35 The Millbank, Ifield, Crawley

September 1961

Mrs Cheal and all the family thank you most sincerely for the comfort of your sympathy and the help of your prayers.

Into the Hands once pierced for our redemption, Thy strong and tender care;
we put our loved one, passed beyond our keeping, and trusting, leave him there.

Our Saviour Jesus Christ...hath abolished death and hath brought life and immortality to light through the gospel. 2 Timothy 1:10.

252 Selsdon Rd, S Croydon

Sept 15th '61

My dearest Chris my heart goes out to you in loving & deepest sympathy as the news of your father's Homegoing reaches you. It was in the Telegraph yesterday, and today the dear weary body is being laid to rest to await the Resurrection, when all the weakness will be gone & only his glorified body will be raised. I know you've been expecting this for some time but nevertheless it still comes as a shock in the end & I know how your heart will be yearning to be at home with your loved ones now. What a wonderful welcome your dear father will have had as he entered into the Presence of his Saviour & heard His 'Well done!' The comfort of his joy will be a comfort to you, and the separation cannot be for very long for surely the Lord Jesus must be coming back soon. But for now I pray He gives you an exceptionally real awareness of His presence to sustain, strengthen & comfort you. Much, much love dear Chris, yours lovingly, Nakam.

Panyam

Sept 15th '61

My own darlings how my heart goes out to you just now, longing so deeply that I could be with you, I feel all numb. So close after A Jo's funeral too. Of course I long for further news of when & how, I'm sure it will come soon. I know you'll be surrounded by loving compassion from a host of friends & dear ones even as the comfort

& enabling of the Lord Himself will be with you. Several folk here have already been along to offer their sympathy, such is their loving way; & Joan came right away & it was her sensibleness that spotted the printed confusion which had to mean it is actually Father who has gone, confirmed then by the arrival of your corrected telegram – post office officials seem to be past masters at muddling telegrams. Joseph Waltu sends his sympathy & now Unaisi is here & wanting me to send her most special greetings. Darlings this attempt at a letter, written in such a welter of feelings brings my overflowing love & concern which I know you'll share with Rene & all at Brookfield, with constant prayer on every breath, your Chrissie.

18 Orchard Drive, Woking

Sept 15th '61

Dearest Chris we rejoice with you at the mercy of God that one moment your dear father was speaking with his loved ones & the next he had passed into the Presence of the One he had loved & served with such steadfast faith. How much more compassionate is our Heavenly Father than we can ever imagine. But we do know from experience that such a translation is a great physical shock to those who are left & so we shall be remembering you all very much in these next days & weeks ahead. Although we cannot get to the funeral we know it will be a time when the Name of the Lord will be lifted up as His faithful servant is laid to rest. Gertrude joins me in sending much much love, as ever, Ruth Henman.

Gindiri

Sept 16th '61

My dear Chris you & all your family are in my prayerful thoughts. I believe that when one from a family goes to be with the Lord, each person in that family is drawn closer to Him. I pray this may be so with the Sura Christian family who will be standing with you through this painful time. With very much love and Phil 1:21&23 from Pixie.

Panyam

Sept 17th '61

Darling Mary I'm sure you have felt distressed that your dear message so thoughtfully sent was mis-typed this end causing some uncertainty as to which of our beloveds had gone Home but please, please do not be troubled any more for there has been Divine purpose in this. I am thankful to have faced the belief that it was she who had gone – as I wrote in her letter – & to have found peace in accepting that news. And, as Joan said, they've been able to explain the Gospel at the post office to the Postmaster himself who could not understand the wording! It is you who have been in my thoughts & heart yearnings since I heard, almost more than anyone else. I know well how the very thought of this particular happening has been a sort of nightmare for a long time. I long now almost with trembling to have the news of exactly how & when it happened but I believe you will have already proved that the Lord in His lovingkindness was there with you. I trust that Rene is with you &

will stay quite awhile, even a prolonged time, and that the Bible Society will be kind & gladly give you leave of absence. You were specially & beautifully upheld in prayer on Friday by the women & by Pastor David this morning; & Ishaku has just been in asking me to send you his strong greetings & that please 'hold your heart fast in patience.' Frances P arrived to be with me, staying for tea & supper, so very kind; and now a dear message for you & me also, in from Moses who remains so bright & cheerful and can do a bit of work with his good hand. Now darling this brings most tender love & care with constant thought & prayer for you, & for Rene, & for Wilfrid & family, as well as dear Mummy in the days ahead, may the Lord bless you each richly, and may He allow Mummy to continue on into a great old age to be a rich blessing to us all – please tell her I keep thinking of her at Redhill Station, her dear bright smile framed by that charming mauve hat, my last sight of her, & your words then, "It's all right." And it was then, and is now, and will still be. I've thought many times of my last moments with Father – how appropriate it should have been at Brookfield, where our very first moments together were spent. He was rarely demonstrative, but as we said goodbye in the hall he stroked my arm so lovingly. That I shall always cherish. C.

35 The Millbank

Sept 17th '61

My own dear darling Chris I know we more or less agreed we would not cable at such times…but what a wonderful help it is to have that little visible assurance that the other knows & is remembering… every letter we've had feels like a hand reaching out to help & a few really special, beautiful ones just lift us up to heaven's threshold. I know you want, and need, details but it feels strange to write them in a sort of detached way; the main sense is of great thankfulness to the Lord for the lovingly gracious way He took F so quickly, not during or as a result of one of those horrid attacks, but so gently & peacefully. On Saturday we'd had a picnic tea in Balcombe; on Sunday Father had been able to be at Meeting and get up to speak! He gave his testimony once again, ending by asking the Friends if they were ready should their Homecall come suddenly. On Monday I had to get some duplicating done in the Office & M&F both came and as we turned into the Nursery drive there was Fred Robinson on his bike (F had only said the week before he'd like to see Fred again) Ralph Peters, Miss Willis & Miss Westaway all came to speak to him, as though he was 'holding court' from the car! Then on Tuesday afternoon M&F had sat out in the sun in the garden together & that evening he'd been fairly conversational, & had a second helping of pudding for his supper, then Mother had tucked him in, kissed him goodnight, and as she went to take her dress off heard a strange noise…and he was gone. Dr Knight came quickly after I phoned and he was most gentle with Mummie. Nurse had been away but just got back that day & came immediately I rang & was very kind & loving, doing what had to be done, leaving Father looking just peacefully at rest. Now my heart's cry is for you to be strengthened & upheld, as we are, yours always Mary.

Daffo

Sept 19th '61

Dear Chris the sad news of your bereavement reached me on Saturday morning. Please be assured of my thoughts and deepest sympathy; I am remembering you in prayer, and your mother, and all your family. It seems to me the closing verses of Romans 8 give such a revelation to us of the extent of the embrace in which our heavenly Father holds His children: 'For I am convinced that there is nothing in death or life…in heights or depths, nothing in all creation that can separate us from the love of God in Christ Jesus our Lord;' now in His fellowship, yours very sincerely, Tom.

Dungate Manor

Sept 21st '61

Dearest Chris how much you are in our thoughts as you will have just received news of the death of your beloved father. Of course you are rejoicing with him in his joy, so wonderfully swift for him, but for you the sense of loss will be great and I care so much about that; especially as you are so far away from your dear ones. We are happy to be having your dear mother to stay here again – Mary is to bring her over tomorrow before she leaves for the meetings she must attend in the Channel Islands. We are so glad to help in this small way. Rene is being so brave but simply hated leaving. Eileen joins me in sending warmest love; we are yours, deeply caring, Madge.

Rodborough Common, Stroud

Sept 22nd 1961

Darling Chris I know that the Lord will be giving you special comfort these days, when perhaps of all the family you have been the most prayed for. What a wonderful man your father was! He told me with such joy about the time he was so ill he needed a blood transfusion, and almost at once felt new life coursing through his veins so he told the nurse he'd like to thank the donor. She said they are always anonymous. Then it came to him in a fresh way that he could tell her his Best Friend gave His blood for him that has brought new life and is available to her also, and he can always thank Him every day! And now he has seen Him face to face & joined the song of the redeemed – how wonderful that must be for him! Dear Chris, the Lord bless you & keep you, for He is thy life & the length of thy days; with much loving sympathy Auntie Lena.

Panyam

Sept 22nd '61

Darlings, of the many sympathetic letters I am receiving about dear Father's passing, this is a translation of the one from Pastor Manasseh which seemed just as lovely as any such letter could be: 'This greeting comes to you in the Name of our Saviour Jesus. I have heard this morning of what God has done in receiving the life of your father. Well Mother dear, we have always known that it would be so one day and I am just writing this little greeting to let you know we are remembering you and all the others of your family in our prayers, that God may give us all perseverance right to the end of our lives as he has done to these old people. May God continue to uphold the heart of your mother and give you peace; Tarifainu is with me in this greeting.' (Tarifainu is his wife.) I've also heard so kindly from Nakam & Mrs Webster, Evelyn Goldstein, and a beautiful one from the SUM secretary Mr Elsey; and Mary darling, old father Lot came to see me with his special remembrances for you; Ishaku in his dear prayers remembers you all; and old father Pofi of Niyes came to send greetings to you, his special friend! Tomorrow I am going to Mongu for the weekend with Frances & together we'll work on the syllabus for Bible enquirers' class; as ever Chris.

Beechcroft, Moira, Lurgan

Sept 22nd '61

My dearest Chris oh how we did feel for you being so far from family when your dear father passed away; when Bernard heard the news of Uncle Ernest passing, it was Cousin Chrissie he immediately mentioned. Mary tells us your mother is being an inspiration to all – as we knew she would be yet she must feel a tremendous loneliness these days. Uncle Ernest will be to everyone he came in contact with, the very soul of uprightness, goodness and strength. I just pray that you may be specially comforted knowing that so many are thinking of you in these days; with very much love & sympathy from Isabel Megarry.

35 The M but really in Guernsey

Sept 25th '61

My darling what a comfort & help your letters have been, thank you so much, I was grieved over the telegram mistake so special thanks for that assurance that you are alright. A lot of the letters coming in here thought A Jo's death was actually Mother, and were then so sad to hear of Father going the following week...I have had many to reassure as quickly as possible. It is lovely & most moving to find so many describing Father in words like uprightness, integrity, single-mindedness, rock-like character – he was held in high regard by so many. Mummie is grieving in looking back seeing him get so tottery, helpless & frail, that is the real sadness; and the rejoicing is in that he was taken without that awful apprehension that turned him icy cold & trembly with the palpitations, but just quite quietly as he fell asleep. That has made the parting so much easier to bear & Mummie able to be so calmly accepting. I see no need for a move from 35 T M & certainly feel we should wait until we know more of Rene's doings – it may well be that she will have to make her home here with us too before much longer. In the meantime I've had such kind offers from our neighbours, and the lovely Nurse, to come & be with Mother while I have to be away, and also M can go to Dungate as they have kindly offered when they have a vacant room for her so I think we shall manage alright this winter. Auntie Elsie, Miss Green and even Edie have all said they could help if needed for a day while I'm out. I am certain darling of the Lord's gracious kindness in allowing things to happen as they have, in order to show & assure us that He is greater & better than our fears and that we really can trust Him absolutely to work everything out now and into the future. I had such a good & calm flight over here and I haven't a heavy programme as I declined schools this time, and go on to Jersey on

Saty morn then home on Wedy but after that mtgs are pretty consistent right up till Christmas. Goodbye my dearest, peace to you this night & always, with my heart's love, Mary.

44 Fitzwilliam Rd, Clapham SW4

Sept 25th '61

My dear Miss Cheal, thank you very much for your lovely welcoming letter. It does not seem so long ago that Miss Rae & I first came to see you about the GLB work in Nigeria and now I have only 10dys before I sail! I am looking forward to working with you all and I do thank you for making all the arrangements & the extra work you have had to do. Did you know I didn't pass my driving test? I am very disappointed, and know I need more practice; I am hoping to be able to have another test in Jos very soon. I was very sorry to hear about your father and have been praying for you and your family, with love from Kathleen McDonald.

Panyam

Sept 26th '61

Darlings it was good to get 3 letters from you last night – a sense of deep thankfulness took possession of me as I read all the strong comfort of your news. I do share with you this feeling of glad gratitude to God for allowing our dear one to slip away so quickly & without fear or pain; we couldn't have asked for anything better could we? You all wrote of somewhat different aspects of the happenings – every bit was so welcome, especially to know that you are all being upheld in cheerful grace & courage. I've been listening again to the tape of when Nakam came to visit you, with the bit on it where Father began, "Well Chris dear…" that was unusual for him wasn't it, for I think 'dear' was always reserved for Mother alone wasn't it?! Yesterday Kefas wrote: 'I am sending these few lines of my loving greetings in remembrance of the death of your father. Let us thank God for Jesus as we know that for those who put their trust in Him death is a happy thing to them.' Actually I put a question mark against that in my mind, but when I read your dear letters I thought it was perhaps not so far from the truth – for Father certainly, a happy thing! What do you think we finished up our supper with just now? A strawberry each from our own garden – the first time I've ever grown them! Bye bye my dearest dear ones, as always your Chris.

6 Rosemont Rd, Acton, London W5

October 1st '61

Dear Chris Cheal two weeks ago I had the pleasure of staying with your brother & his wife and family; Mrs Cheal was extremely kind to have me when she had all the children at home & 3 students were expected who were helping on a church mission in Crawley. I slept on the very comfortable couch-bed in the 'den' downstairs and the students were in the caravan & garden house. Fiona had started on her new domestic science course the day I arrived but she didn't have much chance to talk about it with so many visitors around. I spoke at

Hazelwick & Sarah Robinson Schools where you had spoken before and the children asked some good questions; I enjoyed being there. The Pentecostalists in Gosport were also really warm & loving & the Sunday school classes gave me a £15 cheque for your work so I shall be handing that in to HQ next week. I did not meet your mother while in Crawley but Alison & David told me how absolutely wonderful she was at your father's funeral, perfectly composed and smiling as she talked with all the people there. I do hope you felt aware of the love & prayers of so many people when you first heard about your father; mine were among them; yours very sincerely Margaret Vincent.

Panyam

Oct 1st '61

Darlings the tape has arrived & was so welcome! Thank you for all you have told me on this & by letter – I do feel I have shared in all the happenings as far as it is possible from such a distance; & I know our love & thoughts & prayers have meant so much to each other. Mwantet came to see me again (I was out the first time) & he told me that when he first heard the news about Father, he got out your photos and Dafwash's and then, "we spent the evening with them before us and I said those two – Father & Dafwash – are together in Heaven now." Isn't that sweet?! Today Joyce & I took our wee orphan and his new foster mother to their home nearly 40 miles from here; it is a joy to see how well they have taken to each other. Then we went on to Daffo to meet Tom who needed a lift to Kulere country with a load of school desks for Ambul. A heavy storm turned the road into rushing rivers behind us through which we had to plough back then after tea with

Tom at Daffo we slid along very muddy roads rather thankful the rains are nearly over for another year. I have taken the plunge and bought an Electrolux Fridge! We've been thinking of it since having to return the Batchelor's one upon their return. Joyce was giving 'triple vaccine' to babies as a prophylactic measure against diptheria, whooping cough etc and it has to be stored in the cold. She felt the medical account should pay half so I said if so the fridge would remain here as the property of the Dispensary if any of us left so we three would pay 1/3 of the other half – just £9 each. It is a lovely white & pale blue model and it is such a boon!! Now with dearest love to you all my darlings, Chris.

35 The Millbank

Oct 5th '61

My beloved Chris I'm thankful to say our dear Mary has returned safely from the Ch Is and fetched me from Dungate so now we are home together. Everyone is being so very kind, our dear Doctor called in again to check me over, & I'm glad he gave M a tonic for she is so weary & has little colour now, and the neighbours offer help so willingly but truly I am finding I do not mind being alone here at all, at least during the day. We have agreed to be really honest with each other, I mean Mother not trying to do much because of Mary and vice versa!! Of course in our minds constantly is the thought of our dear Rene. She is much loved at Dungate & one of the ladies there said to me that she could see by R's dear face that she bears a heavy load; with all the love I can send darling, Mother.

Panyam

Oct 20th '61

Darlings many, many thanks for your dear letters & I'm so pleased to note you Mummie seem to be getting out much more with Mary to some of her meetings, & enjoying the beautiful autumn countryside. You asked about Thalazole, it is one of the many M&B drugs used for dysentery & allied diseases; & Frances P suggested it during my recent bout of fever and it cleared me up completely I'm glad to say. Yes, our lovely Gwen & David had their 3rd disappointment last month, the baby was born alright but only lived two days, due we're sure to congenital heart trouble. We are still looking for an adoptive family for the tiny wee prem who is still weighing less than 4lbs but is doing alright. Last night Tabitha Benle gave birth to a 9lb baby boy & Joyce has never delivered one so large in this country before! Tom Owens has been posted to the Bible School in Boi as soon as David W returns, & did I mention that Tom is now engaged to Jean Cooil? The RCC was as usual stimulating & interesting; & to me a great privilege to sit with African brethren & share in their ideas & discussions. I wonder how soon we shall get the African treasurers to be fully responsible for their own church finances?! Phineas has now taken over fully as Schools Manager & I have handed to him the keys to one of the safes. He attended the Edu Sub-Comm for the first time I took him into Jos where he spent £30 in the market buying 1962 school supplies, getting many items a good bit cheaper than I could do! 300 children will be competing for 120 places in the Sr Primary classes – think of the difference since 1950 when we only had 11 boys in school! Mary darling next time you are near Woolworths could you get me half a doz medium hair-nets plse, dearest love Chris.

Panyam

Oct 26th '61

Darlings it is heartwarming to hear of all the loving care showered upon you by so many especially Eileen & Madge; I just wish I could be there with you and share in this ministry but instead I can pour my heart into these letters to you my dear ones. The dear Misses Henman sent £25 to me 'in memory of all my father had been & done' – isn't that lovely! In part I think I shall spend it on two of our lads in very reduced circumstances who are struggling with next year's fees for Theological College, and something actually for myself as a tangible token of this love. Possibly 2 fine spring cushions for the 2 beautiful new wooden chairs I had made in Jos with Uncle Willie's legacy money. The last note from Father was one the end of one of yours Mother where he advised me to get insurance on Monies in Transit. I've had a special pleasure in doing that & suggesting it to others on various committees who are now arranging it also, so I feel that Father is wonderfully responsible for this great improvement! On Tues the West Language Congress sent a grant-in-aid of $250 for the purchase of a Tape Recorder for all the language work I can do here. Of course I shall keep on using the little Cub for messages to you & to Nakam, but on this new bigger one I hope to record not only the languages Prof Greenberg wants me to send him at Columbia Univ in New York, but also the Lord's Prayer & The 10 Commandments & other Scriptures in all the different languages. Then I could duplicate copies for all the outstations in their own vernaculars! Today the new GLB Organiser is due by road, bringing the gift from various divisions in Ireland & New Zealand I think, of an Austin Countryman car. She did not pass her test in London but will take it again as soon as she can here so Daphne Fletcher will drive with her. You remember Kathleen MacDonald came to tea at Brookfield with Miss

Rae; she will be travelling around seeing all the Companies & Sections, probably staying here much of the time. Goodbye darlings for now with blessings on you & my love as ever, C.

35 The Millbank

Nov 4th '61

My beloved Chris we have been thinking & thinking of you most especially today & prayed you might have a happy day with some extra bit of love & birthday blessing from our dear Lord who is ever faithful. I enclose the hairnets with this letter. You know how thankful we are for the gift of your arrival – I still say 'we' for Father seems so near & our lives are bound together still. It is as if he was here now in his chair saying, "It's no use my writing, you give her all the news" after I have said, "You simply must write something for it is her birthday today!" If it is possible for him to be near us darling then I am quite sure he is, and he may be able to help us even more now than ever before – God alone knows. Poor old Mrs G lost her husband some weeks ago – fancy me putting that word 'lost' when I don't believe it all for Father or any true Christian is more 'found' now than ever!! Can I make a cover for the new cushion? I should like to do that for you. God bless you darling & lift up the light of His face upon you, with His peace, Mother.

2 Hawthorn Cottages, London Rd, Crawley

Nov 10th 1961

Dear Miss Christine, please try to believe that we here do often think of you & pray for you, and please forgive me for not writing to you for far too long. Once more I am collecting the SUM boxes and as usual the half yearly totals average between £5-6 but this time I feel it is right to tell you some individual totals as they are very good. Ted Paice & Mrs have collected £25.18.6d since 1945 in sixpences & coppers; and dear Edie Parsons' total amounts to £28.9.3d; and Mrs Barker who did live in Limes Ave brings in 10/6d each half year. I have written to thank them on behalf of the SUM. I thought you would be interested in all this & feel encouraged that the home folk are helping for love of you and the work you are doing. Now may I thank you for the most interesting & enlightening account of your travels & trek into those far off villages & of the people you meet & how they entertain you. I did enjoy reading it & as usual pass it on to most of my box holders, Dorothy has it now. We here, Mother & I, and many box holder friends have sorrowed with you over the loss of Mr Ernest; yet we know our sorrow is only selfish – for him, to be with Christ, is far better. Several times I have seen dear Mrs Cheal, she is being very brave, saying she dare not wear a sad face for she knows Mr Cheal would not wish it & she knows he is now so happy and it will only be a little while before they meet again. The miss in the home life must be very great indeed, as I do know, but Miss Mary is just as bright and as busy as before. My little Mother is fairly well in her general health but 8wks ago she had a fall & broke a bone in her right wrist causing much pain as you will know; & because it was not set the wrist will always be rather deformed. I am so thankful it wasn't a leg. We send you our Christian love and many, many blessings in all your work & a very happy & blessed Christmas & New Year from Kathleen A Willis.

35 The Millbank

Nov 12th '61

My beloved Chris your most welcome letter was waiting when Mary & I got home from Horsham firstly it was Elders Mtg followed at 3pm by Monthly Mtg at which you will be surprised to learn we had two verses sung by a good tenor voice 'In heavenly love Abiding' which sounded grand to me. I felt the need to praise the Lord that such a voice of praise & prayer had been heard in our Mtg then Reg Smith stood and quoted 'Praise to the Holiest in the height and in the depths be praise,' etc. After half an hour of beautiful worship the first item on the Agenda for business was 'A Tribute to the Grace of God in the life of Ernest Cheal' which Margaret Emmott & Richard West had put together. It was quite true & good, a simple record of his life work, spoken out by a few friends who knew him. But Doris got up saying there was one omission in that lovely testimony – no mention was made of his home life which surely must have made a great contribution to his work & service, and his wife & family should have been spoken of. You can imagine my surprise at that! But it was very kind of her nonetheless. Darling your letter was so full of interest & I rejoice over the news of Aristarchus and the splendid address he gave & those other fine speakers at your convention. Tuesday is our SUM Day of Prayer & Mary will take the tape of Daniel Lot's story and your recent letters then we shall be praying for you & so many you write about esp Showul that he may be helped to give up the beer. I feel so glad to have these opportunities of some rides with Mary to her meetings, last time it was Polegate & Tonbridge; she does speak so very well indeed. Please thank Kefas & Jacob for their letters – I will try to write very soon & please give my greetings to Fillibbus and to Shakan; from your everloving Mother.

Panyam

Nov 23rd '61

Darlings all – that's Rene too of course, thank you for your dear letters & specially I was so pleased to hear you had been able to take the tape to Mr & Mrs Hayward & how glad they were to hear all the African voices – I'm sure that gave them much pleasure. Thank you for doing that; and also for the hairnets. On the next tape – it will be a while before I can send it – I managed to record some of Fillibbus speaking with me and with Shakan the girl on whom the rock fell! Shakan is such a sweet soul now, she has a little boy called Emmanuel and she & her husband are both in class for baptism. Kathleen MacD's visit was very pleasant she is a very nice girl, bright & keen & thrilled to be out on the job. We took her to as many places as we could & on a return from Longkat we picked up Emmanuel Dayihir the medical worker now on his way to Maiduguri – he's a faithful soul, never had anything to do with Moslems but now is going as a missionary among them. Do please remember him especially in your prayers. Kathleen did enjoy seeing the GLB groups flourishing in the more out of the way places & thought our Panyam girls were the best!

Rene darling your letter certainly gave me a real picture of your distress and oh how my heart goes out to you. Darling no wonder you feel so terribly anxious, I do too, and I'm sure we are all so dreadfully sorry about all this. Your thought of getting together with all the women who have left sounds a wise & sensible thing but will require much courage. I love your courage in finding comfort in Deut 4:30-31 'When thou art in tribulation & all these things are come upon thee even in the latter days if thou turn to the Lord thy God & shalt be obedient unto His voice, for the Lord thy God is a merciful God, He will not forsake thee nor forget the covenant of thy fathers which He sware unto them.'

You will remember our John Mark who fell away so badly and eventually abandoned his dear wife Grace after making such dreadful accusations which she consistently denied? He managed to get into a study course in Oxford and is keeping up with it. His father Barnaba Kohop came to see me today with a letter JM had written him saying, "When I went to England I was far away from Jesus but now He is near me and I must obey Him." I don't know just what he means but it does show that the Lord is wonderfully answering prayer for what has seemed for a long time to be a hopeless case.

Two weeks ago a heathen woman from Tof gave birth to twins then died a week later. The heathen relatives wanted to throw the babies into the grave with her but Filibbus intervened & persuaded the father to give them to us. We found a young Christian woman, newly baptised, who was thrilled to take the girl so the husband & the natural father both signed the papers, but we still need a foster mum for the boy. The tiny mites weigh 4lbs and 4½ lbs and both are doing well so far. The little chap was my responsibility last night so now I do need to go to bed hoping for better sleep, so goodnight my very dear darlings, blessings on you especially Rene, ever yours Chris.

St Peter's Vicarage, Rushden, Northants

Dec 2nd '61

My dear Chris we are indeed very sorry for this long delay in writing to try and convey our feelings for you in your sorrow & loss. We know you will rejoice for your father as you thank God for his beautiful life & peaceful passing. We wish you could have been at home but the Lord makes no mistakes & we're so glad to hear from Nakam that your mother is able to go on bravely & well. Your sisters and brother will be surrounding her each in their own special way, and 'underneath are the Everlasting Arms.' How good it was that you were able to get back in time for that delightful invitation from the Phonetics Tutor to take your Sura language knowledge to the Ghana University! Here we now have a Deaconess and a married Curate – we can almost retire. We have been able to spend some days at Swanwick, Lee Abbey, Scargill, and finally now at the Old Jordan Hotel in Bucks; yesterday I attended my first ever Friends Meeting a most enjoyable experience, I wouldn't have missed it for anything. We are staying with a cousin of Gordons & we both send our fondest love to you, Louie.

27 The Avenue, Sunbury-on-Thames

3rd Dec '61

My dear Chris I am writing to express my loving sympathy on the passing of your dear father, of course we feel it as a very happy event for him as he has been called to Higher Service with Christ which is far better. But for the loved ones who remain here for a time he will be much missed by the whole family & his large circle of friends. This family tho' spread far & wide continues to flourish & grow and next spring I shall be the proud grandma of 10! And still there come opportunities for which I am also truly thankful, for me to speak to groups about our work in Formosa; and Joan's eldest boy 17yr old Tony, wants to take up medicine 'just like Grandpa.' He hopes to be accepted at The London Hospital. Now dear Chris may God continue to give you encouragements in your work & the good health to carry it out, with our united love & all good wishes for 1962 from your loving Auntie Elsie.

Mongu

Dec 5th '61

My darlings all three again, as you'll see I'm here, with the intention of obtaining a few quiet days to catch up on office work with fewer interruptions. However, tomorrow I'll go into Jos to do the shopping Frances needs while she attends her meeting; then on Thursday we shall go to the Graduation service for the Theological students amongst whom is our Bitrus Yamden! And today was the opening of our Panyam Midwifery Unit which I'd asked Frances to come & open. A huge crowd of women had gathered for this & afterwards we let them all file in to see the interior – it really does look awfully nice! The bedroom has 2 beds made up with new sheets & red blankets, & 2 babies' cots – just boxes painted green on legs with little castors. A green locker for the women's things stands between the beds. The other room is the labour ward with a big cement bed with a sorbo mattress for the delivery; a trolley on wheels completes the furniture. The bathroom is the 'piece de resistance' with a flush toilet – the first in Panyam! There is a room outside for relatives with a small kitchen for them to cook the patient's food, & this completes the whole set up. In your dear letter Mother you mention Brian Hession, just last week I saw he had passed on in Oct & I recently read his book 'To Live Again.' What courage he had. I wonder if now that he is on the Glory side he still feels that he did the best to will to go on living as he did, or whether he thinks 'what an ass I was, for this is so much better!' I am eagerly awaiting news of your Christmas arrangements – if you are going to Dungate Mummy & you Mary up to Scotland? It will be strange if you are all to be in different places but this year it will generally feel a bit strange wherever we all may be won't it. Do remember the Ordination on the 25th of Bitrus Yamden, there will be a good deal of preparation required for that service as you can imagine, but for now I must say goodbye again with my very dearest love to you all three plus a special extra portion to you Rene darling, yours as ever, Chris.

As from 35 T M but really in Richmond

Dec 10th '61

My darling love it's been too long again I know & I'll speak these words to you every bit as much to myself: stop trying to do too much, to fit everything in; learn to say 'no' to some requests; I'm sure we would each get more accomplished in the long run if we could do that. You must slow down at least for the 5 expected days that dear Ant can be with you – what fun it will be; I keep praying he might be profoundly affected by all he sees & hears while with you – I know he is really looking forward to it, as I'm quite sure you are too. This enclosed tape is only for you on one side, the other is Hazel's special message to A; you may have to turn the spool with your finger to regulate the speed a bit of our messages, perhaps on hers too. These past weeks have been so busy; I've had long distances to travel & such a lot of meetings but there are only 4 more now until Christmas which is a relief. This morning I was at the lovely historic Kew Green church where Queen Mary's parents were married; there was a huge congregation & the Bishop kindly gave permission for me to preach!! Also I had to read the second lesson; I was helped to do everything at the right time & there was a good atmosphere & very attentive listening. I was entertained to lunch by a lady in the Civil Svc who has a charming old cottage almost overlooking Richmond Park. It is good that Mummie will be at Dungate Manor over the 24-25th as I feel I must be with Rene she is under great strain

& needs someone with whom she can share the burden. She is earnestly trying to find & follow God's will through, to give Him the glory. Of course it is encouraging news of John-Mark but will he & Grace ever get together again do you think? I had another strange conversation with the woman we both know well JB...isn't it a good thing we don't all think alike! Please greet Unaisi, Joel, Kefas & Godfrey from me & Istafanus & Ishaku too & all my dearest love for you darling as ever, Mary.

28 Abbotshall Dr Cults, Aberdeen

Dec 12th '61

Darling Chris I've been so glad to have your dear letters sent on from 35 TM, thank you for all your love & prayers for us. May you have a most special & blessed Christmas in every way – I will be with you in spirit for the Ordination service. I did get out to the SUM Prayer mtg last evening, only 7 of us but it was good, all were asking warmly after you & praying for you & your work. There is little of any encouragement from here except the Lucia service went off well despite fears it might be boycotted completely; Lucia herself was a lovely Norwegian girl who read part of 1 Cor. 13 v nicely, followed by a little girl of just 9 singing 'Jesus tender Shepherd hear me' which was lovely. I am hanging onto the precious promise in Micah 7:18-20...extraordinarily apt for our present situation. I have nothing prepared for Christmas it seems hard to settle to anything & I have such toothache tho' the dentist says nothing is wrong; but now with a heartful of love to you darling & greetings to all Panyam friends, ever yours R.

Brookfield, Crawley

Dec 12th '61

My dear Chris & I hope Anthony will forgive me for including him in this as there is simply not the opportunity to write separately to him. We are sure you will both enjoy his visit to the full. You have no doubt heard from Mother the details of our somewhat eventful journey up to Nottingham in early October to deposit Alison into Florence Boot Hall at the Univ and come back via Leamington to collect Aunt Ethel to bring her back as Barbara & Margaret hope to find her a little cottage or rooms in someone else's abode. She is not doing too well after U George's demise. And that was all following the rather hectic weeks of September – just to think it is already three months to the day since Father's passing, and Auntie Jo a week before for that matter. It was wonderful that he was taken at such a time when May & I were both on hand, and so many relatives & friends could make the necessary journey. The tributes are still coming in from all sides; they have mostly been certainly very inspiring, with some surprises. Unfortunately I cannot give you as yet a very encouraging report of the Business; economies have been made of course but insufficient to meet requirements. We are re-organising staff and sending out more of the home-staff to earn their keep on outwork of which there is still plenty & more orders are coming in. April is the next deadline & I'm still hoping for an office at Pulborough where quite a lot of building is going on but in reality we still must live from month to month & wait to see how things develop. The Henmans want us to do some planting in the garden of their new house in Godalming & there is a nice order in Horsted Keynes from the Prime Minister's daughter. We do hope & pray you will have a very pleasant & inspiring time together at Christmas both in the work & in your personal lives & that the New Year will be one of good progress for you both, with very much love from Wilfrid – here is B who will add: Well Chris little did you ever expect to have Anthony with you for a Christmas in Panyam! We shall eagerly look forward to hearing all about it. Next week here the struggle to feed the masses will be in full swing (not to be taken as flippant, in light of present famine conditions) Chris I hope Nona will write to you soon, she has done well this term, passed all 14 exams & come top in 3 of them! It has been a tonic to her, & to us. Ant dear please forgive your faithless Aunt & accept her fond love with best wishes to you both for a happy, happy Christmas & lots of love from Barbara.

Braeside, Rodborough Common, Stroud

Dec 13th '61

My dearest Chris very many thanks for your card & letter; I am (we all are) glad you have not stretched to any gifts – your love is the best & most enduring that you can send and we value it deeply. I do so want to keep in touch during these hurrying days; I'm sure you will have a very busy time and I pray that much blessing will be amongst you all there. We've just had another letter from the Pastor who wrote the first one I sent you, from his jail cell; he's the only one left there now & has been sentenced to 6 more years – but he is rejoicing in serving the Lord there and tells of 2 criminals in with him who have been saved! Now with our dearest love & best loving wishes for Christmas & New Year from your A. Lena.

Christmas Eve 1961

My beloved Chris if this letter seems a bit muddled put it down to excess of feelings with so many tangible proofs of the love & kindness of all our dear ones, letters from you, Rene & many others & when we got back from Mtg there was a large box in the garage from our dear Ant – such an unexpected gift with such good things to eat inside the delightful cane picnic basket, what joy there is in thinking of the joy you two will bring to one another, blessings on you darlings. Mary has been to Redhill Hospital to visit poor Edie Parsons who was taken there on Wednesday in such pain from arthritis & now it turns out she has a slight fracture of the 'good' leg is it any wonder she could not walk. We have just heard the last of the Cambridge festival of 9 Lessons & Carols & now there the Praise Service on TV which we like to hear & there is fine singing from Wales. What a great joy it was to welcome your John Mark to this house last Friday morn with Hezekiah & Nakam; I am ashamed of my lack of faith, feeling it was almost hopeless to go on praying & now to see the young man with a shining face & a heart changed by the grace of God! Now I will pray that he will be enabled to go home & make things right with his dear wife and that she, Grace, will accept him back & that they might truly forgive each other. Now my own darling may your heart be filled with joy & blessing & great peace, with no disappointments over Christmas and may your New Year be the most fruitful yet, with dear love from Mother.

SUM Jos

Dec 27th 1961

Darlings, wouldn't it be lovely if we could phone this evening before you go off to Dungate & Aberdeen, then I could tell you what a happy time we've had here together & now on the way to Kaduna for Ant's plane; everything's gone so well. At the Airport 9.30 now having left at 4.30am, not bad going for 173 miles! Just sending my (A) love too! We've had a super time & I enjoyed it all tremendously; Auntie Chris is looking v well & is obviously v fit judging by the way she walked to Tof on Tues! The plane is in now, must stop, dear love, Ant. Well now I'm about to set off again & should reach Panyam by 7pm, yours as ever Chris.

252 Selsdon Rd, S Croydon

Dec 29th '61

Dearest Chris so very, very many thanks for all your kind thoughtfulness, the lovely bag – already in use, the tape nearly worn out with so much use, and your lovely letter, quite devoured. Hez and John Mark arrived on Thursday & we went to see the Perfects for a cup of tea, then on Friday I took them down to Ifield to see your Mother & May. It was a thrilling visit & I watched JM fall in love with your Mother & was so deeply impressed by knowing she has prayed faithfully for him for so many years. He said to me afterwards, "I saw her wonderful face!" and his eyes glowed. That evening we listened to all the tapes you've sent & they were thrilled beyond words to hear all the dear

Panyam voices; and we recorded <u>them</u> for you also! JM was a perfect visitor, delightful to have in the house, even did the washing up! On our day in London he insisted upon paying for everything for all 3 of us and I let him when he told me that whilst in Oxford he gets £51 each month in addition to his Nigerian ADO salary! Chris for this first Christmas without your father on earth I am so glad to know you have Anthony with you & I've been praying that the two of you will really enjoy each others company a lot. Much prayer for your Mother too as I'm sure it was not easy for her to visit Brookfield for Christmas lunch. It has been bitterly, bitterly cold here for days, oh for some Nigerian heat, much love as aye, Nakam.

28 Abbotshall Dr., Cults Aberdeen

Dec 30th '61

My darling Chris thank you so very much for your letters – how often my thoughts have flown to you in Panyam with Ant, I'm sure you had a marvellous time together. It has been a strange sort of Christmas here; Erik went to bed very poorly with the flu & the Dr gave him the 'terramycine' drug I believe it is & would not hear of him getting up, so the blackest depression has settled on him & I've really been quite afraid for him. Christmas morning was bitterly cold & snowing & he still had a temp & now seems to have lost heart altogether & says he can't believe the Bible means what it says where faith is concerned. I arose at 5am to do all that he usually does before early service & set off on my bike, glad the snow was not too deep. I quite enjoyed the quiet ride with not a soul about. There were 25 came out & then stayed for breakfast; I got home at 9.30 then cooked our dinner before starting on the baking preparations for the Boxing Day evening Party which took me all the next day too. 54 came for that and all seemed to enjoy everything; I got home at 11.20 & was glad to fall into bed. It was sad that none of the usual people were at the service or the party, many are simply staying away it is all so sad & so unnecessary. The next day was the worst snowstorm for 40 yrs about 2ft fell across Aberdeen & we had to dig ourselves out, a boy from the house opposite came to help me. The snowplough has thrown up banks about 5ft high either side of the roads. Ingvar has talked to me a little & he is most concerned & has now spoken to E in no uncertain terms; I feel sorry he has to go back to Sweden on the 9th. And I feel E will not be able to take up the work again but perhaps I'm wrong. May God bless the New Yr for you darling & give you health & peace, my dearest love, Rene.

35 The Millbank

Jan 1st 1962

My darling love on this New Year's Day while 5 sledges are sliding along outside our windows – such happy children on them – may God grant you His own best blessing & give you all the enjoyment & encouragement you need, keeping you close to Him always, for there I know you will have happiness & peace. I am quite well but a little weary so will have Mary finish this…Darling, life has a strange quality of unreality these days & this severe weather does not help; but we lived Christmas with you & A – surely the Ordering of God was in his visit to you. Mother is alright but this is the first time she's ever felt unable to finish a letter to you. Her natural turn of mind is that she will soon be Going Home but, as you know, she has a fighting spirit & her desire is to stay here a while yet. The Dr came through snow & ice yesterday to see her & said she's going on well but it is the 'flu injections that affect morale so much. Now darling in the hope this may be a year of special blessing for you I send my heart's love, Mary.

GINDIRI

JAN 11TH '62

Darlings I do hope my Birthday Greeting letter has reached you Mummy & that you are enjoying today to the full. I am thinking of you so much as I toast myself in the welcome sunshine, wishing I could send you some to melt your unpleasant snow & ice. This is our very busy week at GLB Camp, with the main idea of choosing 2 girls to go to England in June to represent N. Nigeria in the Diamond Jubilee Celebrations. There are 22 who have made it thus far & we are testing them in many different ways, & adding that to their past achievements & service in their own Companies, and seeing what more they can learn this week. I think it is quite possible that one Sura girl might be chosen but I must not count my chickens before they are hatched! Tomorrow they must walk the 8mls to Mongu, buy there the foodstuffs they need, return on some public transport in time to cook an evening meal European style in a missionary's house, for 8 people, lay the table & serve the meal. They will do this in 4 groups & each group must have at least 2 Officers at the meal! We finish here on Sunday & should be home on Monday in time for the Faith & Farm Course for 40 of our Panyam women, then schools reopen on the 29th so now darlings my dearest & best love to you both & of course to Rene if, as I hope, she is with you, as ever Chris.

35 T M

Jan 13th '62

My darling love I'm sure you heard from Mary that I've had such a happy week at Dungate while she was away (it was too icy for Rene to get down to us) Getting back here I found a wonderful pile of letters & birthday cards and such lovely bouquets of spring flowers. In Margaret Russell's letter she said she'd seen you at Christmas & you 'looked radiant' – I can quite believe it darling! It was good to read your descriptions of your happy times with Ant & the Christmas Day Ordinations, my heart rejoiced; & I felt your love & prayers throughout the 11th, before, & still on-going, thank you my own darling. What a lovely message came from Nakam's visit here when she told us of the many evenings John Mark, Hezekiah & David used to sit up late into the night talking about "nothing other than the Bible & how we can live it out in our everyday lives." Please do not worry at all upon my account, I am at last feeling much better, but will send this now with all the love in my heart & asking for God's blessings on you, Mother.

Braeside, Rodborough Common

Jan 16th 62

Dearest Chris here is the promised list of prayer requests for other missionaries – I'm sure you also will feel they are vital, but oh how very easy it is to fall asleep in the very act, or at least find one's mind chasing after other things. It is sad to say Frank has given up the college for Baptist ministry training & is at home now hardly at all. Mollie attended a young people's conference at Sunbury on Thames & visited the Tyers family while there. They all go now to a rather high Cof E where the boys are 'servers' & all seem to have contributed towards a chalice; and some candlesticks are to come next. I am sorry about this; & Elsie goes alone to some sort of Free Church. I must not prattle on but go and get the tea ready for the family's return; they would all join me in sending v much love, always your A Lena.

Panyam

Jan 23rd '62

Darlings how lovely to get your dear letters again today, thank you, & I'm so sorry I did not tell you the results of the GLB girls' final test; they did everything they were supposed to do, & within the time, and the meal 'our' team prepared for us was nice, and presented well. Joan, Kathleen & I had the duty of making the choice of the 2 to be chosen for the England trip; we prayed much over this important decision & were relieved that the marks they earned left us in no doubt. It was to be Mary Dabiring of our Sura girls in Panyam and Hawa, a SIM girl from Gure. This was just as we had wished & everyone was very happy & we are especially thrilled about Mary D (she's the one I mentioned previously would have been my personal choice.) She is just such a dear, & went quite speechless when the result was given out. So another Sura should be coming to see you in June; it would be so lovely if the Crawley GLB could entertain her. On Thurs afternoon the women on the Faith & Farm Course will put on a display of their work this week which they seem to have thoroughly enjoyed; they've made a smokeless stove, learned to make rice pudding with milk, & they've made 2 model villages, one clean & one dirty, for their use when teaching hygiene & cleanliness in their own compounds. The District Bible School for men starts here on Feb 5th there is always something else to prepare for! John Mark wrote to me of his visit with Nakam to you in Ifield, specifically your 'charming manners,' Mother, & the wonder he felt at your knowledge of so many names of people you have never seen & the fact that you are regularly praying for him. He also spoke so warmly of seeing you Mary, for the second time now! I simply marvel at God's grace so evident in that young man. I praise God for the kindness of Eileen, Madge & Delia to you each, especially taking Mother into Dungate so happily when you Mary dearest have to be away & Rene is unavailable. Do take care of your dear selves & I pray that you may be kept and blest every single day, so now bye-bye again my very dear loves, as ever yours, Chris.

35 T M

Jan 30th '62

My beloved Chris I must not let the arrival of one beloved daughter hinder me from writing to another beloved one, nor smiling across to the other beloved one here with me! I went to Meeting this morn, the first time since Christmas Eve. Yesterday was one of those beautiful sunny winter days which bring a hint of springtime so Mary suggested a ride to Lindfield to fetch some books & on to see Miss Roberts who is very keen on the Bible Soc & gets up many sales of work etc for it, so had much to say to Mary & I sat by the fire knitting. I had thought to write to you but all the talk made it rather difficult. Rene arrived after lunch and how thankful we are to have her – after such a time of it she has had lately. I am sure she is being given wisdom not her own, & kept in quietness & peace. We have been so interested in all you write about the women's Faith & Farming – what a wonderful change from their old ways of working. We all send you our dear love & with a tender goodbye now my darling from your loving Mother.

252 Selsdon Rd, S. Croydon

Feb 10th '62

Dearest Chris thank you so much for continuing to write to me so fully of your Panyam doings – I devour every word & feel I'm really still with you there, through disappointments & encouragements & all in between. Not forgetting the wonderful extra treat of the photos when they come & of course the tapes, thus enabling me to see & hear so many dear ones – thank you again. I am thrilled about Bitrus & his new ideas of calling the Christians together from all those outstations for organising groups to take the Gospel further – splendid! And your local women composing hymns & singing them to their own tunes, & getting the men to join in! You are certainly seeing 'independence & self-government' growing and in the best direction too, praise be! Now let us believe they will soon want to develop their Church life & Services along their own lines – my heart rejoiceth at the prospect & I know yours must do also! I am sure you will be shown the right time & approach to tackle him in the matter of that hidden sin, which is of course no longer hidden; this is a very serious matter & I suspect a great hindrance to further blessing out in his villages. I can't help wondering if a similar situation might have grown up around the Bookshop workers, to explain it going down so much? Your next letters will enlighten me I'm sure.

Have you heard from your protégé over here recently? He wrote to me & his studies seem to be going well but I felt you should hear his last paragraph, 'I hope you are still praying for me. Although I have come back to the Lord I feel I have not given myself back completely to Him. There are certain quarters of my life in which I have not allowed Him to be Master. Please continue to pray for me because I know it is only when I do give up myself completely to Him that I will have again His real joy, peace & true happiness, as I once had. It is a sad state of affairs isn't it but I am sure there is nothing beyond the Lord's power who gives us the victory through Jesus Christ.' Clearly I must not relax the prayer for him. Chris dear do you know anything of Ibrahim Datok? He hasn't written to me for years & I do not want to lose touch with him. I am so glad you're enjoying giving the OT lectures – & in Hausa too, well done! It will be wonderful if you really can record all the vernaculars for those Languages professors. I can imagine how long the preparation must take you, please be firm about your own daily rest time – your health is vital. How splendid that you found parents so quickly for those orphan twins; & I hope Joyce did get away for her holiday, but maternity work does tie one down rather doesn't it; with much love & prayer, Nakam.

28 Abbotshall Drive, Cults, Aberdeen

Feb 14th '62

My darling Chris I've been thinking of you so much as always, but particularly as you teach giving these intensive lectures – however long did you have to study OT history for this?! You are marvellous. I was so glad to be able to be down home at 35 although it was only a week; Mummy looked quite fairly well but she has gone small, sort of shrunken up tho' usually her bright cheerful dear self. Our Mary looks so tired & so pale, how I wish I could be there longer & relieve her of more of the burden both in the house & cooking as well as just being there with Mummy so Mary can go off to her work with a lighter mind. We had another quite heavy fall of snow yest & all roads are slippery, many blocked completely. For now darling my dearest love to you & blessings on you Rene.

Panyam

Feb 22nd '62

Darling Mummy & Mary I am on my own this week so have been able to catch up a bit with letters & office work. Thank you so much for your dear letters – I love the 'picture' of you two sitting at the fireside with Father's photo on the mantelpiece as though he is still head of the family – which of course he is; and your shared time of reading & prayer together there. How I do yearn with you over Rene in the desperate situation up there & I wonder whether it would be right for her to consider coming away for a few months. It would be a great relief to my mind if she could be with you two, well away from that deadly atmosphere; but as I wrote to her, unless it is of the Lord's ordering it wouldn't bring any real peace or help, so we must go on praying & trusting that she will soon know what is the right step to take. I have told you a bit about Pastor Bitrus' work in gathering the Christians into groups for visiting, now I can add that it is growing wonderfully & greatly helped by the women's enthusiasm for singing the Gospel to local tunes which is spreading like wildfire into so many groups, compounds & Churches! So far there are 6 new hymns, narratives from Scripture and words from the NT, all very antiphonal & repetitive, making it very attractive & everybody can join in immediately. It sounds really lovely but I find it extremely hard to catch the tunes – they are so different from ours. I plan to get it all recorded as soon as possible. My favourite one is: 'Let not your hearts be troubled' & a second group answers: 'O you people of Jesus' then Leader: Jesus says He has gone to prepare a place for us,

Answer: One day we shall see the face of our Saviour,

Leader: There are many mansions, o!

Answer: One day we shall see the face of our Saviour,

Leader: There is no sorrow there o!'

And so on, including, 'There is no adulterer there' and 'there is no drunkard there,' etc. We are expecting the Mannings for the weekend, asking for instructions by road from Lagos, but like so many visitors, without realising just how far we are from a Post Office for answering such requests by telegram in sufficient time to be of help to them! Goodbye for now my dear darlings with so much love Chris.

Crossing the (rough) sea to the I. of W.

Feb 26th '62

My dearest love I am thinking much of you & knowing if you were here with me today you'd be feeling more than a trifle apprehensive about even a short voyage in this tremendous & bitter wind!! It is so very cold you feel as if you have nothing on at all. I've had to be away a lot recently & do not like Mummy having to be on her own so much, especially on my long days. Yesterday she was to have gone over to Brookfield but the wind was so dreadfully bitter she only wanted to stay at home; & another day B&W were to come to her but they did not get there till 8pm & I was back by then. I did talk with her last evening about making more use of the wireless as there are so many worthwhile programmes to hear, & we have both been quite excited over Col John Glenn's achievement in space on the 20th & so thankful he got through safely – Wilfrid told us of the prayer of thanksgiving described in the papers & in a TV interview. Also, I suggested to Mother that she really shouldn't sit listening in a strained sort of way for the phone to ring, but use it to have little talks with other people now & then. On the whole she is wonderful but is looking rather frail & I know it is not good for her to be alone for long stretches. We're so grateful for the dears at Dungate but must not put upon them too often so I'm really re-considering having Edie to stay here with us, if she might re-consider the possibility. I think I am also waiting to see how things continue up in Aberdeen; Eileen feels sure God IS working by strengthening Rene's faith enormously, & that He has the whole matter in hand. Darling although I've not mentioned your work you do know how often I think of you and all of you there & pray daily for you yourself & all the work there, in your busy days & in mine, I'm just so sorry there is not more time to talk on paper with you like we used to; may you ever be helped & guided, always your own & with my heart's love, Mary.

28 Abbotshall Drive, Cults

March 1st '62

My Darling thank you so very much for your dear letter & for all the help & encouragement you give me, & too for the lovely pictures. I'm only sorry I haven't a viewer but I will be able to see them properly when I next go down to home. How I have been pondering what you said, & if I am really meant to leave to go & look after them at 35 The Millbank. Please pray earnestly with me that I may know what is right to do. Though I long to be home with them at 35 I cannot visualise anything past May 18th but once I really felt it was God's will & made up my mind to go I certainly wouldn't want to come back here to live again. It is so baffling, but I know God can alter any situation… It is still bitterly cold with more snow. Please tell Unaisi I pray for her & send my best greetings; & to you too darling with all my dearest love also, ever your loving Rene.

Panyam

March 28th '62

My dear darling May you would I'm sure have been touched to hear Ishaku's special prayer for you last night! My thoughts have been with you since Mummy's letter came 2 nights ago, I'm so grieved that you're having this trouble in your neck but perhaps it is a mercy even in it enforcing you to rest & also giving Rene an unsought opportunity of being with you. I should be happy to think she might be able to stay with you for several weeks to give you a good break, as well as for you to have her help. Do you recall our own name for the Lake Chad project, 'Fish & Chips' & the work put into it by the Carlings, David & Gwyneth from Maiduguri, with many people from Chip. They went on an exploration of some islands on the Lake & they found innumerable tiny floating reed isles on which perhaps 30 or so people live, catching & curing fish & taking them in tiny reed boats to the mainland to sell. These folk are called Buduma, superficially Moslem, & very friendly tho' completely unevangelised. So the Carlings, hearts drawn to these people, are longing to have a houseboat in which tour the Lake, & visit the medical evangelists we all hope will soon be placed in the more strategic mainland villages around the lake shore. Dr McBride from Bambur came to Bill Tett offering a couple of boats which had been used on the River Benue but no longer required, so we are asking at once for the 30ft one! Now we need more medical evangelists prepared to accept training, to be ready when we can open up new Dispensaries. The wonderful thing is we were asked to open more of these medical quarters by the local Government! I have been able to enjoy a couple of days of unusual rest & now have told our Evangelists about our new Chad Project, & much interest with much prayer is already backing it plus some Sura folk are offering to go there at once, Naphtali Dawan, Othniel & Susannah Basan, & 3 other Christian men & their wives will be the only believers to start with in that strongly Moslem area of N.E.Bornu. Pastor Bitrus has just returned from Chakfiem, away south of Mongun, where he has completed his itinerary. He says between 12&1300 people gathered for last Sunday's meetings under the shade trees near the Church – can you imagine it?! This makes me think of your meetings & in a recent letter from Nakam she says, 'May came & spoke at our WF meeting yesterday & I have never heard her speak better; she was absolutely fine & held them all spellbound!' Well done darling! Another wonderful thing is that we have had our salaries raised to £25 per month as from Nov '61 so now I can gladly send another £50 cheque for Rene (enclosed) which I think brings our debt to her down to £400 doesn't it? Darling Mary may the Lord bless you with His healing touch & His peace as you rest; and this also brings my very dearest love to you all three, ever yours Chris.

Beechcroft, 109 Farncombe Rd, Tunbridge Wells

April 14th '62

Dear Miss Cheal, your earlier letter plus the circular, with the recent issue of the Lightbearer have brought great joy to me, particularly the testimony of Daniel Lot; many thanks for all and the inspiration given by you to them all. I am especially interested to know that there are these Sura young men studying in London at the present time; I would like to contact them if possible, & the Sura girl due later on. Will you kindly let me know their names & where they are to be found, I shall make a big effort to contact them somehow. Your mention of Bitrus Yamden is thrilling I wonder if he is a son or grandson of the Yamden I remember from 1918? On the list of my Sura god-children, no.23 is Eliya Yamden but with no date given; Barnaba Kohop figures on that list, amongst many others, God bless them. My wife sends her love & greetings, we hope to see you when you next come home for furlough; greet all the Church for me, God bless you richly, yours very sincerely E. Hayward.

35 The Millbank

April 15th '62

My darling Chris another week has passed & most of my shingles also have, taking most of the pain from my head & face with them for which I am thankful. I am certain the injections of Vitamin

B12 along with the pain medicine really helped, the dear Doctor came in every day to administer them. I have had a very lazy sort of week mostly in bed knitting, reading, with plenty of quiet time for worship & meditation, listening to services on the radio, some good talks leading up to the grand & glorious Easter message. I have prayed a lot for Pastor Bitrus that he may be blessed in his work & witness. Rene has been such a blessing to us as you can imagine she has just done everything to help us so that both M & I feel comfortable & rested but Mary's swollen neck has not disappeared. I am enjoying the book of Dr Grenfell's life – what a time he had with dire poverty & disease there in Labrador, but oh what a blessing his life was! Our loving thoughts & prayers are always with you darling, Mother.

Panyam

April 18th '62

Darlings this is just a quick note to bring you my most loving greetings for Good Friday & Easter, such a joyous time. Our Rogation Service last Saturday was very well attended by so many farmers who brought in their hoes & bowls of seed in anticipation of a good harvest & the new hymns were sung & a good word given by Pastor Bitrus. We are also full of thanksgiving for the first new SUM school in Gwoza and Jim & Jean Hamilton are opening a whole new Mission Station there, all built with funds from here in Plateau Province. Jacob Damut sends you his greetings & Pastor Manasseh is here beside me & sends his too; there are only 6 of us European leaders now, all the rest are Africans & I love sitting with them taking part in their discussions. Rauta Lot, a niece of Pastor David, has today started her work as our first Nigerian midwife, wearing one of Joyce's aprons & triangular cap. She looks so smart & is thrilled to be at work at last after completing the 2yr course at Vom. Her first 'case' has just left the Midwifery Unit with her baby daughter, & 2 others are in the offing. Rauta took the Infant Welfare clinic this morning & tomorrow she must cope with the antinatal clinic; any spare time she will help in the Dispensary. Joyce & I plan to walk the 9mls from Chip to Tal to check up on one of the adopted Tof orphans then on further to Jepniyahal another Chip village I have never yet visited. But I need to be back into Jos for a committee meeting on 30th before going off to Kaduna on May 2nd for the Christian Council of Nigeria so I must finish this for now by sending my dearest love to you two & of course Rene if she's still with you, Chris.

35 TM

April 22nd '62

My dear love I'm actually sitting outside in the sunshine…you'll hardly be able to realise how just how wonderful it is to write that & to feel the blessed warmth of the sun! I do not ever remember a longer spell of cold weather & last week was one of the worst with 3 whole mid-winter grim days. It is quite extraordinary to see even the very hardy people have flagged recently & everyone has felt the struggle against the elements; & even something of the same in the spiritual sphere also. Marcia Cleaver wrote so bravely that the doctors can do no more for her except to deal with the pain when it gets bad. Things for Rene are worse if that's possible. It is so bewildering & I simply do not know how best to help her. And I have said nothing to her or to Mother as they both get so worked up about me, but my neck is no better after all this rest & the doctor thinks the op is my only workable treatment. I shall see what happens after I've spoken at a few meetings after this Easter break & I promise to keep you honestly informed. What a dreadful moan of an Easter letter this is – when it started out so well! We know that God knows quite well what He is doing & He has the matter, all these matters, in hand. Goodbye my darling for this time; God bless & guide you through these busy days, with all my love Mary. I'll be able to use your little story of father Lot reciting his Bible verses memorised so long ago & still just as invaluable in today's situations, it'll be a real message to people over here.

Panyam

May 13th '62

My dearest dears on Friday eve Joyce brought the news that Unaisi Anwet had passed away at 3am; after I left Kaduna she got much worse & on Thurs eve Joyce gave her morphia which allowed her some sleep but then she saw Lois & said, "There's a shilling over there, put it into the Sunday collection for me," & sometime after midnight she lapsed into unconsciousness & then died. Dear sweet generous soul. Her passing has done something to us because for the first time ever in this tribe, 10 or more women went to the graveside & sang one of the new hymns about the glory of heaven. Several heathen came to see what it was all about and Nasik spoke to them before Pastor Bitrus took the service & gave a powerful message. Since then crowds of folk have been in to greet Bitrus Bistu & there has been no weeping or wailing, just a quiet peace & witness to the Lord. Everyone has been recalling her goodness & kindness and Victoria Nasik told me that what she said at the graveside was like was like what the widows did to Tabitha in Acts showing all the good that she had done. Old Daniel Lot still lingers on tho' he has been failing rapidly for the past few weeks; sometimes his mind is clear then he goes off into rambling talk, but mostly he is sleepy. He is not in any pain but just waiting for the Lord to take him. This eve I was over with him & David, we told him we missed him in Church members Class & missed hearing his text so Pastor David said 'his' verse for him, John 14:6 which I then repeated & the old man said, "That verse is in my heart, Jesus will take us to God." It was my turn to give the message in Church this morning & as this year's Census is beginning it seemed appropriate to speak from Revelation 20 & 21 and Malachi 3:16 & 17 giving opportunity to speak on Unaisi & the glories of heaven. Everyone seemed most interested & there was close attention. Pastor David chose such lovely hymns too, 'For all the Saints' in Sura being one of them, & the women sang the one they had sung at the graveside. This must be goodbye for now darlings my dearest love is always with you, Chris.

In the garden at 35

May 15th '62

Darling how good you are to have sent me such a lovely bag for my birthday & it will be most useful. It had rather a stronger smell than some but I've hung it outside on fine days & it's alright now & will be going round with me. At last I've got the tape recorder back & we were able to listen to your messages & the testimonies from Kefas & Filibbus; these are lovely but not really clear enough for anyone but us to hear properly. Your letter from Kaduna has come today & it is so heartening to hear of the ways in which the young African leaders are tackling the problems as well as seizing the opportunities of this present time. You must have been so cheered to meet all those Sura folk & find them witnessing & working so nicely! I feel sure it is very right & necessary to concentrate on giving real teaching about ordinary matters of daily living, personal relationships, business standards etc etc to Church members and the young people who are attending. I feel that here in this country the lowering of standards has happened because this practical teaching is not given. It doesn't do to spiritualise everything, I think we need to be far more direct than we have been. As for you darling, I do feel the Lord is blessing all your years of sowing & that He is using you in a special way just now for the building of His Church amongst the Sura. He will give you even more wisdom, grace & patience to continue this work I am sure. The warmth of the sun here has brought into flower one perfect deep blue gentian & 2 buds beside it; how pleased Father would have been for he had them specially put in by the steps on the top lawn. The Lily of the Valley by the front door is almost out & the polyanthus in the front borders also gorgeous! The not so nice report is that my neck was again swollen & painful during the first week of this month but is not quite so bad now. I saw Marcia & Leslie again last week & they have found great comfort in Daily Light, especially this: 'He spread a cloud for a covering.' Do you think maybe in His all-seeing wisdom even these clouds are a protection from worse things perhaps, all my love darling, ever yours Mary.

FROM A NIGERIAN NEWSPAPER:

DEATH – the death has occurred of Daniel Lot aged about 95 on the 16th May 1962. He was the father of Hon. Pastor David O V Lot. Behind he left 5 sons, 2 daughters, 29 grandchildren and 22 great grandchildren. Daniel Lot was among the first Evangelists in Panyam in 1917 and he retired on pension by the Sura Church in 1945. About a week before he died he blessed his children & grandchildren; may God give him a happy everlasting and peaceful rest "Be thou faithful unto death and I will give thee a Crown of Life."

Panyam

May 20th '62

My darlings this comes with the news of the passing on of our dear old father Daniel. He had a sudden collapse on Tues & we had to search for David who had gone out hunting but nobody knew just where. Finally I went out in the car & found him & got him back in time to see his father & speak with him. Everyone was peaceful & happy about his going because he himself was so well prepared. They made a coffin for him & I took it in the car along to the graveyard & we had a triumphant service to which about 50 women & girls came, singing as they walked to it & on their ways home again. It moved me greatly to see & hear this amazing thing, Sura women never before known to attend funerals, but that changed with Unaisi's burial. It made a deep impression on the heathen too. I did manage to record some of the singing & Bitrus' beautiful message & Polycarp's prayer. This weekend was the close of our GLB session after which Enid took about 60 girls to swim (for their test first then a lot of fun) in a pond at the Fish Farm. The evening feast for them was really delicious – two huge basins of cooked rice with another basin of fish cooked in a gravy of tomato, onion & red pepper. You'd have been amazed to see even the smallest girls stowing away 4 large ladles full of rice & the fish on top! Then we had a campfire on the school playground with games & fun in full moonlight! Joyce's friends were staying with us with their two small children plus new baby, and Granny who is German & doesn't hear much English but seemed to enjoy everything wholeheartedly. After the Mannings earlier visit, Enid brought the flannelgraph to me & got me to use it telling the story to the Bible Classes of Mary Jones of Llanfihangel!! I am sitting on the verandah & a President Hoover rose is full of fat buds beside me, & the Crepe Myrtle tree opposite is simply a shower of delicate white blossom like a bride's veil – I wish you could see them! Bob Churchman has asked if I will write a booklet on old father Lot – perhaps that work will be a job for my next furlough?! Certainly no word yet from the Home Executive people but I think we could start expecting our next reunion about a year from now, depending on circumstances of course. Thank you for your dear letters & I did enjoy reading that you Mummy are so much better at last. The passports for the 2 GLB girls, one being Mary Dabiring, have arrived so now they are all set to travel to England on June 8th with Joan Onions. Don't I wish I were going too!! Mary's sister came here with a little bundle of money £2.17.0 as their family's contribution towards Mary's journey, bless their dear hearts. The mother is a great friend of mine, & a great walker; sometimes I've been able to give her a lift & she calls Fibi 'The Lord's Chariot'! Now goodbye for this time my dear ones, Chris.

Southolme, 19 Park Chase, Godalming, Surrey

May 1962

Our dearest Chris, Mary and Rene, may we share with you a matter which has been in our thoughts lately? It has been our desire for some time that we might be able to do something for our friends in our lifetime which we should in any case want to do by legacy, and this year we believe the Lord has shewn us clearly His will in this matter. We would ask you, therefore, to accept the enclosed cheque as a token of our love & of our Heavenly Father's goodness to us. We send it with grateful remembrance of the many times when our friends, by their love and practical help, have been the messengers of His grace & love to us. We want to do this for two reasons – because we feel the future is so uncertain and we may not always be entrusted with these means, and because we believe that the circle of usefulness will be immensely widened by our friends who love to give just as much as we do. We send you our dear love with Isaiah 63:7 'I will mention the lovingkindnesses of the Lord and the praises of the Lord according to all that the Lord hath bestowed on us;' ever your affectionate Gertrude & Ruth.

Beechcroft, Moira, Lurgan, Co Armagh

May 27th '62

My beloved Chris we had a very pleasant journey here Frid eve, met at Nutts corner by Jimmy Megarry & had a lovely ride through quiet lanes & villages, and after a meal were soon up to bed. So many relatives, so much talking, and so many lovely sights; they took us a drive to Warrenpoint & Rostrevor, high tea at a Country Hotel, and oh the lights & shades on the Mourne mountains were something to remember. Did you know that Isaac sent a cheque for £20 to pay for my fare over here? He seemed so especially pleased to see me, and I him. Later on I will return to New Orchard for a longer visit. And just as we left home dear Gertrude's letter arrived – now how to thank them as one would like is the question. How good the Lord has been to us I pray I may never forget His benefits. I have written to Pastor David, on the same day your dear letter came with the news of his father's death, & we are rejoicing in his joy at arriving safely Home, & also your joy at the women singing instead of communal wailing! Today I believe we are to go to see Frances in the new bungalow in Lisburn – if Isabel can have the car. She, Isabel, asks me to give you her love; she is such a gracious hostess, backed by her devoted husband, they look after Lizzie so kindly & well although there is some feeling of strain which is so sad. L is as usual; I tell her to count her blessings. She has such very fine clothes in very good taste, I do 'feel the difference,' but I am well aware of & so thankful for the richness & heritage I have in love. Mother.

Back home at 35

May 29th '62

My darling love, in between hectic meetings I must mention the wonderful letter from dear G&R though I'm at a loss to know what to say to them; their love & thought is something for which we shall always thank God. Let me know if you would like this invested or an account opened at the Trustee Savings Bank where interest rates are good. I am also thankful that I was allowed to meet dear Unaisi & old father Lot in the flesh, and that you were able to record messages from them which we shall always treasure. Isn't it wonderful that their passing has called forth this expression of faith & joy in the Lord from the women – I believe this will spread! You are being used so wonderfully there darling. Mummie will have written fully to you of our journey & happy weekend together, I met 37 relatives in 2 days, & I'm sure Mummie has a real ministry to fulfil over there, let us pray she is kept well enough to do so. Isabel has promised to give her only the plainest of food so as not to upset her gall bladder. I saw Marcia briefly yesterday, she has failed much & pain is constant. I must dash to Croydon my heart's love always with you, Mary.

Panyam

June 5th '62

My darlings I am trying to visualise you all just now – Mother still in Ireland I think, Rene at home in Ifield, perhaps with Ant too, and Mary dashing in & out between meetings – what a dish of talk you will be having! And how I should love to be in on it! I delighted in your dear letters & Mother's lovely descriptions of her doings there, surely a great blessing to her and I pray she returns well 'set up' with blessing herself. What wonderful friends we have in Gertrude & Ruth, sharing their blessings with such lovely generosity in this way; may the Lord bless them in return more than they can ever ask or think. Mary I should love to pay Rene back in full the rest of her loan, but if you & she truly feel she'd rather keep it at the gradual repayment as arranged, then yes, please invest it. Here the Jos Bank gives 4½% Interest on money deposited into account, but if Trustees or Westminster can do the same or better, I'll leave it to you to decide. I do want to give a tenth to the building of the first Christian school in Limankara in Gwoza. This new school is only possible because of the faithful work of Akila Jalme the missionary to Gwoza from our District. Thank you Mary for your wise expression of opinion on the need for clearer Christian teaching on practical issues, it strengthened my resolve to get such teaching printed & given to Church leaders. SGM have a good little publication,

'Everyday Life,' on very practical matters with appropriate Scriptures for each. I should like to see it translated into Hausa. John Mark & Hezekiah are due to leave England on July 6th & sail for Nigeria, please do keep praying & especially for Grace that she might be receptive to his return. Today I've been chatting with Mary Dabiring, a little briefing before she leaves here for England on Friday! She will be visiting the Crawley GLB company but other visits are not quite definite yet. I've been thinking so much of Marcia, it came to me that a little note may be a tiny cheer so I'm enclosing it herewith as I do not know her address. With my love always Chris.

Beechcroft, Moira, Lurgan

June 9th '62

My darling love yes, I am still here but have my ticket for returning home DV next Wed morn; I pray the day may be fine, but I'm sure the Lord will be with me in any case. I've had the most delightful holiday & seen so much of this lovely country & now about 50 relatives! So many folk with so much talk, & laughter, might have become rather tiresome but there has only been one whose constant tongue wagging was occasionally irksome. Charlie & Frances came in their new Wolseley car, so comfortable, & took us to Donaghadee then Robt & Edie met us at Ballywalter. It was a beautiful day, looking out over the shores of Strangford Lough ah such blue blue sea & bright golden gorse all about, it was grand! On Tues we were at Georgie's lovely garden which Father designed & some of the shrubs came from home so he seemed especially near me that afternoon. Morris took L & me to Richill Quarterly Mtg yesterday where I felt moved to say a few words from Heb 12 remembering past days & the 'cloud of witnesses' & our need to run the race & carry the torch & leave behind us something of blessing for others, but only because our strength lies in looking unto Jesus. I was thankful to be able to give my testimony to the love & faithfulness of God. But before that John Reile had welcomed the meeting & he spoke of our mode of worship on a basis of silence, so I think several non-Friends must have been present. There were several short addresses, all very evangelical & to my mind very good, so unlike an English mtg. Afterwards the MacDonaghs came up to greet me, and George & Annie Chapman, & Helen Jones etc and Robt slipped £10 into my hand sounding very near to tears, so very generous of him; dear love, Mother.

The Royal Ship Hotel, Dolgelly, Wales

June 10th Whit Sunday '62

My darling love fancy me writing to you from Wales! As Mummie is having such a lovely time in Ireland & feeling so well she decided to stay on over Whitsun meaning Rene & Ant & I were free to go a bit further afield for a bit longer in the car he managed to hire & we are having a most wonderful time! How often we have wished you were here with us too & we've decided that by hook or by crook on your next furlough it shall happen somehow! We came via Oxford stopping for our 'brunch' in a little village, sitting on a seat overlooking the cricket pitch, all was peace & birdsong. Then on into the city where Ant parked beside the Christchurch Memorial Gdns, fresh green lawns cut & trimmed to perfection, clematis tumbling over old grey stone walls, borders full of early summer flowers under the Chestnut & Lilac trees still in full bloom. It was so beautiful you could almost cry. In one week we have passed from a very cold & late spring into full summer. It was thrilling to be in Oxford again then we motored on into the incredibly beautiful Cotswold country, along B(minor) roads to Bourton-on-the-Water with its graceful weeping willows at the river's edges, lovely old stone bridges and cottages reflecting the golden sunshine – loveliness I shall never forget. Then we discovered Lower Slaughter(!) a true miniature of B-on-the-W & then up a winding hill to a gorgeous field of buttercups & daisies with a simply wonderful view for miles & miles, perfect for a spot of rest & a bite to eat. Next we went through Tewkesbury taking time to marvel in the Abbey, & find a welcome cup of tea then through the Border country to Prestiegne with Ant telling us lots of the local history. Wilfrid had recommended a guest house there & we were most comfortable over Fri night. The mountain road to Aberystwith was steep & wild & so lovely with the streams racing down glistening in the sun. Lunch was a picnic on Borth sand dunes then on to Dolgelly where we managed to get one double room in a lovely old hotel & Ant got B&B in a Cafe catering for cyclists! But we still had time to go on to Betts-y-Coed, Swallow Falls, & Capel Curig – do you remember?! Oh the grand views over Snowdon, it's all so very beautiful, & back through Beddgellert, Harlech & along the coast road – such a lovely day! The Parish Church only had a service in Welsh so we all went to one of the Free Churches but found it sadly pathetic really with so few in attendance, no joy, altogether rather depressing. But our lakeside lunch picnic was lovely & we drove on to Hereford & could only find rather second class accommodation, but it was at least clean. On Mon morn we started out early for Gloucester where we looked round the cathedral before pushing on to Stroud for a very pleasant visit to Braeside, the house & surroundings just as lovely as ever & Uncle E in his frailty reminding us much of dear Father. We had a good lunch at a hotel in Melcham then on to Swanage arriving with the Myttons at 4.15 in their lovely flat overlooking the sea.

Now it's the 13th & we are safely home again, really feeling as if we've been away for weeks! Tomorrow we go to meet Mummy at London

Airport then Rene & Ant drive up to Aberdeen on Friday. R seems more unwilling to go back than I've ever known her to be & doesn't know how much longer she can continue. All dearest love always M.

Panyam

June 20th '62

Darlings what a pleasure it was to hear all about such happy holidays, Mother's extended Irish one & you 3 on that lovely sounding drive to Wales & back & indeed I do wish I could have been with you. There was a picture of Lower Slaughter recently in one of my lovely calendars; & Mummy how grand that you got to Q. Mtg in Richill & met so many folk; I should dearly love the see the MacDonaghs & Hobsons etc again. We've heard no word from Mary & Hawa so that must mean they've arrived safely & I think they'll now be at the big International GLB Camp at Bexhill – how I'd love to peep in on them! Last Sunday I walked the 3 miles to one of the new congregations which have sprung up just north of here; Jephthali came with me – do you remember his little wife Tarifainu? She was a great help. I've been doing a bit of study in the Chala language of the Baron tribe just west of here, trying to fix up the Lord's Prayer, the 10 Commandments & the Creed. It is amazing how long it takes & the one type-written sheet I sent them they've returned pronounced as being 'without fault'! It is painstaking work & subsequent efforts have required much correction, but so good to see these basic Truths going into another mother-tongue vernacular. So sorry there is not time now for any more, dearest love to you each one & of course Rene, from Chris.

35 TM

July 8th '62

My darling love your welcome letter came on Monday of what has been rather a difficult week for us. We prayed much before Rene & Erik arrived & were able to talk fairly easily though with some strain as you can imagine. He was restless & looked far from happy. Dr Brooks called on Weds as I had to take a special pill that evening in preparation for the Xray next day at Redhill hosp. I had to take everything off & put on a white cotton gown & lie on a cold steel bed; the nurse did allow me my grey woollen cape around my front during the actual xray photos – so why I could not have kept on my long woollen vest & stockings I don't know. She then gave me a barium injection (enema) and after several more pictures she showed me to a toilet where I was to leave all I had been given; then more pictures & it was over. Not a very pleasant affair & so very cold on the back. On Thursday we took a nice ride in pouring rain to Hever as Mary wanted Ant to see the work his great grandfather & grandfather had done but the gardens were not open that day, so we had a lovely tea out in Westerham. You will have heard of the wonderful proposal Eileen has made which, coming just at this time, seems as though it might be God's hand opening a new door of opportunity, we must wait & see. Now darling with all the love I can send, your ever loving Mother.

Panyam

July 14th '62

My darlings I do hope you got my last letter scribbled in haste about Mary Dabiring having at last written to me that she'll be in Crawley from the 16th-20th & that you Mary are going to take her to Bible House. Her mother asked me to send her greetings to you all in my home & she is afraid lest her Mary should be a bother eating all your food! Enid & I picked up our mail on our way to Jos & I had to give her the wheel so I could read yours – I think my thoughts & speech were a bit juddery for there were so many big changes mentioned in it! We've all been praying for so long for the Lord's undertaking regarding Rene that I can only feel now this sense of a parting of the ways is an indication given by God that the time has come to take action. My own first reaction was one of relief as soon as R feels she can really take this step. Then the Little Dungate proposal which is certainly a bit breathtaking, but surely, at this juncture, it can be taken as God's leading the way. If/when Rene can decide to leave Aberdeen it would seem a most wonderful place prepared for her by God and a wonderful place for Mummie to be. As for the flat inside LD becoming our home, well that is something I shouldn't like to make a pronouncement about immediately but let us not turn the idea down for if it is the Lord's will it will prove to be good, acceptable & perfect. Regarding the sale of 35 I would rather that we kept together & shared whatever seems to be the right thing for you & Mummie to do. Therefore if you have to make a quick decision about selling just count my share as one with yours in buying this flat. If Mummie is keen on the idea then we can go ahead & if Rene is to be soon on her own then she must be on her own with us as long as she needs. If there is a room that I can have as my HQ during furloughs, that's grand. There is much to tell about our doings here but no time, so sending you assurances of fervent prayer & my dear love C.

35 T M

July 20th '62

My beloved Chris it is lovely to be home again & that short episode in one's life over & satisfactorily I think. I am not entirely sure what the suspected problem could have been but Mr Stevens told M he found no need to operate. Of course I had further gall bladder Xrays but he did not think there was any need to worry. Everything is so changed from what it was 30 years ago; the anaesthetist puts you to sleep before you go into the theatre – he gave me an injection into my left hand in the veins at the back and the next thing I realised I was getting back into bed. I had had marvellous dreams but cannot remember even one! It is certainly a grand thing to go through an investigation operation without pain; I think of 100 yrs ago when men were strapped down before Drs could operate. It was a somewhat nerve-racking time having to wait till 5pm until it was done but don't be anxious about me. Of course it would be a great comfort to have you here with us but I believe I shall be spared to see you again but if not, all is well, you live in my heart forever, Mother…Well darling (Mary now) isn't it lovely that no operation is necessary or even advisable. I had a word with Mr Stevens & he thinks Mother's uterus is enlarged & it was this that seemed like the lump. There were many muddles in the hospital & some inexcusable things but Mother was unaware of any trouble & survived it all, just so thankful to be home. We had a good day on Tuesday with Mary & Hawa & I took them to Gatwick this morning for the train to London; the Observer has a good picture of them & both have gone off with several copies each. Nakam wrote to us about your John Mark & what answers to prayers we are seeing in him, but truthfully I cannot say 'our' prayers because mine for him have been so weak & feeble that they don't deserve any answer. I'm afraid I have felt him to be a more or less hopeless case;

yet this fresh news of JM is an encouragement to continue praying for them both & to know that NOTHING is too hard for the Lord. Now with all my dearest love, from your own M.

Kano

July 27th '62

My darlings I am imagining you at Winkleberry Cottage & feel sure you will have a merry time in a place with such a charming name! It was splendid to get your letter with the wonderful news of no further op needed – how thankful we all are! Now you can have a very happy time in Dorset with no further anxiety. Here has been a wonderful day welcoming our 2 dear girls back at the Airport at 6.40am. They were among the first of a planeload of 100 school children to disembark & of course the 12 GLB girls & 2 Officers we brought with us were just as excited & sang a special song of welcome & held up large letters saying 'WELCOME.' We were all in uniform & fortunately our 2 got off the plane also in uniform. It was lovely to see Mary back again, looking blooming & telling me your voice Mummie is exactly like mine! And I heard her telling the same thing in Hausa to the other girls. This afternoon there was a terrific Display put on after only a short morning practice – this is where Kathleen McD excels, in organising the Companies. It gave me a thrill to think of the progress since 1945 when I began so tentatively with the first girls, & now so many girls from so many tribes are all happy to work together & have become such a united team. One of the Nigerian Officers, Lieut Halima from Gindiri gave a very good summary in Hausa of what GLB is all about to the assembled watchers.

29th now & last night all the girls were asked to stand & speak giving their impressions and our Mary went to the front & held forth for fully 10 minutes in English, speaking very well of their experiences in England to about 50 missionaries & the many Africans gathered. I was amazed at her calm confidence, fluency & complete absence of shyness, & felt so proud of her. Then Hawa followed in Hausa. They passed around the Observer newspaper cutting, which I thought was very good. In Church M was asked to speak again & did so excellently then all the 13 girls sang 'The Lord's My Shepherd' to Crimmond in 3 parts with descant – it was lovely. Then they all came back with us to the SIM Rest House for cake & coffee & hymn-singing thoroughly enjoyed by one & all! Tomorrow, Monday we return to Jos. Now goodbye my dear darlings, my thoughts & prayers are constantly with you & of course Rene too, as ever yours, Chris.

Winklebury Cottage

Aug 5th '62

My beloved Chris this is my last letter to you from the holiday, sitting in a deckchair in the garden (so called) tho' it's not made up yet, several buddlia shrubs around & a fence covered with roses, we are quite secluded from the road altho' there's hardly any traffic. Such a change from main roads at home; we are very glad of the car however for without it we should be very isolated & cut off. This morning we went the loveliest ride to Shaftesbury having seen a sign to a Friends Mtg where we were welcomed but there was no vocal prayer but the quiet was good. I did not feel much liberty to speak but will trust the little I did manage was in 'right ordering' for as in Rom 1:16 I am not ashamed of the Gospel of Christ, and I am not to judge anyone else only see to it that I am not disobedient to the Word. Mary has taken us some lovely drives through these delightful lanes & villages, to the sea at Weymouth where we did not pause – a mass of motors & caravans had arrived before us – but continued up hilly roads to find glorious far-reaching views. There is such variety of scenery about here in the steep hills with glimpses of sea, fields of golden grain in need of harvesting, charming old thatched cottages with such bright gardens – how often we have wished both you & Rene could be with us to enjoy it all. But there, all my beloved family, and those in Nigeria who have been given you, are all bound up in the bundle of life deep in my heart. That reminds me, 'Deep down in my heart, I know all will be well, for is it not our Father who our lives hath planned?!' (I'm humming but don't recall the tune) What happiness & love has been poured out into mine of His great mercies. This evening we found a Methodist Church in Blandford & the message was from 1 Peter 1 and I'm sure it was good tho' I could hear very little. I did enjoy reading of your Mary & friends receiving such a nice welcome at Kano & speaking so well of their time here – what a chatter there will be & giggling with it! Please write more of John Mark & Grace. I feel now very tired but don't know any reason for it; dearest love from Mother.

Zermatt, Switzerland

Aug 22nd '62

My dear Chris I am sitting in my bedroom looking straight out to the Matterhorn & the most wonderful views, from the amazing gardens down below & all round this Hotel Bellevue, up to the mountain tops & both sunrise & sunset glow it all pink!! To think just two weeks ago I sat by my fire over the perishing cold Bank Holiday weekend while torrents of rain poured down & it blew great guns & got simply colder & colder. Your lovely letter got forwarded to me here at this glorious truly wonderful spot; I've responded at length & with many questions, on the tape I hope to send with this, whatever the cost. Everything is very terribly expensive here, they say Zermatt is so high up & off the beaten track so all prices are up high too. There are no motors here only old fashioned horse taxi things like Queen Victoria's childhood open traps. All horses, cows, sheep & goats have neck bells in different tones & it is all so lovely. I cannot begin to describe the beauty all round so my heart just praises my Heavenly Father's handiwork all day long! The other day I went up Sonegga in a chair lift – my first such experience, & quite amazing! And today it is to be a cable-car up Schwarz-Zee. The weather is perfect, v hot sun almost unbelievable for us poor souls from England, & cloudless blue skies, so I'm drinking in all the wonderfully warm air. I'm coping with some fairly steep climbs, surprising some of the young ones, & I'm truly enjoying every second of each day! It's time for our next excursion so I must go, God bless you, very much love, Nakam.

Dungate Manor, Reigate

17.9.62

Thank you darling Chris so very much for your letters, I'm so conscious of & grateful for your prayers at this strange time of my life. The days are full here from morning till night but I am glad for this, for keeping busy, although I do miss my home, & my precious things around me; & also the fact that one cannot just 'take things easy' or have a day off but there is so much love & kindness & appreciation which I have missed terribly of late years, that I feel my personal losses are more than compensated for – and I do thank God. I believe Mummy told you of the letter I wrote to Erik; eventually he has replied but in his usual non-committal way & spoke rather threateningly again of how short his life is going to be anyway, & not a word of wanting or hoping I'd go back. I told him I had to write to the Committee in Sweden for I cannot bear to go on living under such false pretenses. He said he was glad I had done so. You will know I agonised over writing, and even longer over sending it, & waited another week before doing so, constantly begging the Lord to show me if it was not right or He did not want me to. Now I'm here I spend one full day a week at The Millbank on whichever day Mary has to be out for the longest time so at least I am helping there a little. Thank you again darling & now good night with my dearest & best love, Rene.

Panyam

Sept 24th '62

My darling ones it is good to have Frances back & the opportunity for some good talks with her & of course hearing about her recent visit to you! Also of course respecting her need to start up again slowly as we both know how the first weeks after furlough can be as much of a drain as the last weeks at home. She has agreed medically with me & we feel, looking at all the options, the best would be for you to ask Dr Brooks how soon he can get you into hospital to take care of those gall-stones to stop the pains coming so much; and I have written to Bill Tett to advise him of this and that I might be needing to go home in November but it could be much sooner than that. There are many things planned for these next few months, new Bible studies, committees, developments, buildings etc & I'd like to see them through but I am not indispensable. Let us once more meet prayerfully at the Throne of Grace, trusting that I shall be able to get a flight close to the time Dr B can arrange a hospital place for you to have the op. This morning I cycled to Mongu for their service because one of their keen young Evangelists, who preached last Sunday, was killed by lightning on Thursday & I wanted to be with them. The one who preached today was good & made suitable reference to what had happened, & to Dafwash. Also, we've been planning to start up a literacy drive among women & Victoria Nasik & Enid have been working hard on it. On a recent trip to Jos they called in at Forum & the Lord so arranged it that the women's school was that day in class: 100 women being taught in 16 different classes by 16 literate women, with one woman capably supervising the whole! This is rather how we had thought it should go and there it was, already happening- so encouraging! Now darlings until I hear more from you, with word from Dr B, this brings my dearest love to you all three, Chris.

Panyam

Sunday Oct 7th '62

My Darlings it was lovely to get your dear letters this week & hear your reactions to mine. Tomorrow I hope to get into Jos early, hoping to get an air ticket booking made at once. Bill assures me they are pretty easily got at this time of year, and that the Mission is quite willing to undertake the cost for me. Your telegram has just arrived, after your letters – I take it that the 9th is now Nov 9th? It is so good to know that even before you knew I was thinking of coming, you had felt certain it was right to go on with the op despite your earlier misgivings. I wish you could have heard some of the prayers for you in these past few days: Pastor Ishaya at Chip, "When the day of the operation comes please give perfect victory to the doctor when he does his work inside her." Pastor Joel at Abwor prayed specially about the day of the op & many prayed so sweetly for my journeying & everything connected with my home going. What a comfort to have these dear folk behind us in all our concerns & I know their prayers will be constant. The way Pastor David told the Dist. Church Council about you & your need of me etc was so nice; not a soul has even hinted that it wouldn't be right for me to come to you. Local travels have been badly hampered recently by the shocking state of some roads & a really frightful spot where a big lorry has been bogged down. I believe we were helped to steer around it but it does add exhaustion to all motoring, trying to keep 2 wheels on the central ridge & the other 2 on the edge in attempting to avoid becoming stuck fast in the deep ruts. Just a couple of dry days can improve things so quickly. We had a surprise visit from Rita Shannon, Daisy's niece who also called in unannounced at Brookfield, do you remember?! She arrived with our new SUM Dr Evelyn Jones plus an SIM missionary we know; they had had tea with Frances on route so did not stay long with us. We also have our newly arrived Assist. Schools Manager Simon Akyok with his wife & small daughter happily ensconced in the Dowaki & he'll begin work tomorrow. Joyce had an emergency call today – a note brought in by bicycle – to say Istifanus Jakden has had a bad accident needing hospital. We hadn't enough petrol so Joyce had to go to Mongu first to buy some, then to Daffo & back. She found Isti in great pain with what looked like a fracture of the kneecap; she gave him an injection of pethedine, a strong sedative, and got him onto Enid's lilo (air mattress) in the back of the car, whereupon little Daniel sobbed bitterly seeing his parents driven away, but Mrs Pastor Manasseh took him in & was a great comfort. Joyce got them back here, from where Enid took them on to Pankshin hospital. Now I do regret to say that both Christopher & David have had their birthdays this year without a line from their Auntie Chris, please tell them how sorry I am, with such dear love to you all as always, Chris. PS we are now trying for a booking on Tues Oct 30th arriving Weds morn 31st.

35 TM

Oct 14th '62

My precious darling Chris I'm writing this in the hope it will reach you before you leave Jos next week. Your telegram arrived yesterday morn & rejoiced our hearts to know you can come next Friday overnight; Smallfield hospital visiting hours are only evenings but perhaps they will allow such a travelled visitor in, especially if I am well on the way to recovery by then, since I am going in sooner than first planned. I have been given so many tokens of God's love in the friends He has given us that, most times, I overflow with the hope of Romans 15:13. Darling you know that our love is Eternal, in God Himself, the Father of all Parenthood, & you will realise how much I am thinking & praying for you. And I was so glad to hear of the prayers of those dear friends & the Pastors. If possible I want to let Mr Stevens, my surgeon, hear of Pastor Ishaya's special prayer for him as he operates. I feel so thankful you were brought through those difficult roads safely & now I do commit you to God for every detail of your journeying. All is well, with you & me…whatever the outcome may be…& there must be no mourning, or great sorrow. We will all look forward. Dear, dear, what nonsense I do write, I heard yesterday of an old lady of 94 who had her gall bladder removed & the hospital authorities said, "It was her Christian faith brought her through." I hope they will be able to say the same of me. I hope & believe we shall meet again <u>here</u> DV and very soon

& what a glad joyous day that shall be; as ever your loving Mother, who cannot find words for all the love I want to add to this. God bless you my dear love & keep you ever safe & close to Him, for His will is perfect for each one of us.

~ ~ ~ ~ ~

Malaga, Spain

Dec 11th '62

Dear Miss Cheal thank you so much for your kind greetings. I often think of Panyam & the good work of Miss Webster & yourself. I have built myself a small villa here on a cliffside overlooking a very lovely bay; at present unspoilt & with pleasant adjoining countryside. The simple life & good climate are what I like and I am only 17 miles from Gibralta. I wonder if you would kindly have the enclosed £1 given to my old 'boy' Dogo Kopal from Kerang; & my Xmas greetings to you & to Pastor Lot & all, yours sincerely W.T. Gordon-Marshall, Major.

Jos

Dec 14th '62

Dearest Chris I was so thrilled with your loving gift of that frock before you left for home, I really was thrilled with it, & received it as a most special token of my heavenly Father's love, thank you Dear. Now how thankful we are to know that your dear Mother has made such good progress after her operation, we thank the Lord for His answer to our prayers and we're thinking of you all rejoicing in His goodness. I had a most wonderful week-end at Mongu for the end of their term, the roses & honeysuckle making the air sweet and Frances' guest room is so lovely & she & Christine & Joyce were all so good to me. We also had a happy Break-up at Gindiri too, Mr Wilmshurst spoke at the giving of prizes & Jean Owens gave a lovely message on Ruth with lovely prayers. Those girls are so precious to me now & we do thank the Lord that Hanatu D went to Shirley & apologised for her behaviour – it was Kathleen Mcdonald's splendid message that had turned her right around – our Heavenly Father never makes a mistake! Also, He has opened the way for me to go to the T Chad conference on Dec 29th & Florence & Will are to be there too. My passage is booked for Feb 24th so now I am wishing you & your dear ones a blessed Christmas together, Evelyn.

SUM, Great Portland St London W1

Feb 19th 1963

Dear Chris we are feeling the need for booklets centred on the work being done in Mission Stations and we are wondering if you would like to 'blaze the trail' by writing the story of the Panyam District? The enclosed copies of the outline will give you some idea of what we have in mind & you'll see we suggest Miss Webster's help for the early days & if you agree perhaps you'd send the second copy to her, with your own comments as you see fit; with warm greetings, yours in Him, Tony.

41 Woodland Park Lisburn, Co. Antrim

29.4.63

My dear Chris as the time of your departure to Nigeria approaches, we have you much in our thoughts & prayers, hoping you will have a good trip out & that your work on your return will be blessed in every way. We were with the family last week & all seemed well there; A. Lizzie was telling us that she would like a small bungalow about Lisburn but as usual she will think a long time before doing anything if ever. Now with our united love and all best wishes from us both your affectionate U Robert.

SUM Jos

April 30th '63

Dear Chris many thanks for your letter & we are certainly very thrilled to know that May 31st is confirmed for your return here. Regarding the Morris Oxford Traveller left here by the Bama ladies; it is in good condition with about 20,000 on the clock most of which will have been on tarmac for it is tarmac all the way from Jos to Bama now. Janet Sykes is much better, finishing up her rest time in Gindiri, hoping to come back next week. The first Literature Committee met last week with Enid as very capable Secretary. You will want to know that your pamphlet on Drinking was very warmly welcomed & approach is being made to W. African Gospel Publishing or Baraka Press; failing this we shall likely do it ourselves. Harry was very thrilled, saying it is one of the best positive pamphlets on the subject & just right for our growing numbers of educated Christians. We are very much looking forward to having you back with us and would pray that you & your mother & family will know the peace of the Lord as you prepare for the parting; with every good wish and love from the family here, yours sincerely, Geoffrey.

35 The Millbank Ifield, Crawley

May 2nd '63

Dear Tony I have been trying to get the Panyam Booklet underway & am sending herewith what is already done. Miss Webster has supplied me with a copy of the History of the Panyam Church which I prepared for our Jubilee Year, with the additions prepared by Pastor David & Joyce McQuone up to the beginning of this year. I expect this is rather what you had in mind but you may want to reduce it somewhat. To include lists of Evangelists & Teachers & even Missionaries might well be out of date in a month's time as they tend to change quite often. The number is approximately 145 Evangelists & 160 outstations with schools being led & taught on Sundays; each year these numbers increase slightly. I feel the whole is very sketchy & I certainly shouldn't like it printed until you have added or removed where necessary till it is more acceptable. These copies are the only ones in this country & are therefore very precious, CHC.

Dunsmore, London Rd., Hailsham, Sx

13.5.63

Dear Chris just a greeting & good wishes for Godspeed & bless you as you soon return to your Station. It has been a real joy & inspiration to me to have met you & hear your wonderful stories & see those pictures of God's amazing handiwork. May the Lord bless & keep you & your dear Mother & sisters…'When He putteth forth His sheep He goeth before,' and we who remain at home are all partners together with you so please accept our loving greetings & no need to write back in your busyness, Violet.

Christ Church Vicarage 21 Elmwood Rd, W. Croydon

14.5.63

To all our friends: I am writing on behalf of Ray, Althea, Honour & myself to try & express something of our deep gratitude for all those who have written, sent flowers & gifts, wired & in every way given us loving sympathy & much prayer support not only in England but in distant corners of the earth. Shock, heartbreak & desolation – many of you have trodden similar dark paths – but for each one of us the reality of the Master's Presence & strength has been amazing. On May 1st when I returned from a meeting Dick was at the door & I thought how well he looked. Half an hour later a neighbour with fear in her eyes knocked to tell me he was lying on the pavement (sidewalk) outside her house.

There he lay, the parcel of magazines he'd been to fetch beside him, but he had gone. It was so wonderful for him & what he would have wished, to be taken while busy, as he always was, about his Master's service. After seemingly endless moments the ambulance came with a wonderful token of God's love – I only really know one ambulance man and it was him; I will never forget his personal concern & strong sympathy. The following days were rather a blur but can be summed up in Daily Light's marvellous portion for that May Day evening, 'God Himself shall be with them.' Later it transpired that it was a coronary occlusion, a closure of the artery through thickening, causing him to have died instantly. The service in the packed church was simply triumphant, with 'The strife is o'er, the battle done', leading up to the Hallelujah Chorus; the coffin was turned when the chancel was reached, an old custom which pertains where a clergyman dies while on active service, he must face his people as he always did as their Pastor. Another thing made plain from all your letters is the extraordinary way God uses the life of one ordinary person who quietly & faithfully lives to please Him. So many spoke of their lives having been enriched by his, what they learned from him about prayer & wise counsel and being a good friend. These things are but a fraction of all that has been written & said and they are not recounted to bring glory to Dick, he would have hated that, but to encourage us all in the daily battle to live wholly for God. Our future plans are unknown, to us but not to Him, with love to you all, Eve.

50 Grange Rd, Layton, Blackpool, Lancs

May 15th '63

Dear Chris for many reasons we were sorry not to be able to attend the Annual Mtg in London & foremost among them was that we'd miss seeing you again. Our thoughts were much with you & your mother before your book & letter arrived yesterday; thank you for thinking of us, we shall enjoy the book. Will needs to regain 40lbs to return to normal but still he has no appetite, but he is reading a little now and does take a short daily walk. We hear that your mother has made a wonderful recovery. It was so good that she could go with you to Ireland. We pray she will know afresh the joy of the Lord, as she shares once more in your departure. Quite a number of our younger colleagues are preparing to go forward into the Tchad Republic; we had hoped for a couple to join David Carling on the Nigeria side as well but they feel their call is to Tchad. There is a nurse from NZ who is wondering if she is too old to begin again in Nigeria; we too have both passed the SUM retiring age! But I still have a good deal of work to complete before our Abri New Testament can be printed, so we plan to remain here in England until the weather grows altogether too cold. Please remember us to your dear Mother and sisters, with warm love from us both, yours in Christ, Florence Lunn.

Braeside, Rodborough Common, Stroud

May 26th '63

My dearest Chris we are remembering you especially in these last days before your departure, I'm sure there is always the undiminishing pain of parting. You must also have longed – as have we all – that family affairs could have been settled before you left, but they certainly cannot be rushed & we know the Lord's timing is always perfect. Mollie has contacted a young fellow form Stroud called, funnily enough, Digby Lot, hoping to sail with SUM in Sept to teach in Gindiri. You will like him, a nice sensible lad with an agricultural degree; his parents are not in sympathy & he's an only child which must be very hard for both parties. We all send lots of love to each of you, and a special goodbye hug for yourself, very lovingly A. Lena.

SUM London

28.5.63

Dear Chris just a wee note to apologise for having to slip away early from the meeting but I shall hope to be sending some ideas on the 'Panyam Story' fairly soon once you've had time to settle back into the work. Doubtless you'll be able to revise it as necessary. It has been grand to have fellowship with you over the recent months; & you'll be glad to know that all seems set for a great advance in Ireland as well as elsewhere. It only remains for me to wish you every blessing as you return to the Field & to ask for your prayers as I move into new responsibilities & opportunities amongst young people & in the interests of the Mission generally, with greeting to you all, Tony.

252 Selsdon Rd, S Croydon

May 29th '63

My dearest Chris I am sorry that you are so tired when going back I do wish you could have had some real rest before leaving. Eve & I have just had prayer together for you; we both thought you spoke really well on Monday evening and passed over that wrong slide awkwardness very graciously so don't let tiredness make you have an adverse post-mortem. That is a device of the devil that always plagues me too, but if we have consciously relied on the Holy Spirit I don't think we ought to listen to inward accusations afterwards! Eve is spending some time in here, at present still writing those typed letters & adding bits to each. Today she wants me back with her to lunch then on to a womens mtg; when she implores me to do these things I find it v difficult to refuse while she is so brave & plucky yet so desolate. Be assured of my prayers as you depart, for you, and for your family, & all in the Panyam District eagerly waiting to receive you once again. Of course it will be so hard to leave the dear home folk but may you all prove yet again that His grace really <u>is</u> sufficient. Safe flight & every blessing as you plunge back into the work, God bless you, go with you & before you, and use you mightily, Nakam.

Troutstream Hall, Rickmansworth, Hertfordshire

May 29th '63

Dear Miss Cheal you are much in our thoughts & prayers as you prepare to leave once again for the land of your adoption. We do wish you safe passage & every blessing as you return to the Field. It must be with mixed feelings that you leave home again. We do hope your Mother is by now quite better & that she will be preserved in health during your absence & that your sisters will have all the strength needed to carry on. We do thank you for your visit & pray you will be given wisdom & grace for your great task and that the Lord will go with you in all your ways & use you for His glory, yours in Him, HJ & M Cooper.

Grasmere, Westminster Rd, Foxrock, Co. Dublin

29.5.63

My dear Chris a little note must go to you today to bring our love & assurance of prayer remembrance of you and your dear Mother as you set forth again…the Lord shall bless thy going out & thy coming in…He goeth before…oh and the Amplified of Hab 3:19 I do feel is especially for you. You know how He has laid the Lake Chad project on our hearts too we will be praying into that & looking forward to hearing your news of it. But this wee note needs no reply at all, I mean that! Please do give your Mother our special love & from my Mother also, we send so much prayerful love, Evelyn.

On the bus

May 30th '63

Darlings a wee line to tell you how wonderfully I feel we've been led & helped through these days. I can't express my admiration for the marvellous way you all coped so serenely & gallantly today. It will ever be an inspiration & encouragement to remember. My most grateful thanks to you each one for all your love, the birthday remembrances, & your courageous sending of me forth again. It was lovely seeing Peggy & Irene at Victoria & having a little time with them & Nakam & Mrs Farrant, they will phone you tonight they say. No I didn't have to pay excess! Glorious afternoon & London looks lovely in the sun. Goodbye my dearests I'll finish this now & give it to R&G to post; my heart's love & thanks as ever, Chris.

Central Hotel, Kano

May 31st '63

My darlings it was a non-eventful journey, quite pleasant with an overabundance of good food & at least 50 empty seats. We landed in Rome where I tried to buy something appropriate with Mrs Kennedy's kind gift but all the kiosks had very expensive items so I got an airmail edition of the Telegraph which had a far better picture of the royal honeymoon couple. We landed here at 6.40 to a lovely sunset & temp of 100 degrees! Customs charged duty on the clocks, listed & fussed over every packet of seeds but ignored the roses! And there was Francis Nanle to meet me having waited two hours & we only had a happy 5 minutes of talk as I got my visa renewed for another 2 yrs before the bus came to take me here. It was terrifically hot so I was thankful for a cool bath & lighter clothes before supper & the rooms are comfortably air conditioned. This is where one longs for a phone just to hear your voices again. I cannot express all that's in my heart, for everything you have each been & done to make our time together so happy; earnest hope that the future will open out in blessing for each of us as we wait God's timing; praise to Him & thanks for all grace & help along each day especially the last few. Thank you darlings so very very much for all your love – it is such a blessed treasure. Mary I forgot to mention I put my upper sheet into my case, it was an old sides-to-middle one that had gone into holes again so wouldn't have been worth mending, & the Dispensary will be glad of more bandages from it. Now my darlings farewell for now although I wish you were all here with me, give my love to everyone especially each of you, God bless you all, yours ever, Chris.

Panyam

June 25th 1962

My own darlings I know you will understand the extraordinary amount of work pressures since I returned, and I hope the enclosed typescript, copied to HQ & to Nakam, will give you some idea – it is so good to write of many more positive things than the opposite, & you'll be rejoicing with me at how the Gospel is spreading far & wide and many young people are accepting Jesus Christ then taking His Gospel back to their villages & starting to build churches & schools – such encouragements! And your dear letters keep coming faithfully even when mine are rather infrequent; and Mummie I see the Times Weekly Review so I'll be able to read the full report of the Profumo affair, it is certainly a ghastly revelation. The European engineer at the new garage we are using now, has told me our dear but unreliable Fibi is worth no more than £200 & the hoped for new one worth £400 at least. He strongly advises us to get tubes for the present tubeless tyres. Joyce & I took turn about driving the two cars home & there's certainly no comparison in comfort, the new one simply purrs along so quietly & seems to be rain & dust proof but, even with the luggage rack on top she still cannot carry the loads we have become used to piling into Fibi. Next morning returning Fibi to the garage we took Enid & her moped in the back to Gindiri – not possible in the new car – we had lunch with those on the Course & managed their very spicy-hot African food. On the way back I knew we had a puncture so called in with Frances, only to find the spare also had a puncture so we had to do a mend then & there, using F's vulcanising gadget which was such a help. Polycarp has got the post he was seeking: Assist Provincial Education Officer & he's thrilled but it has meant a good deal of staff changes; Jacob Damut is taking over the school at Pushit & also the Chieftanship. He sends special greetings to you. One evening I was about to start the Bible study – a repeat requested by 23 secondary boys, which I was so glad to do, but Joyce had an emergency midder case & sent to ask for my help. A young girl having her first baby in a heathen home & had been 2 days at it, so they came for a stretcher & brought her in. She was such a brave lass & finally a big baby girl was safely born but seemed to be affected with VD (venereal disease) so Joyce gave penicillin injections to mother & babe. The mother did not hear much Hausa, that's why Joyce needed help with Sura. Now it must be goodbye my darlings all; Rene I do hope your poor foot is better & that elastic stocking is a help, please give my love to Madge & all other friends at Reigate & Ifield. Next time I hope to have news for you of Kefas & Malam Adamu that will be better than that of Mwantet who, according to his nephew who came to see me, has gone back into drink then took wife no4 with whom he spends Thurs-Sunday. The other days I hear he is pushing his other wives back into drink also, but his sons & nephews & their wives are all keeping true & praying for Mwantet, as I'm sure you will too; as ever Chris.

Panyam

August 10th 1963

My darlings just a quick line to thank you so much for letting me know about Rene, & to bring you my loving sympathy in the anxiety that I know you will be feeling about her. Of course I am longing for more news, and have written to her by this same post, putting the Ifield address in case she's no longer in hospital poor dear. I need not write it but be assured of my constant prayerful remembrances throughout all this upheaval. Here the Dearsleys have brought Jean Oliver out to Mongu to stay with Frances & recouperate after her accident. They tell me that since leaving Nguru, Jean has had the wonderful news that I want to share as a cheer for you all: a Hausa Chief & 5 of his people have taken a decisive stand for Christ & have been called to the Moslem head in Nguru to answer for this unheard of thing. They have given a clear statement of their new faith in Christ & that it is their own personal choice with no sort of persuasion being brought to bear; so let us all remember this courageous little group. Yesterday we had a wonderful Dist. Church Comm to discuss arrangements for next year's Bible teaching, & took the decision to ask Pastor Bitrus to be the overall course leader & the retired teacher Ishaku Dabiring to assist him. They will build houses for the 39 students taken from each local church, and make various provisions for their help during the year. Besides this we hope to send some to the 2yr course at Boi and have about 7 more courses running in centres such as Daffo, Chip & Mupun; using those who have finished at Boi plus some pastors & retired teachers to teach these short courses. The Church has provided £450 for this splendid project. The two American Gospel Recordings ladies are hard at work; they've completed 6 languages with still 9 more to go. They keep finding small pockets of folk with different dialects who want to have records also; those who have the completed records are simply thrilled! Motoring along having passed Pankshin, Enid, Winnie, Brenda & I heard a dreadful scraping noise & found the back wheel out of place with the top leaf of the spring broken. How thankful we were it happened there before we started down the steep 2000ft escarpment. We sent a note for help via a passing Land Rover to the Wares, & were directed back just half a mile to a mechanic in the Govt Craft School. I drove very, very slowly there & found the mechanic to be a Christian lad from Forum trained at Bukuru! He took the wheel & spring straight to Jos to be ready for us by Monday. Isn't it so good of the Lord to let us be so near help when these things happen?! The dear Wares soon arrived with a picnic lunch then Frank took Brenda & me back here then took Winnie & Enid on to Kabwir. And at last my case has arrived intact after being held up in Lagos for 2 mths! One more story then I must stop: a teacher in the market had found a little Hausa mother in hard labour. He was surprised to find her willing to accompany him back to our Midwifery Unit for his only transport was the back of his motorcycle; so that's how she arrived & the baby would certainly have died if it'd been born at home. Such dear love, all well here, yours Chris.

Panyam

Sept 10th '63

Darlings your dear letters arrived last night & were so very welcome & I was as relieved as you were to know that our dear Rene was through the op so the biggest anxiety is now over. How I pray for patience & courage for you all, especially you dearest R as you may now have to stay in hospital longer than first thought. I hope you will find an interest in watching all that modern medical science will do to repair your poor body & give you back health & strength. Yes I can imagine how slowly the day of the operation went, certainly for Mother & Mary as I'm sure R was fast asleep. Here's a little fresh picture for you to see how I have spent some of A. Lizzie's gift: £15 bought a new bicycle which then had to be tied to the luggage rack on top of our car, & driven slowly across terribly pot-holed roads to Daffo this morning. There it was handed over with great excitement to the colporteur Dawida (David). His old bike is worn out with much travelling over many hundreds of miles around the western part of our District, visiting markets & tin mines. He is quite thrilled to have this new one, & has been asking for more Hausa Bibles as he has sold all that he had. While in Daffo Brenda examined 102 expectant mums and gave 60 injections against whooping cough, & weighed so many babies! Now the Women's Fellowship wants to build their own Maternity Unit and have their own Daffo Midwife! Since our last visit Isfanus Jakden & Bernard Dabam have treated about 600 people in the Dispensary. During the CC mtg heavy rain came on making it almost impossible to hear one another as it drummed on the corrugated iron roof, but it didn't last long & we drove home safely. Goodnight now my darlings may the Lord comfort & guide your every step C.

In the garden at 35

Sept 12th '63

My beloved Chris I think it seems longer than 2yrs since dear Father reached Home...just think of all the joys that are prepared for us presently, when earth's little while is over. Such a comforting article in the Friend this week, found in a great grandfather's diary, a man who'd suffered great loss late in life, he was depressed in mind, body & spirit until he read this by a missionary friend: *I dreamed I was in Heaven; I was the same in body & soul yet greatly changed. I had none of the feelings of being a stranger – my mind was filled with unbounded satisfaction & with an exquisite sweetness arising from the thought I was once more at Home, so like yet so unlike the home I had lately left behind. Parents, brothers, sisters, friends, who had been separated at intervals from me, were within the reach of my voice, the range of my sight. They welcomed me audibly & with a charm of manner which expressed the tender love they had for me, as if no separation had ever taken place. Some were near me, among them my mother & my wife's mother who came & kissed me as in former years. I soon learned that in Heaven vision is so keen I could see clearly throughout its whole extent & I was welcomed by all the inhabitants of Heaven who were all conscious of my arrival although they were unusually numerous*...etc.

No room to write more of this darling but I thought it beautiful & of great comfort to me. Now you will be glad to know that our dear Rene is making progress & had managed half a piece of bread & butter with her tea, and the next day a morsel of mince and vegetable, which at last has caused a little activity in the tubing which she fearfully loathes, but agrees the Nurses are most discreetly understanding. With very much dear love as ever now my darling from your Mother.

Ward 18 Smallfield Hospital, Horley

15.9.63

My darling Chris the days do slip by but I can hardly believe it's been 3 weeks tomorrow since I came in. I suppose I'm settling down to live with my new condition, at least I can do all the dressings myself & fix on the bag. 12 stitches came out on Thurs & also the glass rod so I thought I should feel much easier & more comfortable but I really don't much. Oh darling I've had such awful dia (can't spell it) then pills to make it more normal then 2 tablespoons of liquid paraffin and quite bad stomach pains plus a high temp. So sorry but it does ease it to write even a little of it to you. Also I have been up for a tiny walk in lovely sunshine. Everyone is kind & I've had letters & cards & plenty of visitors. I am sorry this is all about me but please thank all your dear folk who have been praying for me & I do hope that wee baby girl twin who was adopted is doing well, I try to pray for her. Before too long, some weeks yet I'm told, I have to have the second op to put all this back together again. I do hope it will feel better then; dearest love, Rene.

Panyam

Oct 6th '63

Darlings it was so good to have letters from all 3 of you, thank you so much, especially to know Rene is making a bit of progress. Frances & Brenda both suggested 'Complan' as being a most useful food, as a supplement to an ordinary diet I mean. It is a multiple vitamin product that you can sprinkle on food, & also into drinks. Last Tuesday was Republic Day & we met for prayer & a special service in the morning; Nathan Benle spoke very well indeed mentioning the solid foundation that 'our Mother England' has laid in administration & training Nigerians to take over. We three decided to celebrate afterwards by going for a good walk, leaving the car about a mile out along the road & walking a further 3 miles to a place I'd never been to before, a wonderful rock formation we call the Cathedral. A man kindly accompanied us the last stretch; the views were magnificent looking back over the Fish Farm ponds quite red in the sunset. It got quickly dark on our decent & we had to push through tall grass & crops. We landed up in a compound where I knew a woman & she kindly led us on through some very boggy land where we had to take our shoes off & wade through mud. Then across a river – we were glad to wash our feet, then about another mile along by the Fish Farm ponds in bright moonlight, & finally back to the car. Approximately 6 miles but we enjoyed it very much! Tomorrow Margaret Jolley, a new missionary is to come here to stay for a few days until her posting is decided at the upcoming Field Comm – at which the Nigerian members are really starting to feel their feet & taking more part, following Pastor Bitrus' lead as he makes helpful contributions.

Now the 16th: I'm so sorry for the delay but I've been snowed under but in the meantime more letters from you & what thankfulness that our dear Rene is able to bake scones & sponge cakes once again, and that it looks as though you are to be launched into Little Dungate at last! Indeed it is a step of faith, but a step so well prayed over for so long. Today I am preparing for our Kaduna trip, taking our own foodstuffs this time; Pastors Ishaya & Bitrus are coming with us. At Mongun there must have been 300 women gathered from all the 25 villages in that area; it really was a thrill to see them from those remote places were until recently there were so few women Christians at all. They sang local hymns of their own composition with great fervour & we had such a happy time. I gave them a word from Ex 2 on the influence Jochabed must have had on her children; then a local woman spoke on Eph 6! I had a meal with a pastor-in-training & his wife, then showed the huge & noisy crowd some Kadachromes, & brought back 3 patients who needed a lift, back at 10pm & now darlings I must stop writing, with dearest love to all, Chris.

35 The Millbank Ifield

16.10.63

My darling Chris these notelets are for your birthday or if you have plenty, to give away at Christmas. They come to you with such masses of love & every best blessing for a very happy day on the 4th. We shall be especially thinking of you as I need hardly tell you! I'm writing this on a very grey & dreary afternoon, Mary is away to West Wickham & Mummy has just gone to lie down, as I shall in a minute or two. Early this morn I went to Communion at Ifield Church then M took me to Crawley for shopping & a haircut. Mr Williams has been so very kind in visiting me in hospital, & here since I came home, & sent a lovely big box of mixed fruit plus eggs from their Harvest Thanksgiving. I seem to vary very much from day to day in how I feel & what I can do, today is better than yesterday was. Dr Brooks has put me onto 'tranquilizers' the same ones Father had for awhile – I never thought I'd come to that; and I am to see Mr Stevens again on Monday morning for whatever he will say. Mummy has told you I think of the latest Little Dungate plan after we had such a helpful talk with Madge, Eileen & Delia. It does seem as if it is the right time to sell this house now as Mary can keep the proceeds of sale behind her in case she wants to take Mummy somewhere else instead. All dearest love my darling as ever for Rene.

Brookfield, Crawley

Oct 20th 1963

My dear Chris, peace and at such a time! Your letter has arrived before my hardy annual could even get started but I'll try to get something on the move here. Thanks muchly for writing & bringing us more up to date with affairs your end. I suppose that Oct-December is about the busiest time of your year, and it looks as if you are going to be short-handed during this period. Are you able to apply for help from Gindiri while your usual helpers are away on furlough? I saw the review to which you refer on 'Moody without Sankey,' & actually thought of you when I read it, wondering whether you would prefer it to CHS? I hope it will travel well & help to while away some of your 'spare' hours & giving much pleasure in the process. It will not arrive by Nov 4th I'm afraid but will bring our united good wishes for a very Happy Christmas & New Year and of course the same for your birthday in retrospect. Your report on the roses you took back is made all the more sad because we are unable to send you any more – unless you have a colleague who is due to return to your District before 31st March. If this is the case & you would like us to reserve a Josephine Bruce or maybe a Charles Mallerin rose, or perhaps a different small shrub or two, please let us know fairly soon, say by Christmas. We have just heard the names of the new Cabinet announced, but one never gets more than half the facts even with the present spate of information on TV. Hume seems to be quite a good sort of chap & probably favourably disposed towards 'Kesdom' (Christianity) but one cannot help feeling that this business of relinquishing the title & finding a safe seat is giving ammunition to Socialist scorn & ridicule. Perhaps no-one else could have extracted & received such support from other ministers & Party members, & it remains to be seen how much he can stand up to pressures from the other side of the house. He does seem capable of giving more direct answers than most people in high places. I have not sought my wife's permission to read the lengthy epistle she has apparently written to you, so if I repeat any family doings you'll understand. David has made a reasonable start & is extremely fortunate to have such an opportunity for some study for exams during his working hours, not usually offered in any similar firms it seems. Nona seems to have grown up rather suddenly, she came home for a day off today, this job will certainly give her valuable jumping-off experience for something better. Alison seems to be the envy of all her contemporaries as regards her 'digs' in the best part of Nottingham with a wonderful view & yet very close to the city centre. Jonny has settled down quickly, judging to his letters, & may have a little more push than D did at first. He'll be home for half term next week. As for the Business, again it appears the loss may cancel out last year's gain. We lost £5500 during Jany & Feby in the bitter weather. Such setbacks are nothing new & we did make some profit during the summer, & are getting busy on clearing the land at Pulborough of as much stock as possible. Now we have a lot of planting jobs to be completed by Christmas if at all possible if the weather holds good. Disappointingly there is still discussion over land at Tilgate, Park Farm & Byworth & the 2 old joint cottages & a rough old barn nearby, but trade debts were cleared off earlier than anticipated, a great help. Our week away did us all good, despite the squash & considering it almost certainly is the last holiday we shall have altogether. Now it is high time I signed off with very much love indeed & hoping you have a very nice & enjoyable birthday & also over Christmas, as ever thine, Wilfrid.

Panyam

Oct 25th '63

Darlings I wish there was enough time to tell you all the recent doings in Kaduna giving us such happy times, but overall I can say we have received quite as much, every bit as much or more, help & inspiration, as ever we were able to give. We stayed mostly at the charming bungalow where Mr & Mrs Piepgrass of the W. African Gospel Publication live; met so many new folks & heard many of their new hymns, & sold much literature in Sura, Hausa & English. Also we all went to the home of Mary Dabiring's brother Samuila & partook of a great feast which began outside with coffee, meat pasties, fruitcake, bread – without butter – & biscuits. Then rain came on so we crowded inside & bottles of lemonade were opened. About 10pm great dishes of rice, meat & very hot peppered gravy were served! It was all really very nice & the conversation lovely – mostly about the way they are seeking to spread the Gospel in & around Kaduna. Plenty more good chat with the women, 2 of whom were old GLB girls then we had to leave even thought it was still raining, for we had quite a way to walk to where we'd parked the car. We took Ruda home up through the centre of town & many side streets, but then missed our way & had to retrace until we eventually found our way back to the Piepgrass after midnight. On Sunday I went to the Ungwar Shanu church to meet the group, including some women, calling themselves, 'Hosts of Christian Witness to Everyone,' & Sam Dabiring is one of the leading lights. There must have been 200 people crowded inside with another 100 or so outside around the windows; it was not so long ago that the women in these areas fled from the sight of us!! It was splendid & as a result of this special service 22 new members joined! The 'Hosts' go out to preach in the villages, and in the prisons, to such an extent I felt challenged & inspired myself. They all look so happy & so clean & healthy, a real example of virile Christians with radiant faces & showing such love to each other. I took several photos so you should be able to see them some day I hope. Now more letters have come from you & what cheer they have brought to me & what excitement to think of Little Dungate being now available whether or not 35 The Millbank will sell as quickly as anticipated. But of course there are still many things you left unsaid & I know you cannot yet answer, mainly about our dear Rene & her health & future provision. Now I must prepare to leave again, this time to the Mongun convention weekend with their first baptismal service there; so with dearest love to each of you, Chris.

35 The Millbank

Nov 3rd '63

My beloved Chris I wish you were here spending tomorrow with me, but I do know you are in the place God has chosen for you. You are constantly in my mind & heart for the event of fifty eight years ago is ever remembered & rejoiced over in detail. Oh I hope you will have a very happy birthday with some special token of God's love & thought for you. This evening the sky is rainwashed & clear & tomorrow promises fine, I trust it will be so for your day. Today we had roast beef, potatoes, gravy, cabbage & then tapioca trifle for Eileen Hoyte came here to dinner & she seemed to enjoy it all and the good talk she had with Rene about Little Dungate. Christopher is spending the weekend at Brenda's sisters he was due back here this evening. Mary has been appointed as elder so it is sometimes easier now for me to get to Monthly Meetings & at one recent one the subject of the duties of elders was spoken of, stressing the need for more prayer, Bible study & quiet waiting upon God if our meetings were to be helped. One Friend read out a letter printed in the 'Meeting for Sufferings' publication, asking for help & a clear statement of the Quaker view of sex, then a second letter from a different source & in more moderate terms, but asking for the same help. A matter of no little importance; I wonder how it would be addressed at Ifield? Well goodnight my precious daughter – I mustn't say child – my thoughts & prayers are with you, I commit you to God's gracious care, & pray this next year you are entering may be the best & most fruitful of all. You know how much you mean to me, I hope I might live to welcome you back home next time you can come DV you went back 3yrs ago yest 1960 after coming because of Father's illness & now 5mths have gone since you left this time so only 2½ years to go; I must be patient; with all the love I can send you & very best birthday wishes, Mother.

Squirrels Holme, 27 The Avenue, Sunbury-on-Thames

15.11.63

My dear Chris just a notelet to bring Happy Christmas greetings with this little packet of notelets – I'm sure, like me, you find these always so useful on many occasions. I do hope this finds you well & enjoying life to the full in every sense of the word. Here we go on much as usual; Tony has gone to study medicine – like his Grandpa, at London university Charing Cross Hospital & he is still interested in bell-ringing & rowing. During the summer I have been on a round of most enjoyable visits to the various members of the family; the youngest grandchild, Hazel, is now 21mths. Joan & I had hoped to motor down one day to see your mother but we were unfortunately unable to make it fit in. I do hope Nigeria will settle down happily into the new 'Independent State' and that it will not make any difference to the wonderful Christian work that is going on up & down the land; with love from Auntie Elsie.

Panyam

Nov 18th '63

My darlings thank you again for all dear birthday remembrances. You will remember better than I, certainly Mummy, isn't it just about 33 yrs ago since I first left home to come here? I think it was Nov 17th but not quite sure. Last Tuesday I felt really replete with news for as well as yours I had one of those rare packets of letters from Brookfield, long & newsy from both Wilfrid & Barbara! So our Mary is now an Elder at Meetings – blessings on you dear in your new office, I'm sure you will make many worthy contributions. Enid writes so kindly from her Whitley Bay home of her furlough deputation work & how her people are joining in praising God for what I wrote in the recent prayer letter of the Muslims & Fulanis now coming in to Panyam to see me. Last Weds Pastor David took me & Brenda in his car to Boi & I was so thankful we did not take ours for the road was just about the most awful I have ever been on, & that's saying something! It was so rough with loose stones, great ruts & gullies where wet season rain had washed away so much, & twists & turns & ups & downs through streams & so on. Pastor D drove very carefully & after about 19 miles of bad road we stopped at a mining camp where we found Frank Ware waiting for us in the Boi Land Rover. We all squashed in & the final 7 mls were the worst, I'm sure even David's car could not have made it. It was worth the effort for the meeting was excellent with several women taking part including 2 who spoke on what the Course had meant to them. All the students received Certificates then we all shared first Communion then a very nice lunch prepared by Rachel Turner & Winnie Ware. Now I must work on the next 1-month Bible school courses that we hope to have in Feb '64 so goodbye for this time with my very dearest love to each of you, Chris.

35 T M

Nov 24TH '63

My darling Chris I have spoken at some length to you on the tape that we have all joined in with but you will wonder I have not already mentioned the terrible happenings of last week in the sudden ending of President Kennedy's life. It really came as a great shock to the whole world such a terrible tragedy – so young with such fine ideas for many good things – all shattered in one moment of time. Much pity, compassion & sympathy has gone out to his wife & family. This morning I listened to the early Service in Westminster Abbey the sermon was profound & deep; the Amer. ambassador & his wife were there, also Sir Douglas Hume & his wife, Harold Wilson etc. I think they are on their way now with Prince Philip to attend the funeral tomorrow. It is all so very sad but behind it all God is still working His purpose out & this is still His world. Mary took me with her today to the Women's Service in Purley Baptist, taken entirely by women & afterwards their Secy told me there were over 400 there & that all today have profited from God's word brought to us by Mary. It was wonderful & M spoke in the power of the Holy Spirit on Rom 6:8-14, especially verses 12-14 NEB. Now I see that at last 'Meetings for Suffering' has issued a brief word that our Society of Friends still stands for Chastity (pre-marital) and Faithfulness in all marriages, and yet some 'modern' Friends are objecting! Blessings on you my dear love & hoping the tape reaches you soon, Mother.

In the train

Nov 29th '63

My darling in these 15mins between E. Croydon & Victoria what better way to use the time but in writing to you, if you can read the scrawley bits, for it's certainly past time you heard from me. You must be preparing for your big Lake Chad journey – it is so lovely that you are able to go & see for yourself all the growth & visit your dear Sura missionaries – those sent forth from all that you have sown into your District. Reading your letter telling of this possibility, I just saw you as a Woman Bishop for I'm sure no Bishop cares for his flock more tenderly & carefully than you do. I hope & pray it might be a time of such stimulating happiness for you with nothing at all to spoil it, & plenty of journeying mercies. I'm hoping to have a moment to parcel up the tape we have made for you with contributions from various members of the family. But underneath all the jolliness darling I do ask for you prayers; Rene struggles on with this depressing condition & almost constant pain, & still no reply from Erik, it is hard to know how best to help her for some days she looks so very poorly that you feel she…later: shouldn't lift a finger for any of us but she cannot bear being told 'don't' & this extra bit of tension is having an effect on Mother who is apt to get more confused in her mind than I've ever known her; & you may recall she's inclined to get het up in the approach to Christmas anyway. I wonder how soon you heard the awful news of Pres Kennedy's assassination – it seems surely it can't really have happened. It's been remarkable to hear & read how deeply moved everyone has been and how suddenly we have all realised what a tremendous impact he has made on the world in less than 3yrs & how good his work has been. The horror of the act is as much in the fact that so much good has been lost to the whole world, as well as the personal tragedy. Surely good must come from this as people are shocked into seeing that this good is what we all want but that we can only have if we are all prepared to work for it. Blessings on you my dear love & may the Lord preserve your going out & your coming in; all my love ever yours Mary.

845B Brighton Rd, Purley, Surrey

Dec 1st 1963

Dear Chris no doubt you will be surprised to receive a letter from me for after 24yrs I am hoping to fulfill a deep longing to return to W. Africa – the very thought of which will carry me through even the toughest winter weather. And so I am doing what really isn't done in the best circles – asking if it would be possible for me to spend a few days with you in Panyam? I hope to come out by sea arriving Lagos Aug 13th then have exactly 3wks in the country & so want to find out which dates best fit the friends I want to visit. Few will know me now as it's been so long since my time there but I hope Dr Priestman will be able to show me some of her work, and I must get to Vom & Gindiri but I am most anxious not to be an embarrassment or an inconvenience to anyone. I hope to fly back from Kano about Sept 5th & if I don't stay with anyone too long I shall not upset the routine of very busy days anywhere – I don't know how you do keep up with all you have to do. Unfortunately with the passing of the years I don't adapt myself to change of climate quite as quickly as I once did! Here the term draws to an end & whatever work has or has not been accomplished I am encouraged that each dinner hour about a half dozen first years plus one or two second yrs come to my form room to read the daily SU portion with me. Of course one cannot push these things but at least this small effort, contained in 15 minutes, is not yet frowned upon by the powers that be. Now may I wish you God's richest blessing for the coming Christ-mastide, may you know His real joy & happiness, & all the other Christians in & around Panyam also. Although it is so far ahead I look forward tremendously to visiting you & I do hope you don't mind my boldly asking you; with love & every good wish from Hilda Turner.

30 Sheridan Rd, Worthing

Dec 2nd '63

Dear Miss Cheal it is now more than 12 mths since we had the opportunity of making that unique visit to Nigeria. Since the summer of 1962 a great deal has happened; we were married in July '62 & after a short Italian honeymoon then began the six week preparations of inoculations, last minute purchases etc for the W. African trip and directly on to the Crusader Camp in Ireland. Within a week of arriving home Winnie was taken rather poorly, bringing us to September this year when we were thrilled to have a lovely baby girl; and both mother & baby are fine although Winnie is not 100% yet. I hope this might explain to a certain extent why we have not written, but it comes with apology, for common courtesy required a letter to you after your gracious hospitality to us. We are indeed most grateful for all the trouble you took and the way you were personally involved in our time there. The full result of your most kind cooperation is something we may never know until we reach heaven but we definitely do feel that there will be eternal results from the impact that was made on the lives of those 10 boys we brought with us. From Crusader funds we have sent a cheque to Mr Farrant to cover 2yrs school fees in Gindiri for young Akila; and again our grateful thanks, yours most sincerely in Him, Herbert & Winnie Ramsden.

15 Park Chase, Godalming, Sy.

Dec 8th '63

Dearest Chris this brings much love from Gertrude & me & to wish you a peaceful, happy & blessed Christmas as you shine the light of the Gospel of Peace into many hearts in & around Panyam. We had the great privilege of going to Guildford Cathedral this morning for Bible Sunday to hear Pastor Niemoller give a stunning message on, 'His Name shall be called…the Prince of Peace – the text we had already chosen for our special one this year. After the shock of President Kennedy's assassination one realises how much one had pinned one's hopes on an earthly power…only the Lord Jesus can be called the Prince of Peace. G & I are both well and we do so hope you are Chris dear; with love from us both as ever, yours Ruth.

Braeside, Rodborough Common, Stroud

Dec 9/63

My dear Chris I have this day sent a cheque for you for £5 to your a/c at Bank of Brit. W. Africa, London EC3 which please accept as a Christmas gift from me. It is cold here we could do with some of the warmth that you get. Tim is in hospital at Bristol she had an operation on her tonsils & something else & today we have news it is all over safely. We expect her home in a few days; Mollie will visit tomorrow; Uncle Ernest.

Dearest Chris I must add my word of greeting, my wishes for you are turned into prayer for joyous & bountiful blessings for the Lord's good hand upon you & those for whom He has trusted you with oversight. What a rich, full life He has given you; with much love from your very loving A Lena.

35 T Millbank

Dec 15th '63

My beloved Chris how often have we thought & spoken of you during this past week & we long for news, to hear how you have got on. We can imagine a good deal but expect that surely comes short of the real joy & delight of being there where you're seeing all the dear folks you know, & of seeing the Carlings again, and all that work at Lake Chad that you have prayed for, spoken about & been so interested in for so long. I am so happy to think of you there & hope all has gone well; had you to resort to a camel's back yet? If so will there be a photo or two I wonder?! This letter should arrive before Christmas & just as you arrive back in Panyam I hope, so let me wish you a very happy time & may the New Year bring you a continuing sense of the Lord's goodness, guidance & blessing in your daily life & your contacts with everyone you meet as you seek to be His ambassador. Eddie Swain was here last Tuesday which was very pleasant but the next night Benson phoned that dear Uncle Isaac had left us. It was a relief to know he was now free from all suffering & the limitation of memory quite gone; I feel glad he is safely Home. I may not have seen him often but I shall miss him, he was a lovely person & a very kind brother to me.

Monday 1pm now & no letter from you but a lovely photo of Isaac & Olive, Benson knew I'd be so glad to have this. With all the love it is possible to send you, & picturing you somewhere on the way perhaps from Lake Chad to Maiduguri with Dr C, & praying the Lord to keep you in safety & peace, Mother.

Heath Mount, Rake, Liss, Hants

Dec 17th '63

My Dear Christine thank you so much for your regular PP letters, it is so good to have up to date news & be able to visualise you & Enid & the others as you go visiting place to place – how pleased the Evangelists & their wives must be to see you. We believe there are many places out there still as dark & needy as when we used to travel around so long ago. I love to hear of the Gospel Recording work – so many languages already recorded, & you have been so wonderfully involved in all this. Kay is due back tomorrow from a 3wk deputation into Kent we are hoping to see a bit more of her over Christmas. God bless you Christine, He has greatly blessed & used you there since that day long ago when I first saw you; what changes you have seen & been a part of in our Mission, and how the Lord has greatly helped you all. May you have a glorious Christmas with the realisation of His presence very near; yours lovingly Nellie Maxwell.

Maiduguri

Dec 19th '63

Darlings what joy to get back here (99 miles now behind us) & find your dear letters waiting, thank you so much! And Mary your dear prayer at the end of yours, for the Lord to refresh & replenish me, is being answered this day – thank you! Oh how I should love to slip home right now & spend Christmas with you & share all the news of this lovely trip – but I will attempt to finish typing it all up & enclose it if not with this, then with my next to you. The road to Bama is said to be the best in Nigeria 45 mls of tarmac dead straight & easy & Micah Jatan in charge of the small SUM Bookshop with his delightful family gave us a very happy welcome. Pushing on to Gwoza we remembered the first reports of Ishaya & Naomi Dashwet the first Christian missionaries here, only 10yrs ago before Europeans were allowed into this very unsettled territory. So it was amazing to see the large compound of Hospital buildings, Church, dwelling houses etc! But it is still very very hot there. Florence Chandler showed me around after tea, explaining the places the hosp patients come from, so far apart & up to 150 miles away & so many different tribes. Many were Moslems & had their Islamic rosaries beside them, many of the women had very elaborate & v dirty plaited hairstyles, but all seemed happy to be there & greeted Florence warmly. Two Nigerian nurses from our District, taught in the Jiblik School, were thrilled to entertain us. Two Sura builders are working 26 miles out, on the Basle Mission stn so I was glad to go & meet them & hear more good reports. It is marvellous that now so many Christians are scattered thus all over the place, giving good witness in secular as well as definitely Christian projects. I did get out to Limonkara for breakfast with the lovely Hamilton family who showed me the wonderful school where our Luther Dabiring is the Teacher! He had 23 little ones in a beautiful classroom & was teaching them English so very well, it was charming to see them. Then Akila Jalme from our District, the oldest Evangelist out there, is just coming home for 3mths furlough but took the time to introduce me to one of his converts who has just been baptised, Zaka Mwanbu, & we went on another 2 mls to meet another – his first – who is now an Evangelist to his own people.

Later, safely in Jos & very thankful, after a difficult drive, several breakdowns requiring the help of a lorry we had to stop, and, eventually a convoy including a rear-guard up that steep escarpment in the dark after the rescue car had come out to find us, we got in at 10pm. If this can reach you by Christmas Day how happy I shall be, dearest love to all, Chris.

In the car...

Dec 27th '63

Darling Chris what do you think...Rene & I with Ant driving, are on our way to town to see Laurence of Arabia, last minute spur of the moment!! We loved getting your epistle on Christmas Eve morning, we're all so very glad that it's been such a splendid trip for you so full of wonderful experiences for those you shepherded and for you, & so many now are shepherding others when they themselves were so recently reached. The grace of our God shines from every example, especially that a place like Tof can produce a missionary to send out!

Now it is Jan 6th 1964 and I am ashamed of this long gap since starting this to you. Altho' I have written 41 quite long letters by hand to my B. Soc secretaries this week so have not been idle. And I really hope you have been able to get some bodily rest & refreshment over your happy sounding Christmas celebrations, & are recovering from that marvellous Lake Chad experience. I feel so thankful you could achieve this & I'm quite sure it will be a continuing blessing to them & to you for a long time to come. We still have no word on Rene's second op so I shall not be able to attend the Staff Conf at High Leigh next week as that's bound to be when she'll be called in for it. And also still no word about Little Dungate either. As you can imagine this does create an inner tension for I feel I must give more time this year to the work for which I am paid – last yr was not at all satisfactory in this matter – but I am simply not free to go to work with the home situation so unsettled. But I did receive £5 from A Lena and Eileen, & dear Margaret Clark sent another wonderfully big food parcel, so kind of them. Darling I must go to bed now it is dreadfully late, so my dearest love always, M.

Panyam

Jan 12th 1964

Mother dearest I can't tell you how many times you were especially in my thoughts throughout yesterday & I just kept thanking God for all you have been & are still to us & to many others, praying that He may continue to use you & give you those special moments of enduement or unction – those times which remain as precious memories to me. And your gift arrived safely, no customs duty to pay, such a beautiful tray cloth you have embroidered for me – it is a great treasure, thank you so very much. Joan Onions has been staying here & when her training course for new teachers finished, she took Brenda, who has been feeling so tired, to Gindiri for the weekend but came back without her! Poor B has Dengue fever & has to stay in Gindiri under Pat Cummins' care – and I must leave at 6am tomorrow for 8 days! So now Joan & I have been making up cough mixture & putting out supplies of vital medicines for Samuila in the Dispensary. He plus his helper & Rauta the Midwife will just have to cope on their own & I'm sure they can & will. Now it is 9.45pm and I must stop this & get to sleep, goodnight my dear ones, as ever, Chris.

Jan 14th: such lovely letters from all 3 of you for which I'm particularly grateful in these weeks when I've had little time for any correspondence. After the first week of the New Life meetings in Wushik there is much to report; 18 more people stayed behind to receive the Lord, making 50 altogether. On my walk along the old Kombun road – as Joyce had the car – a young Panyam lad accompanied me & he was one who had accepted Christ that day! On Sunday morning we held a united meeting under the big tree as the Church was nowhere near able to seat everyone; we called on all who had received the Lord to stay behind afterwards to give them a few words of help to carry on. Two additional men joined in having just then submitted to Jesus & wanting to learn…each of them already had 3 wives. What can you say to such? We prayed with them to commit this big difficulty to the Lord and watch & see how He will guide them. Since then we hear of the following places experiencing wonderful blessings, Niyes, Kopal with its 2 smaller villages, Mongun, Jipal & Chakfem, all seeing a great number of new believers. Pastor Manasseh & Pastor Daniel Davwam ask for help & advice with the many known as Christians in their Churches who have come forward now realising they never truly knew the Lord, or confessing sins long hidden, or coldness of heart, all now wonderfully restored, forgiven & filled with New Life. And so it goes on, we are amazed, delighted & so full of thanksgiving. Another wonderful letter came today from dear Daisy positively glowing in the way the Lord is providing for your needs & she feels, as I do, that our family experience of His goodness will prove a real witness to a lot of folk; dearest love as always from me to you all, Chris.

At Bambur

Jan 16th

Darlings, how glad I was to get Mother's letter before we left for this remote spot, very far from the, well anywhere really; & also glad, truly thankful that our car's brake fluid leak was spotted and fixed before we left Jos. Then I understood why I had to take the unwanted & unplanned extra time to detour into Jos instead of pushing on. While awaiting the repair I was able to complete some shopping, join with the Carlings for their picnic lunch beside the beautiful Reservoir then enjoy an afternoon sleep and supper with Kath McDonald. The next day drive here took from 5am to 2.15pm in a selection of vehicles including the HQ's lorry & Geoffrey Dearsley's very nice Opel car which I had a turn driving once the roads improved a bit. We did the first 150 miles before stopping for breakfast sandwiches & very welcome they were too. I am in a 2-bunk bedroom in one of the private houses sharing with another woman delegate – it is such a blessing having a bathroom handy. We heard upon arrival that the Chip school has been burnt down, but I can do nothing until we get back. Here everyone feeds together, Nigerians & Europeans, starting with tea & biscuits at 6.30am; then a substantial Nigerian 'brunch' at 9.15am; tea & biscuits again at 1.30pm and the main meal also Nigerian food at 6pm.

Now it is Sunday 19th & this business conference is mostly over after 3 days of hammering out disagreements, discussions & making decisions. The Kaduna group's (TEKas) 6 delegates are a shining example of what Fellowship can really be; different folks from different ares, some used to infant baptism some not, are happily together under their Lutheran pastors, broadminded enough to have both adult baptisms in the river plus infant baptisms in the Churches, with all attending both! But Jos & Mumbi are not (yet) such happy places. The aim of this conference with its splendid Bible messages was to look at others' points of view, studying 1 Cor. 14 and our Lord's own example in John 13. Planning to start the return journey early tomorrow, & hoping there will be mail awaiting me back in Panyam; as ever yours C.

High Leigh

Jan 18th '64

My dearest darling in these few moments before tea let me tell you I've been thinking of the last time you & I were here together & wishing it were so again now. Earlier today the speaker's main challenge was: do we really think in a Christian/Christ-like way about the world's problems or do we, even subconsciously, accept & adopt worldly standards of conduct? And just before coming here, Renata had asked me to speak on Church Unity at Monthly Meeting! I've not agreed yet but will have to give her my answer soon; yes we have an obligation to learn from others, & to look at our similarities rather than only our differences, but how tolerant should we be? At home there is word at last for Rene – she's to go in to Smallfield hosp on the 22nd for the op on Thursday, not at Casterbridge after all. I am thankful there isn't so much time for her to dwell on it; that Ant is still here with no sign of his visa yet; & Mouse has been accepted at Brighton for the 3yr course, so she won't have him to worry so about either. Darling I am so grateful to you for all you are able to write to us, always so interesting, but I'm afraid I cannot write more now my heart's love M.

Southolme, 15 Park Chase, Godalming

18.1.64

Our dearest Chris your lovely letters have come and we are so delighted to read all your news & hear about this wonderful trip you've had to the Lake Chad project. How good is our God to give such evidence in fruitfulness of the faithful sowing of His Word & His Gospel message through many years; that the Christians in the Panyam area have caught the vision of missionary service to others must be the greatest joy to you. You will have known the sowing in tears but also the reaping in joy. What a journey you took! It was the variety of transport that so filled us with admiration, & we do hope there will be a picture or two of you on that camel but not under those thorn bushes. We hope your arm is fully recovered? And what a revolution the tape recorder has brought, so wonderful that you can capture & replay all those voices and give them some of God's word in their own languages. Nothing gives us greater pleasure than to know you were able to use part of our gift to finance the Chad adventure – that is simply thrilling. And we both really enjoy using the beautiful leather shopping bag you sent to us thank you so much. We are so very pleased to hear of Christopher's engagement he seems so happy & she seems such a nice sensible girl – may they be very happy through many years & find His service their delight. Ruth is busy getting ready for Keswick '64 but joins me in sending our dear love, Gertrude.

35 T Millbank

Jan 19th 1964

My darling Chris so many thanks for your ever welcome letter to me & I note what you say with humble thankfulness but I think it is your loving heart that detects what I don't feel. However, feelings apart, I thank God for giving me such a lovely family. In the life we are living at present with so much inward questioning, & perplexing waiting, your letter cheered & helped me. I know there must be some special purpose for all this waiting; we all seem to need so much patience, Rene for her health & this next op due so soon and her future, Wilfrid says nothing yet I know the Business problems are far from settled, and of course where and when we are to move once more. To me this all stresses the need for more concentrated prayer to go hand in hand with the patience. There are many things these days I do not get quite right & should perhaps be verified, but I am quite sure about that last notion, and this one; we think of you constantly & this brings you all the love in my heart Mother.

35 T M

Jan 26th '64

Darling just a brief note to let you know Rene had the op on Thurs & has come through it alright, the surgeon removed what he said was chiefly causing the trouble – the embedded ovary plus cyst & surrounding bowel and assured us there is nothing malignant so we do indeed thank God for that. R has had 2 pretty tough days with much pain but the nurses are being very kind & looking after her so well. She is still only to take water with a little ribena in it & she does look better than after the previous op. Mother has naturally found it all rather a strain but is so thankful for Brenda being so attentive & thoughtful & as a nurse of course she can pop in every day to see Rene; also it does sound as if Little Dungate is at last vacant. I know you'll be praying with us about that, but now I must go darling, all my dearest love to you, Mary.

35 TM

Jan 28th '64

My beloved Chris there is today a feeling of renewed hope, Rene does not look quite so poorly altho' she does find the Dr prodding daily on her stomach extremely painful. It is a slow business, except of course when Christ touched people here on earth, they were immediately made whole – but I am quite sure He is working on Rene just the same in His timing in His perfect love & wisdom. We called in to Brookfield on our way home from hospital, to make tea & sandwiches for Barbara who has the asthma again all week, and we washed up the dinner things which Wilfrid was beginning to tackle with his overcoat on – he was too cold to remove it. He told me something went wrong with the upstairs cistern last night, it overflowed into the bathroom & down into the kitchen; my poor W that would put him in a fix – troubles seldom come singly at least for him. In a letter from dear Helen Webber in America she tells me she has a blue suit dress plus little jacket, worn only twice and would I like it? Would I not?! I replied yes with great thankfulness. I never thought she'd be able to send any more seeing so much was burnt in that fire, but they are not short I think, & her things are always good. Now with all the love I can send you, Mother.

Ward 18, Smallfield Hospital, Horley

29.1.64

Darling Chris here I am once more & I think the worst is over & I've even walked a step or two beside the bed. I've had my first solid food & very good it was too: cream potato, a spot of mince chicken & baby-food pureed peas but I could not manage the little milk pudding after. They will close the colostomy on Feb 6th & I'll be able to leave here & go to the Convalescent Home in Hove on the 16th all being well. How blessed it will be to be done with hospital; although Mr Stevens says I shall not be able to work for at least 3mths or possibly even longer. I wish I need not so many sleeping pills for I feel awfully dopey in the daytime. Such lovely flowers came from the Tuckers & Mosses, and your very dear letter, may you be kept in safety & peace day by day & given wisdom & strength for all your duties; now with my heart's love, Rene.

Ward 18, Smallfield Hosp.

Feb 10th '64

Darling Chris just a quick note to tell you I've been moved into the nice little side room – where Mummy was so you can picture me here – how I do thank Margaret & Cyril Knott for making it possible because they sent a cheque for £25 to help pay for a private room, wasn't that so good of them?! Mr Stevens wants me to have another barium enema & if this shows all is really well & healing properly inside then he will do the colostomy, but not if the abscess & bladder infection continues to delay it. I've had so many in to visit which is so lovely although rather tiring, & I've told Mary not to come but stay home & rest when she gets in from her long days for she does look so tired out. All those, bar one who died, who came in for their ops when I did have all gone home & I long for that day to come for me too. But I have so enjoyed seeing the pictures of your splendid tour, what a noble one of you on your camel! Dear Mr Williams comes every week to see me, he is a good soul, & this morning I partook of his 7.30am Communion. I heard of the difficulties between some of the missionaries in the Bambur area & we were all so thankful to know the worst troubles were sorted out peacefully before you had to leave there. Oh and poor dear Filippa losing her husband of one month in the dreadful car crash, whatever will she do now we wonder; all dearest & best love darling from your Rene.

16 Sedgefield Drive, Thornby, Leicester

Feb 16th '64

My dear Chris thanks so much for your lovely letter, I'm trying to answer it while waiting here for Enid on the train which is already late. While running for a bus yesterday I fell & have done something to my foot, it hurts but I do not think too much damage was done but I felt a right charley to use a modern expression. When I arrive back to you will there be time to get a few stores in? Perhaps you could ask Brenda if she will be leaving any stores behind which I could buy from her please so you can tell me what these are, and if you could lend me some ready cash, say £5 then I could pay for my pantry supplies. I will then pay you a cheque. Half my January allowance has been paid into my account in the Jos bank & a little more is being transferred today. This will be my last letter, not much longer now DV looking forward to getting back next Wednesday seeing you & Brenda with much love, Joyce.

Panyam

Feb 18th '64

My darlings just a few notes of things I've had put by to remember to tell you & if you'd pass this first one on to Rene please; I had a nice letter from Mrs Fraser of Aberdeen…'I do trust Mrs Forsback is well, we do miss her from our Group here in Aberdeen, I trust she is finding the nearness to home & friends a means of blessing, we send our warmest love to her and to your mother.' Then from Marjorie J the same racy, loving scribble inside a delayed card posted in November! Last week I took a shorter than usual trek out to Ambul to see their school children & check on the Bible classes; we had some interesting discussions but I have done very little walking lately & found this trek to be very tiring so I was thankful to have the time to rest in Tof on our way back. Mary, do you remember Naki from Mupun? Her husband is now teaching in Ambul and she has started a pre-GLB club & it was a wonderful sight to see her with about 100 keen girls so well dressed – no uniforms yet – but so happy, & happy with their amazingly successful leader! Naki herself is thriving on this & had all her own 4 children out there on the field doing the exercises & games with the girls! Another thing Mary, Nakam tells me you spoke at her Women's Fellowship mtg last week & that you were excellent, you fully held the women's attention, 'she certainly has a gift'... well done darling! And I did enjoy your story about you asking Mother how much the 5gals of petrol would come to at 4/9d per gal & she gave you the correct answer having 'done mental' in her head – wonderful! Last Fri & Sat were the big Moslem public holidays to celebrate the end of their fasting; we have to observe these days too although my time could hardly be called a holiday! I had 12 visitors to feed & entertain, starting with David Bawtree at 6.30am on his way by bicycle to see his lady love at Kabwir, needing a spot of breakfast to help him on his way. Frances was able to have a quieter day yesterday so we went out in the evening to visit an old leprosy patient of mine then hers, who is now symptom free & back home in Panyam with a wooden leg after Frances amputated a most troublesome foot. We've been getting Joyce's house spring cleaned ready for her return; but now I must say goodnight my dear loves, yours as ever Chris.

Ward 18 Smallfield Hospital

Feb 27th '64

Darling Chris my very first letter must be to you but please forgive the queer writing as I'm lying nearly flat. It is so wonderfully good to have these operations finished & so to be able to look forward to the future with hope. The Daily Light verse on the op morning was: ... he that trusteth in the Lord, mercy shall compass him about, & those words were still ringing in my ears when I came to at 5pm. The delay has been trying but the date for the Conval Home now seems to be Mar 7th. People have been so wonderfully kind & I was absolutely staggered to find in a letter from Tim, a cheque for £50 & her saying the Lord told her to give it to me; and Mrs Gregory sent Mary £25 to pay the fees of the Conv Home – aren't people splendid! Lying here I have been able to read of all your busy, busy days darling & long, long walks, & pray for extra strength & health for all you have to do, blessings on you my dear love, as ever yours, Rene.

Panyam

6.3.64

My dearest dears what a comfort it was to have letters from you all & to know that our dear Rene is over the last op and doing alright – thanks be to God! How I hope the pain & discomfort will be past so she can really enjoy the time of refreshing by the sea. Here David Carling is preparing for the journey to Lagos with Tsok the very good lorry driver, to haul up the huge boat all the way to launch it onto Lake Chad! The last 150 miles will be tediously long & very tricky, only partly on tarred roads, & the Land Rover will only be able to go slowly; on one bridge there will only be a 9inch clearance. So there is urgent need for daily prayer until this mighty task is completed. I think I told you of the 2 tailors working in Mongu, one a keen Christian, the other a lad who professed conversion some years ago but then became a Moslem. The Christian is trying to draw him back & brought him in for a talk on Sat eve after which I lent them my gramophone & Gospel records which they then played, listened & talked about together late into the night in the Moslem boy's home.

Now it is the 26th & your new letters are with me & I'm so glad you all had a time away at Rustington, & you Rene darling are truly on the mend & feeling stronger. We were at the Regional Church Council at Forum last week & had some particularly good short devotional times each morning. Pastor Damina who is to visit England next year, took the passage in Ezekiel about the building of the Temple on different floors & levels and he likened that to the breadth & expansion of the Lord's work in this land. Pastor David Telta also spoke well, from Heb 11 then the other Pastors including Istifanua Deshi of Kabwir, & Joel, all contributed & this was so very encouraging to hear. We now have to decide who else to send with Pastor Damina. There a growing sense of a keen awakening which is truly heartening; but I cannot write more tonight, just send my dearest love C.

252 Selsdon Rd, S. Croydon

April 8th '64

My dearest Chris very many thanks for your most welcome & interesting letter today. You certainly have been having too much rushing around lately, you really must try to stay in one place a little longer or go away for a holiday for you cannot keep going at that pace for ever! I can of course understand how your increasing 'ends of month' admin days in all the different places are getting harder to manage & yet as you say the contact with all these Church Councils is both good & necessary to keep them all linked as one growing whole. Could African staff not go sometimes or at least alternate with Europeans? Do you think perhaps the time is coming when you might leave them to conduct their own local business each month & only visit occasionally? Such de-centralisation will be good for them & I think would encourage further growth; and you could begin to delegate others to come in and collect their supplies of literature and medicines. It really seems that they are – mostly – established enough for you to consider this, and I do think it wonderfully amazing that every village has now heard the Gospel!! Yes I have heard of the New Life Campaign, I think it is good & I'm glad to know of the part Panyam is taking to get it established. My news is small by comparison but I finally leave here 2 weeks today on the 22nd to live at Rosset Holt, Pembury Rd Tunbridge Wells. I went for a weekend 'on appro" & seemed to have passed for they have given me a warm welcome & a lovely big room rather than the very small one first suggested & which I dreaded. All my furniture that I won't need in my one room there is going to the London City Mission, specifically to a man just home from a lifetime's work with a Red Sea Mission among Arabs, & he has nothing in this country. I know that will bless him so it also blesses me. My new room is being redecorated now & will look fresh but I think it will take quite a bit of adjusting at first, amongst all the old dears who seem so terribly deaf & doddery! I'm sure it is the Lord's leading for me, for as long as He is going to give me, so I'll soon find a niche & settle in; I know you'll be praying for me; now with much love & daily prayer, Nakam.

Panyam

April 9th '64

Darlings I seem to have had no time at all for thinking, let alone writing, for ages, I am so sorry. So it was extra good to get Mother's letter written on Easter Day to tell me Rene was home & able to go out to a service! Now of course I long to know if there is any further development on Little Dungate and the selling of 35? At present all around here there is a lovely, growing spirit of fellowship

& co-operation between Evangelists, I really feel the Lord is moving in our District especially in the remote country places, and it is very encouraging indeed. The whole Mongun Church is now concerned about an unevangelised area to the south of them. I have mentioned the New Life for All Campaign, well it is now coming out to our local area for planning & preparation & Ap 27-May 1st is to be a big Retreat for Pastors & Evangelists to introduce it. Several of our good men have joined 'Ambassadors of Christian Witness' that began in Kaduna & is now spreading to include the home churches from which our men came. Truly the Lord seems to be breathing New Life through us by these various means & I long to see them all coordinated rather than working as separate efforts. Pastor Bitrus certainly sees this need & he is far-sighted and has a good grip of the political trends in the country. You know there is a great deal of pressure being brought to bear by influential Moslems against the spread of Christianity especially in the Gwoza area and Bornu. Bitrus thinks that if the Moslem north is victorious again in the Federal elections at the end of this yr then Christians in the north are almost certain to be in for a time of persecution. Several of his sermons lately have been with that view. About 30 men, mostly Pastors, including David, have launched a new organisation to be called Northern Christian Association mainly to show a united Christian front against the hardening Moslem pressure. A press release has announced the formation & explaining it is not political but it will look into any case of discrimination against Christians, & any unconstitutional behaviour, referring to the clause about religious freedom that David & the Chiefs of Jos & Kagoro got added into the Nigerian constitution. Joyce needed some help today with her medical & maternity work as she had 125 women in the antenatal clinic – a record! I had a happy note from the Christian tailor telling me his ex-Moslem friend Mwanle, is now back with us, & his wife, & they want to buy a Bible, & last Sunday they came in to Church – praise the Lord for that! Now dears, have you heard anything of the 'New Pentecostalism' or the 'Charismatic Revival' as it is also being called? I have read of it, & you know we have Assemblies of God, the Pentecostals, out here & we are supposed to be working with them. Most of our Europeans have either heard of it or not but are taking notice & seem to agree it is clearly taking hold. Pastor B went to an AoG mtg & told me, "They have something that we haven't – freshness & joy in worshipping." In England & America this 'revival' is something with speaking with tongues even in High Churches & P. Brethren mtgs & so on; this is something I can't understand at all. What is the sense, or special significance, what is the value to the Lord; or to the person who uses it, or to others? I'm in the dark on this whole matter. I have written to Ros Manning to order 200 of the Pentecost booklets for our District; maybe that will shed some light. Goodnight my darling dear ones & dearest love to you each & all, as ever, Chris.

Panyam

April 21st '64

My darling Rene it is too long since you had a letter to yourself even tho' I know you know how I think of you constantly & long to hear you are able to be out enjoying the Spring. May I share something that's been happening here that can only be the Lord's doing & marvellous in my eyes. I've written before about a general stirring taking place throughout this whole District which in itself is enough to challenge us to be ready. Still, I don't think I was seeking anything special for myself any more than during all the past years, but for the past few weeks or so I've been conscious of a freshness & new life in my own heart that fills me with joy & gratitude. I'm sure there was nothing that deserved it. It is just a sense of the Lord's presence, great happiness

& peace & particularly a delight in prayer & worship. One night I woke after only about 2hrs sleep, feeling this sense of joy & my mind was so alert, reaching out in prayer to people & needs in a new way. This has happened several times since & gives me special joy because I've so often felt I ought to spend more time in prayer but it has been such a difficult thing to do & now it's not only possible but a delight! There seems to be sort of an undercurrent of joy during the busy days & everything is sweetened & cheerful. Of course I've had all sorts of fears & doubts too. Is this just wishful thinking, a figment of my own imagination & desire? Is it a Pentecostal experience such as I have been reading of lately, and will it lead me into things I don't understand or want? I have brought these fears before the Lord & He has laid them low, so with great thankfulness I have accepted this fresh blessing. I wonder whether it will go on like this or whether it's just a special gift for this time of great opportunity. It has been a special joy to pray for Ant in his new place of need, & for you my darling I have asked if it could please Him to give you some sort of springtime in your own heart like this, to banish the pain & heartbreak of the past years. And I've thought of dear old Madge in constant pain, & asked the Lord to meet her need too. I think I've sung more in the past few weeks than I have for a very long time, & some of the great old hymns seem exactly fitted to express one's feelings. Well this is just an attempt to tell you what is very difficult to put into words, & to ask the Lord to pour His blessings on you dear love, yours as ever, Chris. PS one more thing I think will interest: a letter came yesterday from England addressed to Miss Nachrist Cheal, from Susannah Alheri, a Nigerian girl born on this compound, her father Daniel was the Dispensary Asst when I first came out here. He moved his family to Zaria under CMS but Susannah did Teacher Training at Gindiri & is now at Salisbury College. She used part of her holiday to stay at Braeside & writes so appreciatively of their kindness & of her joy during a students' conf at Swanwick where she was deeply blessed. My, it is grand to hear of 'our own' children from here being so blessed in England!

Panyam

May 13th '64

My darlings I know you'll understand my lack of responses to your dear letters of last week, & possibly the week before also, which still continue to bring me such cheer, & not just for what you tell me of house values having gone up so altho' that does sound wonderful! For us too this has been a time of immense blessing in the preparation for & delivery of the New Life for All Course immediately followed by the big GLB Camp. Both these big events were really great & I'm sure will have eternal effects that we cannot imagine. The teaching from Malam Yakubu & Mr Gerry Swank was in my opinion outstanding; it was teaching the teachers, explaining the course, the handbook, & the best ways of getting it all across to others, enabling the assembled Pastors, Teachers & Evangelists to grasp the truths in a manner suitably reproducible for them to take back to their churches, schools & villages during & after the main Campaign in the autumn. One pastor called Yakubu back to his house to confess that his life & home were not worthy of a Christian or to carry this great teaching to others; and at the end of the final session about 100 folk stood to testify to what the Lord had done for them & so to re-dedicate themselves to Him; and Huldah Yamden was chosen by the committee as the first African woman Director of Evangelism! The Camp was great fun although perhaps not the communal washing in cold water & undressing & dressing together in very small quarters – not exactly streamlined comfort! However, Kath McDonald's amazing organisation, & beautiful programme worked out in detail & duplicated into a small booklet for each girl & officer, was essential, and excellent. The girls put on marvellous displays and everyone seemed to have enjoyed everything & been richly blessed by the quiet devotional times each morning & evening and the excellent talks mainly by Bitrus. On the final evening around the Campfire he spoke from Joel's prophetic words, "prophesy is simply passing on God's message…in the last days I will pour out My Spirit…& your daughters shall prophesy…& your handmaidens…yes the men & sons too but tonight we are thinking about you girls. The end of anything good is the most difficult time & there will be dark days ahead but God is promising to pour out His Spirit onto His girls – you – and send you out as His witnesses." It was a powerful word & all were deeply moved. The Gindiri girls then sang a beautiful finale. Now I'm back from Jos and find more letters from you and I am sharing with you the enjoyment of the wonderful way the house has been sold & for such a price!! Everything just seems to be slipping into place in that perfect way which it does in God's perfect timing. I am delighted by all this and the news of satisfying shopping for some new & well deserved clothes – how that does boost morale! We are expecting David Carling here any minute & we're eager to hear further news of the boat, which is actually on the Lake now! Goodnight darlings with such dear love as ever, Chris.

Panyam

June 25th '64

Darlings just a wee line to bring you such loving greetings as you move into your new home; my thoughts & prayers are with you as you know & I do pray & believe that this is the Lord's plan for us & that we shall rejoice in the way He has led us. I long to hear that you have been able to settle in happily & without too much weariness & strain, & that the new home will be a place of such blessing & happiness to you each one individually according to your various needs: Mary a place of spaciousness in which to house your stock in trade & where you can do your home-work in comfort then relax & rest. Rene a new home of your own in which you can exercise your special ministry for others, & find joy & fulfilment for yourself; and Mummy, for you another home in which you can make that focus of love & prayer that nourishes each one of us & flows out to bless visitors & others around. We have the Elseys here & they are kind & pleasant guests, so appreciative. We went to the Bawtree wedding in Gindiri then on to the mtg of the great conference of Pastors and Evangelists, 650 of them from all over the North. We hear that the postal & transport strike at the beginning of this month is likely to be resumed and so more of our letters may be horribly delayed, like poor Kath McD who flew to Lagos for the start of her furlough but could go no further. But, there is delightful news continually coming in of further blessings from the New Life for All prayer mtgs: a man married to John Mark's sister, was telling of his family even including 6&7yr old children bringing the name of their non-Christian grandmother & praying themselves for her; and most of the women in a remote heathen village who are now Christians, are coming in regularly to the Evangelist's house in a nearby village to pray for the rest of their families. Many of these women said they could not pray aloud, only in their hearts, but after trying a few words they are now praying out loud beautifully & with passion. These utterly rejoicing stories are circulating & in themselves bringing further encouragement, but goodbye for now darlings as ever Chris.

Panyam

June 28th '64

Darlings this will be the second I've addressed to you new home & I'm sending it in case the other didn't get through – how we are all hoping this strike will come to a quick end. Enid & I will go into Jos in the morning & will try to post this there. Joyce is having a terrific time of it in the Midwifery Unit, 65 babies born since she got back at the end of Feb; today she's had one birth & 2 still in labour & Rauta is still on her week's holiday. Enid, Ishaku & I each went to different congregations to take their services this morning, E walked 5 miles, Ish about 4 and I went to a new little place where the church has no seats inside yet, just loose bricks to sit on and 2 tree trunks for pews! But about 60 people crowded in & we had a nice time, 4 of the young men keen to join a baptism class. Between us we three went to 6 more outstations for afternoon mtgs or SS classes & returned rather weary. My plans so far are to leave here on July 23rd for 2 nights in Dutsen Wai & on to Kaduna on the 25th & stay there for 3 weeks with a break in the middle for a short trip to Zaria & Kano taking the Elseys.

Monday early – what a morning, 3 babies born in 15 minutes!! Twins & a girl, all squirming & needing attention & a bath…just done that to help Joyce, now for breakfast; such dear love to you 3 & of course to Madge, Eileen & all the others, from Chris.

Nsukka University of Nigeria

July 5th '64

Darlings this will be the third letter I've posted to your new Little Dungate address without actually hearing of the move! We travelled the 350 miles here on mostly good roads, collecting Pastor Bitrus & Geoff D on the way. We are housed in the students' hostels of this lovely new University; I have a v. nice double room with real innerspring beds & my companion is a Nigerian lady from Lagos where she teaches in the Baptist secondary school. She has 5 children, has been to the USA, & is now hoping to get a scholarship for further study in England! We've heard some excellent speakers & several greatly thought-provoking Papers submitted – one titled, 'A Renewed Church in a New Nigeria' which brought forth lively discussion begun by my roommate who stated boldly that tithing was the best way forward. Today several people have driven 49 further miles to Enugu capital of this East Region, for morning church but I stayed to have a quiet day after attending an early communion service where I sat between a Bishop & a Canon, both Nigerian but neither offered to share a prayer book with me!

Tuesday: Darlings what a joy to get 2 of your letters today & to know you've been so graciously helped over the move & finding your new home so pleasant & lovely. I'm so glad I was able to see it so I can now visualise you settling in & enjoying the spaciousness & wonderful views; & the good fellowship & fond farewells at Ifield with Friends & neighbours and at the Parish Church too. I do hope to hear soon that the gift I sent Christopher & Brenda – a pouffe & a bag – has arrived safely; you'll soon be getting busy with wedding preparations! More good talks here & a feast of discussions on such weighty matters as our relationship with the Orthodox Church, should spiritual healing be included in medical work, and the growing need for pastoral ministry in hospitals. A Nigerian Baptist Minister gave some truly masterly talks from 2 Cor. 2-6 on Christian ministry, on a par with Keswick; a Rev from Port Harcourt spoke out about the dreadful conditions of poverty & that he thought the Communists were evidently behind all the recent strikes, so the urgent need for Christians in industry & trade unions. A Univ. Lecturer from New Zealand asked why 2million adherants/ orthodox church members should now be joining a selection of the new independant and indigenous churches – what do they offer that's not found in our Churches, what do we lack? These prophetic healing groups offer vitality in worship that we are unaccustomed to and personal pastoral care that generally we cannot offer because Pastors are so bogged down in administrative work. As you can imagine this was quite a challenge to us. The recommendation is the Church is urged to take immediate & vigorous action to put its own house in order and start bridging these gaps. A great deal was said about the New Life for All Campaign & the many handbooks & tracts in the vernacular languages & I spoke of the gramophone records as well. For our return journey there were 3 drivers so none were unduly tired; ever yours C.

Miango

July 19th '64

Darlings how wonderful it is that your dear letters seem to be able to follow me around and catch up with me on these various travels, this one not so far away but again a time of solid spiritual business in prayer & discussions & study times. I've met up with the American couple who were struggling so much in their difficult District – mostly the usual problems of professing Christians still stuck in drinking & adultery; they poured out their troubles to me some time ago and we had prayer together. Lately he has been preaching more freely on the Holy Spirit & they are now seeing a remarkable change in atmosphere & attitude, & the fruit of the Spirit is bubbling over from them to their people in such a loving manner. There is a Mennonite missionary here also American but originally a Britisher & strange to say from Three Bridges & Burstow in his youth! He is being wonderfully used in Bible studies on the Holy Spirit & has talked deeply from Ezekiel's vision & living life led by the Spirit. I have just felt what a great privilege it is to be a part of this work at this time and seeing God's hand leading us on and out. Desmond Thomas of Maiduguri has just been telling us about the second visit he & David Carling made last week out to one of the permanent reed islands in Lake Chad. The Buduma people there came out in canoes to meet & welcome them & listened with amazement to the gramophone Gospel records in their own language. David & Desmond treated almost every child, man & woman on the island for some sickness or other. We go back to Panyam tomorrow for a few days before leaving again for Kaduna & the next journeys I told you of in my previous letter, so I know you'll be praying us through – oh how I count on your prayer support, thank you so much; with my dearest love now & blessings on you each & all as ever Chris.

Highlights from Report of Kaduna Visit

July 25th-Aug 16th 1964

The aim of this visit was to offer new short Bible Courses for women in all the Churches expressing interest. The first, on Sunday July

26th was filled with hundreds of eager people & Pastor Habila Aleyideino led the service & preached a very good sermon on the need for fearless witnessing for Christ by life and lip wherever we are. He introduced me to his wife Salome who then appeared early the next morning with 100 women hungry to learn. And so it went on. A Ganawuri woman, wife of a policeman, was forbidden by her husband to attend any Course; he had torn her copy of New Life for All Handbook into pieces & burnt it. Mrs Salome took me to see her & we prayed & encouraged her. During the final week I saw her 3 times in the Church, radiantly happy saying her husband's heart is softening & he had allowed her to join with us. A Sura soldier's wife whom I have known since her childhood, I found in miserable one-roomed quarters with her children. Her husband, once an Evangelist, was away on leave. "This is my bed," she said, "and that one belongs to the other wife." After another Sura woman & I had prayed for her, she then bravely led in prayer. A keen Sura soldier's home was a joy to visit, clean, cheerful & with a well stocked bookshelf, pictures, & a gramophone – for which I had brought for him a set of Hausa Gospel records. He is an elder of the Ungwar Shanu Church & he spent his recent leave in the Barracks with his wife & family helping to build the new Church there. A Kabwir woman is the Unwar Zumunta of the Kawo group; her prayer took up point after point of the Bible study we has just done. A Numan & a Langtang woman were both rejoicing that the Gwari women had all attended the Course, because they had visited them & told them of Jesus Christ. A sweet Pella woman stood up & asked for prayer saying, "I have been ill for 7 years in & out of hospital, I have no child. My husband was patient for 7 years but now he has taken another young wife." We prayed. Later I met the three of them in their tiny 2-room home & was received with much kindness. I found that they had never been married. An Evangelist's daughter from Chip who was a very shy girl in Gindiri School, is happily married to a Chip man working in Kaduna Textiles. She is now Secretary of the Mata Zumunta & took a lead in prayer & reading verses from Scripture in the Course she attended. Two other young Chip couples live in the same row of houses & she has encouraged them into becoming Church members.

I was amazed to find I had travelled 316 miles in & around Kaduna alone – the distance between Kawo in the north & Kakuri in the south of the city is 11½ miles. On the last Sunday after morning service at the central Church the Secretary put a gift into my hand. It was £5 from them plus £6.3.0 from the Women's Fellowship. When I totalled up the petrol and the car repairs needed on the way home it came to exactly £11.3.6d!!

Panyam

August 19th '64

Darlings when I think back to the years of straightness, when I used to long for change & opportunity, and didn't get it, then compare that with this year I am well & truly 'lost in wonder, love & praise!' So many places recently I've been able to visit, and see each with their own interest and blessing. Then this new sphere of work is so fresh & interesting, with the New Life for All project growing all around and in Panyam. Underneath all this is still that fresh personal experience of the Lord that I told Rene about some months ago now; it continues and gives me such joy & peace, even in difficult times, so that I literally don't know how to thank and praise Him adequately. If only one could communicate something of this to the needy folk one meets every day, but perhaps it does happen, if only a little bit, unconsciously, I do pray so.

28th now: oh dear that was the last of my moments to write, I am so sorry for the delay. I have received your letters including that form which I've signed & asked Pastor Bitrus to co-sign as the Minister of

Religion required, and sent it back to you. Pastor Manasseh came to hold a meeting with the men who have been studying the Handbook New Life for All because they will soon have to be examined on it; I am glad to be part of this. Soon after that however I began feeling rather poorly, & quickly unwell; the kitty had scratched my leg which had gone a bit septic, & suddenly it began pulsating right up my leg. The shivers & chills got quite strong so I took a hot bath & went to bed then Joyce came & gave me the first of three shots of penicillin. Next day I was feeling much better & my temp was lower but the leg still pretty swollen so I'm still in bed, but using the time to prepare & send out exam papers. Yes Mother, I do hear you saying, 'When will that child learn to cover up wounds from the dirt!' It was only a tiny scratch, but it will teach me a lesson I suppose! It was so lovely having your dear letters yesterday & now I greatly look forward to seeing the wedding photos soon, dearest love Chris.

Panyam

Sept 17th '64

My darlings, Mummy's ever welcome letter of the 6th is the only one I've had since I last wrote, and how strange to think that Miss Green has passed away before Tommy Smith – what a strange sort of life they lived! Now you're getting ready to take in your first 'oldies' & Rene I am praying for special strength to be given to you; what incredibly perfect timing & such wondrous provision this is from the hand of our faithful God. I am imagining the beauty of early autumn colourings on Reigate Heath & I'm so very glad to have that photo I took on my last evening, of you Rene between Madge & Eileen on the drive of Dungate Manor looking through to Little Dungate. I heard today that your General Elections are on Oct 15th; I think there will be Federal Elections in this country soon but one cannot help wondering how they might pass off for feelings run high over politics these days. We have a very nice American man staying with us right now, he is really on leave but choosing to spend it discovering & learning how life goes on in other Mission stns. We have shared a busy admin day at Daffo, a Communion service at Mongu, & I took him out to a village 4 mls away to visit old Toma & his wife Hannatu who were Evangelists in my early days. We made tape recordings rather like with old Father Lot & we had such fun together doing that. We walked to the car & they came along to Church where their youngest son is in charge. They are a splendid old couple she is taller than Toma, and a great crack. She always used to sit in the Dispensary & listen to everyone's symptoms and add, "Yes I used to have exactly the same as that!" Tonight the American is coming to supper along with Pastor David. Well, the New-L-for-A Campaign is about to begin, the classes for instruction are finished, the Handbook exams being held this week. I have today already examined 10 people including my old ladies who did well except on the memory verses, but Christiana Banput who came to Kaduna with me, is a marvel & knew all hers off pat, 12 verses with references. And now we hear that the 200 gramophones plus 2000 records are in Jos awaiting collection but I must hear the cost of transport & customs before I can give them out. About 120 of our folk have paid the £2 & these records in the 16 languages of this District are eagerly awaited.

Now it's the 21st and your letters with the lovely photos have arrived & oh how I am enjoying them! Thank you everso much for sending them – you don't mention if I have to send them back or not? Everything looks so lovely in house & garden & the ones of you at the wedding are super! The only thing that struck me as extraordinary is Mummy's hat- I've never seen you in such a big one but it is good to have a change! Rene's outfit is superb & so is Mary's & Rene it did me good to see you looking so well & so charming – I should say you could easily be under 40! Ishaku & Yilmak, Joyce's boy, were intrigued with the pictures of the house & the one of Rene in the kitchen called forth many comments: the number & size of the eggs, the Keswick mug on the rack the same as mine here, & so forth. The 'lantrik' (electric light) above your desk Mary, & the handsome cushions were all commented on. It is a charming photo of Brenda going in at the Church door, looking as if she didn't want to keep Mouse waiting a moment longer. I was so sorry to hear she'd come down with glandular fever so soon afterwards, and how wretched that you never got my last letter assuring you my leg is completely fine, you must have been anxious, I am sorry. Joyce has had 3 of her sister's letters go astray. Yesterday we had to say goodbye to Bitrus Yamden as he had a sudden call to go to Ibadan Univ, he gave a very good word in Church & left immediately after. We shall miss him a lot but hope he'll be back for Christmas. Huldah his wife is expecting another baby soon so is staying on here with little Euodia & Bitrus' father. Mipsie darling thank you so much for your dear letter & yes, I certainly will remember your special requests; now with my dearest love to you all, as ever Chris.

Panyam

October 1st '64

My darlings Mother & Rene thank you for your most welcome letters, & I do know that the absence of any from Mary simply means she is just so dreadfully busy. Last Friday Joyce & I were setting off for Abwor then Chip overnight, when a lorry arrived with all the gramophones & records – such a sight as it was with 200 gramos &

boxes & boxes of the 2800 records! Joyce & I grabbed a few of each for the car & off we went leaving Enid & our Station labourer to cope with getting the rest into the store. We've not had a dull moment since, giving out the gramos already paid for with the appropriate records; they are exceedingly good & everyone is thrilled with them, very clear recordings & the messages have come out really well. There are 6 records in Sura – 12 sides that is, some languages have 4 & the smallest 2. Even tho' it's a big job getting everyone satisfied with the right ones it has been a huge thrill to me to get this result of our hard work into the hands of the folk who most need it, especially just at this time. The NLFA Campaign is just starting the main stage of extensive visiting, reaching & witnessing, so these Gospel recordings are absolutely right & already making a profound impression. What a glorious answer to our prayers that they've arrived at this exact moment! The £2 charge is to cover customs & transport for the actual machines & records are a free gift from The Gospel Recordings Inc & their tireless workers in the factory in Australia who make these simple hand-worked machines. I have taken some photos to send to them of the concentration & delight as one after another hears his vernacular recording. Here are a few more thrilling stories of blessing from the NLFA prayer mtgs & instruction classes throughout the District: 12 girls in a remote village who passed the test, so enabling them to go out with the preaching teams; a man & wife were converted then joined a class, took the test & the wife passed! The man plans to take it again & succeed. In one village some old heathen men said they wanted to see this New Life with their own eyes (they first thought it was a person) and, one of my old ladies also passed the test! I have arranged to go for a week's holiday 10th-17th to Rockhaven, Zaria Rd in Jos after the Field Comm next week; perhaps you could get one letter to me there? My very dear love to you each one, especially Mary this time, as always Chris.

Rockhaven, Jos

Oct 13th '64

Darlings on the way here we stopped at B. Ladi to pick up mail & there was another good one from you Mummy, thank you so much. How I wish I could just hop home now for my short holiday & enjoy with you the glories of autumn in Reigate. The FC went well & our 5 Nigerian brethren are taking such an increasingly acceptable part, especially Bitrus Pam & Barnabus Dusu who have been in England & are such nice men with wide vision & also beautiful English! It was thrilling to hear from David Carling of the wonderful development in the Chad Project; leaders of the Canadian SUM & Australian SUM from the Chad Republic are keen to cooperate in the use of the Boat and in opening dispensaries on the permanent islands, permission already granted in Chadian waters. Lake Chad is partly Nigerian & partly belongs to the Chad Republic, so with great joy David is going ahead with negotiations. He has a good Christian nurse who is himself a Chad subject who could lead a team of workers including some of our Panyam missionaries. You'll be glad to know I'm having a marvellous rest in this delightful place, really enjoying myself with the entire sleeping quarters just for me, as the only guest! There are the 5 American Mennonite missionaries who are teachers & live here in this very pleasant compound with 32 school children who all attend Hillcrest School. One book I'm reading is an account of Karl Kumon's journey across Nigeria in 1908 in which he mentions spending a night at Panyam, 'the newly opened CMS Mission Station in a beautifully sheltered nook amongst magnificent rocks, with an attempt at a flower garden, tables with tablecloths, books, papers & easy chairs all make this outpost of European civilisation look exceedingly homelike.' And he adds, 'A district which presented considerable possibilities of developments.' Now dears here are a few more stories coming out of the NLFA as the

Campaign spreads: an Evangelist writes of a man in his village born deaf & dumb who had been ignored & assumed hopeless, but since the NLFA classes & prayer they are now daily using signs to speak with him, showing how Jesus had died for us all, then a dirty and a clean cloth were used & the man refused the dirty but happily took up the clean one, until we are all assured he understands & he now attends all church services & is worshipping God. They are going to teach him to wind the gramophone so that it can be 'his' voice when they all go preaching! A known man came to see the elders in Mongu and amazed them by bursting into tears as he confessed his sin & got right with God. Some Yoruba folk were preaching near Mongu & a Moslem woman overheard them from her house. She was in purdah but after dark she told her husband she wanted to go out & he let her. She got a boy to take her to where the preachers were resting by the Pastor's house & said, "Tell me again all you said this afternoon." They did, and she believed then & there. She went back & told her husband she had become a Christian. In his anger he called the Moslem elders to come & rebuke her. She said to them, "I have been a Moslem all my life but I have never known peace & joy in my heart until now & I am not going to leave this new way." Yes, I intend to find out more about this dear soul for I don't even know her name or where she lives; goodnight for now darlings, Chris.

Braeside, Rodborough Common, Stroud

Nov 4th '64

My dearest Chris I must have a word with you on your birthday though it will be late reaching you, but I greeted you by prayer first thing this morning, & I believe you will have had a happy day. I came across these words the other day & they found an echo in my heart, 'O Lord, give me work till my life shall end and life till my work is done,' but I know that with that prayer there must always be full willingness for the work of His choice day by day. I am sure you will say amen to that as you look around on all the great & wonderful things you have seen & been privileged to have a part in. I do pray that the Lord will keep Nigeria in peace so that the work may not be hindered. Now may the Lord bless you & keep you and fulfil all your petitions abundantly, with our united dearest love, A. Lena.

Panyam

Nov 12th '64

Dear Bill, your letter to hand and herewith what I have been able to produce about Pastor David. It has been done awfully hurriedly so I hope it will serve the purpose & requirement for the next issue of the Lightbearer:

The Rev David O.V.Lot MBE, MHA, MFR. Panyam was hurled out of her ancient tribal life into the modern world in 1907 when the firing of a cannon shocked the brave young warriors into a horrified acceptance of the inevitable. The firstborn son of one of those warriors was strapped in a goatskin on his mother's back when that cannon was fired. His name was Vrenkat and this is his story. Supposed to be making the missionary's bed but when the ominous silence caused Elsie Webster to peep in she found Vrenkat curled up sampling the softness fast asleep! Bubbling over with humour, acknowledged by all as the best educated young man in Panyam, a loyal son to the parents who had become two of the outstanding Christians in the young Church, rejoicing in their first son, that was how David Vrenkat appeared in 1930. He became Headmaster of Panyam School, but the routine job in the one place irked his spirit so when chosen in 1936 for training in the first Pastors' Class he knew that was God's call to him & he responded gladly. From 1938 onwards Pastor David exercised an ever-widening ministry in the Church of the Panyam District. Rapid expansion meant constant travel to new village outstations at increasing distances, for he was the only ordained Pastor in the area. Miss Webster, who had taught, loved & prayed for him from his childhood, guided him through his early years of Church leadership & then slipped into the background, rejoicing in his growth into maturity & wise judgement. In 1951 when Nigeria went to the polls for the first time, Pastor David was elected by a large majority to the Northern House of Assembly & to the House of Representatives in Lagos. So began a career of politics & government of which he had never dreamed. The Pastor from Plateau Province began to be a well-known figure, earning a reputation for honesty & justice. Honours began to come, first the Bronze Medal of the Royal African Society, then the MBE in the Queen's New Year Honours list of 1962. With all this service for his country he still gave considerable time to Church work at home. He would patiently sort out difficult palavers with his Church elders. Many times after long sifting of twisted stories he would suddenly detect a gleam of humour & soon his laughter eased the tension and a solution was found. With the coming of Independence to Nigeria the responsibility for local government was taken over entirely by nationals. The local population at Panyam begged Pastor David to take a post in the Divisional Headquarters of government 18 miles away because they knew they could trust him. So six days a week are now largely taken up with business and on Sundays he travels around his local Church centres administering The Lord's Supper, baptising new converts, & helping the elders. His sermons are always fresh & practical & his reading of the Scriptures a joy to hear. He has a wonderful constitution for with no holidays & very little leisure he keeps going year after year. Nigeria is now a Republic and on the first anniversary of this important day Pastor David V Lot's name appeared again in the Honours list as a Member of the Federal Republic, an outstanding honour for a loyal Christian in a largely Moslem State.

Brookfield, Crawley

Nov 29th '64

My dear Chrisington, incredibly it is almost December & I must at least start this if you are to have any evidence of our existence by Christmastime. Actually I remember that my wife recently atoned somewhat for my lack of correspondence in your direction so you will know something of our family doings. I seem to have heard very little of your doings for a long time, probably largely because of the move from Ifield to Reigate although we ask Mother for your news we don't often see your letters. Comment therefore, on things at your end must be scant. I do try to see Mother each weekend but mutually agreeable timing is not easy. However it is certainly nicer to see them settled there & now helping Rene's old dears to settle well; Mother is playing another of her versatile roles in keeping them on reasonably good terms with each other, and Dr Hoyte evidently notices and values her role. When you have a minute or two to spare I would like very much to hear how recent events, in the Congo especially, appear to Nigerians, whether you feel relatively detached or not, & if you think the American intervention there, and in Vietnam, is assisting or damaging the cause of peace; & if things would have worsened more quickly if they'd stayed at home. It would seem to me from this distance that independence is often coupled with impatience & intolerance; inclined to make these new governments more susceptible to foreign intervention & subversion. The communist influence is making itself felt very much latterly, with one or two notable exceptions, namely your country of adoption & N Rhodesia; but there can be little doubt that the Chinese as a matter of urgency & policy are stirring up as much trouble as possible. Regarding the Business, you can be sure I have kept Mary & Rene fully informed and no doubt they you, but if you need more detail I will of course oblige. Suffice it to say that during Board Mtgs, mostly under Moores's chairmanship, it was agreed that in Sept I should hand over day to day management to Frank Atkinson, and concentrate on production & sales and visiting old & new customers. This has resulted in increased sales, at least locally – nice to think I can still do something! We were only able to move most of the planting to Stopham in March but there is still no sign our moving down there, although that will probably come before too long. The family, as you've heard I'm sure, seems recently to have taken unto itself wings; who'd have thought that Barbara and I would have seen two daughters living in flats in London, and we have driven into Central London on two separate occasions having been invited to a meal by each! Both very interesting and differing experiences, each providing a very good meal! Well my dear this has taken me a long time… 'See how large a letter I have written unto you with mine own hand,' and may it make up in some degree for my long silence, & although it is now a month past the day of your birth, this includes belated best wishes with assurances of frequent remembrances. I really hope this finds you in good health, as we are, we shall be thinking of you so much over the whole festive season, may your Christmas be truly blessed, with very very much love from all of us, Wilfrid.

Dungate Manor, Reigate Heath

Dec 9th '64

Dearest Chris, Rene tells us this is the last date for post to reach you by Christmas – we do hope it does for Stan, Madge & I are full of prayers & good wishes for you. May it be a time of rich blessing for you; living as we do so close to your loved ones makes you seem nearer too. They have made Little Dungate look so beautiful, with lots of loving touches, and they are making the 3 guests so comfy, even tho' Mrs R will never be a happy person unless she lets God change her heart, poor soul. Things are so uncertain in Indonesia, so much unrest, and nothing has been heard of some of our friends still there in the UFM. Madge wishes to greet you so I'll sign off with much dear love, yours affectionately, Eileen…Ah, my dear Chris, first of all a very happy Christmas to you, we know you'll be thinking of us as we most certainly shall be of you. It is just so lovely to live next door to your dear ones, a joy that is renewed every time I go into Little Dungate & feel the loving warmth of their welcome. We do thank God that He has brought them to this new home in which they make Him central as they help the 3 guests to feel 'at home' also; I know they really appreciate the care. It will be so wonderful when you come home too. God be with you too dear Chris, and fill your life with His love; very lovingly, Madge.

Panyam

January 7th 1965

My dearest darlings I was so glad to hear of your happy Christmas with such lovely generosity around you, thank you as always for your dear letters, and especially for your prayers, of which I have been so conscious this week. Humanly speaking everything has seemed in such a rush, with wrong messages making extra difficulties but in spite of this, peace reigned and the first meetings of this new yr have gone off better than anticipated. This is the big week of New Life for All evangelistic mtgs in all parts of our District and I have thrilled at the crowds gathered at each place I've be able to attend. All those in charge of leadership have of course passed the training exam in giving the Gospel message in clear yet simple terms applying to young and old alike, for instance dear old Barnaba Kohop, Rahila Teduwan & Ishaku Sokshak. People seem more receptive than ever & willing to give testimony to the ways the Lord Jesus has changed their hearts & lives. There was a huge open-air mtg in the marketplace of one village & I noted Yoruba Baptists standing with Assemblies of God, some of our EKAS folk all mixed in, to listen to 4 men taking turns on an upturned 44gall drum. Their preaching was forceful & effective on New Life for All – God's way of salvation in Jesus Christ and no other: a Bapt Hausa man from Mongu, then our Bitrus Wetle fresh from the Nakam Bible School, then an AofG Pastor followed by our Polycarp Panzum, it was thrilling to hear them! How we are rejoicing and praising God for this new freshness, and marvelling at the way it is spreading; ever yours Chris.

Panyam

31.1.65

Darlings just hours after I sent off my last to you we heard news of our great old man's passing & the whole world seems to have thought of little else during the past week. Nov 30 1874 – Jan 24 1965 what a wonderful life he had & how wonderful that it was recognised for what it was. Lady Churchill & her family must feel the comfort of having been the home strength & support of one who had such an incalculable influence for good on the whole nation. I expect you, like me, were stirred again by extracts from his wartime oratory. I always remember Uncle Jimmy's rather unQuakerly comment, "Agh, but he puts a bit of heart into you!" Joyce & I were able to get a lift to Chip on the lorry & so enjoyed hearing the reports of all the N.L. for A. and on to Abwor where we heard Godfrey Senlat & Patrobas Yihli making most valuable contributions to the Evangelists' meetings there, then on to a new village Jwak – which means Rock – where Jeremiah Konshik has become an excellent teacher for the young congregation, boldly speaking out the Gospel. Last Weds I had to go over to Mongu & there found Frances & the others full of praise & joy having 3dys of special NLFA mtgs being well led by Africans. Frances greeted me with, "What we've been praying for for years is actually happening!" On their first day 30 people had stood up to make decision for Christ, so we all rejoiced together. But now no more for this time darlings, yours, C.

Little Dungate, Reigate

Feb 7th '65

My darling dear don't ever talk of frustration when you don't write to me, for you know what I feel when the weeks just tear past & I am silent as far as communication with you is concerned. I do truly regret this but we do both understand how the other is placed. At least you know you are never forgotten for a single day, & it's always lovely to have your letters & hear all you news. It is wonderful to know of all the blessing being given through this NLFA Campaign, the Christian Church in Nigeria has surely a most important part to play in the development of the country as a whole & it would seem as though the Lord is using this Campaign to prepare new leaders & strengthen many to give effective witness. In our recent Staff mtg we had Maurice Harvey who is now Circulation Manager in Nigeria under Ross Manning. He told me how he wanted to find out the people's reaction to the offer of Scriptures so he took a selection of Gospels to the first bus stop he came to in Lagos & in 20 minutes sold 103. Another day he was in a market in the Eastern Region & in 4 hrs sold 1000 and wherever he went he received large orders from missionaries & bookshops. I gave him your name & address & he was so interested to hear all about you & plans to visit you on his next trip there. There were other speakers from E. Africa, Brazil & Burma & they all said that despite very difficult political situations in most places, the demand for Scripture is unprecedented. We are all thankful for Mary A who has been given the gifts of leadership, courage, humour, & deep spiritual conviction; but you know how hard it is for men with lesser gifts to accept what a woman like that has to offer. How I wish you could just walk in the door & we could talk about all this, although I do not know where we'd put you to sleep! Dear Ant is here at present but much of his time is taken up with Loretta. Eileen is trying to to find someone suitable to work here for a couple of weeks to give Rene a good rest, and then to do one day a week so R could have a regular day off every week, & I'm sure this is right if R is to be able to keep going. She & I went up to London for Churchill's Lying-in-State on the last night. All most moving & the crowds so quiet, the Great Hall so tremendously simple with just the catafalque & coffin and the 4 motionless Guards; I'm so thankful we went; now darling all my heart's love, Mary.

Testimony of a Missionary

When news of the proposed New Life for All Campaign reached Panyam early in 1964 I had many doubts & fears. I regarded it as a high-pressure project organised by ex-patriates & rather foreign to our Nigerian brethren. I also feared it would cost our struggling Churches a lot of money. I read the programme of events & doubted whether the Christians in our District would cooperate when called to come to a big Retreat in the early farming season. When Mr Jerry Swank visited us to discuss arrangements I was guarded & put to him a counter proposal of more local Retreats. With gentle good humour he pushed my preconceived notions aside, saying that in other places they had found that one big united Retreat to launch the campaign was best. When our Pastors heard these plans they were, to my surprise, in full agreement. My doubts, fears & opinions began melting away as I realised this thing was of God & was quite safe in His control. From then on it was a delight to work in with this movement of the Holy Spirit & see the way in which the Christians of the District were much more easily persuaded to give full cooperation than I had been. Before long I realised that God in His great goodness had a purpose of blessing & New Life for me personally as well as for many others. For a long time my heart had been reaching out to the Lord for a fresh experience of Himself. It seemed to me as if my way had been a long walk by faith, with little evidence of His Presence, & I had been asking Him to meet my need. During April, just before our first Retreat, He answered this prayer with such a sense of His nearness that joy & peace filled my heart. I found that prayer was a delight instead of a perfunctory duty, & praise an instinctive outflowing from my happy heart. As we went through 1964 & on into 1965 in the New Life for All Campaign it was a great joy to recognise that the Holy Spirit was manifesting Himself in the lives of many other Christians too. There was an enthusiasm to pray & to seek the lost that we'd never experienced before; people began turning to the Lord even before the arranged time of visiting & preaching. News kept coming in of old folk now interested after years of indifference, of backsliders repenting, & of full Churches. As we did our little part in praying & witnessing, the Lord was pouring His great power & love into our hearts & out into a multitude of other lives.

You have heard much of the gramophones & 3minute Gospel records in word & song that we have been able to distribute to so many villages & outstations, in all the known vernacular dialects of so many people; it is certain that these records have been used in God's mighty hand as a means of blessing. They have been welcomed everywhere, & those who were previously unconcerned have suddenly listened with ears of understanding; women who for years have resisted all efforts to interest them, are now regularly appearing in Churches to hear more of the Good News that has at last captured them. However not only the gramophone records are responsible, but the Campaign of New Life for All continues to attract many, many folk. Leaders were trained & appointed & sent out to tell of this New Life & the early days were blessed beyond anything I remember in my time out here. It is thrilling to see these men who until a few years ago were still in darkness themselves, now going out to unknown areas of Nigeria & there being used to bring others to Christ. Reports are still coming in as the work spreads & it is clear that hundreds continue to make a definite decision for Christ. All are talking about these remarkable things & we are full of praise to God. On Christmas Day we had the joy of seeing three more of our men ordained to the Ministry of the Church; one, John Mashem, was trained at the Theological College of N Nigeria at Bukuru, the other two were trained at Bambur at the SUM branch there, & all 3 are now in charge of large groups of village congregations; please pray often for them.

SUM, 21 Granville Road, Sidcup, Kent

March 19th '65

Dear Chris may I say how thrilled we all have been to hear the reports from the Field concerning the New Life for All campaign and the tremendous reports of response to the Gospel message. How wonderful to read in your prayer letter too, of the part that has been played by the Gospel gramophone recordings. We shall certainly continue to remember you all in prayer, trusting that in the days to come this wonderful blessing may continue. This weekend at the Conference at Mabledon we have about 25 adults & 25 young people booked in and quite a number of these are keen Christians with an interest in SUM so we are praying they will be truly challenged, and eventually be sent out to foreign Fields. With all the staff here I send our greetings to all the folk at Panyam, trusting you are all well, yours sincerely Jean Millgate.

IN THE TRAIN TO LONDON

MAR 25TH '65

My dearest Love if you can read this squiggly writing, I'm praying for you a most rich & blessed time over & above all you had thought of. We know any Christian work will always have its disappointments & apparent failures, but it gives me such deep satisfaction to feel that you are seeing & taking part in a harvest that has surely been given in God's grace as a result of the faithful sowing that you & all the others have done there throughout the years. Mummy was idly wondering if you could possibly come at the end of December in time to see Ant & Loretta before they leave for his next posting – altho' that timing is still uncertain for they don't yet know if they can marry this July or not till Christmas. Anyhow you know it always cheers her to think of your return, which could perhaps be in a year we think? It is just so lovely to see all the daffodils, crocuses & scillas coming out in quantities around the garden & to be able to wander amongst them at peace – we put the clocks back last Sunday & its light till 7.30pm now, & the birds are heavenly in the early mornings; this really is the most beautiful place to live. If you get this by the 31st please do remember me that morning for I have to address a large hand-picked group of women specially invited to the Deanery at Winchester. I loved your description of the group of children praying for their parents to discover the New-Life-for-All & the one who said it would be enough to give Jesus a feast of joy; and oh, the flow of heartfelt little prayers going up from dear Tarifainu's home! From those young ones clad only in skimpy rags; that they might not fail in school; & praying also that no evil might come to them on their homeward way, as none of them had a lamp or torch & there was no moon. Darling this has filled my heart and I'm sure you will not mind if I tell it to the women in Winchester, but now we have just passed Clapham so I will stop & post this in Victoria on the way to Bible House, with my heart's love always yours Mary.

Panyam

April 3rd '65

Such lovely letters again from you my darlings, thank you so much & yes, all I can say about my next furlough is that it will be DV 'next year!' I felt particularly – & gratefully – that your prayers were surrounding me the past weekend, we did have a wonderful time & the fellowship was sweet & the messages given were first class & the tribal singing before each meeting, a new feature, was very popular. They've been adapting the tribal tunes to the familiar words of hymns & singing then with such fervour. Singing them in Church adds a certain restraint, but when they sing outside they often go beyond what our European sense thinks proper! They get excited & wave their arms about & the older women give high-pitched shouts like cheer-leaders. I talked to two very earnest Christians from Chakfem – a remote area in the south, & asked whether they felt the excitement was worthy & right. "O yes!" they said with shining faces, "We just worship God when we are doing that, we are so happy & we know He is happy too!" Alright, was my response, that's enough for me, I have no further objection. There were so many testimonies of blessing as a result of the NLFA meetings, and much more visiting of the Moslems & Fulanis. A direct answer to prayer came in that 2 men from the Gospel Recordings appeared just as we had lamented the lack of gramophone records in the Fulani language & they were able to address that need at once! I have fixed up a holiday with Joyce's friends in Bukuru next week, then probably on to Vom; as ever Chris.

Chakfem area on Trek

May 8th '65

Darlings this comes to you from a new place, there aren't many now that I've never been to, & as you know I love these opportunities of getting out & about amongst the people, even though my walking is decreasing – I find weariness now after only 4 or 5 miles. About 15 yrs ago I had been to Wubel then the only village in the Chafkem sub-tribe area but soon after that a virulent outbreak of smallpox had decimated the population. The people of a nearby village, Narohos fled when a Nigerian vaccinator arrived, such was the darkness & fear in that area then. I am typing up notes & will hope to send you a copy when all is completed, but the plan is to get to all 8 village congregations before returning to Panyam. Your letter with that lovely photo arrived just before I left & is so nice to carry with me however I see no sign of greying hair in either of my sisters?! While holidaying in Vom I read a most remarkable book called, 'The Cross & the Switchblade,' a best-seller in USA & our Gindiri folk were all talking about it & lent it to me. I do think you must have it too, a marvellous story of spiritual triumph among teenage gangsters of both sexes in New York; the revelation of underworld life of crime is quite staggering. Today I met with the Evangelist at Mandeng who had been away in Zaria for the NLFA conference there, back now & so eager to talk about it all, & he took me to meet the Chief & they offered to show me their rather amazing houses, the like of which I've seen nowhere else. Built into 3 storeys for goats & sheep on the ground floor their nightly shelter, up through a 'manhole' into the living room & bedroom where there is a centre fireplace for cooking, & wide berths for beds all around the circular sides & all sorts of cubby holes for storing personal things; there is no window but then up again through another manhole through which you haul yourself up to the food store at the very top. This also has around the walls, cubby holes which drop right down to the ground for pouring grain, & possibly waste, and with an air-hole in the apex of the roof through which you can poke your head & look down on the world! This has a sort of grass lid or hat which is pulled over at night & for when it rains. Word has reached me that David Carling has some good news in that the sites for sale near out Bookshop in Maiduguri that had been refused us, one at least has now been granted us & permission given to build a Church – think of that being permitted in a largely Moslem town! It won't necessarily reach the Moslem Kanuri people of Bornu, but it will bring Christians from other parts of the country to live & work in Maiduguri & make them a Light to the local folk. It is being suggested that new Churches of this expected size should soon have their own bank accounts and be responsible for their own finances, thus relieving the Mission of a little more work. If this notion really does become reality, and in many places, then I might even start to think about retiring! One morning our walk to the village of Tim was through the most marvellous country but we could not really stop to admire, even tho' the pace was too slow for my liking, but that was because Joseph our leader was extremely cautious for my safety as we had to share the thickly wooded terrain with the wild bush cow – very fierce animals, & Joseph wanted no surprises. As we left Muko on the last morning the Chief took us up a very steep slope to a peak which was more like an Alpine mountain. From it we could see for many miles in all directions down onto glorious valleys & hills & many other hilltops, and every village I had visited was visible. Over to the SW were villages of the Kwalla Church & the distant plains descending towards the Benue River, it was beautiful & the air was like a tonic! The walk back to where we'd arranged to meet Joyce was meant to be no more than 8 miles but it was a lot longer with many rocky outcrops. When we passed a Fulani encampment I was very glad to accept their offered hospitality & while I rested a gracious farmer brought me a large bowl of warm new milk; in return I gave him some medicine for his old mother. Then we went on, to cross a wide river, then on and on till finally we reached Dingwahap, very weary & hot, & there was Joyce waiting with tea, and spam between ryvita had never tasted better! Goodnight now my darlings, Chris.

Panyam

June 24th '65

Darlings I do thank you as always for your dear letters & rejoice at the news of your happy time in Ireland, and Mummy that you're well enough to resume attending Monthly mtg and participating, and that that smoke was only smoke, not a fire. Think I mentioned in my last that we hoped to do another short (?!) trek out to Kulere & Ambul so Joyce could close the GLB there. It was good that some of her girls came to meet us where the road simply ends, and that I had three boys to help carry my stuff & lead me on to another distant village Horom. It took 3 hrs & the last bit was down into a tremendous ravine then up the other side, full of huge trees with trunks some 100 feet high such as I've never seen here; also marvellous ferns & plants & birds galore singing so very beautifully. Horom is perched at the top of this ravine, many Christian homes surrounding the Church & when a bell rings they all emerge from their homes & pour forth immediately for services, SS classes & prayer mtgs. It is remote & isolated, with its own language different from any other – they understand about 3 or 4 other ones but no-one else hears theirs! The Evangelist's wife is a dear soul called Damaris & she brought me delicious food on 3 occasions plus a large basin of hot water for washing – what blessing! They were so very keen that I should sleep in their house with them but I spotted a rat in a bag beside where I was perched in their sitting-room, and as there was no window, I graciously stuck to my original plan of sleeping in the Church! Finally home here via Daffo we were full of thankful praise for good weather, no rain for our walking or motoring on rocky roads. More wonderful reports, from Jos this time, on results from the NLFA mtgs, were awaiting our return, such stories of what God has done & is still doing. A loud & heavy storm for 5 hrs so far, so I cannot write more for now, except to say I'm thinking so much of Rene taking her old name back & all that means, and of all you especially dear Ant, & your happy wedding preparations; with my dearest love to you each as ever, Chris.

Panyam

July 29th '65

My darlings what feasts of letters have come my way, from all of you & from dear Margaret Martin, and each of you gave me different details of the splendid sounding wedding; but let me first send you, Rene, special birthday good wishes for today even though you won't get this till after your day I am thinking of you so much. MM told me how exceedingly charming you each appeared & what you were wearing – I was thrilled to have these wonderful glimpses into the Day, along with the Order of Service to follow along with proceedings, thank you all ever so much. So our happy Ant & Loretta are honeymooning in Sardinia & then starting life together on his posting to Nassau! Thank you also for news of dear Mouse on his Teacher Training course & Brenda in her new position as Acting Sister – with that in mind I thought she would be interested in 2 midwifery patients brought in here recently; one woman in labour was carried about 15miles over rough ground on the crossbar of a man's bicycle & when Joyce examined her she found a wee hand presenting which she managed to push back and took the poor woman straight to Pankshin hospital where the Dr did a Caesarian. Next day I saw her & she was much better & thrilled with a live baby, but unfortunately it died a few hours later. The other woman also in labour was brought in today sitting on the carrier of a bike, but I don't think she has delivered yet. The rainy season has now established itself in full force with the river flooding & rushing all over this compound as it has done on many other years at this time; but inside I wish you could enjoy & smell the marvellous bowl of gorgeous summer flowers here beside me! Pink & yellow antirrhinums, pink dwarf phlox, purple verbena & petunias with lovely variegated leaves. Mary you'll be interested to know that Ishaku's boy Gabriel has been accepted to go to Limankara as a Probationary Teacher for the rest of this year, and Jacob Lot, one of the twins, is going to England this next month – Barclays Bank are sending him for a 2yr course in London, he's a dear lad & a keen Christian, I have given him your address & Nakam's also. Now goodbye for this time with dearest love to you all each one, Chris.

Panyam

Sept 6th '65

Darlings oh thank you so very much for lovely letters and the wonderful packet of photos, so wonderful to see them! You are so good to send me so many. I love the one of you Rene & Brenda, you look simply radiant & without a trace of back troubling you – well done darling! Please do be very careful & take good care of yourself. Thank you too for the news of Ant & Loretta & their new abode – I wonder if they saw anything of the astronauts. One of our young men from the Mupun area now works in Gwoza Hospital & the first hand news from there is so encouraging: a village 12 mls out from there has at last seen break through with 4 people then 6 more turning totally to the Lord Jesus. This was initially due to Moslem pressure for when the people heard a deputation of Moslem high-ups were coming from Gwoza to Islamise them all. The villagers collected all their weapons & prepared for battle, which quite put off the visitors. Now the people are stating they would rather be Christians than Moslems. Tomorrow we are expecting guests & today Ishaku is on holiday so I needed to do some baking but found we have no eggs so I've done two large fruitcakes with soda which have turned out fine, two mango tarts, and a macaroni cheese. On Wednesday Joseph Yariyep is coming to meet the District elders to discuss the follow-up after the NLFA campaign, which is to include the new literacy programme to ensure all new converts can read, using the slogan, 'Reading For All' to follow on after the New Life for All. The newly printed beginners' cards to hold up as prompts are excellent & there seems to be real enthusiasm to get as many Christians as possible into the literacy classes. Also under discussion are the plans for the big new Panyam Church to be the mother church for the whole District; the site commands a position on the main road facing the growing town – invaluable for the future. The first stage will seat 900 with an additional wing seating another 400 to be built onto the side, of permanent materials of course, as the first stage. There is to be a cross on top of the bell tower & a cross let into the east wall, & a smaller cross with 4 faces will crown the entrance porch. The cost will be between £2,500-3,000 and so far we have £350 to start the foundations at once. No more for this time darlings, C.

Jos

Sept 24th '65

Darlings here I am, lodged at our HQs for a little peace to do the writing of the Radio scripts for New Life for All, now that I've been able to meet up with many of the people & find out from them more of the experiences & happenings in their villages during the Campaign. I feel well furnished with information & now need to sort it all out, weaving it into 8min slots told as far as possible in direct speech. They want 13 of these stories for the weekly programme of 'New Life for All,' section of 'Voice of the Gospel' from Jos beamed to & back from Addis Ababa. Mine is not the production of the programme, just the preparation of the stories. Mummy your letter was as welcome as ever & what a mercy that hurricane did not harm our dears in Nassau! To you especially, Rene darling, may I urge a thorough turning of your mind; resting in what the Lord has done for you – bringing you to this happy home and the love & goodwill of so many dear friends. Dearie me this does sound like a preachment!! We have had a short visit from Geoff Dearsley who hadn't seen Pastor Daniel since his ordination so we had a good chat on the way there & back and a picnic tea. I suppose being the most senior British missionary now makes me the sort of vent for folk to use when they want to unburden their hearts! Anyhow G & I had a good talk and prayer together that afternoon. Joyce & I had to go to Daffo on Tuesday & took with us Christiana one of our 2 jolly midwives & they had an all-time record of 197 women at the antinatal clinic & Joyce gave prophylactic injections to 50 babies! Now we have had lunch & I must have a wee rest before carrying on with my script writing; blessings on you all as always & especially dear Rene, Chris.

Jos

October 8th '65

My darling Mary your last 2 letters gave me much to think & pray about, with the intimate news of the Business, and of our dear Rene, & of your dear self too, for I know a bit of how you must be feeling. I think we three girls probably share similar traits of character so perhaps can regard each others reactions with more sympathy than most. I seem to have shot straight into writing about our intimate needs & problems in an almost rude way; so let me say I am earnestly trying to uphold Rene, praying that those deep hurts may be healed – we can be quite sure the Lord knows her every deepest need. But darling I am bearing you up too. You and I have had so much responsibility for organising that we find it so natural & sensible to suggest what others should do, & I suppose with the best will in the world we sometimes seem to some people to be imposing upon their independence. I know too how much it hurts when those one longs to help do not react positively. In further talks with Geoff the matter of my retirement came up in reference to a minute from last year's Field Council that women should retire at 60, anyhow a unanimous recommendation emerged that I should do another tour. I said I'd be willing provided circumstances, home & here, are favourable & health as good as at present. Then when Bible School staffing was discussed David Carling brought out the old argument about women being unsuitable for teaching & leadership of men! I was sitting next to him & after a bit he said to me, "I hope I didn't give offence," "You did!" I replied & of course that gave much to think & talk about. DC was so upset for he is a dear really & he does respect the work we are doing. The Africans I think prefer us women workers in some ways, and DC & others think they have no convictions regarding proprietaries according to Scripture. You can imagine we women after the meeting last night were giving vent to strong feelings! Actually we all feel that a man is more suitable as leader of a Bible School, & we feel that we don't exercise as much authority over the Africans as the men missionaries would do. It's amazing that there are 4 Stations often & usually 'manned' by women only nowadays, & I am sure our men missionaries must be embarrassed about this. But I have thrilled at the strong words of encouragement to the Church given recently by Pastor Manasseh about Christians not being ashamed to witness for the Lord Jesus wherever they are & whatever the cost. This is the bad month for hay fever with grass & crops all ripe & poor Enid is miserable; how thankful I am that I no longer get those awful pouring colds. Now I must close & send so much dear love to you each one, & greetings to the others, Chris.

Panyam

Oct 25th '65

Darlings I'm just back from a lovely restful weekend with the dear Killers whose home has been wonderfully improved with a flush toilet & a full length enamel bath! My main purpose was to write lots of letters but actually I spent much of the time sleeping! On Sunday morning Edith K & I walked to Kombili outstation as the old ex-witchdoctor – converted during the NLFA Campaign – was to be baptised. He grew up in a Panyam compound next to old father Lot then left just before I came out & his great grandchildren are now in the Panyam School! Awaiting my return was your letter with those wonderful photos, what a joy! The one of you Mother with Frances P's mother is just so lovely & when Shadrach saw it he pondered it for some moments then said, "These old ladies hold the watering cans."

I thought he referred to the flowers behind you both, until he added, "By their prayers that water the Seed that is sown in this country!" Wasn't that charming, & such a delightful description of your part in the work of the Gospel out here! And today another letter has come from you with the news of Great Expectations! What a thrill for everyone that Ant & Loretta's little one should be due at the end of May about the same time as you may expect me! We've had some really thrilling reports from David C, Jim Hamilton & Pastor David Telta of the Moslem opposition in & around Gwoza, which only seems to be making the local people more determined to have the Christian way, with many more being converted there lately. The Lake Chad development is very encouraging, with the 3 missionaries at Baga spending Sunday going out preaching & the following Sunday the 3 wives took their turn, leaving the husbands to look after the children for the day! DC asked to have a talk with me to say how unhappy he'd been since that FC that he had hurt us by his comments on women missionaries, so we had a good talk about our points of view! Now goodbye my dear loves & with blessings on you all, Chris.

Nassau, Bahamas

31 October '65

Dearest Auntie Chris I do hope this reaches you in time to bring you our love & many happy returns & our best wishes for a very happy birthday. I'm sure you'll have heard the splendid news that Loretta is expecting a baby at the end of May & now with Mouse & Brenda just beating us to it you'll be a great aunt twice in 2 months! We like Nassau very much, the beaches are lovely, & we have a jolly nice house with an enclosed verandah – necessary because there are lots of mosquitoes – & a substantial garden. We have a maid and a gardener one day per week. We're getting to know lots of people & my job is going well; and the pouffe (squishy leather footstool) looks jolly nice & Loretta uses the bag every day; with much love from us both A & L.

Little Dungate

Nov 4th '65

My Darling Love on this auspicious day I must tell you again what precious memories this day holds for me for more than 60 years. I do bless God for ever giving us such a big bundle of His choice blessings and thank Him again for calling you into His glad service thereby giving us some share also. And I thank you too darling for all the love & thought you give me & which is more to me than words can express. I am writing this in my room where Mary & I have had tea together – her loving thought on this day too – for you will soon have her letter telling you her news which I only heard Mon eve, which came as a shock – until my mind was steadied by the knowledge that even this, so hard to take in, because of all the work Mary seemed able to be doing each day & her appearance of good health & energy, her constant thought for others & as if she had no anxiety or care at all. Yet this has been with her for a year or more & she's spoken to no-one except I'm sure the burden was rolled upon the Lord & He was carrying both & giving victory. So now we cast it all upon Him also & we are being blessed & being drawn closer to one another & Rene seems able for everything & much happier in herself tho' I know she feels very much for Mary & wishes she could bear it herself. We are expecting Frances P this evening; M is going to meet her at Three Bridges station as F is speaking at their PM group; there are so many arrangements to be made but now M wants to add a line so my dearest love & best of blessings, Mother.

My darling I do hope you've had a very happy birthday full of the Lord's nearness & love. I had rather a frustrating time at the hosp this morning only seeing Mr Pitt for about 1½ mins but I am to see the head radiologist on Tues who will decide if I'm to have Xray treatment or surgery. I've never heard of Xray before the op but I will tell you more as soon as I know. Mother has been so calm & unflustered & Rene is being wonderful so we'll thank God for His great mercies; with all my dearest love, Mary.

Panyam

Nov 15th '65

Thank you darlings for writing so often to relieve my mind somewhat altho' the first one made me so grieved & really mad that doctors/surgeons can be so callous & unconcerned over human anxieties & needs. How thankful I was today to hear the Guildford man was so much nicer & that you asked for & got a straight answer about the prospects for the future. Having treatment first is I suppose the wise & right decision & I'm quite sure Mary darling that you will not lack the love & prayer backing of many, many friends as you go through these weeks. Please do not try to do a full programme of work during this treatment; surely a slowing down of your meetings & travel is essential. I do pray these new medical visits will not prove too tiring or painful. As for prospects for next Feb let us hold that in our prayers & see how the Lord leads; it shouldn't be too difficult for me to come home then if necessary. I was so glad you had that pleasant visit from Frances, she writes so warmly, also by this post, about the happy time you gave her & confirms what she said to you Mary that she considers your condition, this kind, need not necessarily be serious. She also told me Rene is eating better than before & is obviously beloved by the 3 old ladies, & Mother she thought you to be marvellous. Now goodbye my dearest dears, may special love & grace & peace be yours each one, for each day, with blessings on you all, Chris.

Beechcroft, Moira, Lurgan, Co. Armagh

Nov 17th '65

My dear Chris as you will see I am here at Kathleen's for Christmas shopping but unpleasant weather keeps me in. I was so sorry to hear the news of May you can be sure I have been praying for her since that God will restore her up to her normal health again & to her useful work, if it is His will. And thinking so much of you so far away but perhaps your due furlough of next year might come earlier as such a comfort this would be to all. Uncle Robert has been keeping well but Auntie Edie finds it very hard to get about on her terribly swollen legs. There were floods about & Sam had to rescue cloth from the factory. There is no more of interest to tell you but I wanted you to know how much I think & pray for you also all at your home so I will close committing you to our Heavenly Father's care that you may experience His peace in these trying circumstances, we all send our love, yours Auntie L.

Bisham, Colgate

Nov 28th '65

My dearest Chris thank you so much for your letter with all its wonderful news of the New Life campaign, so thrilling to hear of so many converts in these days when ones sees so much apathy all around. You must wish yourself at home dear one. I was able to take Mary to Guildford for her first treatment where I gather she is 'marked out' in indigo paint & has 2mins xray on each of 6 places around the area. She had wanted to wait till you came home but the doctor assured her she hadn't waited too long as he would not operate yet anyway, & she has gained a little weight; she is actually looking quite well considering, and this rest before the op is good. Forgive me asking but have you any ideas of coming home before next June? You would be such a tower of strength to them all. Rene is marvellous & will look after Mary so well but of course M does not really want this tho' I hope I'll be able to drive her to Guildford sometimes to save her driving herself. She is so wonderfully serene & calm & has accepted it all as from the Lord – she really is a shining witness. The Bible Society are so willing to do anything for her, they long to be able to help her in any way. Your dear mother is marvellous too. Try not to worry Chris dear tho' it is difficult when so far away. Mary is surrounded with prayers of all her loved ones & many friends. If there is anything you would like us to do please say; now with much dear love from Margaret.

Little Dungate

Nov 28th '65

Darling Chris thank you for all your loving concern & thoughts & prayers; it is a wonderful thing to feel so surrounded & undergirded by the prayers & faith of so many & I'm sure in the wise & loving purposes of God all these things are being woven together to fit into a pattern which will encourage our faith & trusting dependence on God, & be to His glory. I'm glad the waiting is now over. In the hospital I found a real effort is being made to treat people as people & to create a friendly atmosphere – nicer than at any of the previous doctor visits. Only a tiny area of left breast is to be treated at one time, just 2mins of xray on each of the six little places they marked out on me. The young married radiographer was so pleasant; she sits outside the room behind a glass panel & comes in the very tick each burst is finished & she does this from 9 to 5pm every day – just fancy your whole day divided into 2minute intervals! She warned me of likely nausea but so far none, & the treatment is painless, I feel absolutely no ill effects. I shall drive myself here each day for the 1.30 appointments but have had so many kind offers & dear Margaret M took me today. Mother is keeping wonderfully well & Rene is quite marvellous; I can only magnify God's grace & marvel at the way He answers prayer. Fret not thyself darling; dear love as ever yours, Mary.

L D

Dec 5th '65

My precious darling love today has been a wild & stormy morning but the sun eventually came out so I managed a short walk around the gardens for some good fresh air. Things go on quietly & smoothly here, dear Mary is her usual bright self, much cheered by lovely flowers, cards & phone-calls from her many friends, tho' she is unusually willing to rest a little more, we both stayed in our beds this morn & did not go to Meeting. Your letters continue to bring us joy & I am so glad your conference went off well and that you had a few quiet days at home in Panyam for a change, a bit of rest I do feel you need, from all your busy travels, but there, I need not say this. Now it is nearly tea-time so I must tidy my hair, & M wants to add a line, so many thoughts & prayers wing their way to you, may you be kept, blessed & protected always, very dear love, Mother.

Dearest love, your gift arrived in your last letter – I can only say THANKYOU & bless you for such a loving thought. I haven't needed a taxi yet but to know that would now be possible is just too lovely. I know you were with me in spirit through that first treatment, & continue to be so, & you will know I am being kept, upheld, & greatly helped. The only painful part is lying flat on my back on the hard table which at my age I'm not used to! As I wait under that big apparatus I sense that the Lord takes all the daily prayers – of which I'm assured by so many dear people – and He blends them in with the wonderful light rays, putting His hand over all to use them to work out His good purpose. I feel very rich in loving care. Darling it is so wonderful to hear of all your new literacy classes & programmes, well done, and I do hope you get the Bookmobile – I will have a word with John Pearse about that. Now goodbye for this time darling with my dearest love always, Mary.

Brookfield

Dec 12th '65

My dear Chris it was a shock to realise that only 13 days remain till Christmas, hence I fear this must be a shorter epistle than usual. My powers of letter writing have become atrophied through lack of use & opportunity, I am sorry about this. And I apologise also that I do not even know when Barbara last wrote to you but her October visit to the Chairman of Governors at Nona's College seems to have had an impact, for N is now allowed to move into official digs in Golders Green at the start of the January term. By the way, as Dec 15th comes round again does it recall to you our family outing to Gamages being the highlight of the year for us 50 years ago, or maybe more? I can remember it clearly anyway and I think that we were all sick that night, probably delayed emotion! Now what can I say about Mary – at this stage? It does come as more of a shock when it affects our own generation doesn't it. I can't help feeling that it may be the Lord's method of calling a temporary halt on her hectic work activities so that she may be able to continue for longer in time. I have not said this to her in these words of course, for who can tell the mind of the Lord? Our holiday was pleasant except for the weather & the German boy with us who did not add to our enjoyment being mostly silent & unresponsive. And unfortunately I am continually burdened by Business affairs being in an extremely critical state. In fact it was only Mary's timely & most kind intervention that prevented Frank from finally calling a halt. Well my dear this brings our united love & prayerful wishes for a very happy Christmas & the best New Year yet, Wilfrid.

Little Dungate

Dec 12th '65

My darling Chris this is probably the last one I'll write before Christmas so I send such loving good wishes & the hope you'll be able to enjoy the Day with all your visitors & busyness, & really feel the presence & love of Christ lightening & uplifting your heart & soul & giving you His peace. This is what I long for but I seem to get so impatient & frustrated with the constant hum-drum & necessary routine of life – of course this is the constant underlying anxiety about our Mary. I do not go out except for a quick dash out to the shops on my bike. I must say tho' I do think we are all being kept at peace about her & the fact that she still seems so 'normal' & well in herself does help enormously. She is eating & resting quite well & seems not to mind the daily journeys for treatment, thank God. She has even been able to have lengthy talks with Wilfrid, and Barbara too, about the Business, in her position as one of the Directors. What they have discussed, or decided, I do not know, & perhaps it's as well that way, but Mummy does find it rather difficult not really knowing anything. She said wistfully she could not say for she doesn't know enough to say anything, & what a change this is from when Father told her everything; then added, "But one must get accustomed to such changes as ones grows old – and deaf – and try not to mind it too much." Darling I pray the New Year will bring you much happiness; and comfort of heart to us all, ever yours Rene.

Panyam

Dec 13th '65

Darlings how glad I was to get your dear joint letter tho' it took eight whole days this time – Christmas rush, I suppose. Your calm & cheerful courage always reduces my anxiety about you to a minimum & it is just lovely to hear of all the kindnesses of friends praying daily & rallying round to help. Ruth & Gertrude wrote of the wonderful prayer you'd had together & of the guest bed always ready for Mary after treatment if the journey home seems too much or in case of fog or ice on the roads. How good God is to have all these helps in place to share our needs. And it seems to me that I am being able to get through with various important jobs quicker than I expected & make good preparations for others next year so I shall feel happier at the prospect of leaving early if it should come to that. For the whole District in 1966 I am working on an idea that came to me the other night – a scheme of Sunday School lessons on the book of Acts. Most of the printed lesson notes we have out here are very expensive & far too much learning to tackle in one lesson; so Enid & the 3 Evangelists & I have already got the first 19 chapters divided into 52 lessons with a topic heading, word or two of teaching & a memory verse. I want to introduce this to every Sura speaking village & have enough copies ready so every literate person can buy a personal copy for 3d; and then we must work on it all again in Hausa! I took the opportunity of a good talk with Geoff & he is quite prepared for me to go on early furlough, sure that the other committee members will agree to this. Air passages are not too difficult to get at short notice so whether it is to be Feb or May it should be alright. So now darlings my most loving wishes for a Christmas filled with peace and joy & love for you each, & all of us for we shall all be together in spirit, as ever Chris.

Braeside, Stroud, Glos

Dec 14th '65

Dearest Chris, being on the way to recovery – they tell me – I wanted to write to you as we had the news about Mary for I'm sure it came to you as rather a stunning blow. How gladly we would remove troubles from those we love, but when the Lord does not it must be for His best. They all in Reigate seem to be carrying on quietly & I feel sure you are being kept in peace. "*That we may not complain of what is, let us see God's hand in all events; and that we may not be afraid of what shall be, let us see all events in God's Hands.*" Forgive my shakey hand and this nasty biro pen which I dislike but ink in bed is taboo. Dear love from us all here A. Lena.

Dungate Manor, Reigate Heath

Christmas 1965

Dear Chris we think of you so often & we are so thrilled to hear what God is doing in Nigeria. We had coffee last week with Barbara in the drawing room at Brookfield, so lovely that it is still part of the Cheal home. Now in spite of Mary's illness we do pray that when you come back on furlough that it may be a most blessed time all together, until then we pray you are kept in peace; just thinking of your home-coming brings it nearer. Dear Chris distance always seems greater when loved ones are in any sort of trouble and we care for you in this so very much; the family continues in serenity within the Lord's tender compassion.

Several of us are able to drive dear Mary to her treatments but we do understand her desire to do all she possibly can for herself; now with dear love as always from both of us & all the others here, Madge & Eileen.

Little Dungate

Dec 19th '65

Just a few lines my darling love to greet you & bring you our dearest love & constant remembrance & to say how much we look to seeing you before so long DV to show you how much we love you, as if you did not know all this before! It is raining again today but the sun will shine again before too long, it always does; goodbye for now my darling love, Mother.

My very dear Chris our loving thoughts will be constantly surrounding you over Christmas & I do pray that through it all you may know <u>the joy of the Lord</u> to be your strength & the presence of the Lord in your present situation a blessed & most precious reality. I've now passed the half-way mark in the treatment & the Dr was very pleased with me on Weds for the swellings are reducing in size. I have had rather more nausea lately but can still eat mostly normally; & I do get weak in the legs standing about too long so am being very good about resting. Driving is no difficulty & the weather so far has been alright & so many kind people are offering so much help & Daisy writes the loveliest letters each week – I have so much to be thankful for. If an operation is necessary for me – we should know by early January – it will be Mother and Rene who specially need your company & help. Any anxiety on Mother's part makes her restless & her efforts to help tend to become hindrances to Rene who already has her hands over-full. Let us go on trusting His perfect timing for now and for the future, our times are in His hands, ever your own Mary.

Panyam

Dec 24th '65

My darling loves just a wee line to thank you all for your loving wishes & the beautiful calendar too, & the love that binds us all together always & particularly so does the expression of it somehow fit at this season at the end of each year. I'm in my pink dressing gown having just remembered that our mailbag will close in a few minutes so my bath can wait a little bit. There was quite a rush on this morning trying to get everything spic & span for our visitors this evening, so busy that nerves & tempers got a little frayed. I suspect the Nigerians think we are quite mad going to all this fuss! There are 2 large chickens for our feast tonight & Enid has iced the lovely cake her people sent; the guest rooms are clean & sweet with little jars of flowers ready & the verandah is also gay with flowers. We have been plagued by pigeons on the roofs & in the eves – such a noise & mess – so Pastor David came with his gun & shot 8 with 10 cartridges, not bad going! I'll be longing to hear what the Dr decides about you Mary love, dearest & best love as ever Chris.

L D

Dec 27th '65

My darling I kept your parcel to open till last & when I did felt quite overwhelmed, what a lovely gift, so warm & cosy whether I use it in the car or on my bed, thank you from my heart & I look forward to sharing it with you sometime in the not too distant future. I'm to see the Dr again this Weds but doubt he'll commit himself till the day of the very last treatment which is Friday week so not long to go now…sorry darling, as I was writing Birdie came across from the Manor where she's staying for a few weeks. Such an interesting person, from N. Zealand, she does case work at Barts & sees so many men & women who are terribly disturbed mentally or got themselves into the most awful messes. She works closely with psychiatrists & says there are some really good ones & their work is absolutely invaluable, but she goes further & recognises the spiritual dimension & the power of God to do for people what nothing else can do. She is always so stimulating to talk to. I'll write again soon darling but in the meantime may the Lord bless you & keep you in all your going out & coming in, ever yours Mary. Darling Chris what a splendid picnic table! Thank you so very much it will be such a pleasure to use & perfect for teas in the garden or anywhere. Mary & I are revelling in sitting by a lovely fire in the drawing room this afternoon as the old ladies are out, & writing furiously! It is a beautifully bright frosty day outside. Darling don't bring any talcum or soap for coming home for I have four boxes of luscious talc & lots of soap; dearest love from Rene.

Little Dungate

1966! January 9th

My darling Chris your dear letter came for my birthday & I do thank you so very much. The days do seem to be lengthening a little bit now for which I give thanks; it has been feeling rather dark of late. And the news of the temperance question, or should I simply say the drink question, darling I do grieve for you after all the years of work you have put into this and poor dear Pastor David with a wife like Christiana, how very hard for him to bear. I also think you are to be highly praised for your thought & preparation of the SS lessons on Acts; that will be a great help to teachers & children alike. We have been so helped & blessed here over the past six weeks, the Lord has been better to us than all our fears. Dear Margt M is to take Mary to hear Mr Pitt's verdict on Thurs morn so our eyes are upon the Lord for HIS verdict in the matter; this testing time has already been fruit-bearing for our beloved Mary & she's determined to go to High Leigh again on Friday.

Now it is 13th: Daily Light today is just for us, for His Truth stands changeless, a significant word for us all as Mary remains cheerful & bright…it is well, for is it not our Father whom our life has planned. With all the love I can send I'll leave this space for Mary to write, Mother.

My darling, Mr P's assistant says he is extremely pleased with the excellent treatment results but the whole condition is so mobile (??!) that the operation is still necessary & it has been fixed for Feb 7th in Smallfield Hospital. So love I don't know if you can now manage this earlier date but I do so hope you can for your best service would be with Mother during those first days I'm in there. Rene is using up every ounce of her own energy & truly I don't think she has the physical strength to cope with everything on her own. If you cannot come darling I will look to find someone else at least to be with Mummy for the nights. And I am praying that you will find the right people there to do all you had planned so that your work will not suffer, & that you will be led to the right decision for you. Margaret M has been so kind & will take Mother to see me in hosp. Blessings on you my darling & may the Lord guide your thoughts & steps, all my love Mary.

L D

Jany 16th '66

My darling love in starting this letter to you it was to be just a bit of home doings but now we are all shocked with the news about Lagos last night & all the uncertainty it brings as to what actually is happening there. If those two men really have been killed it is so unexpected and awful; and then the Kano planes held up. Dearie me we were thankful the conference last week was got over without any serious incident of this kind. We are so anxious to hear the latest news of your country but we're told BOAC hope to make the flight to Kano tonight as usual. I do hope Mary's day of Feb 7th won't make things dreadfully inconvenient for you to come so soon but it would be a grand mercy & comfort to have you here with us. Now the 7pm news still seems confused as to what really happened & whether that man was taken for ransom or done away with oh I do trust it will soon quieten down. Goodnight my dear love, into God's gracious keeping I commit you once again may He watch over you night and day, dearest love, Mother.

High Leigh

Jan 20th '66

My dearest love how deeply & constantly you have been in my thoughts & prayers, even more than usual lately with the unpleasant goings on in & around Lagos. It is hard to keep one's mind & imagination from running riot & the only possibly alternative is to '<u>stay</u>' it on the Lord, then continue putting you every moment back into His Hand where you are most truly held in peace & security. I'm trusting you will have got my letter, or Geoff D the one I sent to him, so you will somehow know I have to go in Feb 7th & that I'm hoping you might be freed to come home in time for this. But darling I fully understand this may not be at all possible; the Lord will make a way for what He wants. This is such a full conference I must dash in for the next session now; with all my love to you darling & such prayerful greetings to all the others there with you, Mary.

Little Dungate

Jany 23rd '66

My darling I am starting another to you tho' we may see you before you see this, but I must try to get our thanks through you to Mr Tett for his letters assuring us parents & friends that you missionaries are all safe & well whether you were in or near Lagos or not, that was so very thoughtful & kind of him. I had not felt that you personally were disturbed, except of course for the state of the country, nonetheless I did very much appreciate his kindness. Mary is back from H Leigh & took me to Mtg this morning tho' she does not like to talk about her ailment to Friends. I had not seen Gisella for a long time but she asked after you & was the only one to mention the troubles in Nigeria. I've been reading the very interesting story of the Salvation Army & Gen Booth, how he lived with one purpose only: saving souls for Christ in the love of God & trusting in the Holy Spirit's power. We've just listened to one of the best TV 'Meeting Point' on 'What is the Christian Faith?' A Presb. Minister explained his belief as when 40yrs ago he realised his need of Christ's forgiveness & dedicated his life to God & has lived ever since preaching the Truth of Jesus Christ from the Word of God. What a challenge to all those hearing & watching – may it bear much fruit! We commit you constantly to His care & protection & pray that He might bring you safely home to us very soon, your ever-loving Mother.

Panyam

Jan 23rd '66

Darlings, firstly I know you will have had Bill Tett's letter assuring that we are all quite alright; we are all as usual here & nobody seems terribly surprised at what has happened. May God grant a speedy return to normal, or as near normal as possible. Yesterday I was in Jos for the Committee & heard my air passage is confirmed for Friday Feb 4 arriving in London 7am on Saturday. An awkward time time of day so do not come to meet me – unless Mouse or Wilfrid could do so. I'll come by bus to Victoria then by train down & will bring an extra rug to supplement my thin coat in case the weather is still bitter; also a wool jumper, & headscarf as I haven't a hat. It is marvellous to be thinking about winter clothes again! Please could you make me a dental appointment for as soon as possible after I return. I've written asking Frances P if she can come to Reigate before she leaves Feb 16th. Things are well underway here & I'm leaving the Literacy project classes going strong in the capable care of Joseph Yariyep; and the Radio Scripts are complete, likewise the SS class materials on Acts.

26th now: On Saturday Enid, Joyce & I played Scrabble & for once I won so Enid said, "Getting ready to play against your Mother I see!" There is a nurse due back Feb 11th Joyce Pulford, & she'll be here to help our Joyce. It is nice that Dorothy Somerville & Jean Philp are just back from furlough, they called in here for tea this afternoon. Most of my things are packed away now in trunks for storage. The Jos plane leaves for Kano at 11am then I have a 12hr wait there for the night flight at about midnight for London; so goodnight my darlings & goodbye till I see you, blessings on you all & dearest love always, Chris.

~ ~ ~ ~ ~

11 Rose Ave, Coundon, Coventry

August 14th 1966

My Dear Chris thank you so much for your two letters & such nice congratulation on the MBE which as you will know we all regarded as team work in Gindiri as a whole, for what one does the others always are backing up with prayer. My parents of course see it in a more personal light & it has been a great joy to them. We have all been so thankful to hear of the good recovery your dear sister has made; it is wonderful to think she is now back at Bible Society work after two such major operations. Many thanks for the offer of your car; later I shall have to think of getting one but not at present, though I do appreciate the offer for I know what good condition it would be in. We were all thrilled that after all your furloughs you finally could have one this time & I trust it will be so each successive trip home as well. In addition to all the news I've typed up for your return – including how delightful the Panyam garden looks – may I add Chris that you will never know how much your friendship & fellowship have meant to me over all these years; it has always been good for me to be at Panyam; with love & very sincere thanks, Jo.

Southolme 15 Park Chase, Godalming

Tel 930

30.8.66

Dearest Chris, just a little note to wish you Godspeed as you return to Nigeria, & to enclose this little gift for you to purchase something you might need before you go. It has been such a joy to see you in those brief intervals at Keswick, & at home where we know what your presence has meant to all the family. May God pour out His blessing on this next Tour, providing you with the wonder of His Power at work in all the lives around you there; and may you all be comforted as you say goodbye to your loved ones – let us all rejoice in our living Saviour who is nearer to each of us than hands & feet; blessings on you Chris dear, with our love, ever your affectionate Ruth and Gertrude.

The Parsonage, Anslow, Burton-on-Trent

4.9.66

Our dear Chris I think we are just in time to wish you a safe journey back to Panyam & a very fruitful next Tour. How wonderful that your home circumstances are such that you can leave now. We were so thrilled to see your photo in The Life of Faith recently and really glad that you had the privilege of speaking at Keswick a wonderful experience, I do wish we could have been there. All your Prayer Letters are real tonic, read eagerly, & always uplift us so please continue writing – and speaking; with our loving greetings, Catherine.

Greygarth

Sept 66

My dear, just a 'minding' to to wish you Godspeed in the new days ahead; I regret so much that we had little time for relaxing or chat but my love goes with you as you weave God's purpose into the hearts of your dear peoples again. My love to you, all of you in different ways, as you are airborne on Friday and they are left; but we are all linked with you & with them in prayer that this might be the very most wonderful stretch in all your years of blessed ministry. Here's my heart, aye, Daisy.

11 Medina Villas, Hove

Sept 8th '66

My dear Chris just a wee note to wish you Godspeed as you set out once again at His command. I know a little of what it means to be separated from loved ones; our times are indeed in His hands. This next tour of service may well be the most difficult, if not dangerous, for you. Be assured that all of us in this country will be lifting you up & praying for political stability in Nigeria. Thank you for your message at Keswick, all who heard it will never forget it. Please tell your family that I will always do anything to help your dear Mary and any of them. Now with my best love & praying you have a safe journey & a great welcome at the other end, Mary.

Jos

Sept 10th '66

Here I am again, praising God for uneventful flights, altogether a good journey with the plane from Kano to here, well piloted by a Nigerian & Indian crew. I found such a number of dear folk here to meet me: Enid & Joyce, Frances P, Geoff, the Smiths & three Suras: Joseph Yariyep, Shadrach, & Simeon Datak! Then at SUM HQ there was Pastor David & Kath McD with several of her GLB Officers. Kath told me of the amazing time recently at Vom amongst some of the most sophisticated medical staff; Yariyep had two mtgs at which nothing much transpired so he called a third & saw radiant faces as 39 people accepted Christ. I told her & Yariyep that you Mummy had been especially praying for Vom that week. There have already been many enquiries after you & specially Mary's health. It is remarkably cool here & I'm still perfectly comfortable in my English suit & underclothes! How I thank my God upon every remembrance of you all & of the lovely times we have shared together, dearest love to you each & all with my loving thoughts & prayers, Chris.

Little Dungate

Sept 11th '66

My beloved Chris once more I take up pen to write my Sunday letter! By now I trust you are safely back again in Panyam after a journey without untoward incident – I was kept in peace about it & had rest & sleep. Dear Mouse rang up to tell us he had met you and, even if it was at your suggestion, we were so glad to hear & it sent us to bed happy. 4o'c: pause while we took a turn round the gardens – I must go out again & get to work on dead-heading the roses for we are soon expecting Isabel & Jimmy & he will want to take photos. Two more posies left on the doorstep today, one for Mary who is still receiving many and the other for me from Grace W who has remembered your going, isn't that kind. Darling you know how we love you so and oh how we miss you already, Mother but now it is to be Mary:

How constantly you are in my thoughts darling & how increasingly grateful I feel for all you have been to me, & to all of us, during this home time. You used the expression 'more leisured' when you spoke of this furlough but it seems to me you have been more active in helping everybody within reach than ever before. Bless you darling for all your self-giving love, the way you enter into other peoples' problems & give of your very best. How we all thank God for you & pray that you will be greatly enriched in your own life work. Mummy has been so obviously & wonderfully upheld from the moment you left; & she really enjoyed the visit from the Irish relatives who loved the gardens & John & Helen had a splendid talk with Rene which really cheered her too. Business matters are very nearly completed now; I am still typing the last letters approved by the Solicitors & which Wilfrid must sign; I know you'll be praying with us that it all might be settled really quickly now after dragging us through so many long months. Goodbye my precious Chris, may you be specially helped & guided as you turn your mind from this to all the work waiting for you there; always yours with my heart full of love, Mary.

Redhill Station Waiting Room

Sept 27th '66

My darling I've just remembered the other thing I told you in my last I'd forgotten: when I took Mother to Dorking to collect the notices I was having done she was reading the paper while waiting the few minutes in the car. As we started for home she asked, "What do you think about this Maisie Tongue?" I could hardly drive for laughing – as I'm sure you know she meant Mao tse Tung. We yearn for more news of you but we have gladly received the circular from HQ assuring us all is well with missionaries in these rather startling events. We lift you up to the Lord constantly asking that you might have special wisdom to match the hour & that soon a way through these new difficulties will be found. I pray the Christians may be enabled to demonstrate true forgiveness & the God-given power to live in honour & at peace. Please tell all those who have been praying for me that we will continue to hold one another up & thank the Lord for the answers He gives. The morning I had to go to Guildford the check-up was delayed 45mins then the Registrar spent 7½ of my 8 mins telling me how impossible it was becoming for them all to work under the NHS. He was the one who had insisted on me having that second op. Then he glanced at my chest with one finger as it were & said no need to return for another year. Dr Johnson was no better pleased with me that than I was. However I am thankful to be managing all the motoring & so many mtgs but I do get more tired than I like after speaking & then having to talk with many people afterward. I usually recover quickly & this too is an answer to much prayer. Regarding Business we are as we were – & yet still firmly in the Lord's hands. Wilfrid has to go to Chichester hosp tomorrow for an ECG to see about his chest pains; dear love M.

L D

October 2nd '66

My own beloved I'm starting this week's letter later for we have been glued to the news of more troubles in Lagos, Kaduna and even Jos I must wait to hear more at 9pm on TV. And tonight we just are hearing a very terrible thing happened in some Methodist Church Rene thought it was, where the Labour Conference was meeting. Mr Wilson was reading the 2nd Lesson from Matt.5 when a group of young people jumped up & began shouting at him 'Hypocrite' & many other unpleasant words flew about before the Police came. Oh such awful doings & in a Church service & on a Sunday eve, is this England? I am trying to knit a cardigan for Madge but the pattern seems quite beyond my powers: 15 minutes to knit one row of 97 stitches – life is too short to spend all that much time on one row, I must find something simpler. Goodbye for now my precious Chris we do miss you a lot & I send all the love it is possible to send, ever your Mother.

Panyam

Oct 6th '66

Well my darlings things are rather uncertain these days altho' here everything goes on as usual & we are as busy as ever. When you next write could you tell me if there's any news yet of my car having been sold? I was called to help a family to safety requiring a round trip of 50mls but that has been our only contact with the stark realities of other parts. There have been few in our area from the east & the affected family was not of the tribe that has been attacked, but even so they were beaten up, all their possessions taken and they had to spend 3 nights out in the bush. I was glad to be able to help, & take them in to our DO for protection with the Pastor's help also. Strong measures are now being taken against those who were responsible for the troubles but that hasn't prevented a lot of dislocation including our Field Committee being postponed for 5 wks & we do fear a petrol shortage – I was thankful to get 8galls yesterday. And having our internal radio system is a comfort with our different stations talking each morning; with dear love to all, C.

TT College, Gindiri

6 Oct 1966

Dear Madam I am writing to give you a warm welcome back to you from England I think you have been here 2 times this week but there wasn't possibility to meet you. You have come back to meet our country at this crucial time, indeed a time of sincere prayer. We are praying for that peace which the world cannot give or maintain; our leaders themselves can cry peace, peace while there is none. Let us pray God will give us that peace which we are longing for which passes understanding; may He guide the Military head Yakubu Gowo & those we know to be his sons. I hope you are settled down & relaxed from bodily tiredness from the journey & may God help you in the undertakings for our District in serving Him amen yours in Christ, Fredrick.

Advanced Teachers' College, Kano

Oct 9 '66

Dear Nakris it is a pity I could not see you but I had to leave for Mongu immediately after morning service. I write to assure you of our safe arrival we travelled in Muazu's bus to Kano at 6.30am Monday with a lot of stopping on the way of course. Every time we were checked to see if anyone is armed. Here in Kano every Christian and pagan is being called a liar, that there is no truth in people who do not face the east. Kindly pray for us for we are few now in the Church. This is the time we need more strength to stand firm for the Lord. We shall also pray for you & all the refugees still finding their way out of the north. God has a purpose for each & every one of us whose lives He has saved during this disturbance. I hope you there are all well and fit for the Maker's use; it is yours sincerely Tabitha Guyit.

Little Dungate

Oct 9th '66

My beloved Chris I wish there was real Peace in your District – then I would probably have a letter to reply to, but as it is I am still glad to sit down & write to you & very much hope & trust it will find you well & happy & busy just as at other times. Our News here of your area has not been very good & we hear Jos is still under curfew, which had been lifted in both Lagos & Kano. Mr Tett sent another letter saying we would be kept informed if necessary. I feel that you are well, but cannot help hoping your travelling will be now just in your immediate area – surely this is a time for keeping quietly in your own place. I know you will write when you can. I hope I am not indiscreet for writing any of the above. While alone here I kept busy finishing the pram blanket for little Annabelle, buttons on the front flap, petersham binding and zip up the front, forgetting Miss Collinswood was coming to tea, only just got the kettle on in time. We were having a pleasant teatime when someone else rang the doorbell it was her sister – whose arrival she did not appear to welcome. But I may not have judged rightly. When at last they had both taken their leave I returned to my sewing but found it increasingly tricky so decided to put it aside for Brenda to finish. I retired to bed early with rather a bad head.

Mon morn: it is better today, but I shall leave all 'finishing' of garments to the younger folk for I must remember I am getting old. There is still no Business news to tell you. And still no letter from you. As you know our thoughts & prayers are with you so much and we believe all is well, I will rest REST in the sure knowledge that you are in the Lord's care always, as I look upon my lovely picture of you it brings such happy memories; with my heart's love, Mother.

Rosset Holt, Pembury Rd, T. Wells

Oct 17th '66

My dearest Chris thank you so much for your more than usually welcome letter assuring me that you are fine, all is well & things are settling down – a great matter for thanksgiving indeed. Dr L has given a terribly pessimistic view of it all & told stories of ghastly butchering etc which I thought was a great mistake because there were four mothers of missionaries in the audience gathered to hear him, plus some young hopefuls who will have been put right off applying to the Mission Field especially when hearing the committees are trying to decide whether to send missionaries back now after their furloughs. He also said he thought this would develop into a religious war bringing more murders, massacres & persecution; let us hope & pray he is not in any way prophetically correct. I am to be taken to Sidcup on Thursday for lunch with the Tetts & it will be good to talk things over with them. Jacob & Mary Lot came to visit me soon after their wedding; it is so lovely that they are here, & such real lovebirds; he is so thoughtful of her in every way & she had on the shortest mini-frock I have ever seen! With much prayerful love to you & to Joyce, God be with you, Nakam.

L D

Oct 22nd '66

My darling Chris we were so thankful to get the letter from you, thank you, & we will believe that things around you are getting back to normal. We need to be praying for governments, do we not, as we're reminded that the Christian faith is not only a matter of theology but has to be applied to the current situation wherever one is. Our 'current situation' is still much as it was when you left; Worrell has promised an answer but is, as before, held up by someone else not doing what they promised first, and so we go on, & the solicitors have disallowed anything further till all is properly signed. This is so hard on all of us especially Wilfrid. I hope I may have the opportunity & wisdom to say what needs to be said. Rene stays outwardly calm, reminding us of God's sure knowledge of all this & what ours hearts long for, quoting Psalm 84:11. There is still no buyer for your car. Last week while I was taking a mtg, some car or lorry hit my wing & scraped it horribly – I was very fed up – because of course no note was left, and now the repair is to take 2 more days. Dear love to you always darling your Mary. Now it is Mother, to tell you Mrs Smyle has joined the Heavenly Host, in her 103rd year! I feel the loss of a dear friend but rejoice in her joy. At her memorial service her favourite quote was read out, "My dear, never give out stale bread!" Meaning we must get fresh food each morning from the Bible & always be ready to distribute it.

Panyam

Oct 25th '66

Darlings you will be glad to know the family I had to rescue are happily re-settled, with many of their belongings restored to them & apologies from the local chiefs. However the story is not so good from Bukuru where a European is dealing with the aftermath of 60 of his employees being killed last month & his English colleague's departure taking his family with him. But to reassure you I will quote some lines from the letter from our HQs, 'Although we grieve with those who have been bereaved or maimed, remembering the students who have had to change schools, there can be few if any of us who have not found these past weeks challenging and we praise God for the comfort of His Holy Spirit. We must be much in prayer as we consider possible changes in policy, with clear guidance necessary in these unreliable circumstances. After two visits from the British High Commissioner, we do not consider it to be time for women & children to be sent home; the safety of our Mission families is of course priority. Essential services are being maintained and we remain at all times in close contact with our London HQ. Mr Tett is to visit the Field and plans to be here just before Christmas and to visit all the Branches. Wherever we are, we are assured that God shall supply all your need…He knows our needs…and hitherto hath the Lord helped us…and there had not failed one word of all His good promise…He is Jehovah – Jireh, He will provide.

And Nakam writes that Bill Tett spoke so well at a conference she attended, giving a resume of Nigerian political events leading up to & including the latest troubles. But no details of horrors were given & the subject not referred to again, except for prayer for the leaders & Nigeria as a whole. Thinking of Rene so much as her holiday comes closer; with my dear love to you all as ever, Chris.

Nassau, Bahamas

Nov 8th '66

My darling Chris can you believe that I am really here and that I didn't forget you on the 4th! Such huge planes those Boeing 707s are, & almost full we still flew at 580mph at 31,000 feet with delicious food & hot flannels handed out before & after eating. At about 3pm I needed the lav but the Captain warned us to fasten seat-belts for we were heading for turbulence; so I waited but nothing much happened & by then I was quite anxious to go. No sooner had I got into the tiny room when everything began bucking, bouncing & tossing around – I could only sit tight & chuckle a little & cling onto the washbasin for what seemed a long time but eventually got back to my seat. After tea we landed in Bermuda for just a short stop then on again to Nassau & there was dear Ant waving a welcome at me & soon we were back at their lovely luxurious home with Loretta & darling William! The weather is lovely & so warm that I wear neither vest nor corsets nor stockings! There are wonderful grapefruit, oranges & lemons in the garden & also coconuts! I did not feel in the slightest unwell on the plane; & now the dears all join me in sending so much love to you, from Rene.

Panyam

Nov 16th '66

My darlings here is a small piece of history I think you will like, but first thank you so much for all most welcome letters it was especially nice to hear from Rene & I know she has written to you also about loving the warm sunshine! 'And has left off some clothing in consequence' – your comment did make me laugh Mummy then you added that you never thought she or Mary ever troubled to wear much at any time!! In 1953 in a Regional Church Council mtg Dr Barnden told of a visit he'd made with Frances Priestman through Maiduguri into Gwoza to the thousands of people entirely without the Gospel. He threw out the challenge to the Nigerian Church because at that time Europeans were forbidden to settle there due to the unstable state of the people. I remember him making this appeal in the Panyam Church. Well, yesterday one of the first Gwoza converts was married to a Mupun girl in the same Church! Among those who so jubilantly danced around them as they came out of Church was Naomi Dashwet the first woman missionary to go to Gwoza & her husband Ishaya joined us later, also Luka & Hannatu from Gwoza & Limankara, the pair who travelled the 500 miles for the year in the Nakam Bible School. The dear bride wore a veil & gloves &, like her two bridesmaids, just a simple white cotton dress with a bouquet of flowers from my garden! Everyone brought gifts of food and it was a really happy occasion with much dancing & singing. It was also the last day for the Bible School students so that celebration followed the wedding with more joy and an evening Display on the playground by the light of my Tilly Lamp, acting out some Bible stories. Then Nathan Benle one of the Teachers, gave an excellent summing up of the whole year, reading the Good Samaritan story & reminding all that there will be a special collection in Church for the Nigerian refugees.

Sunday morn now and it was a Goodbye Service & they sang 6 hymns to new tunes brought by different students; the favourite seemed to be, 'Jehovah is in Heaven, so I won't be afraid any more!' Then we all sat down to a shared meal of rice & mutton with very hot peppery sauce, cooked by the young wives & of course gruel to drink – the non-fermented kind I mean. There was such a happy spirit about & they all seemed really sorry to be parting & one wife said to me, "Now you must open a two-year Course here for next time!" Chris.

Little Dungate

Dec 15th '66

My beloved Chris I hope this reaches you in time to bring my undying love & Christmas joy & peace, merriment & good cheer all through this happy season with God's blessing over & above all for that is what brings true happiness. Mary & Rene have so many jobs to see to but today M is in hospital just for another routine checkup. I have prayed so much about her condition and the state of the poor Business & I know we must accept these happenings & frustrations as being 'allowed' by God for our good. It has not been an easy lesson to learn. And I am not sure that God ordains or wishes these very thoughtless acts of solicitors etc, but these things must be amongst the ALL THINGS that work together for our good. Maybe she is writing to you at this moment as she waits, of our doings yesterday, we are so thankful that all seems finally finished with that part of our lives at any rate, J Cheal & Sons – no longer. So very sad, but we are thankful it is over & now Wilfrid will be free to be with his family more, he certainly needs a rest. I was so very cheered by your last letter, thank you darling; I do sometimes feel I have got to the place mentioned in Ecclesiastes 12:5 of the grasshopper becoming a burden, for my mind seems tired & I hate myself for not wanting to write any cards or letters, just think of it, I am wishing, tho' without enthusiasm, for the wings of a dove. It is a relief to write thus to you & I think you won't mind & you will understand, I am growing really old. 'Nough said. I am resting on such lovely words as, 'Nothing can separate us from the love of God, life, death, things present etc and it is that love that unites you & me in an Eternal bond for all time & Eternity, so outwardly tho' I send you no gifts to show it I am glad you know it in your heart goodbye now my darling love, your loving Mother.

Spindlewood

(When the final move had to happen from the Nurseries, my parents were enabled to move to this delightfully ancient thatched-roof cottage in the small village of Amberley, in the Sussex Downs)

Dec 19th '66

My dear Chris it's now three months & more since you went back & yet the actual event you were hoping to see is less than a week past. Probably Mary has told you much of the happenings, frustrations & delays, but after more than 6mths since we had the beginnings of the final finality it is now very difficult to persuade myself that it has happened. The terms offered were harder than at first expected but we had to grin & bear it for the alternative was worse. I did not thank you nearly enough for all you did in August to help the general situation. I cannot answer with any clarity regarding what next. Did Barbara write to you from Cornwall? We spent the first 10 days of November there in St Mawes. Naturally I hoped to leave going away till stopping work but we had to make the break then. It did us both a lot of good; it was wonderful walking country but as regards weight I lost some ground I had made as the food was so good. Tomorrow morning I have to see the doctor again in Arundel re the chest discomfort. This brings our very warm & loving greetings from Wilfrid, Barbara & all the family.

Little Dungate

Christmas Day 1966

My darling, Mother & the oldies have gone up to bed & Rene & I are sitting quietly by a lovely fire writing letters, wishing it was possible for you just to walk in. We're staying up because we want to watch the first of a new series of Dr Finlay's Casebook which comes on at 10.30 tonight. It has been a lovely bright day with the bare branches of the silver birches looking so beautiful against the surprisingly blue sky & the hills so clear. All I can say really now the Business is no longer ours, is that I have spent much time writing letters to those concerned to try hard to iron out misunderstandings which I do hate for they can so easily become 'roots of bitterness' so if they can be cleared up at once I think it is right to take action. I think I also hate money for what a menace it can be, or at least it can be the cause of a great deal of bitterness. Now Rene has a line or two to add so I'll just send you my special thoughts & prayers & my dear love for the New Year & all the way ahead, ever yours, Mary.

Darling Chris thank you so much for the book which looks really good & I'm so glad you liked the cardigan, it seemed just right for you. How we've been thinking of you as we know you will have been of us. We had some lovely gifts this year except perhaps for five calendars & enough handkerchiefs to stock a shop! Mary has had a rotten cold & cough & I had so hoped she could go away for a few days, after all the anxiety over the long drawn out Business troubles etc, possibly to Burrswood, but she says NO most firmly. I must go and get tea. The children are coming for lunch at New Yr and then we 3 go down to Amberley for tea there. What an eventful year 1966 has been, 'When all Thy mercies oh my God, my rising soul surveys…I'm lost in wonder, love & praise…unnumbered comforts to my soul…when worn with sickness oft hast Thou with health renewed my face...revived my soul with grace...' I do thank J Addison for writing those dear words so long ago; such dearest & best love now to you darling as ever from Rene. Oh & Mummy wanted me to say our Christmas pudding this year was v good, Mrs Craddock's new recipe on TV was voted the best ever & M said she quite expects many other homes in the country were enjoying the same thing, except we didn't 'mix everything together & leave overnight' as recommended!

Panyam

Dec 31st '66

My darlings, here is my last letter of this year so full for us of anxieties, suspense, great happiness & much of the ordinary inbetween. Please forgive this copy of the copy but there is not a spare moment to write individually this week & I do want you to hear about the 3 new Pastors ordained yesterday. The Panyam Church was packed full with many folk sitting outside. Pastors from the District sat either side of the Lord's Table & the 3 ordinands sat facing them a little in front of the congregation. Years of preparation went into this day for Patrobas Yilhi, Aristarkus Yilmak & Bitrus Mallo and all had heard God's call early in their lives. They have all completed years of training either at Bukuru Theological College or at Ayu in the Mada Hills Church, after working as Evangelists or Probationary Pastors. To Bitrus Mallo the purpose of God on his life was especially real for he & his wife & their two young children were spared from death in a serious lorry accident only two weeks ago. The Senior Pastor, David Lot led the service from the pulpit; after hymns, prayer & Scripture readings, Rev Damina Bawado stood to put the searching questions to the ordinands & each in turn answered these in the words of their solemn vows. As they did so the hearts of many in the congregation were stirred to make their own responses of self-offering to God. "Do you promise by the power of God to show forth a Godly character, to keep your own heart, to teach and admonish your children in the way of the Lord, so that you and your family shall show forth a holy witness to all other Christians?" In turn the 3 men came to kneel while the hands of two Nigerian Pastors & two European missionaries were laid upon their heads as the ordination prayer of dedication was offered up. Each man was then given a beautiful copy of the Bible with a word of exhortation to use constantly this Sword of the Spirit, this guide for life & service. Elders from all the District Churches came forward to shake hands with the new Pastors to signify support & loyalty. Pastor Damina then preached excellently on 2 Tim 1:8-14 followed by the final act of worship, the remembrance of our Saviour's death. The quiet of that big congregation during the Communion was simply beautiful. When it was all over we then shared a communal Nigerian meal in the main Bible School building. It was a very special day indeed & hearts are truly thankful & this one now needs her sleep, with such dear love as always, your Chris.

Panyam

January 19th 1967

Darlings, posts are still rather uncertain still, since the troubles back in the autumn; we are continuing to get Christmas mail posted in England in early Nov so if I don't comment on something you think I should have it's probably because I haven't got it yet! When the 15th passed over quietly we were thankful as we'd heard rumours of further trouble on the anniversary of the coup. The proclamation from the Ghana Conference in Accra with the Regional Leaders seems to have given a sense of renewed security & hope. On Sunday morning radio we heard a special prayer service in memory of the leaders who died Jan 15th '66. Enid's packet of watercress seed is giving us tiny tastes of it in our salads – I've never heard of it growing in this country before! We are facing a problem over the girl meant to be helping Kath with the GLB. She is a very strange sort of person – most gifted in leadership & with a tremendous knowledge of the Bible & ability to teach it, and yet psychologically all tied up & most queer. We have asked advice from the Warden of Gindiri on how to go about trying to help her into a more stable attitude. But now I have had a new message in from poor Kath to come & talk to this girl who is refusing to do any work. Apparently she is no longer willing to accept any orders from anyone now except God Himself. I'm not looking forward to this for it is a grievous situation; the girl could be such a blessing & a power for good, but at present poor Kath is tense & weary with the strain of trying to work with someone so difficult. On the other hand Jean Cameron has settled down happily & has written a poem about all the different jobs we keep giving her! Goodnight for this time dear ones, as ever yours Chris.

Little Dungate

Jan 29th '67

Darling dear I do not know how you can make even a little time to write to us when your hectic times seem even busier than mine & in addition you have emergencies to cope with, late arriving visitors, lorry accidents & baby births at night, not to mention assistant staff who only assist in more difficulty, but oh how we thank you! I do think somehow you have to devise a plan or ways of conserving your physical strength so that spiritual help is available when most needed, unhindered by a tired body. I know delegating responsibility is hard, always with the sense that the job won't get done quite so well, so I'll just continue praying that all of you on the Station may be helped to find ways through these difficulties, as I know you'll be praying for me in mine. At one of our recent mtgs I asked why we must spend so much time talking about the issues & not praying, do we just rely on others praying for us? I was uncomfortable for 97% of those present were ordained men but I felt it had to be said. One thought that for us to do so would seem like a sign of panic; one other spoke up suggesting we should recommend the use of the prayer booklet more than it was currently used, but entirely bypassed the idea that we as staff should pray together for our specific needs. I then very much wanted to ask the leader whether when his wife was recently going through her treatment & then operations did he just use perhaps the collect for the day? Darling we must also continue praying for our dear Rene who battles bravely on. Now with my dear love to you as always your own Mary.

Mongu

Feb 6th '67

Darlings you may be surprised to see I'm writing from here; it was a sudden decision to ask Frances if I could come for a few days while she is away & look after myself in her lovely peaceful empty house. It's a great opportunity for me to rest & then get on with some overdue office work, so here I am. Arriving for lunch just before she left meant that we had some good talking time which we've not had in a while. The Killers are in the other house only a few minutes walk away & it is nice to be near other folk even while enjoying solitude. They have asked me to supper both nights so far & I plan to entertain them, having brought my own 'chop-box' that always comes on treks with me. Shadrach, Frances' good boy is nearby on holiday in her absence but sweetly comes along to see I'm alright. It is bliss to be quiet & not have to talk or listen to talk for hours on end, and I can stay till Saturday! Now one other word about the troublesome assistant to answer your query Mother, no she is not European but a Nigerian girl & it is more difficult to deal with, for with the former I could tell her where to get off in no uncertain terms but with Nigerians you have to be so careful these days in case it would seem like race discrimination. But as with anyone, we gave her another chance to state her points of view & air her complaints before we tried to deal with the matter. Even with better understanding, the conclusion – after 2 further hours – was that she will have to be suspended at least until her wedding, which itself seems to be the root of the trouble.

Later, back at Panyam: all seems well here except that goats have stripped the verandah rose plants again and mice are in the store shelves, & cockroaches everywhere! It was lovely to come back to your dear letters & hear Mr Stevens' views Mummy & I'm so glad to know he is a Christian as well as a skilful surgeon so we can trust his advice. If you do need this further op we will take it in our stride as you say for we are in Safe Hands, and may calmness, courage & patience be given as you need it. I was reading in Daily Light of the trees of the Lord being full of sap, fat (!) & flourishing & bringing forth fruit even into old age – that is just you Mother & I know will be the experience of all hospital staff looking after you, should it come to that; now with my dearest love to you all three as ever Chris.

Panyam

Feb 24th '67

My darlings just a short note to thank you for letting me know so quickly after the Xray report, how I wish I could be with you to discuss all possibilities but it does seem we are of the same mind as your first reaction, "Let's get it over & done with." Mr Stevens knows Mother's age & marvellous constitution & still feels it is a reasonable risk to take to relieve her of this wretched gall/bile duct pain. The Lord has brought us through emergencies in the past & we can safely trust Him for this one; and darlings you know I will be as with you in spirit & as involved through constant prayer as it is possible to be, with best love, Chris.

Jos

March 8th '67

Darlings I am sorry you are still waiting for an op date for Mother but so glad to hear you are settled in mind on the rightness of it. Today I was reading Psalm 71 what wonderful words, wonderful truths & wonderful comfort therein; share it with me and you too will be helped & given a heart at peace and gay courage! You mention big firms closing down in voluntary liquidation and yes we can indeed be thankful for the mercies that have surrounded us all through the past difficult years & how truly marvellous it is that we didn't have to come to that. We came here into Jos for Council mtgs and further car repairs so while I wait I'll tell you of the great numbers of 'ladies in waiting' we've been having in our Midwifery Unit, every bed full of those who have delivered & some waiting outside. Joyce was called out one evening to a difficult case of the woman had given birth to one twin, the other still unborn. Several hours later I went along to help Joyce struggling with the retained placenta & lots of bleeding after the second delivery. By 11pm we went off to hospital & worked together till 2am & 3pints of saline drip did revive the poor mother a wee bit; knowing her to be a Christian we were also of course praying with her. Frances then had to do a manual removal & we mopped up but half an hour later the poor patient died. Oh so dreadfully sad, but at least we knew we had done all we possibly could, and the young husband was very grateful. Now we shall need to find new homes for two more little motherless infants. Do you remember Polycarp Fian Datok who was Interpreter for Billy Graham's N. Nigerian Crusade? He was home last weekend & preached a fine message on Sunday before getting ready to go on a year's course to Australia! And Mary you will remember Unaisi Angwet, it is her youngest daughter Lois here in Jos with me with her 3 little girls, waiting for her husband for they are going today as new missionaries from our Church out to Limankara, they are a fine couple! Now my darlings you know how dearly I love you all & will be with you in spirit during these days; the Lord bless you each one & make you all a blessing to each other & to many others; part of me is always thinking of you & imagining what is happening to you these days, praying His peace & love will be very real to you, Chris.

Panyam

Mar 16th '67

Darling love how wonderful that your letter came this evening & Pastor David is going into Jos tomorrow & can take this wee line there to post for you bringing all the love in my heart for you today & we can be so close in spirit. You may be coming round from the anaesthetic about now and M&R will be phoning Smallfield hosp to see how you are – I do wish there was a line to Panyam too! I am continuing to trust that you have been kept in perfect peace throughout, as I have, believing that all will be well. Another instance of His tender loving care is the dear Christian woman who has earnestly requested we remember her next time we need a home for an orphan and this very evening I have received a brand new baby boy. His mama just got her Homecall & her poor young husband kept thanking God for us; he only had an old heathen relative with him & in such hands the wee mite would invariably follow its mother. Rauta is giving him a bottle now & I'll have him in my room tonight & tomorrow we'll go out & find the woman who offered. Now darling, the Lord bless you and all who are caring for you, in the hosp & when you get home, yours as ever C.

Jos

Mar 31st '67

Darlings I'm here again, this time for Field Committee & there is a moment to write & tell you I was more delighted than I can say with your letters Mary & Rene, with even those two lines from Mother herself – bless you all & many thanks indeed! Your lovely 89th birthday photo went all round the Commt. table during our coffee break with many admiring comments & fresh assurances of prayer. The newest Comm. member is Luther Dabirong Chishak who was born in Panyam the year I first came out! Mary will remember his father Joshua. There has been a bit of tension & fear of possible outbreaks of violence again, so we gathered Church leaders from across the whole country, including our Pastor Damina, 3 weeks ago & issued a joint statement. This was then presented by a few in each Region to the Military leaders, urging patience & to refrain from bloodshed & also urgent & earnest prayer by all Christians every day at midday specifically. Right after that was our Church members' convention & it was one of the best I remember. The Bible School students sang a few hymns for us using the big reed pipes as accompaniment; the practices they had beforehand would make you think they were performing in the Albert Hall! Pastor David gave a very fine message from Matt 5:9 on peacemakers, pointing out the opposite are those who fan the fire of hatred & division. Another message included the disciplining of an Evangelist found making the intoxicating gruel then this was added, "We have taken action on Eph 5:18 but we have forgotten the second part and we are ALL guilty of disobeying that." Later Akila Wantu preached on Rom 8:31-39. Who shall separate us from the love of God? He spoke of the possibility of the persecution of Christians in this country in days to come, and coming closer; and of the Evangelist in Pilka who had seen two men murdered but many more had accepted Christ. Chris.

Panyam

April 10th '67

My darlings I still go for 'petticoat strolls' outside on these very warm nights occasionally & tonight I'm sitting here in my petti trying to keep cool! It is very hot inside with the Tilly lamp burning away, but I'd always rather have it hot than cold. This aft letters came from Mummy – at home – and Nakam, & Pastor David who is clearly enjoying being back in England again! He said that to be at Little Dungate with you was like being in Panyam because of your knowledge of it all & kind enquiries about so many of his people. He described the beauty of the countryside, the garden flowers & your views of the hills' early morning frost, cows etc in a quite remarkable way. He is looking forward to his week in Ireland with the Belfast Hamiltons & hoping to meet some of our folk too.

Later: in a nice letter from A. Lena she wrote that she loves hearing about the NLFA work & prays constantly that the Lord will restrain the powers of darkness so that the vital work may not be hindered & the Light may spread. And in another letter from Nakam she writes that after David spoke at Keswick a girl from S. Croydon was led to make a definite offer to SUM; and that he was able to visit Mr Hayward – what a grand visit that must have been for both men! An additional urgent need that is challenging us now is the problem of boys & girls leaving primary schools but not qualifying for further education or training. These disappointed young people drift off into the towns seeking for paid work – anything rather than remain at home to farm with their fathers; they could have done that without any education. At our Field Comm we considered & discussed this at length, envisioning a youth hostel in both Jos & Maiduguri, plus an English Bible School with agricultural emphasis in a rural area, with plans for courses on new home projects and correspondence with the youth away from home. That must be all for this time, with my dearest love as always, Chris.

Kagoro

May 1st '67

Greetings darlings to you all with a special lot of birthday love to Mary today! We've had such a good time here with the GLB Officers' conference, nearly all dispersed now after 9dys together. Well over 100 Officers from almost every province in N. Nigeria – just think of 25yrs ago when Marjorie Burrough started the first Company in Kabwir & I followed suit with the 2nd in 1945! It's been good having Miss Rae here with us for the Council Mtg with Geoff D & Barnaba Dusu & the 10 women members who were at conference for one decision among many that had to be made was regarding the unhelpful assistant I have mentioned. She too attended the conference & when called in she calmly 'wiped the floor' with all of us in turn so there was no doubt remaining that she is not the right person for this job so we terminated her appointment. Sadly she left us all aghast with her proud rudeness & Mary Dabiring was not alone in feeling ashamed. Poor Kath has twice been in tears, in private, but I think we have been able to encourage & reassure her for we all feel she is doing a splendid job in every way. Getting back to Jos today we are hoping to take delivery of our new car since the present one is simply getting too expensive in frequent repairs. My dear love to you each one as ever Chris.

Panyam

May 8TH '67

Two more dear letters from you Mummy this week for which many grateful thanks; you can hardly know what it means to me to have them coming along so regularly & that you've been spared to continue this ministry! And I'm sorry I never mentioned how relieved I was to hear my old car had finally been sold – many thanks to Mary for that. I do hope you have a very happy visit to Spindlewood for the birthday party. Our new car was waiting for us in Jos & it was a great pleasure to drive her home. She's a bit smaller than the Morris Oxford but the back seat lets down so we can still take lying down patients to hospital. She is white with maroon upholstery & looks splendid for she's a 1967 model with the latest gadgets; I've named her Fibi PilangNan – praise God which pleases all our folk here. Geoff saw us off last Monday with prayer & the next day the Panyam folk joined in thanksgiving for such a lovely car for God's work; she's a dream to drive, with much better springs for our jolty roads, & does 40 miles to the gall! Another delightful letter came from David in Belfast with no mention of the cold except that old Mr & Mrs Hamilton who took him to see the Lord Mayor of Belfast, had given him an electric blanket and 6 others, and that they looked after him like an egg! (a Sura expression) Also, at the CU at Ballymena Secondary School several children bought copies of 'His Workmanship' & 3 girls took SUM collecting boxes. Yesterday in Church here Pastor Bitrus who is still struggling, gave a terrific sermon on Exod 3:5 the preparation for hearing God's call, he was truly inspired! He seemed quite well & strong even after the strain of preaching twice, then in the evening returned to Gindiri on the back of a friend's motorbike; dearest love from Chris.

Snr Pr School, Panyam

15.5.67

Dear Madam Mrs Cheal many greetings in the name of our Lord Jesus Christ, sending our greetings through Miss Nakris Cheal is not enough for this. We become very sad when we hear you are not well now we are very happy to hear you are well or discharge from hospital. We never see you personally or you see us but love of God put us in one family and prayer holds us together. We give thanks to Almighty God very much that you are better from what had happen to you we pray He will keep and care with you. We need your prayers too for direct our leaders in the right path to rule the country. My wife and our 6 children are sending their lovely greetings and wish you more strong in your health we wait Pastor David Lot back from you to bring us news about you. I enjoy teaching children Scripture in School and Sunday school and my aim is to put them on a strong foundation which is Jesus Christ that they know and take Him as their personal Saviour when they still young. I write and talk a lot Bye madam I am Malachi Z Banwat.

Panyam

May 25th '67

My darlings what a feast of lovely photos in with your letters thank you so very much, no wonder we all dote on Rene's grandchildren – William and Annabelle are both simply lovely! And Mummy I'm so pleased to know that Mr Stevens is pleased with your wonderful recovery, what a great mercy this is for all of us. You mention Wilfrid's work at Arundel but don't tell me what he is doing there. Last weekend we, that is 2 students keen to ride in our good little Peugeot to Jos, from where I went on to Bukuru at the kind invitation of the Fausts who were giving a dinner party for Ed & Nellie Smith as Nellie will possibly not be returning here after their furlough. We are by a long way the oldest missionaries out here on the field now & between us we have done just about 180 years! Three of us still have our mothers, & we all agreed we owed a tremendous debt to our faithful families sharing our lives here & constantly praying for us. It was a super supper & I spent the night in the Faust's charming guest room & left after a splendid breakfast – a most pleasant occasion altogether. At a recent Finance Comm mtg we heard from John Ducker the MAF pilot briefly in Jos & needing to discuss the many & v frustrating problems regarding flying regulations around the Lake Chad project. He told us of yet another incident they regard as a miracle; another pilot, Gordon, was flying back when his engine failed & he had to make a forced landing on very rough ground full of trees & rocks & the only damage was a mere scratch on the undercarriage. Adding this to the marvellous Chad rescue operations by John D back in Feb they are encouraged by the signs of the Lord's amazing power & goodness to them. Our prayer took wings as we asked again for the difficult & limiting regulations in & around Chad to be soon removed. However in Daffo on Tuesday we were plunged into an unpleasant palava when I went to the car during a break in the morning's proceedings, and discovered a tin of 1000 of Sulph. dim tablets which was not ours. These days there is a terrible amount of stealing of drugs & illicit selling of same in the markets and I found out this tin had been sent by a man from Chip who works in the Dispensary to Istifanus Jakden – whom Mary will remember – who works in Daffo. They had managed to get a young man who has only worked here 3 weeks to do their dirty work – he had come with us in the car to Daffo – & naturally he was frightened & denied all connection with the men or the medicine. Sadly it has transpired that there are more fingers pointing at Isti for he has been seen giving illicit injections to folk in the Daffo market. We had to spend all day gathering members of our Medical sub-committee together, including Pastor Aristarkus, to deal with the matter. Now I am sure you will have been following the Nigeria news as anxiously as we do, although we hear very little except through the wireless. I do know that the Christians are all praying for Yakubu Gowon & the whole country more than ever before. The breaking up of the Federation into 12 States may mean that our work in Bornu & Sardauna provinces will face new difficulties as they will be in a different State from us in Plateau Province. We heard yesterday that Christopher Lot had a motorbike accident & is in hospital with a broken thigh; Joyce is taking his mother in to see him. Dearest love to you all, Chris.

Panyam

June 23rd '67

Darlings I'm so sorry there has been so little letter-writing time recently but I do continue to be so grateful for all your faithful letters coming in to me. I must tell you though of the interesting visitor the other day; do you remember Satdi Baki the boy you supported while he was in Gindiri Secondary School? He is now at Ahmadu Bello University in Zaria studying social administration, a tall good-looking lad & a keen Christian I should think. He talked most intelligently about the state of the country, & their hopes & fears. They think MajorGen Yakubu Gowon is a man of great restraint. They know he is always being badgered by different people to follow their ideas & it is extremely difficult for him to steer a straight course between them all. They hope very much that sanctions against the East will succeed, but, if not, he is sure war will inevitably follow & be very costly in lives. I asked if Christian students are praying for the country & he said their Univ CU has 3 prayer mtgs a week & he never remembers one where the leaders of the country were not covered with prayer, which was encouraging. We just listen to the Radio & when day follows day without any special news we are glad. But I believe the beginning of July will be a critical time when oil dues are to be paid. The Federal Govt says they must be paid to them, and Ojukwu says they must be paid to Biafra, so we shall see. Don't worry about us for I doubt we should be greatly involved even if hostilities did break out. Various plans are made in case of emergency, & you know how thoughtful the SUM has been in letting our relatives know how things are going. Our own plan for the Pastors' Retreat in Mongu is going ahead for July 12 & 13th & Pastor Manasseh's new home is quite spacious enough to house all the expected guests. Goodbye now my dear loves blessings on you all, Chris.

Panyam

July 3rd '67

Darlings, more welcome letters from you, and one from Wilfrid telling me a bit about his job in Arundel which seems to suit him admirably – showing people around is just the sort of thing Father loved also, & I think I share that enjoyment! I've had a lovely time taking Pastor David around the District these past 2 weeks, covering about 400 miles visiting 9 of the centres where we hold monthly gatherings. Of course until 1957 David was the only Pastor for this whole area so it is wonderful to see the growth in the last 10yrs. In each place he has given a splendid resume of his 3mths in England, including the spiritual stimulus of meeting so many people who pray regularly for all of us here, and all the amazing things he saw. Some of his highlights were getting tickets for the London Underground by putting 2/- (2 shillings) in a box that gives you back 1 ticket and 6d (half a shilling) change! The lifelike figures at Madam Tussauds, snow in N. Ireland, the crowds of motors & the traffic lights guiding them at crossroads, & when he tried to see the top of a multi-storey building his hat dropped off backwards! And of course he speaks of you Mother, the one who has prayed for him for nearly 40 yrs, with the phenomenal memory for the names of Panyam people, and with Mary's request to ask the people of Panyam to pray for us in England at least once a week. You have given him this fresh idea of the need for Nigeria to pray for England & her needs, especially the trials of those newly offering to SUM to come out here but without the support of their families; and the very young folk who can give very small amounts which do add up, so we need to teach them young! He presents all this with such joyful humour that captivates his listeners and tho' I have heard it 9 times I am not weary of it in the least! Now the news has just come in of an explosion in Lagos with 4 deaths & many injuries, but no further details yet. Darlings I'll write more when I know.

July 8th: Well my dear ones it seems we are for it now, as I'm sure you've heard on the news this morning civil war has broken out. The area mentioned is about 400 miles away, very near Nsukka the university town where I went for the Christian Council mtgs in 1964. I doubt it will be over as quickly as the Israel-Arab war, but perhaps one could hardly call that over yet – what a world we live in! Darlings I'm sure you feel a bit anxious but we know well where our comfort & peace lies in all uncertainty & we have proved so often God's goodness & mercy. I am so very thankful that Ant is no longer working in Port Harcourt. We shall just carry on our work as normal as long as we are able but I do feel it is up to us to make every possible preparation for our work to go on as well as possible if we did have to evacuate. I am so glad we have the plans already in place for the Pastors' Retreat next week. With my dear love to you each & all as ever from Chris.

Braeside, Rodborough Common, Stroud

July 12th '67

My dearest Chris we remember you very often these days, we are told to preach the Gospel but it is never our right is it, to ask to see the results, but the Lord has certainly let you see much of the harvest, at least in its beginning, how good this is! "You might tell how many acorns there are upon an oak tree but you can never tell how many oak trees there are in one acorn!" Now these happenings in the Near East tell us in no uncertain words that the Lord is at hand, this trouble is not unique, just as in Psalm 118 …'they compassed me about' several times then each time they are cut off, it is the arms of the Lord that triumph. The Shofar horn has already been blown at the Jerusalem Wall as a call to prayer and thanksgiving – Christ's second coming is more than ever the only hope for this distracted world. The family all join me in much dear love & constant prayer for you & your faithful work out there, your dearly loving A. Lena.

Panyam

July 14th '67

Darlings our P Retreat is over for another year and truly I can say it was wonderful. Eight of the Christian women cooked food for us all to share & brought it along in big bowls; we had tea & kosai (bean cakes) at 6.30am and tea & biscuits at 4pm and a hot meal at 10am and 7pm always very nice meat in gravy over rice but often too peppery for me to eat as much as others did. That kind gift from Mrs Edwards plus a wee bit more, was enough to pay for all that and give a small thank you gift to the splendid cooks at the end. The fellowship was warm & friendly with rich times of prayer together and excellent messages & testimonies given. It was really a thrill to look around at them all & think of how they have all been brought in, and along, and grown; each is a good man serving the Lord in his appointed place with real dedication and desire to teach others to follow on. We talked and prayed through big topics so relevant to all, such as boys & girls who take each other without Christian marriage; marriage feasts that are becoming a racket for making money, the need to enlarge the Bible teaching courses; keeping the registers and the finances in good order; and the limits of pastoral authority, and so on. Everyone was tired at the end, but all expressed happiness & gratitude. Today I heard that Yakubu Gowon has a sister in Kaduna who is a very keen Christian & as he is no longer allowed to go out anywhere to Church for security reasons, she sends him a weekly tape recording of our friend Mr Piepgrass's sermon! Angus McDermot the BBC reporter in Lagos has twice referred to him recently as 'an obviously honest man.' I met a brother of his last time I was in Jos. Blessings on you darlings each one & love to all as ever Chris.

Little Dungate

July 23rd '67

My Darling love we are finding there is more news in the papers than on TV and tonight there is mention of the Federal army being just 20 miles from Enugu and I know you have been there – oh how I wish all wars were over! They raise so much ill feeling and sorrow & loss. Our prayers go up to the only One who knows all and who, despite all, will continue to work His purposes of good…if only we & all the world would cooperate and not hinder. I am so glad you had a grand Retreat darling. It would seem unlikely that the Fed army will settle peaceably there near you or in the Arab-Israeli war either. I must stop this and go outside and remove dead heads from the roses in hope of second blooms. Did you know the Bible Society is going to have Bible readings in different public places across London? I think this must be to counteract the wave of apostasy & lawlessness. I'm sure Mary has told you our holiday in Ireland is booked & I'm sure you will write to us there. Do pray it may be a fine evening for the journey, the plane journey, I do not feel courageous but the Lord deals very graciously with me in my times of need. Once more I am committing you to the care & protection of our loving Heavenly Father, as ever your own Mother.

Panyam

July 31st '67

Darlings this should reach you before you leave for holiday 'across the water' bringing my best wishes for a lovely time there & my love to all the relatives you'll see. After our Sunday morning prayer mtg I told them I'd just heard that 500 European missionaries had decided to stay on in Biafra; if such a situation arose here what would they think we should do? This raised a lot of talk then finally David spoke, "I would advise that you should go back to England. I know how anxious your families would be for you; & how could we support you all adequately if no money could get into the country? You are not involved in this war so I would say withdraw; you could keep in touch, and pray, then return when things get easier. It would be different if the Moslems were fighting against us Christians – then you & we would be in it together & we would face it together; but not in this civil war, there would be no sense in you risking your lives." Chris.

August 10th: I love to think of you over in dear old Ulster enjoying the warm family fellowship and many a laugh with good crack! The civil war has taken a dramatic turn with the conquest of the Midwest Region this week & of course we all wonder very much what will happen next. One of our dear girls, sister of Hezekiah who visited you at Brookfield, came back in rather a hurry from her College in Warri in the Midwest region that is now in Ibo hands, so I suppose she won't get back there again. She was hoping to study medicine so will now try to continue that in Gindiri. The river is flooding again as it does many years at about this time & even tho' the water rushes right through this compound it soon goes down often leaving stranded wildlife in odd spots. A bandicoot, the outsize type of rat, got marooned beside our guest house, and I found a snake behind the door of my office the other day. The only other time

I've seen one actually in the house was two days before Mary arrived but I did not tell her till afterwards! Ernest Killer is making plans to go by road to Kaduna to collect two new couples coming out from England & bound for Gindiri; it is a difficult time for new folk to be arriving, with Jos airport out of normal service as Kano has been. Now darlings I must go to sleep for tomorrow is a long day of committees, so my dear love to you 3 and all the various relations, Chris.

Panyam

Sept 25th '67

Lovely to keep getting your newsy letters, well, except of course the sad news 2 weeks ago of Geoffrey Bloss' sudden death – I did write to poor Mary & have been praying for her and the children, and Margaret & Sidney too. And yes Mother I typed the Sura Dictionary in Brookfield kitchen and the prayer book in the Millbank lounge. I was just thinking of the Brookfield kitchen this morning and of how many important crises have been connected with that room: especially facing 2 almost impossible situations of having to find a house to move to from Brookfield, and then last year with Barbara there when Frank phoned her that it really did look like the end for the Business but then Wilfrid came in saying he'd seen the Bank Manager who had told him of a possible buyer; that was the man who eventually bought the Business. All of that was shared in the kitchen that day. On both those occasions I remember how prayer just seemed the only thing to do & how wonderfully the Lord heard our cry, now that we can look back on it, and praise Him. On Friday I spent nearly all day 'laid on one side' – I know you'll remember that expression! – with just a spot of fever and probably a bit of overdone-ness & was quite fine again on Saturday. At one of our services last weekend Bitrus Mallo's closing word was very good and I believe touched a lot of folk; it was from 2 Kings 6 when the axehead fell in the water – the young man was distressed because it was a borrowed axe but the 'Great Physician' was there with him & able to help retrieve the lost iron & all was well, but what about you, where have you fallen? Show the exact place to Jesus the Great Physician & He will work a miracle for you too; just be honest and show Him that hidden place where the trouble lies and let Him do His work for you. That was the gist of what he said. Yesterday after services I went out with my old ladies & we gathered a small crowd to listen to some gramophone in a compound that stank of beer. Panyam town on Sunday evenings is like a stagnant fen of drink with crowds of shouting, inflamed, intoxicated people and little children playing about amongst them & that ghastly stink of their beer. And yet, individuals of them call to me to go on praying for them because they know it is wrong; in haste again now, all love as ever C.

Jos

Oct 14th '67

Darlings here are some snippets that deserve whole letters of their own but need to be jotted down while I have these minutes, & the best is that excellent report the doctor gave Mary at her check-up, what a great uplifting praise this is! Yesterday was Fri 13th & at our shared breakfast prior to the committee mtg someone commented on the date and I had to respond with "What my Mother would say of it: this is the day the Lord has made & we will rejoice & be glad in it!" And Mummy

I am so delighted you were able to go with Wilfrid to Arundel Castle & see a little of what he does there and some of the treasures on display before it all closed to the public at the end of Sept. Is it really possible that one table could be insured for £25,000? It seems incredible; but I quite agree with you of course that our inheritance, & that of every true Christian, is far greater than anything in that Castle! At the morning mtg David Carling brought us some encouraging news from Chad: the first convert from Tataverom on the northern tip of the shore -after 8 yrs of work & witness - in one of the lake side Dispensaries has openly confessed Christ & several people from the Chad Republic Church are interested & offering for the Project, but the need for more missionaries there, both Nigerian & Chadian, is very great. David C took the boat up a river off the Lake and discovered several quite big towns with thousands of unevangelised people till then unheard of. I told you about the drinking hordes on Sunday eves in Panyam town and market-place; so after discussing it with Pastor David we held a big open-air meeting there last Sunday early evening, bringing a large crowd of men, women & children from the Sunday Schools, & the amplifier. We sang several hymns then put on a record or two then Pastor Bitrus gave another splendid message which David followed in Sura. Many more people came first out of curiosity then to join in; it all went off happily and I hope we can repeat this. Sometime ago I believe I told you about Maina's wife who stuck to her heathen ways and refused to come near us. Fairly recently, and unusually for her, she got frightened & stranded out in the bush one night, quite alone & lost, so she prayed for the first time then slept under the stars. In the morning she was so surprised at her safety & to find her path easily, in every sense, for she gave up all heathen ways then & there to follow God's way, and has not looked back! There is no particular war news but oh we so much hope to hear of an end to the hostilities soon; yours, Chris.

Panyam

Nov 30th '67

My own darlings I know you forgive these infrequent & sometimes scrappy letters. Last week I had to race back from Gindiri admin business & committee mtg to attend a posh wedding between Alfred Nanle & Rahaba Lot, the grandchildren of Andarawus Kakiyes & Daniel Lot respectively, then straight off from that 15 miles west to a little village called Mile7 where a crowd had gathered to give me a lovely welcome into their newly built Church. I was especially pleased to see again the young deaf & dumb man who was converted at the NLFA Campaign; I had brought for him an EAWoods picture book and he was delighted! I came back along a new road to a village I've wanted to visit for years, called Bwai where the Evangelist's wife was one of the first little girls I remember treating in the Dispensary when I started work in 1930! This month I've been doing the auditing of the Church accounts in as many places as I can get around to, some are ever so good but some are terrible. Now I think I must set up a Course for Treasurers to help them understand how to keep an account book & why it is so vital to get an overall picture of church finances; and for the good ones to be able, & willing, to help the bad ones get better. I shall try to take a student Pastor with me each time as a splendid introduction to this course & perhaps they can help me write it. It was lovely to get in this evening after another really busy day and find letters from you dears, thank you so much but I'm nearly dropping asleep so no more now but my dear love as ever Chris.

Panyam

Dec 5th '67

My darlings another dear letter from you Mummy cheered me so, thank you – you sound fully recovered & really well again! I wish you could see the roses on our dining room table; one is I think a Crimson Glory with the most heavenly smell & the other is Peace. They send drifts of scent all over the place; how gorgeous roses are. A smaller Masquerade is starting to flower on the verandah with several buds so maybe we'll have some for Christmas. I do not know how we are going to manage to continue with all these expectant mothers; Joyce & Rauta Lot examined 800 in the antenatal clinics just in November, but our good Rauta is leaving shortly to get married. And the Native Authority Dispensaries are almost empty of medicines, saying they have all been sent to the battle front; so crowds of ordinary patients come along here hoping for treatment as well. The triple vaccine for babies is increasing also & Joyce gives hundreds of these injections each month. In the middle of all this one of our bright new medical workers who we had spared to part time to do his training at Alushi, completed his training then left without notice for a job in the new Roman Catholic hospital 300 miles away where he can earn far more than here. So we have an urgent need for at least 2 more Nigerian midwives and more medical workers. Some grand news from Bukuru where they recently held their New Life for All Campaign; I was there one day last week when some young boys came up for a chat. We sat outside & had such a happy time as they told me how it helped them and their shining radiant faces echoed their words and they told me they meet for prayer in one or other of their homes every eve with an average attendance of 40! They begged me to go & join them & I should dearly love to. It is wonderful to get these reports from across our District and all over the country and the amazing spread of interest in NLFA to virtually all West & now East Africa. The plans to extend to E Nigeria are by no means forgotten but have to wait for cessation of hostilities before getting going with the programme there. Also a wonderful work of God is going on among Univ students at Ibadan, all very encouraging. We have four of our dear women all lined up to go for a month to Gwoza but sadly some objections have been raised because they are women! The feeling is though that when they discover who these women are, such splendid senior women, & two of them elders in their Churches, that they will change their objections to welcomes. If they don't, I will have to "tell 'em what they can do with their tin 'elmets!" – that's from Gert & Daisy, & a frequent quotation out here! Dearest love always Chris.

Panyam

Dec 20th '67

My darlings as we fast approach this most special time of the year you know my heart is with you and I send all the love in it. In lieu of actual gifts, which I am so sorry not to have sent this year, here are two happy tales to tell and greet you with for Christmas! Pastor Bitrus has given another of his splendid sermons, this one on the Lord Jesus coming down to be born into the filth and poverty of that stable in Bethlehem, showing us how He is prepared & ready to be born into the poorest & wretchedest heart anywhere in the world, and there to grow and bring New Life, until at the end we can say, with Simeon, "Now lettest Thou Thy servant depart in peace, for my eyes have seen Thy Salvation." There is an old Panyam man called Sebu who used to be the Judge in Court & has been an attender at Church services for a long time, listening to many, many sermons. Suddenly he told Pastor David he now wanted to come right out as a Christian and follow Jesus, so he was given the opportunity to stand up in Church & give his testimony, which he did, to everyone's amazement & delight. Afterwards the Christian women were a bit troubled for this old man had nobody to cook for him as one wife had died & the other was a leprosy patient at Mongu. However the next day Frances P came over from Mongu bringing home a patient she had discharged, none other than Sebu's wife! The remarkable thing is when she first went away to the Mongu Colony she was most hostile to the Gospel, but has listened to words from Pastor David's brother Yariyep, & others, and now is a definite follower of the Lord Jesus & here she is back, quite well, and willing & able to look after her husband again! She did have to have a foot removed, but Frances fitted her with an artificial one on which she is quite able to walk. The welcome this old lady got was sweet to see, and she now thinks nothing of walking the half mile to Church with her husband for every service; and he wants to enter the class for Baptism & she has agreed also! Now darlings you know how much I love you & that all my prayerful thoughts will go from here to you each one, goodbye & Happy Christmas dear ones, Chris.

Panyam

January 8th 1968

My darlings I am sure by now what I wrote for Mother's 90th has arrived, & even if not you will know I will be celebrating with you on the 11th – congratulations again Mummy what a day! I really do feel those special words in Gen 12:2 & in Psalm 92:13-15 & those particularly in the Amplified OT truly are your own, & I believe that DV we shall be spared to meet again next year or whenever it is to be! The other day on my way back I was met by a frantic messenger announcing a woman had delivered in the road so I hurried in to find the young girl who helps in the Midder Unit had somehow got the woman indoors & onto a bed and had cut the baby's cord. The poor mother was bleeding profusely & I was frankly worried, but a tablet of ergometrine, given by this untrained girl before I'd arrived, began to help, & we kept her still & calm till Joyce arrived by which time she was alright. I was in working on my accounts when I was called out again to a nasty accident where a lorry had tipped over & the driver was very messy from a severe head wound. We got him cleaned up & were bandaging him when his passenger was brought in with a broken collar bone. As soon as Joyce was free we took both chaps to Pankshin Hospital.

Later 20th: What a pleasure it has been to get in from another really busy day of visits & meetings to find lovely letters from you & have 5 minutes to sit out in the sun & pour over all your dear Birthday details; I could just see it all – the lovely flowers, cards, gifts, and mainly Mummy's shining blue eyes as bright as when she was 25 and meeting Father! Please dears do get a good photo taken if you've not already, of her in that new rig-out plus the pearls – I mean a proper portrait done in a shop! After that I made lots of l-curd & l-ade for our sensible boy had squeezed nearly a full box of lemons so they would not be wasted. Then he & I went down to the garden & picked spinach, 2 crisp cabbages for salad, plus 4 beetroot & some young beans for supper, and by next week we should have masses of tomatoes also; and about 1000 watercress seedlings have sprouted in my old bath & look very happy. It is lovely to have these things so fresh from the garden. There have been a few difficult palavas to deal with lately: a young unmarried Teacher, converted last year at Ambul, has now been named by a young school girl there as the father of her expected baby. He denies absolutely, she maintains that it was he; and a very similar case here in Panyam too. Then last Sunday eve Victoria Nasik told me of complaints brought to her about the 5th woman so recently added to the 4 preparing to go to Gwoza; she had behaved very harshly & said some awful things. Victoria did the right thing after speaking herself to the offender she then took the 4 to see her & apparently she treated the whole thing very lightly & remains very keen to go on the special mission trip to Gwoza. We are praying, for many now feel this 5th woman should not be allowed to go. If she is prepared to go to those she has hurt and apologise there should be no reason to leave her out. Bye bye now darlings with so much love as always, Chris.

Panyam

Feb 15th 1968

Darlings we have had unexpected visitors today, and out of it a spontaneous gathering of a few elders plus the 2 Pastors & Ross & Chris Manning; after tea Ross talked to us about the Nigerian Bible Society & the organising of it. This was set in motion almost 3 yrs ago with Sir Francis Ibiam as Chairman in those days; but of course very sadly it has all had to be held in abeyance during the war. But Ross & his helpers in Lagos have kept busy; the work has been going on although here in the North we have heard little of it. Now he is on a sort of deputation tour & it is clear a lot of our folk are interested in getting on now with Auxiliary and membership & so on. Pastor Bitrus Yamden was chosen as District Chairman to coordinate the work of local Churches to encourage the transportation & distribution of the Bibles, & Frederick Shidda is the appointed Secretary. So I expect this visit will bear much fruit. I took Chris up to see our big new Church & came back to find

Joyce had returned from her GLB day in Mupun with the gift of a fine cock which then made a super supper for us all. Now dears before I forget again I must talk with you about shoes. Those that I brought out with me don't seem to have lasted very well at all & I'm already on to my last pair of new ones. I asked Mollie Tett if she could kindly get me a pair & get it to someone coming out by sea, possibly a pair of Scholl's driving casuals as advertised in Reader's Digest but I think I ommitted to mention my size 6½ you know. I wonder if one of you could kindly give Mollie a ring, the number is now 01-300-1109 ,whatever that means!, & let her know in case I did forget. Many thanks. On Friday afternoon the Postmaster came in for a long chat, telling me his sad story; he was brought up in a Christian home, & school, & married a good girl, but she died of smallpox, & 11 days later their only little child died too. Soon his father also died. He then went all out for worldly pursuits to try to forget his sorrows. He knew it wasn't right, & he wasn't right, but you could sense his pathetic desire & need to get right & find the secret of living right. I gave him some booklets & a copy of the story of Pastor Yona of Rwanda & some of our English tracts but could not stay longer with him; please keep praying for him with me, I'm sure word of him will soon come in; as ever Chris.

Panyam

Feb 28th '68

Darlings there is good news to report from the 4 would be missionaries to Gwoza who became 5, then the great heart searchings because the 5th had wounded the 4 so badly with her tongue. They faced her once more with this and finally she went & made her apologies to them; a hard thing for her to do as she is rather a leading light & does not like being thought less of by others than she thinks of herself. Surely the Lord was answering prayer that this came to light when it did so this trouble was not carried with them to erupt again later, & they could all go as clean vessels in His service. They all forgave her, so the 4 became 5 again. I took them along to the NLFA Office where they were warmly welcomed for the necessary 'briefing' after which they got transport for the next 366 miles to Maiduguri and on the final 90 miles to Gwoza. From there on the next Monday morning I got a Radio message via Laurie Chandler to say they'd all arrived safely. Now we hear that all 5 women are very well & each living happily with a Nigerian missionary family, thereby creating 5 teams of two women who go out visiting together. Last Friday Joyce & I spent a night in the Midder Unit at Daffo in order to speak at the first 2 early meetings of the convention then back later on Sat to Chip for their big weekend. Oh it was terribly hot there but a very worth-while time; then on Sunday eve back to Richa for their monthly mtg on Monday – what a life! George tells me I ought to cut down on so much travelling then straight into business mtgs at the end of these journeys. So I think, with all your frequent suggestions along the same lines, that I really should slow down a bit (!!) Pastor Bitrus Auta at Gindiri had a narrow escape for death – he was trying to snatch grass matting from an oncoming fire when the wind blew it right around him setting the grass alight. He was trapped in it until someone helped him escape. Now I'd like to tell you about Malam Ya'u, an Evangelist in the Hospital. As a young nomadic Fulani boy he got hold of a Bible and by simply reading it he saw the Light and accepted Jesus Christ. He then left everything connected with Islam & now is a glowing witness for the Lord. "Who helped you to understand?" I asked. "No human," he replied, "Just the Holy Spirit." Mary darling I am of course honouring your request for confidentiality re your retirement, and about all these big changes going on in your lives. I have told our District Church Council that I am expecting to retire at the end of this tour; it seemed best to tell them in good time. Please write more fully when you can so that I can share more deeply with each of you; my dearest love to each one of you as ever Chris.

Panyam

March 25th '68

Darlings how I wish I had more time to write to you without the feeling of rush – please take the word for the deed, there is so much to tell of our Gwoza trip, but here are two or three of the highlights. It took me actually three days before I felt fully rested after that very long trip but it was well worth all the effort & I am so glad to have had even a tiny share in the great things being done in that far distant Mission. On our return we were host to 11 Committee people for the Friday evening mtg & meal but Enid was away & our boy Sila never returned after taking his holiday. I have learned how to do this sort of thing with minimum fuss or trouble so I prepared a large pot of potatoes cooked & another of rice, and a good sort of stew of onions, tomatoes, meat & gravy, served out onto plates with a spoon to eat it with, Nigerian fashion, with water to drink, made a sufficient and very tasty meal. In Jos at the big Provincial Building I found one of our men at his desk -it is good that we have some outstanding Christians in this Government starting the new Administration April 1st. Polycarp Fian Datok is now in an important post in the State Education Dept., he seems to be going on strongly & steadily with the Lord. You remember that his wife Dinatu is a daughter of old Father Lot. The day we finally arrived in Gwoza, 2 of our women on the NLFA team Naomi Dashwet & Christiana Banput, came to us at the run, arms outspread & just hugged us. A happy reunion & they were thrilled with news from home. We pushed on & got to Limankara at 6pm & Enid & I got ourselves unpacked & sorted, giving thanks in the terrific heat for very welcome sleep on the mosquito-proofed verandah. Most of Sunday's messages were translated in Hidkala the local language. To break our return journey we stopped at Molai where the Carlings entertained us to supper with gorgeous glasses of ice cold water! We sat out in the moonlight & several others joined us for coffee & chat. I was greatly delighted to meet the first convert from Lake Chad. I'd been praying for him for over 2 yrs before we knew who it would be of course. He has been having a lot of persecution from the Moslems there so David decided to bring him to Molai for awhile; he has learned good Hausa from the 2 missionaries at Tataverom but his wife knows none but she has got rid of all her Moslem charms, and kept shaking hands with us all! Mainland life is strange for them & she had never seen bananas or yams before! We also met the Langtang Evangelist, such a nice man, telling us that so many homes & even the prison in Nguru town are open to him now because of his knitting! He is an expert & knits while walking along which intrigues people & they ask him to teach them, which of course invites new contacts. Next morning we had to make several stops to rest due to the heat & we got to Bauchi just at tea time but could find no tea available, just bottles of Fanta! Enid & I got back here mid-morning on Thursday having motored 1060 miles, E's car behaving beautifully all the way – until she needed it again & it was fully conked out so she's gone with the European Road Engineer, a Mr Liggett who comes from Co. Armagh and knows Moira well! Goodbye for this time dear ones, with all my very dearest love to each one, Chris.

Panyam

April 24th '68

My darlings since writing after our long journey & Enid's car conkout, it's been repaired & well used, & it took her safely to Bauchi & back. But returning from there she overtook a turned over lorry & stopped to find the poor chap had both his legs broken & one foot hanging nearly off so of course she got him into her car & detoured back to Bauchi Hospital. On Saturday I got delivery of E's car – repaired again, and went on to supper with the Fausts after which we had the pleasure of seeing three films on the Life of our Lord as Alan Chilver was showing them to the students. I'd never seen any of them, & they really were beautiful; made in the USA & so a bit un-English, but everything was beautifully acted. I'd never seen a play with the impersonation of Christ in it before, but this was truly impressive; it gave one a warm & also an awed feeling. The Birches came to spend Sunday with us to see what they are coming to; Pastor David gave them a good introduction & welcome in Church. I was so glad to hear of the happy time you had in Eastbourne, & I'll be thinking especially of you all this week as the big changes come for each of you, & Rene as you move into Dungate Manor and begin working there. Thank you so much for the gorgeous photos of your little darlings, William & Annabelle both arrived here quite safely even though their envelope was rather torn. I have asked Karl to take this to the post office now in the hope it will reach you in time for our dear Mipsie's birthday – I trust you've already got my card and letter specially for you darling girl; this, like those both, comes with my dearest love to you. Chris.

Jos

May 5th '68

Darlings before leaving to come here for the GLB conf there was another most welcome letter from you Mother; I really rely on you for news of everyone for I realise it's hard for the other two to write, and it's ages since I heard from Barbara – I have written to her & W for their birthdays. In September there is going to be a World Conference of the Girls' Life Brigade & Kath McDonald is going to be at it – it now operates in 36 countries! We have three Methodist couples staying here; they work very near the eastern area where the war has been, & now have to come 300 miles to get their cars serviced here. One couple is Irish & I find they know B&E Gallagher well! Last week was thankfully dry again after that unseasonal rain that ruined over 1000 of our newly made bricks, so the building of our new Guest House can continue; & the big new Church roof is also on at last although there's still a tremendous lot to do.

12th now & last Sunday Joyce & I went to a new outstation the other side of Daffo where they've built a lovely new Church to seat 500 – the people are pretty well off being so near the tin mines so they were able to spend £800 on this. When asked to speak I was able to remind them that when I first came out in 1930 there was not one Church or one Christian further than 8 miles west of Panyam…now there must be 80-100 village congregations in that direction alone. I know you will like to hear about Tada but I'm afraid that will have to wait till I can write again so my heart's best love to you each one, Chris.

May 22nd: Darlings I'm enclosing for you a typed copy that's going to several others so you won't have to wait any longer for this. 'Last year during the NLFA Gospel Team visit, Tada was brought to faith in Christ through the man who went to his village of Bazala, some long distance from Gwoza itself. After the team left he was so persecuted he went back to his old ways but this year another team member went to Bazala to look for him. Tada asked whether it is possible for one who had failed to be restored, and was assured yes so he gave himself to learn all he could. He learned to read and bought a Bible which he is avidly reading. Matthew the team member left and the persecution began again. Tada's father had died years ago but his mother organised a gang of senior relatives to come & persecute him; they took away his wife & gave her to another man then the mother threatened that the gang would come & kill him & sure enough that night they came to find him. It was very hot & he went to sleep outside with his Bible & a blanket to keep the mosquitoes off. He wakened hearing men around & saw them looking for him in the granary & in his house; one shone a torch near where he was lying but never saw him. So he rose up & ran, leaving the blanket but clutching the Bible. He had £2 in the pocket of his shorts & when he reached the motor road at dawn he was able to get a passenger lorry to Maiduguri & on to Jos. In his Bible he had the address of Mathew the only Christian he knew, so he determined to go to him. The £2 just paid the lorry fare to Jos but Matthew had moved away to Miango but another Christian took Tada to Wilf Belamy. Wilf asked him why he had not gone straight to Gwoza Hospital to Dr Chandler & Tada replied that he knew his people would hear of his whereabouts & nothing would stop them killing him as soon as they found him. Others confirm this as being very likely. He kept saying to Wilf that all he wanted was more knowledge of Jesus Christ, so Wilf asked if I could give him a place in our Bible School, with NLFA paying for his food & fees. The other Pastors all agreed we should accept him as long as Dr Chandler is asked to investigate the truth of this in Bazala, so we don't take him in under false pretences. One of the Mongu Teachers heard all this and agreed to meet the Gindiri lorry on Weds & give Tada a night's lodging, sending him on to Panyam on Thursday morning. This all happened to plan! Tada has been thoroughly mothered & fed by our women & given a home with Eliya until Bible School re-opens at the end of the month, "To let him know," said Deboratu Yariyep, "he has come into a new family now!" Several of our Teachers have suggested we all provide his food between us so that NLFA will have less to pay out for him. Oh how nice it would be if the war was over and loving-kindness such as this could be shown by all Christians for those in need. The news these days makes one heart sick oh for a ceasing from the useless loss & bloodshed; dearest love to all Chris.

Panyam

July 3rd '68

It was a special pleasure to get letters from you Mummy, and Auntie Lena, for there has been a gap of several weeks now, due I believe to the BOAC strike. I was delighted with A. Lena's lovely comments on everyone & everything – she thought you all looked so well & happy in the new set-up, especially Rene looking better than in years, coping so well & the Manor so peaceful & she mentioned the pleasant ride to Spindlewood family & on to Newhaven etc. Here the whole countyside is overflowing with beauty these days & nights with the scents of flowers & uplifting birdsong. How blessed we are to be living in peace here & able to enjoy these things, compared to the terrible conditions in Biafra – I wish we could send relief but there seems no communication at all between here & there. One special event of last month was the visit from Gerry Swank & his American friend Dr Peters to hear our impressions of the New Life for All in this District. 10 Nigerian leaders came to this mtg in our sitting room & it was a most worthwhile time I thought. They said that they felt it is time for another all-out effort across our district before long, particularly for the encouraging numbers of Fulani who are really interested but not yet fully ready to commit, although several have, and now entered Baptism class! The visitors enjoyed their lunch as much as what they heard!

Later: oh how gladly I received more letters when I came in this evening, 2 from you Mummy & ah dear Mary yours complete with enclosures, thank you so very much – I think the strike must be over now. While we were rejoicing over our new Guest House being not only finished but occupied this weekend, the sad news came in of a faithful Christian in a nearby village was struck & killed by lightning. Pastor David went directly there to preach in their services & was told that the previous Sunday that man had preached excellently on the need for readiness for the Return of the Lord. On a panel for Church Relationships, 2 Nigerian speakers were open & blunt about ways they have been offended by white people; it was a measure of the fellowship we all enjoy together, that they are willing to be so frank with us. They also spoke of their appreciation of this understanding which is growing between us. The script of our newly revised Sura Hymn & Prayer Book – the fruit of over a year's typing work, needs checking & re-checking. I told Peter Dominy the Anglican minister that we had changed or omitted certain controversial phrases from the Baptism service: 'seeing this child is now regenerate,' and 'sanctify this water for the washing away of sins,' and he was in full agreement! By the way Mummy, I noted in a Jos newspaper's list of Ahmadu Bello Univ successes, the name of Sati Baki Gutip – the boy whom you & Father sponsored through Gindiri Bible School, now he is a BA in Administration! Thank you again for your lovely care & share in the ongoing work out here! It is after 10pm & time for some sleep, so dearest love as ever from your Chris.

Panyam

August 26th '68

How could I not send a line to you Mother on this auspicious day to greet you as I'm sure you are back in 1903 for a little ponder today…perhaps just leaving for Moira, then that special train stop for the bridal pair?! What a wonderful day it must have been! And I'm so glad to think of you, Mary & Rene going for the week to Broadstairs – is the Dumpton Lodge Hotel the one where we all stayed so long ago where the 'other three sisters' were in charge?! Thank you for this most recent letter & all its other newsy bits too. Next Saturday I expect to go to a party!! The Fausts have invited me to the dinner party that their son is giving to celebrate their 40th wedding anniversary, at the Vom Catering Rest House – a very posh & expensive place! And they've asked me to sing a solo, 'King of my life I crown Thee now.' Then I am invited to stay the weekend with the Chilvers at TCNN where I spent my week's holiday earlier in the year. Jean Chilver wants me to speak to the wives of the Pastors in Training on the Monday morning. The Bible School just started up again for their last term; Tada has done really well in the exams and his wife in with the women, stood up with her Reading Card to tell me all that is written on the first page. Everyone is so pleased to have her, & their loving interest will be a big influence in her life and in Tada's also. I was surprised & a bit sorry to learn that Tada had been baptised before he left Gwoza for in this Church no-one would be admitted for baptism until they had had more time to to show a true Christian witness and comittment & to take important steps such as Christian marriage first. Now I must stop this and write a special note to our Mary, & sending my love to each of you always, Chris.

Panyam

Sept 6th '68

Darlings your letters again brought me such cheer along with the newsy bulletins – another wee buggin expected next March; and oh the mentions of our old haunts in Haslemere, Shottermill and Rake – the fun we used to have there – I am glad you were able to see those places again! On the party night I arrived at the Chilvers' home in plenty of time to have a bath in their gorgeous bathroom with an electric heater & masses of hot water, then taken to the Catering RH with 29 others for the delicious meal of soup, two enormous turkeys done to a turn, enough for most of the men to enjoy huge second servings, then peaches with cream, coffee & a super cake made & iced by Jean Chilver. The 'programme' was filled with song, recitals, anecdotes, tributes, solos & finally a Bible reading and prayer. A splendid evening & I wore the nice green Tricel dress you sent & felt quite comfortable & happy in it. One day recently on my way home from Darowa I was able to call in to see Stephen Adamu, a Mongu chap I'm especially interested in. He was a boy in school here with us, then a probationary Teacher in Joan Onions' time, then he got a job as a scribe in Tof, by which time he was married with a child. The next thing I heard he was in trouble over embezzling money & had run away leaving his wife who then went off to another man. Last year however he wrote to me saying the Lord had met him & urged him back into repentance so please would I pray that his wife might become willing to return to him. Pastor Manasseh & the Mongu Christians did all they could but nothing would persuade the wife. After many folk had been praying for a very long time, a Judge in Mongu Court got her released from her parents' influence which had been the real reason for her refusal, and she went back to Stephen. The Churches in the Darowa mining settlements all joined together in a feast of rejoicing to celebrate her return, as in Luke 15:23, and their answered prayers. I was so happy to find where they live & they were both there so we had a few minutes of happy conversation in which she told me openly, "We are happier now than ever we were before!" Quite a crowd had gathered around to share the joy, with a great many small children & some Sura folk, one of whom belongs to the Assemblies of God Church. He told me all 3 Churches are full every week & they have happy fellowship together, & they meet together for a NLFA mtg every Monday! What an example to us in our horrid divisions which create such suspicious fears of one another. There was just time for another stop to greet two Hausa women that Enid has made friends with; they are more or less shut in according to the Moslem rule, so especially pleased with the visit. They are friendly & charming, as are several others in their Hausa homes in the market area. Please pray with me that their glimmer of interest in Christ may grow. Last evening David Wilmshurst came to supper & to tell us of his first week as guest of the new Governor of this new State – one of his old boys from Gindiri Secondary School! DW was flown to Lagos to have 2hrs with General Yakubu Gowon & Eric Meyer Editor of The Christian also an invited guest. Gen YG was sincere & honest & finally asked Mr Meyer to lead in prayer. They were then flown to Enugu & Makurdi to see there what is going on, and now DW is on this quick tour of SUM Stations – so no wonder he feels rather in a dream.

Now it is the 7th & our dear old man Bitrus Bishtu, Unaisi Angwet's husband, got his Homecall & went this morning. He lived alone, cooked for himself & was such a courageous man & still did his bit of farming. He made ropes from local hemp, & the Girls' Brigade use hundreds of them for skipping. Goodnight my darlings and richest blessings on you, with my love always, Chris.

Panyam

October 7th '68

My own darling dears thank you each for your dear letters this week, I was looking forward so earnestly to having them & hearing the news, & now I can share with you much more deeply in the problems & the anxieties of knowing how we shall be led in the days & weeks to come. I think of you all especially for I know we & the dear ones at Dungate Manor are all so sweetly tied up in our plans & I shall now be eagerly awaiting your next letters to see how all this has progressed. We have faced various crises in the past & been brought through them & we have never found the Lord to fail about giving us guidance about His best way forward just when we most needed it. I often think of the day Mary saw the advert about 35 The Millbank when we absolutely had to leave Brookfield; & when B & I in the kitchen at Brookfield with nothing to avert bankruptcy then W came in with news from the Bank Manager & so on till it all worked out. Perhaps this crisis is not quite so acute but I know we shall be shown a way through it, and thus be able to plan for the future and how best to care for our dear Mary; I long to hear that this new treatment will help, & give real pain relief particularly in her poor legs. Now I want to say darlings you know I am ready to come home earlier than expected if I am needed, even though I know you will not want to suggest this; but if it is the right thing it will come as no shock or disappointment to me. As you can see I am gradually taking my hands off from things here & although always kept busy, I don't feel it would be too difficult to slip away if I could have a month or so in which to make final preparations. I hope I have made it clear to you all, ever since my last furlough really, that I plan to retire next year anyway, & the Mission is certainly expecting me to do so. The SUM rule has always been retirement for women at 60 so, as Geoff D says, I'm on reprieve for this extra tour! From here there is a wee bit of both kinds of news, the bad first: Kefas has been imprisoned at Pankshin after fighting with the Police Chief in a pub. We've known he is drinking & so have been praying more fervently so perhaps this is the Lord's way of bringing it out into the light & leading him back into full repentance. Of one of the couples recently received into Church membership, the man was converted by reading in a NLFA tract the verse, 'Every man shall give an account of himself,' then he went into his village Church the next Sunday & stood to testify of his previous bad thievery & asked the Church to pray for him. After that his wife joined him & they have been married and baptised – to God be the glory! Goodbye my dearest dears with all the love in my heart, Chris.

Panyam

Nov 5th '68

My Darlings it was just lovely to have your gifts to open yesterday & I was really pleased to see such beautiful things, thank you for the love & kindness that come with them and the special letters too. How glad I was to know Mary that you have been a freer from the pain in your legs, this was such happy news and a wonderful answer to prayer. Among all the cards around me is a perfectly gorgeous picture of Tra-na Roisan Bay, Donegal, from Peggy Fryer whose mother used to live at Banford House near Portadown, but my prize card is Rene's of Hunca Munca & her babies in a shoe or possibly it is Lucinda's cradle – Jane was the other wooden doll wasn't she? We are expecting that nice Fulani man & his wife, he's now a Christian Evangelist & they're coming to spend a month in our District, visiting the many Fulani who gather in the market each week –we are praying for a real wave of blessing among them this month.

We went it's the 9th now to meet Enid's plane but had to go away & come back later as it was to be very late. When it finally came we all had to wait even longer for her luggage because the ground staff were busy trying to get a lion in a large box into the plane to go on to Lagos. It had been ordered by Yakubu Gowan to give as a present to Algeria! Now I'm finishing this – the first time of writing to you from Kwalla – where I am having a sort of holiday while visiting the many Panyam folk who have moved to settle down here. Mary Sansbury drove, & I travelled in the big Landrover with Lilian Blenko & the Dispensary worker's wife & Mary did well even as the bumpy roads got bumpier the nearer we got to Kwalla. Several times we had to stop to adjust the loads in the back which kept shunting forward & nearly burying us. We had to cross the wide Shermankar River which usually keeps them shut up in Kwalla for 3 months during heavy rains. Lilian & Mrs T decided to wade across so I stayed with Mary as we bumped over the rough stone drift under a foot of water then up a steep wet sandy bank on the other side. It was another 16 very rough miles till we got in at 7pm in the dark –we were all mightily thankful it was over & so were able to enjoy the special song of welcome they had composed for us. The dispensary copes with even more patients than we do but their fridge is nearly full of snakebite serum – there are many snakes down here; it is also very hot indeed. Lillian has been doing the majority of the Teaching & I marvel at the amount of work she can get through; I've been having a lovely rest, with lots of good reading & I find the temperature generally not conducive to anything else, or any activity. I hope to post this on our way home; enclosing all my love & an extra wee dose for Mary, C.

Panyam

Dec 10th '68

Mary darling how wonderful it was to see your dear handwriting again last week & how I wish I could convey to you the beauty of Pastor David's prayer for you at our early Sunday morning time – your heart would have been warmed. He asked the Lord to bless the medicine they are using for you now & that in those inner places where medicine cannot reach, the Lord's special healing touch would reach right there! Then I remembered dearie that I've not asked lately how your eyes are now, so please do tell me just how you are feeling & if you are getting expert advice? Now Mummy thank you for your letter and kind knitting offer, what I should really like most for when I come back home is a woolley pair of pants! The bright red ones Mary gave me last time were an absolute Godsend for keeping my cold legs warm in English temperatures. May the Lord spare us all to have another joyful meeting on this earth before too much longer & rejoice together again in all His goodness & loving kindness during these past nearly 40 years! With my most loving good wishes for a lovely & very special Christmas and my heart full of love for each of you, C.

Panyam

Jan 4th 1969

My darling Mother this is especially for you in good time for your 91st Birthday next week; what a lot of love I send you as my thoughts go out to you now & how I praise God for these long years that you have been spared to bless us and so many others. By way of a gift let me share with you the really excellent sermon preached by our Bitrus Yamden last Sunday; it was from Matt 2 about the wise men then and how wise men ever since have recognised God when He has revealed Himself. He spoke of the 3 Astronauts and the verse in Gen 1 which they read & the prayer they offered from outer space, contrasted with the Russian astronaut who 'didn't find God in space' and the Scripture that promises that when we search for God with wholehearted sincerity, He will be found. And next perhaps I can describe our beautiful new Church to give you a better picture of it, and the team of 3 wonderful old women in their woolly caps and brooms who have offered to sweep the building weekly to keep it looking just right. The inside is 80ft long & 50ft wide with the east wall plain white with the wooden Cross in the centre; two tall windows on either side of the side walls throw light onto the Cross most effectively. The side walls have strong grey stone buttresses at intervals in between which is painted pale pink & wedgewood blue; with tall, narrow windows in groups of three. Seating is just cement benches on either side of the central aisle; the pulpit & Table are the same wood as the Cross, and the Table, prepared for Communion, also has two jars of lovely flowers, as it was made ready for the Dec 27th Ordination Service. That was a beautiful occasion: Geoff D offered up a prayer of dedication of the new building before the service began, and it was very moving generally & I found it particularly so because I have watched the 5 ordinands growing up in spiritual stature over the years of preparation for dedicating themselves to this high calling. One dear woman said in awed tones to me afterwards, "As I sat there in the midst of that great throng I wondered whatever it will be like in Heaven?" Yes, a really moving, lovely time; now with my very dear love to you darling, Chris.

Maiduguri

Feb 3rd '69

Darlings you really are super to have sent mail here to greet me, thank you so much! This has been a pleasant journey so far, the SIM plane to Nguru landed on the tarmac road in thick haze but all was well, then on here to M'guri just 1¾ hrs in the air instead of all those motoring miles. We went straight out to Molai to the Womens Training College & Secondary School where 10yrs ago there were 8 Christian girls & the rest all Moslem but now with the new State arrangements so many more students can attend from Missions This afternoon we had a baptism service at the Leper Colony, now to Gwoza, then to Chad next week. Great problems, great opposition, call for great prayer.

Later: Coral, in whose house I was sleeping, dislocated her jaw while yawning at 4.30am; I had to go and call up Dr Laurie & after unsuccessful attempts we all went off to the theatre where he gave her a whiff of chloroform & quickly put the jaw back in place. I'm sure you remember Tada with his mother who persecuted him so bitterly; she has now started to attend Church services here! The new Midwifery Unit at Daffo may have got off to a slow start due to the midwife's illness, but is now a busy & attractive centre; & the new Dispensary at Panyam is at last under construction – the old one has been in constant service since 1931 & is far too small for present requirements. A Vom-trained Nurse, Malam Emmanuel Makut has taken up Panyam work & is settling in well. There was a terrible lorry accident one night on the bridge below the Dispensary & all our Medical workers were involved for four hours. Eight people died & 30 others were treated for injuries, several needing to be taken directly to Pankshin Hospital.

Back in Jos: where I simply had to buy a pair of shoes as my last pair was just about ruined by the deep sand of Chad and the water seeping up into the floating islands! Also, I found your 3 letters waiting for me, thank you so much for all news & especially the report of our dear Mary's further xrays. Darlings let me remind you again that I am now ready to come home whenever you feel its right to ask – my heart longs to be with you now, & now that this splendid journey is over I feel I must start to prepare things here for my departure so that I can be ready to go when you give me the word. God bless you all my dear loves, giving you daily grace and strength and courage; dearest & best love from Chris.

Little Dungate

Feb 21st '69

My own dearest love I'm sitting by myself in front of the drawing room fire to have a grand chat with you & to say how thrilled we are to hear that your journey to see the progress at Chad, and so many places on the way & way back, was such a happy & blessed time for you especially, & all involved. What farsighted & courageous plans for the future for these dear people & places; and what stories you will have to tell when you come home, & I've no doubt your pen will be busy too with new articles and booklets. I do hope you can bring your typewriter as I have none now. Rene is writing full details so all I will say is that Ant & Loretta have another son born 5 wks prematurely but all is very well with both of them! Now darling, I have finished the course of 7 deep xray treatments & saw Miss Mellor, the Director of the Centre, afterwards. Dr Johnson tells me she is recognised as one of the very top people in this branch now; & she is noted for giving personal, individual care to her patients. So I am very thankful to be under her, & had already felt her concern for me as a person; she reads your reports & records before seeing you, rather than while talking to you as so many others. She feels the treatment has been satisfactory & does not consider any further operation on the jaw. She is concerned over the rapid increase in my breathlessness in the last few weeks, despite the recent chest Xrays showing little change in lung condition – extraordinary to me. She suggested a series of 5 injections of a very new thing which has proved beneficial to those who've already had it, & I agreed, so I had a blood test & the first inj before leaving. They are large & intravenous & have to be given by a Dr. By Weds morn I was just about laid out with a dreadful headache & vomiting from empty stomach. Dr J came & gave me an anti-nausea inj which was a great help, & she came again this morning, & wants me to wait till seeing Miss M again at Redhill on Tues before any further new inj. The Xray treatment always causes a lot of unpleasant nausea & a horrid taste in my mouth so perhaps the new inj was too soon after. I'd like to have another try at them, with the anti-nausea stuff, if it will help my breathing I should be alright. The other thing Miss M put to me was an operation on the pituitary gland to arrest the softening of the bone condition, mostly in the jaw & back – this is what gives the pain in the legs. There are two ways to do this op: a major abdominal one which she doesn't recommend because of my breathing; or a lesser one where the incision is made between the eyebrow & top of nose. I confess neither of these appeals to me at all & Miss M says it's only something to think about at this stage. It would mean taking cortisone & thyroid for the rest of one's life; I did ask how long she thought the effects might last & she said I should have possibly 2 or 3 more years of life. Mother & Rene feel as I do so please let me know what you think, dear love always Mary.

Panyam

Feb 28th '69

My darlings I am so deeply grateful to be told all that is happening & send such dear love to you each one & sympathies untold over the mouldy time our dear Mary has been having & with that reaction after the new injection. In Jos I was able to speak with Geoff, Bill & Frances about whether I should plan to go home sooner & they all agreed on sooner & Bill suggested booking a flight at the end of March to be changed if needed as there is no extra charge to do this. Now I am in full assurance that this is right & so have asked them to book me for March 25th for you know I've been thinking along these lines for awhile now, and making preparations. I shall write to all the Pastors asking them to tell their people the reason for my rather sudden going; they will all understand. When I have thought of September I have dreaded the idea of a big send-off, so perhaps this is a kindness from the Lord for me! Blessings on you each one my darlings, our trust is in God & His changeless mercy, & that together with our love for each other will be our strength & help all the way, as ever your Chris.

Little Dungate

28th Feb '69

My darling I don't know a lot more than I did when I wrote last week but I did see Miss M again on Tues & she is leaving it to me & Dr J to decide. I am willing to try the injections again if it will really help my breathing which is a major source of concern to me now. I am to see this Consultant Surgeon at the Westminster Hosp as he is the man who does this op on the pit gland; which prob means me being in for a few days under observation first. She assures me that to go & let him see me like this does not commit me to having the op though in her opinion I should derive great benefit from it & for maybe 2 more years have much more activity & freedom from pain. So I have agreed to see this man; I think it is right to take one step at a time, so I'll take it, but I do realise his decision whether or not to operate must depend on the lung condition. Dr Johnson was in again this morning & spoke with Mother too; specially wanting to reassure us that there was no question of the brain or mental condition being affected in any way by this op. She is so very kind & helpful in every way. Darling if I were to have the op I know your presence with us at that time would be the most tremendous strength & comfort to us all especially to Rene & Mother, for the suffering on behalf of those you love is always harder than going through it yourself. If I don't have the op I think the time is coming quite soon when I shan't be much help to Rene, rather the opposite, & the care of the whole household plus me will be very heavy for her. Mother is wonderful but her efforts to be more helpful usually end disastrously; so if you feel you really could come home fairly soon – but only when you have done everything you should do before leaving, and if you can be quite certain this is the Lord's best timing for you – then for us it would be simply wonderful. One of us will tell you as soon as I am called up to the Westminster; now darling such dearest love to you always and special thoughts & prayers, ever your own Mary.

L D

March 2nd '69

My beloved Chris this will be a short note for you know how we are placed here but I can tell you Ant arrived safely at HeathRow, met by Christopher in his new red car, the Christmas present from Ant. Of course he will see Loretta & baby John first, and then I'm sure he'll be down here to see us just as soon as he can. In the same way that I know you will come to us just as soon as you can, only when it is entirely right for you to leave. Mary has written to you but I heard her say to the Dr this morning that she will not agree to the new operation until Chris is here, & we still have no day for her to go into hosp for observation. She is going on quietly – she is an inspiration to us all with her courage & strength – doing what she feels able for, resting between times a little more; she is bright & cheerful all outward seemingly well, trying a little sewing but finding seeing the detail rather difficult. Her new electric sewing machine was a gift from a Bible Soc area person, how kind they have all been to her; she was greatly loved, honoured & respected by them all. We have been listening to <u>such</u> a good sermon on Matt 11:28-30 that finished with his simple account of how he came to Jesus following that Scripture, when he was 21, in his words, "I came to Him, I confessed my sin, & thanked Him for His love in dying for me on the Cross to <u>take away</u> my sin, I believed His Word is Truth, thanked Him again & went to bed. Since then life has been so different, with so many experiences of His guidance & His work in my heart, that I <u>know</u> He makes all the difference, in every life – in every person who will come to Him & follow in His Way." Now goodbye my precious love, it will be a joy if you can come, I think of you constantly & I'm praying for direct guidance from God so that you may be able to say, when it is time to leave, about your life's work in Africa, 'I have finished the work

Thou gavest me to do' and with all the love it is possible to send you, your loving Mother.

L D

5TH MAR

My darling love can it really be true that in 3 wks you might be here with us?! Especially for our Rene this is one of the most blessed answers to prayer she has ever had. She is so good & gentle with me but does get very nervous that her care might not be sufficient. The thought of you here means more to us than even we realise, to have you turn up & walk in the door will be the most blessed relief. Nothing from Westminster yet but several times this week I've wondered if the Surgeon will ever do the op with my breathing like it is now. I've had 2 further half strength injections with no ill effects, but no noticeable benefit either, so tomorrow it will be a full strength one. Lovely to see dear Ant here, just the same as ever; he is going to go over the books now at the end of this first yr of us running Little Dungate on our own, he'll do all the business things. And he'll see the solicitor about getting my will sorted out; aren't these further wonderful signs of the Lord's loving provision for our need? Such dearest love darling & many many thoughts as you do all your preparations, longing to see you Mary.

LD

March 5th '69

Darling you letter came yesterday & has so filled us with gladness that we are to see you, God willing, so soon & our beloved Mary shall have the joy of your companionship, not to speak of Mummy & me! I have been trying to realise what it is going to mean to you – after so long & useful a life as you have lived it will not be easy to leave all your dear African friends and children – may you know special grace and comfort & above all peace of heart as you come away from them. Yesterday Mary had a bath after breakfast but I think it was too much for she was so very breathless all day & went back to bed after tea; she listened to her radio and knitted. Darling if you were to have waited until September I fear it would be far too late. Be sure of the biggest & lovingest welcome possible – Ant has already 'bagged' to meet you at London Airport – and most constant thoughts & prayers as you say farewell over there in order to come here & bless us, thank you darling with all my love, Rene.

LD

Mar 11th '69

Darling Chris thank you for your letter of yesterday which gave me a good deal of thought; I've not shewn it to Mother for she is having a difficult enough time these days but I have spoken to the boys & L & B. We all feel that for our darling Mary's sake you should not delay.

I'd love to say yes by all means stay on till April but our Mary is having such a hard struggle every day now. The injections do not seem to have helped & her general condition has deteriorated rapidly even this week; she takes 40 minutes or more to dress herself & can only move so slowly. She cannot drive the car for she is too weak & shaky & her appetite is very poor for the food seems to get 'held up' somewhere although the difficulty is not in swallowing. Her breathing is so bad now that altogether I feel most anxious about her. I'm only telling you all this so that you may know how things are with her darling; Brenda, especially, feels that unless she is able to pick up a bit soon, the end cannot be far away. May God help her over these trying days and give us all the understanding, sympathy & guidance that we so badly need. Mummy is doing her best of course but does get terribly anxious & it is not easy for me to give them each the time they need or want as well as looking after the other old dears. Please darling don't be longer than the 26th all my love Rene.

Rosset Holt

March 12th '69

My Dearest Chris this is just to bring you my very loving sympathy – the news of Mary sounds very sad, I'm sure they must be longing to have you home with them. I can understand how torn you feel, & also what a rush it will be for you to get everything settled up & all your goods disposed of in time for your flight. To leave in a hurry in a way may be a help, with the time for anticipation cut short – but on all sides you are in special need of the Lord's strength & wisdom & grace and you can count on my deepest sympathy & understanding prayer. 'My times are in His hands' has been much in my mind this last week, & may your heart & mind be kept in perfect peace as you rest on that unchangeable fact. Chris dear may you feel surrounded with love & help & strength both physical & spiritual, and much grace, all my loving sympathies – I can know a little of what this is costing you, yours most lovingly, Nakam.

Gindiri Teachers' College

Mar 15th '69

Dear Mother in Christ your letter telling us of your sudden going touched my heart & I went back in deep thinking. Thank you for all the great work you have done for Jesus in Nigeria & specially here in Panyam area. We owe you words of thanks for the extention of Churches across our District, God has blessed your work & as you are going away the blessing is your forever & ours. You have led me on right paths; I will never forget 1953 when you asked me to come & repeat my class, and 1968 when you asked me to accept the call to Limankara. Now I am counting my blessings & name them one by every one to see what the Lord has done for me. In case I may not have chance to come I wish you a safe journey back home we may meet again in person or surely before His Throne God bless you amen Francis Bila.

SUM Maiduguri

March 16th '69

Dear Chris we were very sorry to hear the news of your sister & that you must go home early; we sympathise & pray the Lord will give you peace as you make arrangements and pack. For one who has been so closely attached to all the Christians & all the folk, for so long, it must be so difficult to leave & we know everyone will be very sad to lose you. The sorrow of the Church and her people is shared very much by us also; not just the personal help & encouragement you have given us, but your whole life & attitude to missionary work has been a real inspiration to us and we pray that the Lord will so work in us that in some small way we may be able to follow your example, Peter…We cannot imagine a Panyam without Chris, so many will feel their 'Mother' is leaving them. I echo everything Peter just said, and although we don't know where our next posting will take us, we shall be always grateful for meeting you at the start of our time here, & now our heartfelt prayers and love go with you always, Janet.

LD

March 16th '69

My beloved Chris this will be my last letter to you in Nigeria; it is one thing that I do not feel unfaithful in the doing of, which has been both a joy and a privilege and I think I've not missed many weeks. This is even truer of you for you have been so faithful & given us much joy in hearing regularly of your wonderful work & service for the Lord. Mary has word at last from the Hospital she is to go in Mar 24th & it may be for a few days while they study her. She does not drive the car any more and kind offers have helped her to get to the appointments. Ruth sent some money for taxis so that is how a recent time was managed, and the charge was 13/6d so Mary offered £1 and he took it with a 'thank you very much madam' but she did not mean him to give nothing in change. I think she was not up to a discussion. She is in the hands of the Great Physician & tho' my faith grows weak at times I still know He is able to do exceedingly abundantly above what we ask or think – even if the answer is not always yes – and I am at peace as I leave her in His tender care. You know what I feel about our dear Mary but God is able to supply all our need so we will trust and not be afraid, darling I am so longing for your arrival home, ever your loving Mother.

[NO ADDRESS]

17.3.69

Dearest Chris as you leave I'd like to feel you could buy yourself something you wouldn't normally be able to, I know it's an English £1 but you could use a Nigerian one instead, it comes with much love & deepest gratitude for all you have meant to me down the years. You have consistently encouraged, showed me an example of steadfastness & dedication which has been a challenge & a blessing. I am very grateful to the Lord for that privilege of the nine months with you at Sura. I read this poem in a book by a missionary nurse in S Nigeria – do you know it?

'The sun goes down as a Christian dies, not in defeat but in

SPLENDOUR, the sun sinks only to human eyes, the Christian only to render an empty shell to the sin of man while the life of the soul continues, His servants shall go on serving Him without a break, but unhampered by the shell.'

I just love that SPLENDOUR! May the Lord be to each of you all you need; the grace is there always but we must take hold of it; dear love to you all & constant prayers, Kay.

TCNN Bukuru

March 17th '69

Dear Madam yes Madam we knew of your going to UK on retirement near the end of this year, but you newsletter tells your departure has become urgent due to your sister – nothing to say but she has God's hands around her to bless. May He keep & direct you throughout your journey & please take our greetings to your mother, sisters, relatives & Nakam for we always remember those who pray for us. Please continue to pray that we shall be always directed by the Holy Spirit and obedient to God the Father. Da Nan Wuri le diret ka yi asak ki yem lu fi mo jir amen A wan la fi, Luther D Cishak.

Panyam

March 19th

Darlings, just a wee final note which might reach you before I do! I think Sidcup HQ will have phoned you to say I am planning to come on Monday! BOAC arriving 7.30am at London Airport. 26th was full, so booked for 27th – people often drop out at the last minute – not literally! & I just felt it was worth trying for the earlier date, and so it has happened. We are getting through everything marvellously here, nearly ready, all news when we meet, it will be splendid if Ant can meet me, dearest love as ever Chris.

Katul Primary School

Mar 20th 69

Dear Madam I am glad to reply to your lovings letter which I got todays morning. Very sorry Mary is not well again and you are going back home for help. Madam though I have been long without writing I have felt your prayers for me. You know it was through drink that Satan looked for my downfall. I wish I had not been taking this then none of it would have happened. Thank you for praying God would show me this is not good for me. I am sorry for I may not see you. My last word of this letter is a thank very much for the work you have done in this land for the Lord, in keeping us up to know Christ as our Saviour and Lord. Give my loving greetings to all the people in your family, yours Kefas Katya.

Ahmadu University, Zaria

March 20th '69

Dear Madame to know you are leaving Panyam for good pains me a lot, for seeing you around always gives renewed joy. My own desire is that you need not retire at all but who am I to question God? After the long years of work I do know you need rest. I thought I could visit on your return from Chad but not possible now & I wish I was home to say the 'dang mu kat' to you in person. May God give you a safe journey home & be with you and bless you, and our greetings please to your own people, yours in Christ AL Lohor.

Ahmadu Bello University, Samaru, Zaria

March 20th '69

Dear Nakris we learnt of your sudden going away, it is a pity we shall not see you now it has come so sudden. I wonder whether we shall ever meet again on this earth before we all meet at the feet of our Lord Jesus. Anyway He knows it better than us. We shall continue to pray for your Mary & your Mother & rest of them & your brother & his family. The Lord has really used you wonderfully in our District & what you have done will never be forgotten. May He continue to use you at home & wherever you go until His Coming; how you will be missed by all our people & especially the old women who always enjoy your company. We pray the Lord will send somebody to continue His work you are doing, may it be His will to grant you journeying mercy with lots of love from Chris & Mary.

Gindiri

March 24th '69

Dearest Chris this is an unforgettable day for you I know, & only the Lord & those who have been through it know all it means. I've just been reading Act 21:1 'when we had torn ourselves away from them' and I know you have just experienced this – but also that He has borne you up with His loving understanding. You are probably waiting in Kano now, and your three dears must be counting the hours; you are like Billy Graham – greatly prayed for. Eph 3:16-19 and 1:19 are such tremendous words for pondering upon aren't they, life words really.

Now it's the 25th and you are home, strengthening poor Rene & your dear little mother just with your presence and I know Mary will have been absolutely thrilled that you made that extra effort to get to her in time to strengthen her for her preparation for going Home – what a welcome she'll get! You must be glad to see all the flowers & signs of spring as constant reminders of the Resurrection Life so very much in our thoughts at this time. Please greet Rene & Mother Cheal for we are all family really & when one member suffers so do the others & yet we can all rejoice triumphantly together in our Father's provision of love. Now you won't mind if I write the last page to Mary?

My dearest Mary, yes indeed as you wrote, His strength is fully completed in our weakness, & we know that you have been strengthened in your soul as you continue to hold on to Him, strengthened by the Holy Spirit with power penetrating to your inmost being & that was what the Lord was doing when the radiation was turned on, and is doing now through the prayers of all of us who love you. What a blessing you've been to us and to so many, and what a challenge your life has been, and what a welcome you're going to receive from your Beloved Lord when you see Him face to face in the Morning! And what joy that Chris has been able to tie off all her ends on the foreign Field & come home to bless you all with her always strengthening presence. To His gracious love I commit you Mary, and all your dearest ones, with so much love to you all from Kay. Hold fast!

Jos

March 28th '69

Dear Chris on Monday last I was bereft of speech; the nearer the friendship the more difficult it is to express oneself; in a way this is right & understandable for one doesn't need to be always chattering – Nellie & I know something of companionable silence. Our duties make demands and your absence here means so much to your dear ones there. Nellie's presence with her parents was a must; she'll be returning tomorrow DV. I know she joins me in trying to say to you, 'Dear Chris' which has a top quality all of its own, to us, and to many, you have been an anchor; a place of deep content; a calm confidence imparting itself to us from year to year. Distant in miles maybe, but very real, God's own child; gift from Him to Nigeria; THANK YOU! In His love E & N Smith.

Shortly after noon on Tuesday 22 April 1969...

...at The Westminster Hospital, London, Mary went to be with her Lord and Master whom she loved so dearly & had served so faithfully. Those of you who knew her will have your own indelible memories of her. Please remember her Mother, her sisters & brother & their families, & may the gap in the family circle left by Mary be filled with the presence of the Risen Saviour. Various family members were with her during the afternoon of the 21st & she was then giving herself oxygen when she needed it. She said thank you to everyone for their prayers, and asked for the evening's portion of Daily Light to be read, which included the words 'Enoch walked with God'...'If, when we were enemies, we were reconciled to God by the death of His Son, much more, being reconciled, we shall be saved by His life. And not only so, but we also joy in God through our Lord Jesus Christ. Our fellowship is with the Father, and with His Son Jesus Christ. The grace of the Lord Jesus Christ, and the love of God, and the communion of the Holy Ghost be with you all, amen.'These familiar words, inspired by the Holy Spirit & by His infinite love, gave assurance and peace, truths accepted by faith. Mary repeated the words 'Enoch walked with God.' She had walked throughout the years so close to Him that there could be only a brief 'shadow' of death; on this last little bit of the journey she must have beheld the sunshine of the joy so soon to be hers. The next day the nurse said Mary had had a good night but at dawn she lapsed into unconsciousness. They sent for Chris & her nephew joined her later. She did not regain consciousness and the end of her earthly journey came peacefully just after noon. We had been remembering her & her family that morning at Bible House prayers & as we sang the last verse of Charles Wesley's hymn the words had special significance: 'Changed from glory into glory, till in heaven we take our place, till we cast our crowns before Thee lost in wonder, love & praise. (Taken from words written by M K Abel 24.4.69)

SUM HQ Jos

May 25th '69

Dear Chris we heard that you sister has gone to be with the Lord 'which is far better' although it is sad to be so separated from loved ones we are however assured that this is part of God's divine plan which He unfolds to us continuously. Please accept at this late date our sympathies & prayerful wishes that the Lord may comfort all of you and your aged mother, while you bear the loss. I also want to seize this opportunity to thank God for enabling you to give so much of your time & energy in His service among our people. You have been faithful in answering His call obediently, now I pray we may be so obedient for Him to use us wherever we may be. The work is hard with many struggles could be termed Corinth but we find personal example is better than too many words. You wanted us to focus on young people and now we have Reading Sessions well attended, a Youth Centre being built, and the Young Farmers Club is growing & has a garden and poultry. The Lemkes are full of these good ideas. Fibi and I send you very warm greetings & best wishes, yours very sincerely Barnaba & Fibi Dusu.

Little Dungate, Reigate Heath, Surrey

September 1969

Dear Prayer Partners, I wrote my last letter to you as I was leaving Nigeria in March. We marvelled at God's timing for I arrived on the very day that my sister Mary was taken into the Westminster

Hospital, and I had just four weeks in which to visit her there before the Lord took her Home to be with Himself. Now I am living at the above address with Mother & helping my younger sister Rene Parker with the running of our home which is shared by three old ladies. I should like to ask for your continuing remembrance in prayer as I hope to try & further SUM interest in this area. If you would like to continue to pray for the Lord's work in Panyam please fill in the form below & send it to our Sidcup HQ. Thank you for all that your prayers have meant to me personally over the years, Christine H Cheal.

22 Woodcote Rd, Wanstead E11

Sept 22nd '69

Dear Miss Cheal it was sad to receive your final letter for my sister & I have been privileged to be among your prayer partners since the original. Our prayers for you will continue & we were both grieved to learn of your dear sister's Homecall, for your sake, not hers! It was my privilege to know her in the Bible Society as I spent years on the HQ Staff. We also understand what a wrench it must have been for you to leave your beloved African Church. May God bless you always, yours sincerely Kathleen Street.

5 Stourwood Ave, Southbourne, Bournemouth

Sept 25th '69

My dear Miss Cheal I've just read your 'final letter' but I shall not cease to pray for you; after all those years of devoted service are you to be abandoned? Rather, since you came home I have prayed for you even more than ever; for such strong ties cannot be severed without a sort of 'homesickness' for all your spiritual children and the country of your adoption. It cannot be easy for you to adjust to quite another set-up at your time of life, no offence meant, but I am 66 & you cannot be much younger. I have dealt with the requested slip at the bottom of your letter and now I remain yours very lovingly, Mary Griffith Edwards.

SUM 75 Granville Rd, Sidcup, Kent

Sept 1969

Dear Chris we did much appreciate having you with us yesterday at the British Home Council & on behalf of all members I would like to thank you for the very thrilling account you gave of the work in the Panyam District & its relation to the total missionary outreach in the Northern States. You made your presentation so well; and your contributions in consultation regarding the future Field Administration enabled the decision to be taken for more integration with our African brethren by disbanding the P & F Committee. We are also grateful for all the service you have given to the Mission over these past 39 years which I am sure will continue in the days to come in prayer & fellowship, yours sincerely, Bill Tett.

SUM Jos

October 20th 1969

Dear Chris I have been asked by members of the Girls' Brigade Council of the Northern States, to write to you to express our appreciation for all your many years of service to the GLB, now known as Girls' Brigade in the North. We do thank you for your great interest & for so ably acting as President & Chairman of our Council. We were only too sorry that you had to leave Nigeria so much earlier than expected & so were not able to be at our last meeting. We are going to miss you very much but know that you will join us in prayer for the girls of this country that they might be brought to knowledge of the Lord through the work in our Companies. As you will know Kathleen McDonald has now moved into our new Brigade House & we would very much like to have a photograph of you in uniform that we could have framed and inscribed. We should be very grateful if you could send this to us or perhaps it would be better to send it out with someone. With our very best wishes – may the Lord bless you abundantly; yours very sincerely Maye R. Harris, sec.

Little Dungate

Nov 4th 1972

My darling Love how glad I am to be still here with you to celebrate your 67th birthday! This morning I have been thanking God for you and all that your life has meant through these years, and still means. It is a joy to know that so many who think of you, knowing it is your birthday, will also give thanks to God for you, and pray for His blessing to continue with you – and how much more then your loving & thankful Mother. I am so grateful for your loving thoughtful care for me, and your continued patience. You bring encouragement, joy and merriment even in my failings. Somehow I feel that Father, Mary, and little Ruth are all close to us, joyful in our joy. God bless you my darling and continue to use you more and more; with all the love it is possible to send...no, give you, your loving Mother.

Department of History, AB University Samaru, Zaria

17.11.72

Dear Miss Cheal thank you for your reply letter, I gave your greetings to Monica Datok, Mrs Dadirep, and all of them and they were very pleased. I find it necessary to contact you more for our research on Education & Social Change in Panyam District because in the questionnaire Pastor D Lot has listed names of past missionaries: Mr H Wedgwood, Rev. & Mrs E Hayward, Miss C Burnett, late Miss

EM Webster, & C.H. Williams. The Department felt that we could find information through these old people & it is likely late Miss Webster's family might have papers regarding the Nakam School and others. Prof Gavin suggested some missionaries, most likely late Miss Webster, might have had a confidant with whom she exchanged letters? Perhaps you can help us with this, and if these papers not already deposited in the Rhodes House Library possibly you could do this and, with donor permission, we could receive microfilms of them for this research. I am very grateful and I appreciate your help so much, may the Lord bless us and keep us to do more of His will, yours in His Name, N. Gutip.

Chaplain Dept HQ 9Inf. Benin City

August 1973

Dear Miss Nakris Cheal thank you very much for your letter has certainly shown that you have not forgotten me & my family but I am very sorry about my silent communication please accept my apology. It is indeed good news to learn your dear Mother & Aunt of 95 & 90 years old respectively are still living and praying for us? Oh God may they have more years, if possible longer than Sarah in the Bible. Yes Madam you ask if I am still serving in Nigerian Army, my rank is Lieutenant, and Luka Tang whom you knew well is my lay reader & is doing well. I do not lose contact with my Church at home, Pastor Bitrus Malo will say about me. Thank you Madam, we shall never forget your part in which you played contributing to growth of Churches during your evangelical missionary works in our area of Ron/Kulere particularly and Plateau in general, we wish you more years of fruitful. My regard to your old age Mother & your sister; my wife and children here in Nigeria salute you there in UK may the love we have in the Lord Jesus continue to show us His will & build our faith in Him amen. Please write to me again, all the best, yours sincerely in Christ, John Nashem Lieutenant Rev.

Nakam Memorial Secondary School, Panyam

July 5th 1975

My dear Chris greetings in Christ's Name! I am covered in kumya because I haven't written much, but not for a single day have you been out of mind. This whole place shouts of you, & almost literally too as I play your tape to try to learn Sura, you are still the best teacher! Firstly, on behalf of the whole school, & with all my heart, thank you for your wonderful gift, we will use the money for a large blackboard with easel, which can also be used in the Church, we are all most grateful. I am preparing a 2sided tape to answer your questions and to send you many Panyam features; we played your message, and your mother's in Church last Sunday morning and the people were absolutely thrilled. My wife & I know this is where we belong & the Lord has poured His blessing on the school & on us; but the whole situation is ridiculously impossible. Now there is no likelihood of grant aid for at least a year after inspection, & they won't do anything till we have put up more buildings. But our Lord specializes in the impossible & we have already seen answers to prayer, certainly in agriculture. I am hoping to make us self-supporting in dry grain food for the whole school – we have 6 acres planted of maize and a further 8 acres of beans. Forgive more now, all news in the coming tape, God bless you all there, yours Derek.

Nakam Memorial Secondary School, Panyam

June 26th 1976

Dear Chris it's high time I wrote again & will enclose the annual report for you. You'll be happy to know the Govt is very pleased with Inspection & intends to grant us N50,000 towards building aid. This hasn't materialised yet so we are not counting chickens but praying that finances like this will not spoil the wonderful fellowship & unity we've experienced from bearing difficulties together scraping along on virtually nothing! Pray the spirit of faith continues & grows. And yes, Gill has the flowers all round the house in almost as wonderful a way as you had in your day, she has described it to you on the tape we are doing for you. People delight to come to stay in the Rest House & many come regularly for holidays, it is almost always occupied. All 14 of our subjects have at last been inspected so we shall be allowed to take WASC for the first time in 1979! The Braille Hausa Bible is still a dream but we do have a library copy in Sura; few people here can afford a personal Bible so mostly listen to tapes, which is great for our 5 blind boys – we shall have 10 next yr DV – we are in contact with the RNIB in UK. How you succeeded in uprooting I do not know – I feel I could not bear to leave my people now, but I suppose I may have to discover one day. You are in our hearts all the time, but I fear you would be ashamed of my efforts at the Sura language. You knew over-filled busy days so you will understand lack of study time, with school all week and churches all weekend; I have visited as many as I can get to & keeping in contact with the pastors – you will know this; our love & warm greetings, Derek.

Box 5324 Nairobi, Kenya

23rd March 1980

Our dear Chris we are sorry not to have written sooner but maybe the flood of letters will have subsided a little now so this will be especially welcome. John and I are praying for you & your family as you re-adjust to life now that your dear Mother has gone to be with her Lord. Easter and the spring time will be particularly special for you this year. You are much in our thoughts and prayers as we praise God together for His Resurrection life, His gift of Eternal Life to us, and for all that we see, and have seen, of His life in those we love. With our special love at this time dear Chris, J.&J. Dean.

Epilogue

1984 marked the 50th anniversary of the founding of the Nigerian church in Panyam, and, at the request of the congregation there, Chris made one final visit to participate in the celebrations. The highlight was the service on Sunday June 17th when COCIN (Church of Christ in Nigeria) was overflowing with two thousand people in attendance. They heard their Nakris preaching in their language, apparently word-perfect even after many years away. When Chris returned to England, her health began to deteriorate and less than a year later, she was Called Home by Almighty God who first called her to a life of serving Him.

www.ingramcontent.com/pod-product-compliance
Lightning Source LLC
Chambersburg PA
CBHW031942260626
47157CB00017B/2005
* 9 7 8 1 6 4 5 3 8 0 6 0 3 *